THE SECURITIZATION OF SOCIETY

The Securitization of Society

Crime, Risk, and Social Order

Marc Schuilenburg

Translated by George Hall

With an Introduction by David Garland

NEW YORK UNIVERSITY PRESS

New York and London

NEW YORK UNIVERSITY PRESS
New York and London
www.nyupress.org

References to Internet websites (URLs) were accurate at the time of writing. Neither the author nor New York University Press is responsible for URLs that may have expired or changed since the manuscript was prepared.

Library of Congress Cataloging-in-Publication Data
Schuilenburg, Marc, 1971–
The securitization of society : crime, risk, and social order / Marc Schuilenburg ; translated by George Hall ; introduction by David Garland.
pages cm. — (Alternative criminology series)
Includes bibliographical references and index.
ISBN 978-1-4798-5421-9 (cl : alk. paper)
1. Crime prevention. 2. Crime--Sociological aspects. 3. Public safety.
4. Internal security. 5. Law enforcement. I. Title.
HV7431.S376   2015
364--dc23   2015000542

New York University Press books are printed on acid-free paper, and their binding materials are chosen for strength and durability. We strive to use environmentally responsible suppliers and materials to the greatest extent possible in publishing our books.

Manufactured in the United States of America

10 9 8 7 6 5 4 3 2 1

Also available as an ebook

Translation of this book was financed by the Department of Criminal Law and Criminology, VU University Amsterdam.

CONTENTS

Introduction

DAVID GARLAND

The concept of *security* is familiar enough by now, even if its multiple meanings (crime prevention and public safety but also risk management and control of the future) and its multiple contexts (physical security, military security, economic security, environmental security) sometimes trip us up. And many readers will be aware that the criminological study of policing and crime control has recently given way to a broader, more sociological concern with the diverse ways in which security and urban safety are produced or undermined. But what exactly is the "*securitization of society*" to which Marc Schuilenburg's title refers?

"Securitization," in Schuilenburg's usage, is the spread of techniques by a multiplicity of actors and agencies that are aimed at "making the future secure and certain," as he puts it. It is a spider's web of prevention, inspection, and policing that has attached itself to the routines of urban life and social interaction and that seeks to direct conduct toward ends that enhance public safety and commercial profit. Or, to employ a different metaphor (borrowed from Gilles Deleuze), it is a tangled rhizome of controls that has grown organically in the rich soil of city life, nourished by various authorities in their concern to tend public space and private property, and serving to root social action in a law-abiding culture.

Schuilenburg's analysis begins from the premise that our societies have undergone a shift from a criminal justice system of crime control, monopolized by the state and its uniformed police, to a hybrid system in which multiple actors and agencies have become jointly responsible for delivering security. The old top-down process of state policing, focused on apprehending criminals, has become a more horizontal, collaborative network chiefly concerned with prevention, risk management, and cost control. As Schuilenburg writes, "Insecurity is no longer a matter for the judicial apparatus alone, but also for schools, football clubs, housing corporations, hospitals, care and welfare institutions, job agencies, shopkeepers' associations, insurers, energy suppliers, and citizens." Multi-agency policing, third-party policing, public-private partnerships, the enlistment of private actors in the production of security—these are the by-now-familiar reference points from which this inquiry begins. And Schuilenburg embraces the insights of Clifford Shearing's "nodal governance theory," which insists that the government of security today occurs largely beyond the state, activated by multiple, diverse nodes or centers of activity.

But where Shearing and others are chiefly concerned to describe the newly emerging organizational forms and structures that increasingly characterize police work, Schuilenburg points to a different line of inquiry. He insists that our current theories are too static in their concerns, too neglectful of the dynamic aspects of security work, and too removed from the "molecular" or micro-level of analysis to effectively capture the perpetual motion of the securitization machines that have been put in place. So, instead of tracing the spread of these new arrangements, or asking about their forms or their effectiveness, he poses a different question, How, in fact, do these complex arrangements work? On the ground? In reality? According to Schuilenburg, this is a question that has been neglected: "few scientific facts are known about the dynamics of public-private partnerships," he points out—and as a result, the literature "lacks a sense of reality."

So Schuilenburg sets out to study the new terrain of hybrid, public-private security practices. But instead of assuming that the formation of this new nodal governance network has put in place a formidably powerful system of surveillance and control, he pauses to ask whether such entities are indeed capable of carrying out their own programs according to their own designs. We have often been warned about the panoptic reach of these new arrangements; about their remarkable capacities for control; and about the totalitarian possibilities that they entail. But less has been said about their intrinsic limitations and contradictions, about the practical difficulties of implementing their rather ambitious programs, and about the day-to-day problems involved in working *across* organizations and *between* disciplines rather than within them. It is precisely these hidden, unscripted aspects of the new security practices that Schuilenburg seeks to bring to our attention.

Instead of looking at the programmatic aims of the new security practices, or at their effects, this book examines the processes of implementation, the working practices, and the resulting tensions, conflicts, and forms of security staff deviance that inevitably shape what gets done. This is what Schuilenburg means when he talks of adopting a "dynamic" approach. His focus is on change—or perhaps we should say "change in use"—and his interest is in how the implementation of programs and the operationalization of policy involve unprogrammed choices and departures from the organizational script. His claim is that interagency cooperation always creates space for the motivations and interests of specific actors to derail the agency's practice. His focus, therefore, is on improvisation, on impromptu creativity, on the workarounds and rule departures that tend to occur when complex programs are being carried out, especially programs that entail cooperation and coordination across agencies.

So instead of seeing "security" as an ordering principle of contemporary society—a rigid pattern of control imposed on the flux of social action—Schuilenburg asks how, and to what extent, the supposed orderliness of security is actually accomplished. And instead of assuming that security *is* in fact accomplished, or even that it might be, he starts from the theoretical premise that such orderliness is impossible. Outside the planners' utopias, real actors stray from their scripts and diverge from their program, especially when these actors originate in different agencies and bring with them different habits, interests, and motivations.

To think in terms of orderliness and the imposition of order is, he says, to be "insensitive to the subtlety of a reality that is permanently in motion." So when Schuilenburg talks of the "securitization of society," he intends it in much the same way that Foucault does when he writes about the "disciplinary society"—he means a society in which security mechanisms have been pervasively established, not a society in which security has been successfully achieved.

Schuilenburg's concern is to refocus our attention on the contingent, the unexpected, the unscripted actions prompted by personal motivations and choices—and shaped in the course of interaction among collaborating actors—rather than by agency programs or bureaucratic rituals. He insists on the fluid, changeable aspects of social reality and objects to static oppositions and our tendency to process reduction. And though he might have grounded his dynamic analysis in a sociological tradition such as Norbert Elias's "process sociology," he draws instead on the work of Gilles Deleuze and Gabriel Tarde, using Deleuze in particular to rethink Foucauldian ideas about security and render them less static.

Gilles Deleuze (1925–1995) will be known to many Anglophone readers as the author (with Félix Guattari) of *Anti-Oedipus* and *A Thousand Plateaus*, and as the Freudo-Marxist theorist of "desiring production" as the universal primary process and capitalism as a system of deterritorialized flows. And criminologists may be familiar with his "Postscript on Control Societies"—in which he develops a more fluid version of Foucault's concept of discipline and argues that controls are no longer located in closed institutions but are more mobile and more modulated. As Schuilenburg writes, "While the disciplinary society [of Foucault] works via closed and fixed spaces (walls, boundaries, gates), each with its own specific function, the society of control works through constantly changing networks. Mobility, flexibility and acceleration are qualities of these networks. The carved spaces of the disciplinary society thus make way for what Deleuze and Guattari call a 'smooth space.'" (Schuilenburg gives a nice illustration of the contemporary city as a smooth space of patchwork controls when he recounts his Sunday afternoon journey from home to a soccer game, in which he moved from one secured territory to another, passing through five quite different security systems in the space of twenty-five minutes.)

The work of Gabriel Tarde (1843–1904) is less well known, though some readers will recall Tarde's debates with Émile Durkheim about sociology's proper object and method as well as Tarde's insistence that *imitation* is the basic social process. Schuilenburg presents Tarde as a theorist of the contingent and as a source for thinking about unscripted action and the social processes that generate it. "Tarde draws attention to social reality's ongoing dynamics and possibility of transformation" and, by theorizing the creativity of social interactions, helps us to "visualize the dynamic character of security."

If Deleuze and Tarde are valued as "philosophers of difference" and dynamic thinkers, they are also the source of some important concepts, chief among which is the Deleuzian idea of an *assemblage*. This idea plays a central role in Schuilenburg's argument, and security assemblages are, he insists, a vitally important feature of the contemporary urban landscape.

What is an assemblage? The term was originally an artistic one, describing a composition consisting of found objects, but here it is Deleuze's reworking of the concept that is invoked. An assemblage is, Schuilenburg says, "a fabricated coupling of heterogeneous elements"—a "recurrently changing configuration" that "somehow functions together." The relations among the diverse, conjoined elements are contingent, a product of the process of assembly. Assemblages are thus functioning apparatuses that have been patched together, forming an irregular and often temporary configuration that is nevertheless made to work.

The appeal of this conception for Schuilenburg's dynamic approach is obvious: the idea of an assemblage draws attention to the fact that the practical significance and operational function of any specific element tends to change when it is brought into relation with other elements. The conjoining of different entities, or the alteration of an entity's working environment, results in a change of meaning and effect. And, of course, the concept seems custom made to capture the nature of the multi-agency, public-private security partnerships that seek to mobilize diverse actors and heterogeneous agencies in a coordinated program of regulatory action. (Richard Ericson and Kevin Haggerty were thinking along the same lines when they wrote about "surveillant assemblages" in the late 1990s.)

The idea of an assemblage is quite similar to Foucault's concept of a *dispositif* (about which Deleuze wrote a notable essay in 1992), but it seems clear that Schuilenburg would like to distance himself from Foucault, whose concepts he regards as insufficiently fluid and dynamic. And in an important respect, the present book succeeds in moving beyond Foucault and posing a series of questions that are absent from the Foucauldian problematic.

Foucault's object of study was *the program*: the discourse, the rationality of governing. But as Schuilenburg insists, no program is ever self-implementing, and the implementation process will often give rise to deviations and departures from the programmed script—particularly when that program brings together the employees of different bureaucracies and seeks to involve them in joint, cooperative action.

It is this dynamic, deviant action that Schuilenburg wants to get at. He wants to look at the interactions and choices of diverse agents as they unfold in the assemblage context—and discover how these actions differ from the announced programs that supposedly guide the work of security. Instead of studying programs and discourses with Foucault, Schuilenburg seeks to examine the actual conduct of the actors who are brought together within these assemblages. As he notes, there is much talk of the "integral approach," but he questions whether this approach is truly in place "in real-life practice."

To answer these sociological questions, he shifts from the level of the program to the level of the practices—from the molar to the molecular level, as he puts it—and asks a series of questions: "How do the authorities give substance to the agreements made? How do they interpret and evaluate official policy? Which emotions and feelings play a role in such interactions, and how are these elaborated in practice? Do new aims arise in the partnership over time?"

None of these questions, he insists, can be answered through study of the formal structures of preventive partnerships or the programmatic aims that they declare: "The conclusion that a security program is an ordered entity with a clear preparation, decision, and execution is too simple. There will always be activities and interactions that collide with and tumble over one another without the authorities having much grip on them." So, in an inspired and productive move, his study shifts into an empirical, ethnographic mode, bringing realist sociology into conversation with the governmentality framework. By studying four Dutch security assemblages up close, he is able to uncover a molecular reality of clashing interests and visions, diverging personal motivations, problems of trust and dysfunctional interaction, all of which belie the programmatic aims that the agencies announce to the world.

These four case studies—which are a highlight of the book, each more interesting than the previous—introduce us, in turn, to the worlds of multi-agency "urban intervention teams" and their behind-the-door home visits; of shopkeepers in The Hague and their efforts to enforce a quasi-criminal "Collective Shop Ban" for undesirable customers; of the "road-traffic crime-prevention" initiative wherein police, insurers, and loss adjusters seek to reduce the crime risks associated with road haulage; and of efforts by police, energy companies, housing departments, and tax authorities to "combat marijuana cultivation," which has grown from its domestic beginnings to become a full-scale illegal industry. In each case study we see how the component elements of the assemblage pull in different directions as the carefully scripted program of cooperative action eventually gives way, under pressure of events, to the dynamic play of power games and the clash of competing priorities and sensibilities.

Marc Schuilenburg's book is itself an assemblage of sorts—a creative merging of diverse elements drawn from philosophical argument, social theory, and empirical observation. And he has made that intellectual apparatus function to generate new understandings about an increasingly important aspect of our world. *The Securitization of Society* delivers a series of insights—about the dynamic and unstable elements of the security world, about the difficulties of interagency action, about the fragility of even the most powerful security assemblages—that, having now been stated, will quickly become our new common sense. Had we paused to think of it, we might have "known" that things don't work out in practice as smoothly as security policymakers (and their critics) suppose. But until now our theories were not constructed in ways that gave a place to this knowledge. Schuilenburg's book has changed all of that.

1

The Problem

Security is an ordering concept. We order our lives in the hope of ensuring a safe existence. The last two decades have witnessed radical changes in the way in which this occurs. Traditionally, the government was the entity responsible for our security. But now, an increasing number of other players have assumed tasks and responsibilities relating to our safety and security. In some cases, they have taken over these duties completely. Private guards at airports and in shopping malls are a well-known example. But schools, sports clubs, and housing organizations have also embedded the concern for safety and security in their policy. To paraphrase Mike Presdee (2000), a loud and exuberant carnival of detectives and security guards has burst loose. One consequence of this is that the concern for safety has begun to direct its efforts toward affairs of a personal nature. In the Netherlands, intervention teams have been given the task of improving security and livability in the cities. They come visiting, spontaneously, to discuss income, health care, and children's education with various residents. This is referred to as getting "behind-the-front-door." And it is also the case that increasingly invasive security measures are being taken when rules are violated. For example, shopkeepers in The Hague can issue a shop-access ban to offenders for a period of one year. This ban then applies to all shops that participate in the Collective Shop Ban agreement, a new, self-generated initiative of cooperating businesses designed to combat crime and disorder. In addition, the newspapers are reporting on similar sanctions that are now being introduced in other cities, through denials of access to tram, catering, or cinema facilities.

Although security is regarded as an important ordering principle of society, the ordering power of security is anything but a uniform and simple process. The concern for safety and security is much less homogeneous and static than we tend to think. The ascribed developments in the field of safety and security—(1) new parties, (2) increased attention to domains such as education and health, and (3) the introduction of exceptional sanctions—which are covered here only briefly although present for a much longer time, are not drawing to a close soon. Therefore, it is important to look more closely at the complexity of the safety and security issue and to gain insight into the changes that are happening in this field.

Security as an ordering principle

Rapid perusal of criminological literature indicates that theory forming with regard to the ordering power of security is still in its infancy. Although research in this field has a relatively short history, the findings of most scientists do not diverge to a great extent (see, for example, Crawford 1999; Bayley and Shearing 2001; Johnston and Shearing 2003). What links these studies despite their mutual disparity is the ascertainment that many public tasks and responsibilities in the field of security are performed by parties other than the government. In the last few decades, new initiatives have arisen in which not only the government—and the police as an extension of government—fulfills a duty in this field, but various national and international players are also active to such a degree that it has become self-evident that they, too, take responsibility for security issues and develop and implement security measures autonomously. In this framework, there is mention of collaboration with the government to a greater or lesser extent.

The "responsibilization" (Garland 1996; 2001: 124–27) of parties other than the police is an important strategy: it creates a new distribution of responsibility for security. In this way, the approach to insecurity in many countries is no longer a matter for the judicial apparatus alone, but also for schools, football clubs, housing corporations, hospitals, care and welfare institutions, job agencies, shopkeepers' associations, insurers, energy suppliers, and citizens. The responsibilization of these parties emanates from the insight that the traditional judicial slant is too restricted to allow for an effective approach to the current security issue. The underlying thought is that crime levels are and will probably remain high in an open and prosperous society, and that the government has only limited possibilities to deal with this situation. Tasks in this domain are increasingly being transferred to other parties who tackle them in their own particular way. On the one hand, social organizations close to the population are made responsible for the security problem. On the other, commercial parties are increasingly being assigned "police-type" duties, such as the monitoring of shopping malls, airports, and gated communities (Shearing and Stenning 1983; Rigakos and Greener 2000; Wakefield 2003). In the most ideal circumstance, successful responsibilization leads to the generation of a degree of self-reliance among the parties that have been made accountable for security concerns.

The consequence of all this is that solutions to security issues are increasingly being sought in a multidisciplinary approach in which players other than just the government are involved. In many cases this requires a joint effort by the government, businesses, and civilians to tackle urgent security issues. This approach may have a relatively simple structure, as is the case with the Dutch Civilian Net (*Burgernet*) project, which has the aim of enhancing safety in the living and working environment of ordinary citizens. People who have enrolled for this project receive a message from the police when a child is reported missing or when a burglar is active in that neighborhood, for example. These messages are sent to participants who are situated within a certain radius of the incident. When the participants see anything that appears to be relevant to the matter at hand, they can call the general police number and convey what they have seen. But the collaboration among the various parties may be more complicated than the "two-party" Civilian Net system. The composition of anti-marijuana-cultivation teams is a good example of this. In addition to the police and civil servants from the municipality, the team also contains personnel from housing corporations and energy suppliers, and is engaged in the detection and dismantling of illegal marijuana plantations in Dutch cities.

The examples of Civilian Net and anti-marijuana-cultivation teams appear to be very different, but they also have much in common. Whereas the enforcement of safety and security was once a primarily vertical affair in which the government enjoyed a monopoly, public and private parties now seem to have gained equal standing. This being the case, the collaboration in network-like structures between public and private parties has significantly stimulated the horizontalization of mutual relations. Various terms have been introduced to describe this horizontalization: "gray policing" (Hoogenboom 1991), "multilateralization" (Bayley and Shearing 2001), "preventative partnerships" (Garland 2001), "third-party policing" (Mazerolle and Ransley 2005), "pluralization" (Loader 2000; Jones and Newburn 2006), and the like. Although each of these terms involves a slightly different emphasis, they correspond in the observation that the implementation of *policing* is no longer exclusively reserved for *the police*. Other organizational forms have arrived in their stead. In administrative terms, this is referred to as a transition from "government" to "governance" (Crawford 1999; Pierre 2000; Newman 2001). This shift has been accompanied by new regulatory institutions, mentalities, and techniques. The implementation of security measures, for example, is increasingly taking place in networks or arrangements among the government, companies, and citizens. The formalization of the collaboration occurs by means of contracts or similar agreements such as protocols and covenants. A covenant is a much-used means to record the most important tasks and responsibilities of the participating parties, such as the aims to be pursued and the results to be achieved, as well as the way in which information should be exchanged among the parties. The argument is that the agreements made will be more closely observed in this type of contract than they would otherwise be in unilaterally imposed obligations ("commanding power"). This is reinforced by the idea that such an agreement leaves no leeway for informality.

In general, these developments appear to evoke few questions. Most studies on the central role of security in society mainly cover the judicial system and its most prominent actors: the police, the Public Prosecutor's Office, the Department of Justice, the prison system, and rehabilitative programs. In this framework, most attention is paid to the activities of the government and the effectiveness of judicial intervention—that is, the Penal Code as the ideal means to make society safer, and to protect the general public against crime and disorder. Although change has gradually crept in over the past few years, much less attention has been given to the role of housing corporations, shopkeepers, insurers, and energy suppliers, and research into the cooperation of the same parties with the government is rather scant, to say the least. There is a substantial lack of scientific insight and knowledge about how new parties are actually dealing with their responsibilities and about the way in which cooperation functions in everyday reality. How do the new parties acquit their tasks, which punishments do they mete out, which truths do they propagate?

How

This book, too, covers the ordering principle of security. It wishes, however, to broaden existing analyses by adding the aspect of *how* changes in security take place. I deliberately use the word "how" to overcome the restrictions of a "causal approach." I return to this topic in more detail later; at present it is most important to establish that, in the literature on security, the issue of how changes occur is seldom discussed or conceptualized and questioned in a creative way. Changes are simply observed. My idea is that this leads to obscurity with regard to the processes that actually enact the observed changes. On this point, the literature on security displays a lacuna, and consequently requires supplementation. The conclusion that the security problem has changed is rather obvious. A much more thorny question concerns the way in which changes take place and what the consequences of this may be for safety and security. With this question, I do not sweep the complexity of the security issue under the carpet—in contrast, I place it at the center of my analysis. Change, as I would like to logically argue, is not a temporary or transient phenomenon, something that suddenly ceases to function, or something that policymakers and politicians can set aside, but is rather a basic fact of human societies. Change is inextricably linked to social reality and, accordingly, is inherent to the ordering of society.[1] Regardless of whether we are concerned with security in a spatial, programmatical, institutional, or other sense, changes will constantly occur. This being the case, it would appear to be logical to start from change itself when examining social reality and the implementation of security measures.

In this book, I shall focus on the changeable character of safety and security. I believe that this is necessary because the analysis of security threatens to become static and sterile. Concentrating exclusively on those changes that have led to the new situation in security systematically deprives the latter of the opportunity to be changeable *in itself.* The existing situation is affirmed, without consideration for the processes that could perhaps neutralize those same changes. Accordingly, rather than determining which changes form the foundation of the current security situation, I aim to uncover the processes that are inherent to those same changes. This means that an investigation into the basis of the appearance and disappearance of modifications in security must be made at a more fundamental level. Instead of attempting to demonstrate that the explanations in the relevant literature are inaccurate with regard to the new situation, I wish rather to place them in a more general perspective on change. In this way I hope to relocate the emphasis on some aspects of security as outlined in the literature, and to demonstrate that the issue of change has not, as yet, been fully investigated.

What I am not going to do in this book is to examine *why* the security issue has changed. At first glance, the difference between *how* and *why* would seem to be a semantic matter, with little practical significance. That is not the case. The question *why* is mainly related to broader social developments such as individualization, globalization, and the rise of new information and communication technologies that have changed the economic, political, and cultural context. In this way, these developments have consequences for the position of the government and the approach to problems of insecurity, whether this involves diminished confidence among the population with regard to the capacity of the government to resolve problems or populist discussions on the severity of punishments meted out. Although analyses of such developments provide fruitful insights into changes in security, and the way in which security is currently embedded in our society, I wish to approach matters in a slightly different way by investigating *how* changes in security actually occur. A more process-orientated explanation is necessary in order to obtain a good understanding of the changes in security that we are currently experiencing (under the influence of individualization, globalization, and information technology). In other words, my suggestion is that we shift our attention—for the time being—away from the broad range of transformations in social ecology that led to the current situation in security management, and instead concentrate more narrowly on the dynamic processes that directly produce specific outcomes in the management of security (see also Valverde 2011). In order to explain these outcomes, it is essential to zoom in on the issue of change itself, without having to fall back on broader social developments.

Classic antitheses

The world never stops. "Nothing can ever happen twice," wrote the Polish poet and Nobel Prize winner Wisława Szymborska in *Calling Out to Yeti* (1998: 20). Tomorrow will welcome new changes, as it always does. It is for this reason that I wish to develop a general explanation of processes of change in relation to security. In doing so, I shall question—at the very least—the numerous static concepts embedded in the literature on security. Many static concepts or ready-made structures are deployed by security experts in order to form a view of reality. This happens by, for example, creating conceptual pairs such as "micro-macro," "subject-object," and "public-private." These concepts are mutually opposed as each other's negation, and a number of fixed features are attributed to each pole of the opposition. In the case of "public-private," these features coincide with a specific form of law enforcement. When the choice between public and private is whipped up to extreme proportions, elements such as government, criminal law, guilt, repression, population, and nonprofit organizations come into play with regard to public enforcement. Private enforcement, on the other hand, is characterized by contract, risk, prevention, group, and profit aims.

This dichotomy can be seriously questioned. One disadvantage of this opposition is its narrowness and absence of nuance. For instance, the one synopsis directly ratifies the features of the other synopsis. In general, people do acknowledge that these antitheses are not always equally applicable but claim that they are nevertheless useful for sketching the latest developments in security with a few loose brush strokes. In real-life practice, however, the distinction between public and private is often difficult to apply. Most diverse partnerships between the government and the business world are much too complex to describe in terms of public and private. Indeed, the distinction between public and private seems to be fading in the current security landscape, to make way for "hybrid" connections in which the involvement and responsibility of the participating parties are reinvented, reformulated, and relegitimated. As a consequence, it is all the more confusing and inaccurate to continue to use such dichotomies when the facts cast doubt upon the characteristics of these terms.

A second objection that can be raised about this kind of antithesis is that an important problem regarding the security issue—namely, the process preceding every order and by means of which it is formed—is adroitly but disappointingly avoided. It is a formalistic distinction that does little justice to social reality, which is a good deal more complicated. For example, the distinction between "public" and "private" can say something about the features of both poles, but it provides no insight into how these characteristics actually arose. The discussion is based on a fixed point or already-constituted category, so that people tend to dismiss the idea that social reality in itself is never stable or static. Alfred North Whitehead (1964) referred to this as the "fallacy of bifurcation." To him, this term signified the human tendency to divide the process-oriented and changeable aspects of reality into—viewed conceptually—strict distinctions or previously demarcated principles. One shortcoming of this type of approach is that it cannot clarify how a certain ordering has arisen, or has acquired exactly these properties and not other ones. An important question is, then, how can we investigate changes in reality without beginning at a fixed point that is always applicable as *an invariable*?

By posing this type of question, I wish to draw attention to the fact that very few theories have been formulated with regard to this domain. After all, the general characterization of security as an ordering principle takes no account of the continual changes that occur within that domain. In fact, the constant factor of change is not taken as the starting point of analysis. And precisely because people cling tightly to fixed and ready-made structures, changes in security will never be examined thoroughly or be sufficiently recognized. The issue will remain one of loose observations, such as "security is a complex and internally conflicting notion" or "governing through security is difficult to organize in an open society." Accordingly, analytical instruments are needed to identify and elucidate changes, while the previously mentioned disadvantages are neutralized. To be more specific, a dynamic perspective that can give a better understanding of the complexity of current security issues is needed, one that can provide instruments with which to investigate the most relevant changes that occur within that framework. From such a perspective, we should be able to draw conclusions about "how" security is being constituted in a variety of realms.

Theory and practice

In this book, I wish to build up, step by step, a dynamic perspective on the issue of security. I have already mentioned that security is an elastic concept. The geometry of the concept is so variable that everything can be dropped into its flexible confines. Everything that is even slightly related to security, ranging from food production to climate change, can be classified under that heading. Although a host of meanings is attached to the notion of "security" and there are many types of "security" to examine, I shall primarily deal with the situation in which the classic nation-state is relinquishing its responsibility in the field of crime fighting and settling differences among citizens, companies, and the government. Security control covers, then, the assortment and use of goods and services that are intended to prevent and punish crime and disorder and to limit the damage these cause (Manunta 1999; Zedner 2003). Whereas tackling these forms of insecurity is mainly seen as one of the duties of the state, the clear demarcation of governmental tasks and tasks of other parties is coming under increasing pressure. The previously sketched social developments have resulted in a situation in which the organization of security has been spread across many parties. This problem not only has consequences for the concrete execution of security tasks but also impinges upon more abstract concepts such as citizenship and the spatial infrastructure of the city.

In order to acquire a clear picture of what has changed with respect to such issues, I believe it is necessary to perform more research into the background of our current society and into the issue of security within this society. To this end, the following chapter first covers the most relevant changes in security and then develops a more general perspective in order to analyze changes—in this place and in this form—more precisely. This perspective can also be used to examine the consequences of those changes with regard to citizenship and urban space. In that case, a response must be given to critical questions concerning whether or not involving private parties in the governance of security might lead to the exclusion of certain groups from sections of the city, and what certain changes signify in terms of equality of rights for all citizens. With that same perspective, one can also perform empirical research into everyday activities in the approach to security. With reference to the methods used, I wish to point out the following.

(1) Theoretical research

The most important aim of the theoretical research is the development of a dynamic perspective that can be used in response to the question of how changes in security occur. It will be self-evident that there are various options and scientific directions that can be taken to work out this problem.[2] In the field of criminology, to mention the most obvious discipline, there are elements that dovetail neatly with the issue raised in this book, although they may often not be fully elaborated and underpinned. For instance, various authors draw the conclusion that the study of security ought to reach beyond the traditional mutual opposition of the "P" words: "public" and "private" (Kempa et al. 1999; Bayley and Shearing 2001; Marx 2001; Crawford 2006a; White and Gill 2013). But in general, these authors have written little or nothing about what this implies at the theoretical level, or about the conceptual problems with which this observation is confronted. Therefore, they provide little of substance in the exploration of the issue of what it means to start from the changeability or the process-oriented character of reality itself.

Other points of address can be found in a philosophical approach to the issue that aims to gain a better understanding of how processes of change actually work. This issue is largely a philosophical one, and the answer can contribute to further social-scientific research into the dynamic character of security. In this framework, I agree entirely with Anthony Giddens, who stated that "the social sciences are lost if they are not directly related to philosophical problems by those who practice them" (1984: xvii). The philosophical movement that seems most applicable as a source of inspiration is the French philosophy of difference, and specifically the work of Michel Foucault (1926–1984), Gilles Deleuze (1925–1995), and Gabriel Tarde (1843–1904). Along with Jean-François Lyotard and Jacques Derrida, Foucault and Deleuze are among the most important representatives of a philosophy based on thinking in terms of differences (Oosterling 1996; Kimmerle 2000). Together with Friedrich Nietzsche, Henri Bergson, and Martin Heidegger, Tarde can be regarded as an important precursor of the contemporary French philosophy of difference.

The most relevant aspect of the philosophy of difference is that representational thought is rigorously questioned, as I previously illustrated by mentioning the conceptual coupling of "public-private." Representational thought places primacy on the unity or the identity of things, and therefore has difficulty with changes or unexpected occurrences. It excels particularly in the idea that the creation of order is a matter of organization, classification, definition, and discernment of all kinds of transparent patterns and general categories. In their criticism of this, the French thinkers of difference emphasize the *raison d'être* of "difference." They regard reality as something in which everything constantly differs, and in which new qualities are consistently produced and other significances arise. For this situation, Derrida invented the word "*différance*," a neologism that is "neither a word, nor a concept" (1972: 3) and in which the meanings—"to differ" and "to defer"—of the verb "*différer*" resound. The underlying notion is that what *de facto* appears can only exist as such due to the fact that it figures in a context with other, mutually divergent elements. Because this context is constantly changing, the significance of this alleged factuality is also consistently different. As a consequence, there is no longer a fundament on which to base any difference. At most, one could speak of a tension that defines the origin, and in which justice can only be done to difference when it cannot be reduced to an opposition within a unit or identity. The consequence of this is that thought can never make itself absolute and shut down. It is situated in a field of irresolvable tensions, paradoxes, and aporias and can only maintain its integrity when it displays its own shortcoming.

I believe I can find, in the work of Michel Foucault, Gilles Deleuze, and Gabriel Tarde, the greatest number of points of contact required to study the full complexity of the problems mentioned above. What these authors have in common is that they focus upon the process-oriented and changeable elements of reality. They wish to comprehend a world that, in principle, never stands still. In doing so, they allow space for issues that are not clear-cut, and they examine the relationships between a consistently fluid reality and our ideas about this reality. Their insights and vocabulary can make a contribution to an enrichment of the debate on security and are thus useful, in my opinion, for an adequate treatment of the issues raised in this book. For this reason, I aim to apply the thoughts of Foucault, Deleuze, and Tarde to the question of how changes in security occur. In my treatment of their thoughts, I shall work in a way that does full justice to their texts. I shall later discuss the choices that I have made in this framework. I do wish to remark, however, that I do not regard their work as a bundle of ready-made theories that are waiting to be applied to the issues in this book. Thinking is not the same as reproducing. My goal is to think within their thought patterns and to add something to these. This means that the philosophical problem that Foucault, Deleuze, and Tarde were engaged in must first be recognized. Subsequently, their concepts can be reviewed and can be transformed into new instruments of thought by means of which the dynamic character of security can be investigated. In contrast to the early Foucault, who tended to be oriented toward structuralism, I present him in my theoretical research as a thinker consistently trying to identify the way in which power actualizes itself in concrete situations. In this approach, it is not power as an empty concept that explains its application, but rather the diverse ways in which power manifests itself that give content to the concept of power. Moreover, by relating the thoughts of Foucault, Deleuze, and Tarde to the context of security, I believe I can gain a better grasp of their philosophical concepts. The consequence of this is that the train of thought of Foucault, Deleuze, and Tarde will also change, without every similarity to their work disappearing from the ultimate result.

(2) Empirical research

The aim of the empirical research is to generate knowledge and more insight into the collaboration of parties with different backgrounds (mentality, language, technologies) in the governance of security. Literature from the domains of public administration, management science, and organizational psychology refers to problems that may occur when institutions organized at different levels and having their own angles of approach, opinions, and interests collaborate. That is why I am so inquisitive about "what is happening on the ground." However, little research has been performed on collaboration of public and private parties in the domain of safety and security. Our understanding of the causes and correlates of crime is substantial, but our knowledge of the management of security remains rather primitive.

In order to set up a useful research project, I assume that the public-private partnerships to be studied are not passive entities but are "active processes of sense-making, symbolic communication, and contested understanding" (cf. Ferrell 2013: 258). Indications of this can be found in the fact that the partnerships are exposed to economic influences, political pressure, public expectations, and internal social and power mechanisms. Despite formal restrictions such as laws and covenants, there is always scope not to apply the agreed-upon measures. This scope is linked to the complexity of social reality and the degree of policy freedom that players enjoy in a specific context (Lipsky 1980). At a more abstract level, this means that all kinds of forces are active in which parties can assign meaning and that produce a certain effect and serve a certain objective. In this context, we can refer to the trust that parties must have in one another's actions (Coleman 1990: 177–96; Crawford 1999: 112–13; Edelenbos and Klijn 2007). Personal beliefs and emotions may also play an important role (Fineman 2000). In general, these issues are difficult to record in writing and are not legally enforceable. It is striking, however, that much research is actually devoted to quantifiable outcomes of security measures (usefulness, profit, efficiency, policy effects), but not to the players that have to implement these measures.

The empirical research, therefore, does not have the aim of providing an "objective analysis" of everyday reality. The emphasis does not lie on measurable output (defined policy aims) and outcome (desired social results) of the executed interventions in terms of arrests, success percentages, or improvement in the subjective feeling of safety. Evaluation involves more than the instrumental question as to whether something works or not. It also involves examining the ratio of the dynamics and mechanisms of fighting crime. One way of doing this is to look at the interactions among the actors on the ground. How do they relate to one another and how do they regard one another? Which kind of language do they use, and what do they hope to achieve? How do they interpret the agreements made, and how much importance do they attach to their observance? Thus, attention is paid to the perceptions, styles, and values of the parties, the interpretations and meanings they assign to their behavior and the direct environment, the language they use, the emotions they nurture, the frustrations, joys, and shame they experience—

in short, everything that makes life unpredictable, variable, and, above all, so changeable.

In the knowledge that great progress can be made in this field and that qualitative research lends itself to a study of the sense making of such processes, I investigated four public-private partnerships in order to discover how parties give substance, within the formal and legal confines of every partnership, to the agreements made. In this matter, it is important to mention that not all Western countries demonstrate the same development with regard to sharing responsibility in the field of crime fighting. For instance, there is still a clear distinction between governmental and private parties in various Anglo-Saxon countries such as the United States. In the Netherlands, since the last third of the twentieth century, there has been a visible tendency for the government to collaborate increasingly with private parties in tackling crime and disorder. Recently, similar developments have been present in other European nations but have not yet produced the same scale and impact as in the Netherlands (Edwards and Hughes 2005; Crawford 2009). Accordingly, it was interesting to take the Dutch situation as a starting point for this research.

In the choice of public-private partnerships, I first concentrated upon Netherlands-based research directed toward the cooperation of the state with nonstate actors such as business companies and citizens. Much has already been written about citizen participation in the approach to public safety (Scholte 2008; Terpstra 2008; Van Calster and Schuilenburg 2009; van Stokkom, et al. 2012).[3] There is less information directly available on partnerships in which the government collaborates with social organizations and business companies to combat crime and disorder. I charted as broad a range of parties as possible, with a preference for governmental collaboration with unusual partners such as energy companies and housing corporations. In earlier days, such parties had little truck with security issues. It is self-evident that there is an indirect relationship, but their core business is not really about security. Urban intervention teams that pay house visits to check whether or not the residents are observing rules and regulations, and that simultaneously pay attention to the social and psychic problems of the residents, form a good example of this type of combination. Another example is the tackling of organized marijuana cultivation.

The police and judicial organizations will deploy additional strategies in the coming years. This will take place by means of an integrated approach in which collaboration among the City Council, the Inland Revenue Department, housing corporations, and energy suppliers will be set up.

After this, I examined whether or not it would be possible to gain access to the participating parties in order to perform the necessary research. For example, my request to be embedded in an urban intervention team in Rotterdam met with serious resistance, and ultimately the municipality did not give permission for this type of research. As a result, I had to shift my focus to Amsterdam in order to study the phenomenon of intervention teams. Finally, I examined the type of interventions the parties had at their disposal, in accordance with the points specified in agreements with the local authorities. Did it merely involve addressing passers-by about their conduct in public, or were the measures more drastic in nature? An example of the latter is the Collective Shop Ban, which enables shopkeepers to refuse offenders access, generally for a period of one year, to all enterprises that have signed on to the measure. Ultimately, on the basis of these criteria, I selected four public-private partnerships involved in combating crime and disorder: those involved in the effort to reduce marijuana cultivation, partnerships designed to tackle road transport crime, urban intervention teams, and the Collective Shop Ban.

Structure of the book

In the chapters to follow, I explore the idea of a dynamic perspective on contemporary practices of security. For a long time the issue of regulating the governance of security has been framed as state-centric or organized around binaries such as public-private. However, it is increasingly the case that a multiplicity of actors are brought together to organize security in different sites. With the term "the securitization of society," I refer to this mobilization of a range of actors—health, education, spatial planning, welfare, the retail sector, energy utilities—whose aim is to make our lives safer and more secure. The book is organized into four parts and eleven chapters. Parts 2, 3, and 4 are preceded by a short introduction outlining the theoretical background of the chosen approach and the method used. In this first chapter, I have provided an introduction to the research as a whole.

In part 1—"A Politics of Fragmentation"—I examine, in chapter 2, the major changes that have taken place in security management since the eighties. I do so on the basis of the most current and up-to-date criminological theory on the topic, the nodal governance perspective—a theoretical and normative aspect developed by Clifford Shearing in conjunction with colleagues such as Les Johnston and Jennifer Wood. This means that, in this chapter, my goal is to provide a general elucidation of the new situation in the governance of security. In doing so, I outline the background for the rest of this book.

In part 2—"From Panopticon to Patchwork Quilt"—I develop a dynamic perspective on the issue of security based on the work of the key "theorists of difference"—Michel Foucault, Gilles Deleuze, and Gabriel Tarde. In chapter 3, I offer a first hint of an answer on the basis of the work of Foucault. I do so by elaborating on the fight against smallpox. In covering the medical approach to smallpox, I direct attention toward the governance of security. In chapter 4, I elaborate this angle of approach further via the thinking of Deleuze. Leaning on his conceptual apparatus, I elaborate on the various aspects of the concept of "assemblage," and I examine the lateral connections with Foucault's idea of power. I conclude part 2 with a chapter on Tarde. In that chapter I cover his concepts of "imitation" and "invention," and I explain how these forms of interaction consistently ramify and multiply. After this, I introduce the conceptual duo of "molar" and "molecular" in order to be able to study public-private partnerships.

In part 3—"Among People"—I present the results of the empirical research. In my opinion, research into the activities of actors and the effects of these on the collaboration with other parties can make a useful contribution to knowledge about our current security situation. This part consists of a description of four case studies: the tackling of marijuana cultivation (chapter 6), the elimination of road transport crime (chapter 7), urban intervention teams (chapter 8), and the Collective Shop Ban (chapter 9). In each chapter, I deal with the interactions among the authorities that implement official policy.

In part 4—"The Era of Invisible Fissures"—I think through the implications of this research for social understandings of public space and citizenship. In chapter 10, I pose the question as to whether the classical concept of citizenship still satisfies the security landscape. This brings me to the introduction of a phenomenon that I call "*terroir*." I present that concept as a useful alternative in the deliberations on "the right to the city," in which the loss of public space is discussed. The study ends in chapter 11 with a reflection on the findings and critical remarks about what has and what has not been accomplished in safety and security management.

PART I

A Politics of Fragmentation

2

Nodal Governance

Although security is currently a dominant theme in politics and receives much attention in the media, it has played a major role in political-philosophical discussions on the way our society is ordered for quite some time. The writings of thinkers such as Cesare Beccaria and Thomas Hobbes in particular have encouraged us to regard security as a central responsibility of the state. In *Leviathan*, Hobbes (1963) argues that social order is not a given. Instead, the natural state is one of universal violence and an unbridled pursuit of power. By means of a social contract, a governing body is created whose function is to put an end to this situation and to assume responsibility for the safety and protection of citizens. However, the last few decades have witnessed radical changes in the field of security, and these have shaken the firmness of this standpoint. For instance, a large number of private parties are currently developing activities to make life safer, and are collaborating with the government to prevent and combat crime and disorder. To emphasize the difference with the classical term of "enforcement," which refers to the exercise of power "in the name of the law," the term "policing" is now being used. The extension of the meaning of this term lies in the fact that the legal authority known as the "police" has an increasingly loose connection with the actual activity of "policing" (Bayley and Shearing 2001). With this, the government's monopoly on the implementation of security control is coming under discussion.

Horizontalization

Criminologists Clifford Shearing and Jennifer Wood have made extensive analyses of the organization and execution of security management in modern society. These analyses show that social, cultural, and economic developments have engendered a drastic change in the position of the government, as well as of security as a public commodity. The organization and implementation of security is no longer exclusively in the hands of the government and reserved for specialized state institutions. Organizations beyond (commercial service providers), below (citizens' initiatives), and above (transnational institutions) the national state have taken over a significant share of security management (Loader 2000). A consequence of all this is that responsibility has been spread across many public and private parties, with government (and thus the police) being only one of the relevant parties. The state is merely "one of the players" and no longer has a monopoly on resolving challenges to security (Johnston and Shearing 2003: 144; Johnston 2006). This does not mean that the influence of the state has diminished, but it does mean that security issues can no longer be approached from the standpoint of the government's exclusive right: "The king is dead, long live the extended royal family" (Burris et al. 2008). Shearing even speaks of going "beyond a state-centered paradigm" (2006: 26–28).

The most important changes that have led to the new situation in security date from the past thirty years. A reversal with regard to the execution of public functions has become clearly visible. In a trend toward self-dependency and privatization, facilities that had been largely in the hands of the government for quite some time—such as tasks and responsibilities in the fields of security, transport, drinking water, and energy—have been taken over by private investors or disseminated across a gamut of public and private parties (Graham and Marvin 2001; Megginson and Netter 2001). For instance, the police force is increasingly being surrounded by numerous police-like organizations, of which private security firms are the most conspicuous. In the jumble of new parties, a distinction is made between "auspices" and "providers" of security (Bayley and Shearing 2001). Striking examples of "auspices" are wealthy inhabitants of gated communities who personally hire private security firms in order to protect themselves against crime, nuisance, and other unwelcome behavior. The reinforcement of mutual control and everyday security measures plays an important role in this framework. David Bayley and Clifford Shearing also refer to cultural authorities (Vatican, Black Muslims) and film and pop stars who are accompanied twenty-four hours a day by people who function as both drivers and bodyguards. "Providers" are individual citizens and commercial security firms who adopt or supplement the task of the police.

For example, in 1981, the Netherlands had more than ten thousand private security agents, in comparison to almost twenty-seven thousand police officers. This number has now tripled in twenty years' time and is approaching the current number of public police functionaries, estimated to be forty-nine thousand (van Steden 2007: 65–66; Heliview Research 2011).

The rise of "mass private properties" (Shearing and Stenning 1981; 1983) is an important reason why the responsibility for safety and security and their implementation no longer rests in the hands of one and the same party. An exceptional feature of such domains is that they are generally privately owned but simultaneously have a public function. Examples of mass private properties include shopping malls, amusement parks, sports stadiums, business estates, and university campuses. These are function-linked locations or "mono-functional areas" (Hajer and Reijndorp 2001) that have an unambiguous identity; in other words, people can seek relaxation there (amusement park) or go shopping (shopping mall) or work (business firm) or study (university). Although these areas fulfill a public function—they are places where people meet other people and spend their leisure time—they are frequently owned by wealthy companies and the security problem rests in the hands of private security firms.

Another exceptional aspect of the phenomenon of mass private properties is the recalibration of the concept of security. For instance, the scale enlargement of private ownership indicates a specific development in which a greater role is allocated to the private, commerce-oriented security industry. In such a situation, more space is created for a more preventative approach, whereas a more repressive approach had been employed up to that time. This is connected to the fact that, in contrast to the police service, private parties in such locations pay less attention to the phenomenon of crime itself. They are much more concerned with matters that could lead to damage or loss. Although it is true that crime may be a cause of loss, they do not coincide in this respect. Loss can also be incurred by a leak in the roof of a shopping mall or by negative publicity about the allure and atmosphere of the shops. Parallel to this, many private security firms direct their efforts to regulating the behavior of those present by means of a blend of measures and interventions. More attention is thus devoted to the prevention of possible infringements of security, and to the exclusion of potential risk factors, while less emphasis is placed upon measures and means that are primarily repression driven (Young 1999; Flint 2006).

The rise of mass private properties and, in the extension of these, of shared spaces such as gated communities that are managed by private parties and are not publicly accessible can be seen as an influential catalyst in the increasing complexity and pluralism of the security landscape. In addition, other developments that play a role in the fragmentation of security can also be identified, starting with global developments such as the network society that has radically restricted the legitimacy and influence of the nation-state with regard to the structure of security. To gain a good understanding of the causes of this development, the Spanish sociologist Manuel Castells investigated, in three large volumes with the title *The Information Age* (1996; 1997; 1998), the changes taking place in economics, politics, and culture, and analyzed the relationships between states, organizations, and citizens—under the influence of the technological revolution that information technologies have created—and the accelerated globalization consequently set in motion. Castells observes that the advent of the network society has fundamentally altered the position of the nation-state. Confronted with international networks of organized crime and terrorism, the state can only remain a force factor of any significance in a relationship with other public and private actors. This necessitates a different political structure and leads to new parties filling the power vacuum that arises.

In addition to the impact of globalization, in which network logic has become dominant, changes to public governance also offer an explanation. Commercial thinking in terms of measurable output and outcome has become characteristic of current governing rationality. The literature on this topic refers to "managerialism," "market governance," or "new public management" (Garland 2001: 18–19). Neoliberal processes of deregulation and tendering out are being coupled to effective and purposeful governmental action, stimulating the execution of police-like responsibilities by private parties. An increasing "formalization of social control" (Jones and Newburn 2002) is closely related to this, meaning that the number of professions with supervision and order maintenance as their secondary task—receptionists, concierges, wardens, janitors, platform guards, tram conductors—is declining rapidly. These jobs are being taken by private security guards, with the important difference being that the primary task of the latter group is to engage in monitoring and to enforce order.

Finally, ideas from the United States, such as "zero tolerance policing" and the "broken windows" theory (Wilson and Kelling 1982; Kelling and Coles 1996), also play a role. In these directions of problem resolution, interventions such as prevention and extensive control mandates are regarded as being more effective in preventing "evil" than the classic control method of criminal justice. Accordingly, numerous European cities have been inspired by the zero tolerance policy in New York, introduced under the leadership of former mayor Rudy Giuliani and police commissioner William Bratton. With respect to the English context, Trevor Jones and Tim Newburn (2007) have pointed out that the imported policy is not grounded on an exact copy, but rather the governing attitude and rhetoric have been adopted. René van Swaaningen (2008) has demonstrated that this also applies to a large degree in Dutch security policy. For instance, the municipal elections of 2002 in Rotterdam formed the basis of the introduction of new professional groups and a broader arsenal of measures to make urban quarters safer. In this process, there is mention of a military discourse that makes it clear that there is no way back. There are no "project managers" but rather "urban marines"; no "goals" but rather "targets"; no "neighborhood teams" but rather "intervention teams"; no "security policy" but instead a "security approach" (Tops 2007: 293).

Network theory

In order to gain a better perspective on nodal governance, I believe it is important to study the abovementioned book by Manuel Castells, *The Information Age*. The rise of the network society and the accompanying changes to society in general and to the nation-state in particular form crucial points in the analyses of Shearing and the other nodalists. For example, Wood and Shearing (2009) state that their nodal orientation harmonizes with Castells's trilogy from the 1990s about the network society. Scott Burris writes that "the theory of nodal governance is intended to enrich network theory by focusing attention on and bringing more clarity to the internal characteristics of nodes" (2004: 341). And even the Dutch police draw the conclusion from Castells's analysis that they should position themselves in the flows of people, goods, money, and information, which Castells refers to as the "space of flows." In the vision document "The Police in Evolution" (*Politie in ontwikkeling*, Politie 2005), the Dutch police point out that these flows have received too little attention in the organization of the security function. According to the authors of this document, the police are conventionally strongly oriented toward locations rather than toward movements. For example, the organization of the police has always placed emphasis on working in area-based structures. The increased significance of "the space of flows" advocates, however, a different organization of the police function. Now taking the disappearance of borders and high mobility as a starting point, the police will have to pay more attention to flows and locations where flows converge, the so-called nodes. For this line of approach, the Dutch police use the term "nodal orientation."

To help clarify the advent of the network society, Castells draws a distinction between the abovementioned "space of flows" and the term "'space of places." I shall deal with these concepts briefly, before discussing their mutual relationship. In *The Rise of the Network Society*, the first part of *The Information Age*, Castells writes that our society is organized around flows, which he defines as "flows of capital, flows of information, flows of technology, flows of organizational interaction, flows of images, sounds, and symbols" (1996: 442). The space of flows consists of three layers. There is a material basis formed via a circuit of connections that send electronic impulses: micro-electronics, telecommunications, computer processes, and the like. In Castells's view, this network has a spatial form, like that of "'the city' or 'the region' in the organization of the merchant society or the industrial society" (1996: 442). Then there is a second layer of "nodes" and "hubs" by means of which various locations with their own social, cultural, physical, and functional features are mutually linked. The third layer of the space of flows consists of "dominant managerial elites" (1996: 445) who determine the direction of the flows. This framework includes successful businesspeople, for example, who move around via an interlinked spatial network of offices, VIP lounges, private jets, hotels, and golf courses. In such places, they conclude business deals with one another and determine which investments should and should not be made. In his book *The Ticklish Subject*, the Slovenian philosopher Slavoj Žižek points out the reverse side of this nomadic existence:

> On the one hand, [there is] the cosmopolitan upper- and upper-middle-class academic, always with the proper visa enabling him to cross borders without any problem in order to carry out his (financial, academic . . .) business, and thus able to "enjoy the difference"; on the other hand, the poor (im)migrant worker driven from his home by poverty or (ethnic, religious) violence, for whom the celebrated "hybridity" designates a very tangible traumatic experience of never being able to settle down properly and legalize his status. (2000: 220)

Characteristic of Castells's story is therefore what one might call being "lost in space." Translated into spatial categories, this concept involves "safe zones" that are far removed from the inquisitive eyes of urban citizens. They are the places to which the homeless and drug addicts are assigned so that they can eat, sleep, and wash without being immediately arrested by security personnel. In the Netherlands, people speak of the "bed, bath, and bread arrangement."

Besides the new spatial logic of the space of flows, there is the traditional space of places in which people live, work, and relax. "Place" encapsulates the idea of the presence of others and refers to form, function, and meaning within the boundaries of a physical setting—neighborhood, district, village—in which social activities occur. In this context, changes in the physical space are inextricably connected to changes in the space of flows. Social activities and technological processes are not separate from one another, but are interlinked. Anthropologist Arjun Appadurai writes about this kind of situation in *Modernity at Large* (1996). He demonstrates how narratives and images from television, the Internet, and films contribute to the fact that people leave their own country and head for a different destination. Although the interaction between the space of flows and the space of places determines everyday life, the degree to which Castells accentuates the difference between both spaces, which he underpins from a Marxist angle of approach, is quite remarkable. The people live in a space of places and the elite make the important decisions in the space of flows (1996: 446). In this way, identities ("the self") in physical places are subject to pressure, while power becomes embedded in a network logic, subsequently giving human activity form and direction in the space of places. This structure dodges the political system and eludes the democratic control of a national state.

Like Castells, Saskia Sassen is also interested in the way in which the process of globalization has arisen and in the effects to which it is leading. In that field, she refers to the phenomenon of "global cities" (1991). Cities such as Tokyo, London, and New York form the primary hubs in the current worldwide information economy. With regard to physical space, this results in the financial districts in New York and London—Wall Street and the City, respectively—occupying their own strategic positions because they are already partially disengaged from their direct surroundings. Their location is no longer connected to their direct surroundings in any primary way. Because they are embedded in a broadly distributed network, global cities can no longer be reduced to a demarcated piece of ground, as a part of a country. A different kind of spatial geography has arisen instead, a "translocal network of global cities that is equally sharply delineated and structured" (Sassen 1999: 130). The reverse side of this development is expressed in regions, cities, and territories that are not embedded in the space of flows. These places have been robbed, to use Castells's words, of the technological structure that is necessary to communicate, innovate, produce, and consume—in short, to live in the wider context of the world. The shadow sides of life accumulate in what he calls "the black holes of informational capitalism" (1998: 165). These are areas, just like the abovementioned safe zones, that do not dovetail with cultural, social, or economic facilities. Viewed from the standpoint of the global information economy, these places no longer represent any economic value.

Although criticism has been articulated with regard to Castells's Hegelian dialectics on the relationship between the space of flows and the space of places, as well as on the relative autonomy that he assigns to the virtual flows in the network society, it is interesting to see how these flows exert influence in issues of safety and security. An excellent example of this is Schiphol airport, which is exemplary of the nodal orientation of Dutch security management. For instance, the physical space and organization of Schiphol are fully entrenched in the global infrastructure of the flows of goods and people via aviation, railway transport, and road travel. Every year, almost four million travelers go to, from, or through Schiphol. The surface area of the entire terrain amounts to 2,787 hectares (6,886 acres), and almost sixty-five thousand people are employed there. With regard to security at Schiphol, it is striking that the parties involved (shops, private security agents, police) have been combined for a number of years in the "Schiphol Platform for Security and Public Safety," on the basis of which various tasks and competencies in the field of inspection, order maintenance, and investigation can be coordinated. This being the case, what can be said about the concrete substantiation of the tasks and competencies of all these parties in real-life practice? To be able to give a response, we must first examine the features of the security programs that have been agreed upon by the various parties.

Security program

In the first chapter of *Governing Security*, Johnston and Shearing discern five characteristics of a security program (2003: 7–8; Burris 2004). The first element is a definition of order. Order may have numerous shades of meaning but generally describes a way to ensure that things are "the way they ought to be." This means that there is agreement on a set of explicit or implicit norms about acceptable public behavior (Wood and Kempa 2005). In that framework, the Penal Code, which determines which activities are forbidden, is a basic point of reference. But in real-life practice, behavioral rules are also recorded in civil contracts, such as covenants and protocols. Take the mass private properties of football stadiums, for example, where rules apply and punishments are meted out that are much stricter and heavier than a citizen normally experiences in day-to-day life.

The second element is that there is at least one actor active in a program. In nodal language, an "actor" refers to a node, which is positioned in a horizontal network and, being connected to other nodes, ensures supervision, control, and order maintenance. The word "nodal" refers to the Latin word "*nodus*," which means "knot," "lump," or "swelling." The meaning derived from this is "hub" or "knot." As such, it concerns a structure or organizational form that organizes and combines people and things. But Johnston and Shearing are referring to something other than merely a physical place (such as a shopping mall, for example) or a virtual environment (such as ebay.com). Nodes are formal or informal organizations that are interested parties in a concrete security program. They may be companies, ministries, or the police, but youth gangs, households, NGOs, or journalists also fit the definition (Burris 2004: 341–42).

Tools or technologies constitute the third feature of a security program. These are instruments that can insert a node in the implementation of control, supervisory, and investigative tasks. "Technology" usually refers to a whole range of innovative inventions or discoveries. A good example here is biometrical control at airports. For example, Schiphol and John F. Kennedy airports initiated a trial period with biometric data in May 2008, for American and Dutch travelers with a low security risk. Travelers who wish to participate are additionally screened with regard to security risk. Once registration has been approved, a chip pass with biometrical data is made. In this trial, use is made of passport, fingerprints, and iris scans. On the basis of the biometric chip pass, travelers can subsequently easily cross the border without being held up for questioning or physical control at the airport (Romein and Schuilenburg 2008).

In addition to physical instruments such as handcuffs, cars, weapons, and truncheons, Johnston and Shearing distinguish three other instruments that can be applied in a security program. There are legal instruments employed within the framework of criminal research, such as inspecting posts, eavesdropping on telephone calls, and searching premises. But Johnston and Shearing also mention symbolic instruments. In this context, one can think of the respect or esteem that a node enjoys in society or among other nodes. Finally, there are the personal instruments of an actor, such as his or her communicative skills, charisma, and intelligence. Parties that are relatively weak, in the sense that they do not have legal and physical technologies at their disposal, therefore do have possibilities from the perspective of nodal governance. After all, it is not only these instruments that make an actor strong—symbolic and personal instruments, too, may be valuable. By mobilizing these instruments and combining them with the technologies of other nodes, an actor can reinforce his or her position in a security program.

Exactly which technologies will be used and how this will be done depends on the parties involved and the objectives of the security program. In real-life practice, the ideal mixture of technologies will have to be calculated each time. In the case of Civilian Net, for example, the Dutch government is represented by the municipality and the police. The police are responsible for Civilian Net's technical system and the operational deployment of members of staff and participants. The municipality is responsible for the communications and relation management of the participants. If the police initiate a search action in the neighborhood, the people in this neighborhood who have enrolled for the project are sent a message by the police coordination desk, usually by telephone, which gives a clear description of who and/or what is being sought. The police ask the participants to hold surveillance from their own living or working environment. A separate telephone line is subsequently set up by means of which suspicious situations or pieces of information can be reported. With these data, the coordination desk can lead the police to the right place.

The fourth and perhaps most important feature is the mentality of the node—in other words, the manner of thinking that determines one's view of the world and the way one reacts to situations and circumstances in everyday life. A mentality not only provides a framework within which to define aims, interests, and success but also ratifies the technologies to be used. An example of a mentality that results in a certain action is a "punishment mentality" (Johnston and Shearing 2003). This concerns a *post-delictum* initiation of action, in terms of tracing misdemeanors, determining the guilty parties, and punishing the perpetrators. This mentality harmonizes with the classical state monopoly on security in which punishment is the most important instrument available to promote security in society. Broadly speaking, the enforcement of order is typified by the protection of individual legal rights and goods, such as life and property. It is up to the state to protect these goods by the exertion of physical force in the form of an imposition of a lawful measure that may only be applied if the same objective cannot be achieved through a less severe measure (the *ultima ratio* or *ultimum remedium* principle). The literature speaks of "governing the past" or of a "post-crime society" (Zedner 2007).

The risk mentality stands in sharp contrast to thinking in terms of guilt and responsibility. This mentality is oriented to the future and is often applied after negotiations and in agreement with other parties (Shearing 2001; Johnston and Shearing 2003). Despite the fact that this mentality has scarcely been delineated, it involves techniques to manage and minimize risks in the real world. The punishment of harmful behavior is only important when it leads to a reduction of the risk. Two kinds of technique are exceptionally evident here (Von Hirsch and Shearing 2000). The first is based upon personal profiles. It is assumed that certain individuals have specific characteristics that indicate a heightened risk of criminal behavior, such as "man," "young," "colored skin," "sunglasses," and "hood." Although no rule-breaking act has yet occurred, the risk of one actually taking place is regarded as being high enough to ban such people from certain places or facilities. For instance, some people have been banned from flying with certain aviation companies because they are regarded as potential hijackers. In contrast to the first form, a second kind of technique is directed toward the rebuffing of people who have already been convicted of violating certain rules, such as football hooligans and shoplifters. Despite this gradual difference, the similarity between these forms of exclusion is evident. Both concentrate on the identification of "evil" in the form of potential threats or possible security risks.

Besides the punishment and risk mentalities, Johnston and Shearing discern two other mentalities: a "restoration mentality," which advocates a problem-oriented approach to the victim and perpetrator, and a "welfare mentality" in which the emphasis is placed upon the "normalization" of perpetrators. This latter mentality is linked to what David Garland referred to as "penal welfarism" in his book *Punishment and Welfare* (1985). This practice was first propagated around 1890, and enjoyed a peak in the 1950s and '60s. The basic modernistic attitude is the instrument of penal welfarism *par excellence*: belief in progress and improvement. Of course there are differences of opinion and scandals, and a serious institutional crisis breaks out regularly, but the organizations that are involved in and around this practice share one important objective: the return of the perpetrator to society. In order to enable the perpetrator to participate fully in social interaction, matters such as diagnosis, individual treatment, and social work are given particular emphasis. Research into the causes of deviant behavior shows that social reform and economic welfare lead to a reduction of crime. Crime originates mainly from the maladjustment of individuals and families, as well as from social arrears in the form of poor economic circumstances or insufficient access to the labor market. These notions form the basis of a solid state monopoly on the implementation of punishment and eventual care for the perpetrator: "The state was to be an agent of reform as well as of repression, of care as well as control, of welfare as well as punishment" (Garland 2001: 39).

The fifth and last element of a security program is the interaction among the abovelisted characteristics. Johnston and Shearing speak of "practices" (2003: 13). The combination of those characteristics results in concrete activities that are undertaken in a security program. Which practice will ultimately develop will have to be investigated on the basis of empirical research.

Power

The previous part of this book has made it clear that the issue of security is currently being tackled in a different way than has been the case up to the present. It now involves not only parties other than the police and the Department of Justice but also a different approach to security, one that does not only rely on tracing and punishing perpetrators of crime and disorder. This being the case, the complexity of security is linked to the number of organizations that are attempting to resolve issues of security, and to the nature of the measures employed to tackle the problems. Another relevant aspect is the fact that the organization of security is no longer governed top-down by the government as the director and executor of security issues, but is increasingly being implemented by ever-changing partnerships and complex network structures. No single party is the self-evident center of gravity in this situation, and no party is assigned priority in a partnership. Partnerships may change in their makeup, as do the responsibilities and objectives that ought to give these same partnerships consistency, coherence, and direction. The party that occupies, for example, a certain position within a security program may not necessarily occupy the same position in a different program. In other words, there is mention of a hybrid security model, with a rich and varied picture of responsibility and representation.

The theory that the government is merely a node within a security network and that punishment is no more than one of the many instruments used to enforce order shows many correspondences with the power analysis of Michel Foucault, for whom, write Wood and Shearing, "power is understood as being everywhere, not because it is exercised everywhere, but because it is viewed as coming from everywhere" (2007: 9). In his work, Foucault invalidates a number of myths about power, including the idea that some people are born with an exceptional talent or capacity to exercise power. To Foucault, there is no essential connection between the person or instance that holds power and power itself. Power is not something that one source can have exclusively at its own disposal or something that is exerted from a single point but is, rather, in the words of Wood and Shearing, "decentral or nodal" (2009: 13). Because Foucault's analysis of power will be dealt with extensively in the following chapter, here I shall only briefly outline his concept of power in order to expose, *in abstracto*, the overlap with the starting points of the nodal orientation of Shearing and his colleagues.

According to Foucault, "power [is] not an institution, a structure, or a certain force with which certain people are endowed; it is the name given to a complex strategic situation in a given society" (1976: 123). Even in his early work, this approach led to a critique of more everyday representations of power, and particularly of the legal-discursive and Marxist representation of power. In Foucault's view, the analysis of power ought to be independent of issues of legitimacy and consensus, and also of violence and suppression. Neither the autonomous subject nor the political sovereignty of the state provides an adequate starting point for speaking about power. "What we need is a political philosophy that isn't erected around the problem of sovereignty, nor therefore around the problems of law and prohibition. We need to cut off the king's head," writes Foucault (1980: 121). In his lecture series entitled *Il faut défendre la société (Society Must Be Defended)*, he prefers an elaboration of what he calls "Nietzsche's hypothesis" (2004a: 16). This means that, at each instance of institutionalized exertion of power, the genealogical question as to which power struggle preceded the present one can be posed. Therefore, a specific sociocultural field should not be sought in terms of the law or repression, but first and foremost in terms of strategies of "conflict, confrontation, and war" (2004a: 15). Only when power relationships have come to a standstill and have petrified is there "a form of domination [*domination*] (ethnic, social, and religious)" (1983: 212).

In his lectures at the Collège de France and in his books *Surveiller et punir* (*Discipline and Punish*, 1975) and *La volonté de savoir* (*The Will to Knowledge*, 1976), Foucault developed a new theory of power and indicated which classical postulates he wished to abandon. First of all, there is the *postulate of property*. Here, power is owned by a person, group, or entity. Power rests in the hands of, for example, an absolute monarch or ruling class. The consequence of this is that the state, as Foucault sees it, is seen as "a kind of 'meta-power' which is structured essentially round a certain number of great prohibition functions" (1980: 122). In contrast to this, he declares that power is not a "thing" but rather an anonymous strategy that is exercised via tactics and techniques in concrete practices. The anonymity indicates that power "exists only in action" (2004a: 14) and that no entity, person, or group can be designated as its owner.

Second, there is the *postulate of localization*. In this context, power is regarded as something that can be localized in a state system (police), ruler (monarch), or institution (government). Accordingly, power is always exerted from a certain point or place. But, according to Foucault, power does not exist as a coherent whole. It ought to be analyzed "as something that circulates, or rather as something that functions only when it is a part of a chain" (2004a: 29). For this reason, a specific power effect will have to be explained on the basis of the entirety of relationships that mutually connect various elements. Regarded in this way, the term "local" has a double meaning (Deleuze 1986: 34). Power is local in the sense that it is never global and "is produced in every relation from one point to another" (Foucault 1976: 122). But this does not mean that power is localizable. Foucault regards power relationships as being always unstable and fluid, and consequently always capable of reversal.

Third, there is the *postulate of subordination*. Power is a derived function of this. In Marxist theories, this recurs in the notion of retaining current production relationships in society. The economic infrastructure is the determining societal force; in other words, it is the force that ultimately determines the life and functioning of power. In the political philosophies of Hobbes and Beccaria, the idea of subordination recurs in the fact that power is a right that one can discard by transferring it to a political entity. In contrast to this, Foucault states that a power relationship is not economically or politically determined. It should really be seen as a social function that is innate in the field within which it is exerted.

Fourth, there is the *postulate of essence* or of *attribute*. In this context, power has an identifiable essence and is a property of those who possess it. This group distinguishes itself from other groups or persons who have no power. In Marxist terms, it concerns the oppressed, for example, or the nonowning class. In contrast to this, Foucault states that power has no essence; it is simply operational. Power is produced in the relationship among forces that are always dissimilar and changeable. This means that power is a relationship that should be studied by examining "how that relationship itself determines the elements to which it is applied" (2004a: 45). Thus, the relational character of power does not lie on a binary opposition between the dominators and the dominated, but rather on a dynamic network of relationships that intersect, influence, and reinforce one another.

Fifth, there is the *postulate of modality*. In this framework, power refers to an instrument that can be used in a repressive manner (violence, suppression, exploitation, propaganda) on ideological or political grounds by a system or entity. It is a power that excludes and forbids, and entails a series of negative effects, such as "refusal, limitation, obstruction, censorship" (1980: 139). However, Foucault holds the opinion that power should not be defined in negative terms, but should rather be seen in a productive light. This means that it is a relation that itself generates a reality and is connected to practices in which people are made into coherent subjects.

Sixth, there is the *postulate of legality*. Here, power is regarded as an articulated rule, embedded in law or in a contract. In that way, it is presented as an alternative to war or chaos. But to Foucault, power is actually equivalent to war. He reverses the classic formulation of the Prussian military thinker Carl von Clausewitz and claims that "politics is the continuation of war but by other means" (1975: 170). Speaking of power in terms of war gives it the character of a permanent struggle that comes to fruition at the level of concrete physical processes and happenings. As a result, Foucault's analysis of power does not remain caged in abstract considerations of "society" and does not take a minimalist concept of humankind as its point of departure, as do the writings of Hobbes, who, in *Leviathan*, reduces the state of being human to a longing for freedom. According to Foucault, there is nothing more material and physical than the exercise of power. At the same time, this postulate also makes it evident that the law also creates all kinds of illegalisms. The law "administers" (Deleuze 1986: 37) illegalisms by allowing, tolerating, or regulating them. This means, in the words of Foucault, that "a penal system must be conceived as a mechanism intended to administer illegalities differentially, not to eliminate them all" (1975: 124). For example, legal prohibition demands organized supervision by the police, the Department of Justice, and relief workers, who constantly monitor and control the population.

In a supplement to the six previous postulates, I wish to add a seventh. A relevant aspect in this context is the fact that it is impossible to conceive of power without resistance. Although Foucault did not write much about resistance, he has always made it clear that power cannot be understood without resistance coming into the equation somewhere. According to Foucault, "there is no power without potential refusal or revolt" (2000: 324). Resistance is impossible without power relations. In *The Will to Knowledge*, Foucault states that in our relationship with power, there is not just one place of—as he articulates it—the "great Refusal, the soul of revolt, source of all rebellions, or pure law of the revolutionary" (1976: 96). Instead, there are diverse forms of resistance, each of which has its own background, each a special case: "[r]esistances that are possible, necessary, improbable; others that are spontaneous, savage, solitary, concerted, rampant, or violent; still others that are quick to compromise, interested, or sacrificial" (1976: 96).

Criticism . . .

The nodal approach to the governance of security allows four conclusions. First of all, we must avoid giving priority to the state in the organization and implementation of security management, and must examine which other parties are engaged in this field and which relationships exist among the various parties. After all, security is no longer governed on the basis of one dominant party or center, but rather on the basis of a network of separate programs in which the most diverse nodes can converge. This implies, as a second conclusion, that governance is not an outcome of one single party, but should instead be seen as the outcome or the property of a hybrid model. An associated fact is that governance is the result of ever-shifting relationships and alliances, and is not the result of a government that occupies a central position and guides the other "rowers" (cf. Osborne and Gaebler 1992). The consequence is a tangle of relationships and mutual influences far removed from the classical security thinking that harmonizes with the characteristics of a hierarchical, vertically structured approach. Finally, it must be emphasized that governing is a human activity and consequently embodies normative implications. This must consistently lead to questions about who is responsible for the organization and implementation of security, and the way in which the interests of citizens can be optimally cared for (Johnston and Shearing 2003: 148; Wood 2006).

Up to this point, everything appears to be pretty convincing. But let us look a little more closely at the starting points of the nodal approach as presented by Shearing and his colleagues. These starting points are certainly not undisputed and are even the issue at stake in a lively scientific debate. In this context, the criticism is not directed to the observation that a shift has occurred from a state monopoly on security toward a fragmented management of this issue, but is more oriented toward the consequences of this shift for the provision of security. In this connection, I discuss the views of Ian Loader and Neal Walker (2007), Trevor Jones and Tim Newburn (2002), and Lucia Zedner (2009).

Nodal orientation, as articulated by Shearing and others, is characterized, in the opinion of Loader and Walker, by a skeptical attitude toward the state that implies that preference should only in the last resort be given to the state above other parties in the implementation of security. In their view, this attitude refers primarily to the shortcomings of the state, meaning "that it lacks the situated knowledge and therefore the capacity to deliver security across a diverse array of local settings" (2007: 117). In the view of Shearing and others, the state works too bureaucratically and, in contrast to private parties, is less capable of excluding potential risk factors and of preventing the erosion of security. Although Loader and Walker conclude that this type of view ("state as idiot") does hit the nail on the head in some instances, they also declare that "state-skeptics have tended to be inattentive towards continuing positive contributions of the state" (2007: 143). This causes friction because, according to Loader and Walker, security should be approached as a "thick" public commodity that every citizen should be able to access in equal measure while, in the light of a democratically functioning society, state intervention is also an elementary precondition of the social division of this commodity. In addition, Loader and Walker pose the rhetorical question as to whether or not Shearing's nodal vision is even possible without the state. Everything seems nice and easy, but what do you do if there is genuine conflict among the parties? Who then determines the rules? Klaas Rozemond (2010) also refers to this problem and states that Shearing's nodal orientation necessarily presupposes the use of violence because the alternatives to classical criminal law can ultimately only function effectively when the state defines and enforces private rights. However, this does not alter the fact that Loader and Walker also acknowledge that, besides the government, there are many parties engaged in the organization and implementation of security management. The major difference is, however, the starting point of each analysis. In contrast to Shearing and his colleagues, Loader and Walker express the conviction that state interference is necessary and desirable in the provision of security. In that context, they speak of "anchored pluralism." The state ensures security as a public commodity, but allows as much scope as possible for other parties and alternative security programs.

Another set of criticisms with respect to the nodal governance perspective comes from Jones and Newburn. In their article "The Transformation of Policing" (2002), they refer to continuity in security management in addition to elements of change. In more specific terms, they oppose Shearing's notion that there was once something like an absolute governmental monopoly on security. Their research shows that the number of private security guards in the United States and the UK in the 1950s was almost as large as that of their public counterparts. The claim advanced by Shearing and his colleagues that there has been substantial increase in the quantity of private security guards is thus not grounded in empirical and historical studies. Indeed, such a monopoly has never existed, according to Jones and Newburn. Other authors have also assumed the standpoint that the findings of nodal governance do not indicate great changes in issues of security. With regard to the Dutch situation, Bob Hoogenboom (2009) states that the discussion on the fragmentation of the policing function reaches back to the early eighties, with numerous studies on administrative supervision, as well as studies on the rise of parties besides the police in the field of surveillance and order maintenance. Hoogenboom refers to the continuity of the public policing function and concludes that this has not essentially changed since the beginning of the nineteenth century: "There has been little change in the way in which everyday policing is executed through surveillance, emergency aid, relief work (referral) and local community care" (2009: 66). The last observation provokes the question as to whether or not this is an argument relevant to the above-discussed nodal orientation. In contrast to what Hoogenboom suggests, Shearing tends to direct his attention toward the issue of what it means to the configuration of security management when the government is seen as simply one player among other players.

Slightly less extensive but no less fundamental is Zedner's criticism (2009: 158–63) of the recurring attention paid, in Shearing's nodal orientation, to the tackling of security issues in the poor neighborhoods of South Africa, also referred to as the "Zwelethemba model." In this model, named after the community near Cape Town where the first project was set up, solutions to problems of crime and social difficulties such as water shortages and access to health care, for example, are sought at the local level (Johnston and Shearing 2003: 151–60; Shearing and Wood 2003a; Froestad and Shearing 2013). An important role has been assigned to the so-called peace committees, which are comprised of residents of the neighborhood and have among their tasks the facilitation of processes in which local conflicts can be mediated. Here, the emphasis lies on a bottom-up approach: operating from the lowest level, resting upon the input of knowledge and experience by concerned inhabitants in order to enable a more just distribution and more effective form of security observance. Zedner regards the problem-free way in which the Zwelethemba model is recommended as being "overly optimistic, even dangerously so" (2009: 161). Apart from the fact that this model is clearly derived from the economic and political postapartheid situation in South Africa (and not from Europe, where the welfare state is still relatively strong), there is always the danger that local communities will be exclusively governed in the name of security. In addition, there is the risk of the less attractive sides of informal resolution or conflict conciliation arising as a form of "private justice" and of deliberate defamation of certain groups or individuals on the basis of race or social status. In this respect, Monique Marks and Andrew Goldsmith (2006) emphasize the importance of security as a public good in countries undergoing radical social transition, such as South Africa, with its movement from apartheid to democracy.

. . . continued

Although the above objections and qualifications must be taken seriously, I believe that they do not preclude the nodal approach serving as a useful starting point for obtaining a better understanding of the latest developments in security management. Nodal orientation rightly points to the cultural, economic, and political causes of fragmentation, and provides them with a vocabulary with which to analyze the implementation of security measures and new collaborative forms between public and private parties. In doing so, it largely follows the points of departure of network theory, with the proviso that interest is primarily focused on the way in which security is governed by private and public parties. An important aspect in this perspective is the shift from fixed structures to the features of the nodes that are active in concrete security programs. At the same time, it poses the question, "What is the best way of coordinating and integrating the various nodes of security governance, and how should this nodal arrangement be funded?" (Shearing 2005: 61). In this context, I wish to reemphasize that, in nodal governance literature, there is a great deal of obscurity surrounding this topic.

Although the above-discussed criticism is very diverse and is directed toward various starting points of the nodal orientation, another important point has been largely ignored. It is obvious that Shearing and his colleagues nurture a rather simple presupposition about the way a security program works in real-life practice. Literature on nodal governance offers many details about mentalities and the structure of nodes, where attention is primarily paid to the differences between private and public parties. But, at the same time, it is difficult to dismiss the impression that these same differences in a program can be simply discarded in order to achieve a concrete aim, such as the improvement of security, for example. The nodal approach seems to be based on a harmonious whole or, in other words, on the idea that nodes engage in a program when they negotiate with one another about what they will or will not do, and about the use they make of certain technologies and structures. For instance, the parties are expected to make realistic and well-considered decisions that are founded upon sufficient available facts and alternatives. In doing so, they keep close watch over the goals of the collaboration and they distinguish between main and side issues. This may well be the case in theory, but it is doubtful if this is always the case in real-life practice. For the time being, the idea of a harmonious whole comes across as a somewhat romantic representation of the way things work in a security program, and of the capacity of the parties to solve a concrete security problem. The classical concept of humankind as engaged in enlightened thought is typical of such an approach.

The problem with this concept of humankind largely concerns the presuppositions on which it is founded. It claims that humans are rational and calculating beings who weigh the costs and benefits of an action and decide to act when the benefits outweigh the costs. This dovetails with the more general notion that humans act purposefully and are therefore predictable. However, it is debatable whether or not such generalizations can be formulated—consider the work of Nietzsche, Marx, and Freud, for example. Regardless of how different the ideas of these "masters of suspicion" (Ricoeur 1965: 40) may have been, they nevertheless share a strong suspicion of a long metaphysical tradition in which hierarchical antitheses place the true above the false, reason above nonsense, and the rational above the emotional. At the same time, they strip the subject of the narcissistic delusion that he or she is an autonomous and transparent being, and redefine the subject in terms of human activities in a material, sensory world. For instance, in his explanations of human behavior, Freud relies heavily on the subconscious. This subconscious is a silo full of urges, longings, instincts, and traumatic experiences. Marx emphasizes that human existence is not primarily determined by the conscious but rather by a complex whole of economic and political relationships. And Nietzsche exposes the subject as a fiction and as a grammatical function, and describes it as "the best doctrine on earth" (2007: 27). Behind the subject, according to Nietzsche, there is a play of forces that he characterizes as a "will-to-power."

The nodal approach has enabled us to realize that there are differences in mentality, structures, and technologies among the nodes, and that nodes in a security program converge according to network logic. But we actually know very little about the way in which the dynamics in a program function. Little or no attention is paid in the literature to the diversity of the people who implement the tasks. There is a suggestion, more or less, that all these people are similar and that any differences among them can easily be removed. The interactions among the people are also hidden from view, and this contributes to the presumption that all these actions are similar too. Because these issues are inextricably connected to the use and application of a security program, I will deal with them later on in this book. On paper, the theory of nodal governance would appear to be correct, but it remains debatable whether or not sufficient account has been taken of the equally dynamic and complex character of security management. After all, behind formal reality, various processes are always churning—sometimes result driven, sometimes disruptive, sometimes emotional, sometimes affective, sometimes conflictual. The question is, What is the effect of all this on the collaboration among the actors involved in modern security policy? After all, this policy acquires form in security programs of a strongly relational nature.

In my opinion, placing the accent on the relational aspect of security is of major theoretical and practical significance. It is even determinative for the organization and substantiation of security. For this reason, I wish to study the relational aspects in more depth in the next part of this book, on the basis of the French philosophy of difference. While Jennifer Wood (2006) states that more attention should be paid to the way in which actors relate to one another in a security program, we are still faced with the problem that the literature contains very little reference to the fact that there are always struggles and conflicts among actors, too, and that clashes of interest and sensitivities are also present on the work floor, emotions and frustrations can gain the upper hand in many situations, prejudices can obstruct the realization of good agreements, and all kinds of resistance can arise. In the abundance of security problems and programs, these issues seem more relevant than ever. Studying them can make a useful contribution to the issue of the governing of security and the effect of this on everyday life.

* * *

The government is slowly losing its (partly assumed) monopoly on security. Parties other than the police and the Department of Justice are becoming increasingly active in the market for security and the prevention of risk and crime. Inasmuch as one may speak of partners in crime, citizens, community organizations, and companies now belong to this category. These changes are attributed to global developments such as the network society and a form of neoliberal thinking that sees itself as offering a series of *simple rules for a complex world*. In addition, there are developments such as the rise of mass private properties and the formalization of social control. The consequence of this is transition from a monopoly model to a hybrid security model.

Besides the many new parties, this development also entails other problems. How can equilibrium be established between horizontalization and the democratic division of the organization of security? How can the interests of all citizens be guaranteed within this structure? How can democratic control be attuned to the new parties that are now part of security management? One good question deserves another. How do parties give substance to their responsibility? With regard to this last question, nodal orientation makes use of a rather classical concept of humankind, and approaches security programs as if they were hard and fast entities. Scarcely any attention is paid to the relationships among the authorities in the implementation of security control, and therefore to the dynamics within a security program. Regardless of how obvious it may appear to be, people seem to forget that the substantiation of security is also determined by emotions and sensitivities, and that these are dependent on the specific circumstances and actors involved. On this point, literature on nodal governance lacks a sense of reality.

The route from formulating abstract characteristics such as mentalities and structures to everyday reality is a long one, littered with philosophical problems and dilemmas. But philosophical problems have never had much significance within criminology. This can be explained from a standpoint largely oriented toward policy making, but it is disappointing from a scientific point of view. In my opinion, it leads to a strongly reductionist way of examining the issue of security. For this reason, in the following part of this book I wish to take up the challenge of developing a new perspective from which to study security. The substantiation of this perspective is based on the work of the major figures within the French philosophy of difference: Michel Foucault, Gilles Deleuze, and Gabriel Tarde.

PART II

From Panopticon to Patchwork Quilt

In this part, I shall develop a new perspective that provides more lati-tude for the dynamic character of security. I seek the constituents of this perspective in the work of Foucault, Deleuze, and Tarde. It will be self-evident that these thinkers place different accents on different view-points, and that they direct their attention to diverse matters.[1] Foucault is no Deleuze, just as Deleuze is no Tarde. But, in addition to the many differences, there are indeed the necessary similarities. All three authors distance themselves from a long metaphysical tradition in which a uni-lateral orientation toward, and an appreciation of, unity and totality are the central features. They champion a form of thinking that is not directed toward a recognition of the identical; instead, it is situated in a reality in which everything constantly differs, without that difference being subsequently categorized as a particular case of something more common or even universal. Moreover, in their work, all three cling to an immanent thinking in terms of relations, without making this imma-nence subordinate to transcendence. It is impossible, within the limited confines of this book, to give a complete picture of all their ideas. For this reason, I wish to elucidate briefly the choices I have made in my treatment of their work.

Michel Foucault is well known to social scientists. No philosopher has enjoyed so much attention in the past few decades. Libraries are full of writings about the disciplining of the individual and his view that prison is more than a "house of detention." In an extremely original way, Foucault worked out a new set of instruments for the exercise of power. This resulted in *Discipline and Punish* (1975) and *The Will to Knowl-edge* (1976), two books in which he describes the power relations that make people productive and efficient individuals and involve a certain manner of speaking. In doing so, Foucault demonstrates that in schools, barracks, and prisons—he refers to them as "disciplining practices"—various methods (timetables, exams, exercises) are applied to teach people desired or appropriate behavior. However, I believe that, in his oeuvre, there is another point of interest that has received much less attention but is nevertheless relevant for the treatment of the problem addressed in this book. It concerns the concept of *sécurité*, a new form of power that Foucault introduced in his lectures at the prestigious Collège de France between 11 January 1978 and 4 April 1979. Unfortunately, Foucault did not come to a profound elaboration of this concept. He devoted only a few lectures to the topic and scarcely dealt with the question of what it means to the functioning of power, let alone the perspective it could possibly offer in the wider context of a theme such as the managing of present threats and risks. Moreover, in the early eighties, he shifted the focus of this study to what he called "the governance of the self": practices in which people actively attempt to turn themselves into ethical subjects. Partly on the basis of the recently published lectures at the Collège de France, it is possible, I believe, to further elaborate the content and implications of *sécurité* as a power concept. In more specific terms, it can be shown how this new form of power leads to other insights, taking the above-described changes in the organization of security as the point of departure. For this purpose, I have studied Foucault's entire oeuvre, and now place the accent upon what one could call his "second period," in which he combines his previous archeological approach to knowledge with a genealogical approach to power.[2]

Gilles Deleuze is a different story. His thinking is diametrically opposed to the need to keep life simple, neatly compartmentalized, and straightforward by means of dualistic oppositions such as "private-public," "micro-macro," and "subject-object." However, the impact of his work in the Western philosophical community, particularly in France, the UK, and the United States, is in stark contrast to the reception of his work within criminological circles. The latter is largely confined to a few quotations from his extremely concise article entitled "Post-scriptum sur les sociétés de contrôle," dating from 1990, in which he gives an elucidation of Foucault's historical analysis of the shift from disciplinary power to a controlling power (Rose 2000; de Lint and Virta 2004; Haggerty et al. 2011; Hallsworth and Lea 2011).[3] Nevertheless, his work offers the necessary footholds for a dynamic perspective that can give insight into the way in which changes take place in social reality. In this framework, I refer primarily to Deleuze's concept of assemblage, which I provisionally define as a fabricated coupling of a number of heterogeneous elements in a unique consistency, which changes character as soon as new elements are added or old elements are removed.

Just as with Foucault, a complete study of Deleuze's rather complicated oeuvre is necessary for any elaboration of the concept of an assemblage. Various arguments can be advanced here. In *Mille plateaux* (*A Thousand Plateaus*, 1980), the book that Deleuze wrote in conjunction with psychiatrist Félix Guattari and in which the term "assemblage" appeared for the first time, Deleuze devoted so little space to the elaboration of the concept that it is impossible to speak about a fully elaborated concept. He is also rather frugal in his concrete descriptions of an assemblage in the empirical sense of the word. In his work he studied classical philosophical systems of thinkers such as David Hume, Friedrich Nietzsche, and Henri Bergson, and primarily analyzed the general characteristics of an assemblage. In addition, the concept of "assemblage" is closely related to other concepts in Deleuze's work. It refers to a series of problems, and for this reason the philosophical thoughts that are raised with this concept must be extended to other concepts such as rhizome, diagram, and control, for example. Moreover, in Deleuze's opinion, concepts do not have universal significance in the sense of an Aristotelian essence or a fixed relationship with an object or state of affairs, but must always give an answer to the immediate question, Why here and now? This starting point is also expressed in his philosophical system in which everything is interwoven with everything else and in which concepts are consistently related to concrete circumstances. Consequently, a linear construction of an assemblage is impossible because concepts, to put it in a Deleuzian way, are "hewn" from life in an immanent movement that also changes life itself into a new consistency. The result of this is that Deleuze continues to develop and refine the notion of assemblage in his work, and the consequences of this as a whole must be taken into account in the further elaboration of the dynamic perspective on security.

In chapter 4, I shall argue why Deleuze's thinking opens up new domains of reality. However, as was the case with my remarks on Foucault, this chapter does not pretend to discuss his work exhaustively or to give any kind of encyclopedic overview (for such, see Romein et al. 2009). In the introduction, I indicated that I was concerned with the elucidation and revelation of philosophical concepts, and with seeking resonances of these in thinking about safety and security. The aim is therefore not to test, let alone falsify, Deleuze's philosophy, but rather to approach his oeuvre as a toolbox full of instruments with which to tackle the issue of security. In this way, I hope to come one step closer to designing a new perspective that explains the way in which changes in security work.

The arguments that I have presented above to justify taking the work of Deleuze and Foucault as a point of departure also apply to the last chapter of part 2, which covers the work of Gabriel Tarde, the most philosophical sociologist in the French philosophy of difference. Tarde was one of several nineteenth-century philosophers, led by Alexandre Lacassagne, who developed crimino-sociological thinking, which assigned exceptional weight to the integration of social environment in any explanation of delinquent behavior. A most relevant element of his train of thought is that Tarde points out the driving force of series of interactions behind changes in social reality. Although Tarde penned his ideas about human existence and actions more than a hundred years ago, I believe they still offer valuable insights that supplement the contributions of Foucault and Deleuze. They can also be used to investigate the dynamics of security issues in an empirical way. Strictly speaking, one could also do this by means of more recent theories, but from the perspective of a philosophy of difference, I have opted to work with the ideas of this French theorist, whose long-disregarded work has recently received more attention and has now been largely revalued in a positive way. Thus, chapter 5 is the concluding section of the theoretical part that should lead to a new set of tools with which to visualize the dynamic character of security more clearly, and to structure the data collection of the third part of this book.

In the subsequent three chapters I will deal with a specific element of the work of Foucault, Deleuze, and Tarde: *sécurité*, assemblage, and interactions, respectively. In discussions with these thinkers, I wish to uncover how they interpret these concepts and what they mean when changes in social reality are involved. I seek equilibrium between respect for the particularity of these thinkers (their ideas, vocabulary, literary style, humor, relations with other philosophers), on the one hand, and the nerve to go beyond their work and to speculate and stimulate, on the other. This kind of perspectivism appears to me to be the most productive way to approach their work, first of all because I recognize the input of their own philosophy of difference in this approach and also because it allows scope for several conceptual genealogies without the necessity to determine the essential meaning of a philosophical concept. In the elaboration of this objective, I shall consistently refer to current substantiations in security practice and relevant notions in criminology. Strictly speaking, their train of thought is not perfectly honed to such developments but, to avoid being completely detached from the issue of security and to steer away from rather abstract formulations, the choice of this approach seems to me to be both constructive and legitimate.

3

Securitization

This chapter represents the first step in realizing a dynamic perspective on the issue of security. I take the work of Michel Foucault as a starting point. The fact that the perspective of nodal governance harmonizes with Foucault's analysis, in which the power to configure society is removed from the hands of the government and the police, provides a solid and germane basis.[1] In this chapter, I direct my attention to an elaboration of the lectures entitled *Sécurité, territoire, population* (*Security, Territory, Population*) and *Naissance de la biopolitique* (*The Birth of Biopolitics*), which Foucault gave at the Collège de France between 11 January 1978 and 4 April 1979. In these lectures, he speaks of a new power relation that he refers to as security (*sécurité*) and that entails a different way of thinking about how to oversee life and the living circumstances of people (*bios*), namely, in terms of prevention, certainty, normalization, and risk. Whereas the prominence of security in contemporary society is often explained by reference to social, political, and cultural changes, developments in that direction concur with the broad contours of Foucault's analysis about the issue of public health, and more particularly with the approach to smallpox. The domain of what can be said about changes in security is thus greatly enlarged.

Leprosy and the plague

The most eloquent pages in Foucault's *Histoire de la folie à l'âge classique* (*Madness and Civilization*, 1972) and *Discipline and Punish* (1975) discuss the outbreaks of contagious and fatal diseases in Europe in the seventeenth and eighteenth centuries. Countless overseas wars took their toll, but in Europe itself it was leprosy and the plague that claimed the most victims. Leprosy is traditionally regarded as the disease that occurs in the Bible as a "scaly affliction." The underlying notion is that the sufferer has turned away from God in one way or another. Symptoms such as swelling, rashes, and light-colored patches just under the skin indicate the presence of the disease. A priest determines the leprosy infection by declaring the diseased person "unclean." In *Madness and Civilization*, Foucault describes how leprosy was gradually banished toward the end of the Middle Ages. It had claimed enough victims, had behaved as an indomitable beast in a civilization that was increasingly embracing humanistic ideas and ideas about the forming of humankind. Exactly why leprosy vanished from Western Europe is still not fully known. Foucault speaks about "the spontaneous result of segregation and also the consequence, after the Crusades, of the break with the Eastern sources of infection" (1972: 16).

Whereas leprosy is the disease that God imposes as an individual punishment, the plague is regarded as a collective castigation for the overindulgence and debauchery of a whole community. In the introduction to the *Decameron* (1835), a ten-part collection of tales from the fourteenth century, the Italian poet and scholar Giovanni Boccaccio states,

> In the year 1348 after the Son of God's fruitful incarnation, into the distinguished city of Florence, that most beautiful of Italian cities, there entered a deadly pestilence. Whether one believes that it came through the influence of the heavenly bodies or that God, justly angered by our iniquities, sent it for our correction, in any case it had begun several years earlier in the east and killed an innumerable mass of people, spreading steadily from place to place and growing as it moved west.

Estimations by historians diverge, but it is certain that the disease claimed the lives of tens of millions up to the nineteenth century. Between 1346 and 1354 alone, the Black Death wiped out a third to half of all Europeans. It is not certain that all deaths were due to the plague, however. Research into the disease's spread pattern and routes of infection indicate that African viral fevers, caused by the ebola virus, could also have been responsible for much of the misery. But the great difference between leprosy and the plague is not the number of victims, regardless of how overwhelming the quantities and size of the endemic area may have been. The diseases differ from one another in the techniques by which they were tackled. The approaches to leprosy and the plague conceal "two ways of exercising power over men" (1975: 200) to prevent the infection of people.

In the case of leprosy, the victims were isolated. They were frequently banned from their village or town, driven out into the big wide world, or pushed off to sea in "ships of fools." In the view of Foucault, the leper is rejected, exiled, and dissociated: "He was left to his doom in a mass among which it was useless to differentiate" (1975: 200). The lepers lived in no man's land as beggars. Occasionally they were granted admission to a town, as on Copper Monday (the first Monday after Twelfth Night). As they entered the town, they were clad in special robes and adorned with bells and rattles to warn the inhabitants of their arrival. It is self-evident that the authorities wanted to keep the plague sufferers at a safe distance, but in Foucault's explanation of the fight against this disease, it is clear that a different technique was used than the one deployed to combat the dangers of leprosy.

In the case of the plague, the town was divided into various districts that were subdivided into neighborhoods. Each of these fell under the authority of a civil servant who was responsible for all kinds of domestic situations. At the same time, soldiers patrolled every gate and street corner to ensure that nobody could leave his or her house. In addition, a register was created to ensure that all the inhabitants of the city were shut in. It was only after the shut-in was complete that steps could be taken to isolate the plague sufferers in a sealed space. In addition, various towns established plague houses to accommodate the sufferers. In Amsterdam, this building was in the middle of the city, within the city walls. In this way, every inhabitant of the city was permanently localized, classified among the healthy, the ill, or the dead.

Behind the image of leprosy and the plague, various techniques have been devised to minimize the risks of infection. Leprosy leads to exclusion (in this context Foucault speaks of a "religious model"); the plague leads to enclosure (a "military model") (2000: 146). These techniques are grounded in different types of societies. According to Foucault, combating the plague took place in the disciplinary society of the seventeenth and eighteenth centuries. In contrast, the fight against leprosy was exemplary of the sovereign society prior to that. It is exactly on those two points—techniques and society—that important changes have taken place in the past few decades. These changes are predominantly visible in the controlling and regulating techniques applied to combat smallpox. The question arises as to which techniques were used in this framework, and which form of power best describes the techniques that were then deployed.

Smallpox

The most conspicuous aspect of Foucault's lectures *Security, Territory, Population*, is that, with the term "security," his analysis of power takes on a completely different connotation. Unfortunately, security is not a completely elaborated power concept and only comes to the fore fragmentarily. On the one hand, this is related to the fact that Foucault never had the intention to produce a fully elaborated theory of power. He regularly admits that his investigation of power relations is not directed toward a "theory of power" but rather toward development of an "analysis of power relations" (1976: 109). In other words, Foucault is not interested in questions about "what" power is, or "who" possesses power, but wishes instead to develop a certain method with which to study power. On the other hand, the lecture series gives the impression that Foucault himself is still searching for an answer, in order to distinguish his new analysis of power from previous formulations of sovereignty and discipline. While his first three lectures cover the power relation of security, this is scarcely referred to in subsequent lectures and makes way for a comprehensive study of what he calls the "genealogy of the modern state" (2009: 354).

This being the case, Foucault has not produced a refined analysis of the way security works and what the term precisely entails. This makes it difficult to point out occurrences in which we can justifiably speak of "security" rather than of "discipline" or "sovereignty." This does not alter the fact that his lectures can be used to position the concept of security within his general power analysis, as well as to link it with the question of how changes work and what the consequences could be for contemporary security. I wish to respond to these last two issues by analyzing the coherence between power relations on the one hand and the ordering of society through security on the other. In reviewing the societal fight against smallpox, I seek concrete footholds from which to spell out that interlock. In contrast to leprosy and the plague, the fight against smallpox cannot be understood in terms of a sovereign (exclusion) or a disciplinary (enclosure) exertion of power.

Whereas people originally believed that smallpox was caused by stagnant water or rotting waste, the insight gradually grew that the disease was connected to invisible viruses, the so-called *variola major* and *variola minor*. These viruses are spread through human contact. Viral infection can only occur as a result of the virus being able to survive a certain period outside the host, in someone's clothes, for example, or being carried by a person. If someone else inhales the smallpox virus, he or she will begin to suffer from fever, muscle pain, and dizziness after about a week. This is followed by a rash over the entire body, and red spots appear everywhere. These spots subsequently become blisters and fill with pus. If the victim stays alive, the pus dries out with the passage of time and the body is covered with scabs. When the scabs disappear, the body is littered with small scars. The person is further immune to the disease.

To prevent the number of infections from increasing explosively and the disease from acquiring epidemic proportions, the authorities in several countries applied a wide range of techniques, including medical campaigns, quarantine, and obligatory vaccinations. The last technique is the most well known, but was also the most controversial, as it turned out. The fight against smallpox was linked to extensive reports about the social and hygienic circumstances in which people lived. In this process, as Foucault describes, "unhealthy places in the city were localized and, where necessary, destroyed" (2000: 154). The systematic and successful tackling of smallpox will nowadays generate very few questions, but this practice was actually inconceivable in terms of medical rationality and medical theory in the nineteenth century. What made the fight against this disease so exceptional?

First of all, Foucault speaks of the "preventive character" (2009: 58) of the approach. The only effective treatment of smallpox is preventative vaccination, a discovery pioneered by Edward Jenner (1749–1823), an English doctor who vaccinated people with a strain of the cowpox virus. Although the Frenchman Louis Pasteur recognized the general applicability of this approach in 1881, the name of the procedure reaches back to Jenner's discovery. "*Vaccinia*" is derived from the Latin word for "cow" ("*vacca*"). In his lectures, Foucault did not deal with this treatment in great detail, but the vaccination of citizens is a political decision *par excellence.* It takes place under the authority of the government, which thus interferes in the personal lives of the citizens. In the course of the nineteenth century, more and more European countries made vaccination obligatory. Within the space of a few years, the method was being applied in Paris, Vienna, and Geneva. Not long after that, it became common in places such as Constantinople, Berlin, and Boston (Pols 1997). Various countries passed special laws to make this treatment possible, as did Germany in the second half of the nineteenth century. The great success that was achieved with the timely vaccination of the population is striking. Eventually, the World Health Organization announced on 8 May 1980 that the world was officially free of smallpox and, on 1 January 1982, it scrapped, smallpox from the list of diseases subject to quarantine protocols in the International Health Regulations: "The world and all its people have won freedom from smallpox, which was the most devastating disease sweeping in epidemic form through many countries since earliest times, leaving death, blindness and disfigurement in its wake" (World Health Organization 1980).

Second, the fight against smallpox was directed toward the entire population of a country. In the application of the measure, the state made no distinction between victims of disease and healthy people, between abnormal and normal. More specifically, there was no opposition between "good" and "evil" at the basis of the politics. It is characteristic that all inhabitants were regarded as a single entity. In the extension of this, Foucault indicates that the conditions under which people live and the way in which their bodies function as bearers of biological processes (public health, birth and death, average lifespan) become a component of a national politics that makes use of the sciences, such as statistics, for example—whose etymological meaning refers to "knowledge of the state, of the forces and resources that characterize a state at a given moment" (2009: 274). The same development leads to the population gradually becoming an independent object of knowledge and power. In the words of Foucault, the population becomes "object of surveillance, analysis, intervention, modifications, and so on" (2000: 95).

Third, a normal mortality rate can be attached to the disease. Not only do the statistics of the eighteenth century demonstrate that "the rate of mortality from smallpox was 1 in 7.782" (2009: 58) but also various "normalities" can be compared to one another. The mortality rate can thus be calculated for every age and every profession, in every region, city, or part of the country. For example, children younger than three years had a greater chance of being infected and of dying than people in other age categories. This fact can be deduced from two charts. The first chart shows the average mortality rate, while the second shows the risks for each category. It is important to observe that this discovery of "the normal" (2009: 57) does not begin with the "vague area of nonconformity" (1975: 181), as is the case with discipline, in which specific techniques are exercised in order to come to a "normation" of a sociocultural field. In fact, it distances itself from a disciplinary power inasmuch as this is linked to "the power of the norm" (1975: 186). Whereas the norm manifests itself as a coercive principle within disciplining facilities such as schools, prisons, and factories, "the normal" comes to the forefront in the techniques of security. This normalization does not work through discipline and in the internal ordering of certain practices, but rather realizes an effect by deriving the norm from statistical data and subsequently spreading these, from outside, over the population with the aim of identifying people, groups, or fields that form a potential risk for one another or for society as a whole.

Security as a power relation

The major changes within the domain of health care paved the way in the nineteenth century for a transformation from disciplinary mechanisms to a power relation that Foucault calls "security" and that is further concretized by modalities such as prevention, population, normalization, and risk. In the context of my analysis of the modern approach to the issue of security, the French word "sécurité" immediately gives problems. The term is not only a variant of the other French word for security ("sûreté"), but is also etymologically related to the "certainty" of a community—"securitas" in Latin, which was used in Roman law in combination with "pax" (peace) and "libertas" (liberty) and was personified on imperial coins as a female form. On the one hand, the term "securitas" expressed the protection of life and goods within the national state. This primarily concerned the safeguarding of streets, and markets. At such places, citizens had to be shielded against malevolent individuals. On the other hand, "securitas" stood for the safety of a certain community. In this sense, it was understood as what is now seen as "defense": the protection of a city, state, or nation against forces from outside. In the *Dictionnaire de Trévoux* (Trévoux Dictionary), published in Paris in 1757, "*sécurité*" also denotes a condition of belief. This demonstrates that the concept also has a subjective dimension, which recurs in feelings of insecurity, for example, among the citizens. It refers to the trust or conviction of being in a position of security against a background of potential danger (Piret 2002). In this way, the French word "*sécurité*" "elides the English safety-security distinction, in which safety denotes the concrete fact of being removed from danger, whereas security merely denotes the presumption that one is safe, whether this is true or not" (Hamilton 2013: 186).

Zygmunt Bauman provides a different elucidation of the words "safety" and "security" in his work *In Search of Politics* (1999). He states that "safety" is concerned with the protection of someone's body and his or her immediate surroundings (property, home, neighborhood) while "security" covers the position and living situation of a person, what the person has achieved, and what he or she can claim or may be entitled to. Related to this, Bauman also refers to the notion of certainty, which involves "the difference between reasonable and silly, trustworthy and treacherous, useful and useless, proper and improper, profitable and harmful" (1999: 17). In other words, certainty is related to the competency to discern between sense and nonsense, and the ability to make decisions that one will not regret later. Thus, certainty refers to a degree of predictability that ought to dispel the uncertainty of the unknown. It gives self-confidence and creates status and identity. A shortage of safety and security can lead to anxiety. Uncertainty and insecurity make people afraid.

Although it is extremely difficult to determine the boundaries between safety, security, and certainty in concrete incidences, the collective application of this heterogeneous trio by a multiplicity of actors forms the core of what I call the "securitization of society."[2] In the current framework, this term covers the gradual occupation of society, since the nineteenth century, by techniques whose function is to bring the future under control. A crucial element in this formulation is the emphasis on securitizing the time yet to come, which Anthony Giddens (1991: 111) described as "the colonization of the future." In this way, an as yet unmaterialized reality—or, to put it better, a negative future scenario—becomes a subject of reflection and a focal point for action. On the basis of this orientation toward the future, an increasing number of living areas are explored from the point of view of security, and security techniques are being applied to an ever-growing extent. Accordingly, completely different fields, such as health and education, become structurally and functionally "homologous," to use Pierre Bourdieu's words (1979). This means that these fields are problematized in a similar way and obtain a certain coherence due to a number of basic principles. For instance, the most important programs in those living areas are increasingly configured according to the abovementioned modalities of prevention, population, normalization, and risk.

As I argued, security techniques distinguish themselves from techniques of discipline, which Foucault describes as being methods to turn individual bodies into productive, efficient, and obedient units. The distinction lies in the fact that, due to their reflective nature, they point to the future, making it possible to predict occurrences and thus prevent them. For example, it is not the criminal but the future criminal who is the object of intervention. This being the case, securitization lies in the extension of criminological notions such as "actuarial justice" and "risk justice." These focus not on the return of the convicted perpetrator to society through a process of resocialization but on the identification and classification (and *de facto* rendering harmless) of activities or behavior that could pose a threat to the social order. Malcolm Feeley and Jonathan Simon (1992; 1994; Simon and Feeley 2003) have demonstrated that the techniques that are used for this have a basis in the world of insurance.[3] In the functional rationality of insurance mathematics, the premiums and payments are systematically determined on the basis of risk evaluations and considerations founded on prevention policies, and sanctioning takes place with reference to legal stipulations (Reichman 1986; Simon 1987; 1988; Ericson and Haggerty 1997).

However, securitization is a wider and more pragmatic concept than "actuarial justice" and "risk justice" because it does not place the emphasis on the position of the judicial apparatus or the state, but makes it clear that the pursuit of security takes place in a plethora of practices and environments. In addition, the starting point here is a medical model with the accent on soft resources and care and the living circumstances of the population. Also, "securitization" focuses more on the continuity and diversity of these developments than does a term such as, for example, "new penology" (Feeley and Simon 1992), which refers to a break with "old" forms of punishment. Viewed in the long run, many of the present changes in the governance of security are less unique than is often thought. I shall return to this topic in the third part of the book.

Although Foucault talks about a "society of security" (2009: 11), he does not go so far as to declare that all exertions of sovereign or disciplinary power have disappeared. In his view, it is better to speak of a triangle: "sovereignty, discipline, and governmental management, which has population as its main target and apparatuses of security as its essential mechanism" (2009: 107–8). In intellectual terms, it is tempting to further elaborate the differences among sovereignty, discipline, and security. Nevertheless, it is probably more meaningful to clarify the exceptional way of ordering that occurs in the process of securitization. The above quotation indicates that the issue of security is closely related to the entire body of questions that are provoked by the phenomenon of "governing and governing oneself, of conducting [*conduire*] and conducting oneself [*se conduire*]" (2009: 364). Foucault outlines the techniques and procedures of ordering on the basis of the neologism "governmentality" ("*gouvernementalité*"), a term that was first heard in his lecture of 1 February 1978. In contrast to state-centered approaches, as conveyed in the political philosophies of Niccolò Machiavelli and Thomas Hobbes, Foucault does not place the emphasis on the government's monopoly on enforcing social order, but rather on the "art of governing" (1997: 27). In other words, the ordering of society, in the sense of governmentality, is not regarded as a perfect reflection of the divine ordering, or explained in terms of the relationship between the monarch and his subjects, but is rather a matter of all techniques and procedures that are involved in the managing of social relations in society, such as "the government of children, of souls, of communities, of families, of the sick" (Foucault 1983: 221).

Governmentality

Foucault's considerations of governmentality deviate from the traditional liberal-democratic definition by shifting the focus from the legal (rule of law) and representative (rule of the people) framework within which political decisions are formulated to what a modern government actually manages and regulates, namely, life itself (Laermans 2009). In fact, one can go a step further. The everyday lives of people and the methods for configuring their living circumstances to an optimum degree form the most important elements of the notion of governmentality. To avoid reducing the issue of governmentality to vague abstractions such as "representative democracy" or "constitutional state," Foucault seeks a connection with the definition of "*gouvernement*" given by Guillaume de La Perrière in his text entitled *Le miroir politique* (*Political Mirror*), which dates from 1555: "Government is the right disposition of things arranged so as to lead to a suitable end" (qtd. in 2009: 96). It is striking that La Perrière speaks about concrete affairs and not about the power to govern an area of land. In the latter case, governing refers to an exertion of sovereign power or, in other words, to the power relation between a ruler and his territory. According to Foucault, this power is an asymmetrical right and claims the right to decide "on life and death" ("*jus vitae et necis*"). The sovereign exerts his power over life and death "by exercising his right to kill, or by refraining from killing" (1976: 178). The relationship between life and death changes with the regime of governmentality. Governmentality reverses the right over life and death, as it were: it is of a contrary order. This modernist form of power is directly focused on life, while death falls out of its scope. In other words, "the ancient right to *take* life or *let* live was replaced by a power to *foster* life" (1976: 181).

In a series of pedagogic texts by La Mothe Le Vayer, dating from 1653, the issue of governmentality is further concretized to three different forms of rationality: first, the governing of the self, a domain that falls under the category of morality; second, the governing of the family, which is a part of the economic issue; and third, the science of good governance by the state, which traditionally belongs to the political domain (2009: 93–94). An important element here is that the economic issue—in other words, the management of individuals, goods, and welfare—is progressively incorporated into the government's political practice. In this way, the aim of governance is less and less oriented toward the practice of governance itself, as in the sovereign manner of power exertion by the ruler, but rather toward what a modern government actually manages and regulates. This being the case, the aim of governance and the instruments that are deployed to enable this must be sought in "the perfection, maximization, or intensification of the processes it directs" (2009: 99).

According to Foucault, the governance of people's lives and living circumstances in the modern state arises as a result of embedding a specific form of power in society: pastoral power and the figure of the shepherd (see also Welch 2010). This pastoral power is a benevolent and caring force. It is directed toward the welfare of the believer and entails total and permanent obedience. This power not only forms the introduction to governmentality but also provides an elucidation of how security could become such an important theme in our society. Although the theme of the shepherd is also present in Plato's *Statesman*, its core cannot be found in Greek or Roman antiquity: "It is not a Greek nor a Roman idea" (2000: 300). The Greek and Roman gods, in being transcendentally distant from human affairs, were never understood as shepherds. This form of power reaches back to early Christianity and even to pastoral guidance in the pre-Christian East. In *Security, Territory, Population*, Foucault declares that the shepherd not only watches over the herd as a whole, but he also looks after every individual sheep, ensures that the sheep do not suffer pain, goes looking for animals that have gotten lost, and treats animals that have been wounded. The image of the shepherd who shields, leads, and protects is continued into Christianity and, later, in the institution of the church and the pastorate, with the most important goal being ensuring salvation for every individual in the afterlife. Moreover, techniques such as confession lead to a hermeneutic opinion on and relation to the soul. This makes it possible for individuals to see themselves in a new way as the subject of their own actions. In "Omnes et Singulatim: Toward a Critique of Political Reason," Foucault (2000: 308–11) summarizes the characteristics of pastoral power and the pastoral function, which I describe as follows:

1. The pastor or shepherd is not only responsible for every individual member of the community or herd, but also for all their behavior, all the good and bad to which they are exposed. In other words, he ensures the welfare (or the health) and the survival of the group as a whole and of every individual sheep. This involves integral care in the

sense that the welfare of everyone [*omnes*] and every individual [*singulatim*] is of paramount importance.

2. The bond of the pastor with every member is a personal one. His will is obeyed by everyone, not because his wish is our command or because his will is therefore a law, but purely because it is his personal wish. The obedience thus issues from the community itself and is not dependent on the power of argument or on a coercive manner of imposing a rule.

3. Knowledge is individual. The pastor or shepherd is aware of the needs of every separate member right down to the finest details and, whenever necessary, he will satisfy these. He knows what is going on in the soul and minds of every member, and has knowledge of everyone's most intimate secrets, because he is moved to do good and to care for his members.

4. The goal of pastoral power is that every member should work constantly on his own "asceticism" in this world. This "suitable end," as De La Perrière described it, is not about death itself but about the relationship of someone to himself. It forms an essential component of Christian self-identity in which someone comes nearer to God due to an extreme physical state of detachment.

In contrast to most historians, Foucault does not see a hiatus but rather clear continuity between the pastorality, the Christian function of the pastorate (otherworldly salvation), and the governmentality that has been dragging the social system into the modern state since the eighteenth century. The transition from the pastoral art of governance to the imposition of the governmentality of the modern state, in Foucault's opinion, is nothing other than a transition from an "economy of souls to the government of men and populations" (2009: 227). Whereas the function of the pastorate and its institutionalization is directed toward individual salvation in the Christian church, this salvation has now shifted to the care and protection of matters such as "health, well-being (that is, sufficient wealth, standard of living), security, protection against incidents" (1983: 215). This means that care is directed toward the circumstances under which people live and the way in which their bodies function as bearers of biological processes. Foucault refers to this as "biopolitics," a form of power that regulates social life from the inside. Modern exertions of power are thus synonyms for "biopower."

Biopolitics

Foucault describes biopolitics as a modern form of power that is situated and exercised at the level of life through control of the population. The term first appears in a lecture entitled "La naissance de la médecine sociale" ("The Birth of Social Medicine") that Foucault presented at the University of Rio de Janeiro in October 1974. "For capitalist society," states Foucault, "it was biopolitics, the biological, the somatic, the corporal, that mattered more than anything else. The body is a biopolitical reality; medicine is a biopolitical strategy" (2000: 137). The concept subsequently returned in *The Will to Knowledge*, the first part of *The History of Sexuality*, and in the lecture series *Society Must Be Defended*, both of which date from 1976, in which Foucault connects the concept with the conditions under which people live and the way in which their body functions as a bearer of biological processes. Finally, the theme is covered in his lecture series *Security, Territory, Population* and *The Birth of Biopolitics* at the Collège de France from 11 January 1978 to 4 April 1979. In these lectures, Foucault defined biopolitics as "the set of mechanisms through which the basic biological features of the human species became the object of a political strategy, of a general strategy of power, or, in other words, how, starting from the eighteenth century, modern Western societies took on board the fundamental biological fact that human beings are a species" (2009: 1).

According to Foucault, the first major theorist to cover the concept of biopolitics was Jean-Baptiste Moheau in his text *Recherches et considérations sur la population de la France* (Research and Considerations on the Population of France), dating from 1778, in which he talks of interventions by the national state in the environment of the population. On this point, the concept of population refers to more than the traditional significance of "the people," "the subjects," or the "number of inhabitants in relation to the inhabitable surface area." For a proper understanding of the concept, the "population" is increasingly regarded as a collection of individuals among whom cohabitational relations and structures exist and who, in that context, form a *sui generis* reality with its own characteristics and needs.

What Foucault demonstrates here is that, since the eighteenth century, power over life ("biopower") has been organizing and developing along two lines: anatomic and biological. On the one hand, Foucault speaks of humankind as an object anchorable in disciplinary practices such as schools, factories, and hospitals. These "anatomo-politics," as Foucault calls them (1976: 183), attach themselves to the individual body and train it through a systematic division of space and time. By systematically bringing insights from the humanities into practice, individuals are turned into specific subjects. On the other hand, regulatory mechanisms arise that direct themselves to the population as a whole. Within such frameworks, individuals are treated as examples of a biological kind. Foucault defines this life management at population level as "biopolitics" (1976: 183). Whereas he suggested in *The Will to Knowledge* that both power forms were becoming increasingly intertwined and exerting ever greater mutual influence, he made a more explicit distinction between these forms of biopower in his later lecture series *Security, Territory, Population*. In addition, he reinterpreted the interaction with the population as an object of political policy on the basis of the more general notion of governmentality. This partly explains why his use of the terms "biopower" and "biopolitics" in his work remains largely limited until the period 1976–1978 (Laermans 2009).

In Foucault's view, the characterization of the population as a collection of individuals with specific features first becomes visible in the functioning of a medical police who have been assigned the task of supervising the inhabitants of a state. Nowadays, the word "police" evokes ideas of tracing crime and criminals through the public authority called "the police," specifically set up for this purpose. But in the eighteenth century, the word did not have the meaning that is now attached to it. The activities of the police entailed more than "the surveillance of dangerous individuals, expulsion of vagabonds and, if necessary, beggars, and the pursuit of criminals" (2000: 94). Instead of being a separate institution, policing concerned a way of governing that is specific to the state, the "domains, techniques, targets where the state intervenes" (2000: 317). In other words, it is about a whole set of techniques that must produce order and is related to matters such as security, urban hygiene, and health. In Foucault's words, "the biological traits of a population become relevant factors for economic management, and it becomes necessary to organize around them an apparatus that will ensure not only their subjection [*asujettissement*] but the constant increase of their utility" (2000: 96).

Specifically, the attention of the police is focused upon five different points of concern (2009: 323–25). The first of these is the number of people who are living in a national state. This point embraces the idea that the power of the state is significantly dependent on the number of inhabitants. A second point of concern, closely related to this, covers the necessities of everyday life. Having a large quantity of people at one's disposal is not sufficient to engender power; the citizens must have enough food, water, and accommodation. Moreover, attention must be devoted to the quality of the food and the water supply. The third point of concern is the prevention of unnecessary waste of societal strengths. Those who can work, for example, must work. Unemployment undermines the power of the state. Accordingly, the emphasis of the police should lie on living beings engaged in working and trading. In addition, attention must be paid to the circulation of commodities in a society. This fourth point concentrates upon improving the infrastructure. In this context, we can consider the quality and construction of roads, the navigability of waterways, and street cleaning. Besides these physical preconditions, there is a whole battery of rules, conditions, and restrictions with regard to the trading and selling of the commodities themselves. The fifth point of concern is the abovementioned public health. Health is not only an issue in times of plague or leprosy, but the everyday health of every individual is a constant object of concern and is a reason for state intervention in the lives of ordinary citizens.

In this framework, an extensive administration is set up to obtain more knowledge about the health of the population. Data and observations on matters such as births, health, illness, and death are collected in series of reports and registers. The construct of the "healthy citizen" is needed in order to govern life effectively and efficiently. This knowledge, as Foucault states in *Security, Territory, Population*, rests upon four relatively new concepts: case, risk, danger, and crisis (2009: 60–61). "Case" does not involve an individual case ("something in itself") but rather a means to individualize a collective problem, on the one hand, and to incorporate an individual case in a collective problem, on the other. In the case of a disease, it is important to examine the possibility of "risk of infection." For instance, statistics may help to calculate that the risk of smallpox is not the same for everyone. This means that the medical police will be able to identify what is "dangerous" and what has a chance of developing into a "crisis"—in other words, a situation in which a certain phenomenon will suddenly break loose.

The development around the medical police and the health issue of hygiene and medicine fit into a broader biopolitical framework in which the population is treated, by means of specific forms of knowledge and techniques, as a collection of coexisting beings with their own biological and pathological characteristics. Moreover, the appearance of the population on the political stage is linked with the advent of new governmental practices. In the Netherlands, urban intervention teams are typical examples of this. This topic is dealt with in more detail in chapter 8. Such teams have the aim of improving local security and of reinforcing social bonds in the neighborhood. These teams pay visits, either spontaneously or by appointment, to families at risk in order to check how they are coping with living conditions (finance, social disorder, fire safety), work and income, health, and security. However, increasing control of the population provokes the inevitable discussion. To what extent should the government be involved in the citizen's freedom of action? Is there a collective interest besides an individual interest? And, if so, how are these two related to one another?

Controversy

One of the yardsticks for a civilized society is the way in which it organizes its public health care. In this context, it is again interesting to devote attention to the fight against smallpox in order to understand fully the process of securitization. In fact, the approach to this disease is at odds with classical liberal ideas about the ordering of society. According to the liberal approach, society should be governed according to its own principles. In addition, the social space—the being together of people and the way in which they relate to one another in a natural way—must be exempted from intervention by the state as much as possible. This space can function relatively separately from the political space because it has its own rules and patterns. A typical feature of this domain is therefore not the structure of the sovereign, the legal subject, and the exertion of power but rather the starting points of "self-organization, free transaction and interests" (Simons and Masschelein 2009). This returns in, for example, the idea of the invisible hand, postulated by Adam Smith (1976), which has become synonymous with an economic notion in which absolute freedom of action has priority—or, in other words, the idea that a market ought to be able to regulate itself without intervention from outside, and ought to be able to offer resistance to threats that could disrupt its equilibrium or functioning.[4]

It requires little effort to understand that the endeavor of the government to improve public health clashes with the individual freedom of citizens to arrange their lives as they please. To a great extent, this is related to the obligatory inoculations demanded by the government. For an outline of the interests and dilemmas that play a role here, I turn to a study by American historian Michael Willrich (2011) about the fight against smallpox. Objections similar to those now being heard in the Dutch context of urban intervention teams were already being expressed in the United States of the nineteenth century. In contrast to European countries, in the United States the governmentality of the health care issue led to much more social discomfort and vehement discussions about the legitimacy of the measures. Such discussions were primarily heard in southern states such as Kentucky, where the disease claimed many victims among the African American section of the population and poor white inhabitants. These groups had little or no access to medical care and lived in densely populated areas. Poor nutrition and unhygienic circumstances made many of them more vulnerable to the disease. Moreover, supervision of public health lay in the hands of the police, which thus had the right to interfere in individual affairs to serve public welfare. Fines for avoiding inoculation even amounted to as much as a hundred dollars. Jail sentences of forty days were not uncommon. In addition, people who refused to be vaccinated were sentenced to carry out public work on the roads and streets. The agitation about government measures to fight smallpox had various aspects. They can be partly traced back to tensions between white and black population groups. One part of the black population regarded quarantine—imposed to reduce the risk of infection—as an expression of white power, and attempted to avoid complying with this measure. In turn, a part of the white population put the blame for the disease on the African Americans. God wished to punish the black population for its sins. These racist-driven theories were stirred up by rumors that white people could not get smallpox.

The objections to social regulation by the government increased greatly in a short time, and opponents united in an antivaccination movement: a group of people who displayed active resistance against what was called "state medicine." This resistance was founded on the idea that vaccination is an infringement of the individual's personal freedom. Some parents held the opinion that their authority within the family was thus undermined. More generally, the antivaccination movement turned against growing interference by the local government in fields such as education, family life, personal beliefs, and freedom of speech. Their attitude encapsulated a libertarian approach, and they underpinned their main objections by quoting passages from *On Liberty* by John Stuart Mill (1989) about the rightful freedom of the individual, the limits of governmental action, and the sovereignty of the body. On the basis of a strong aversion to government interference, the scar left by vaccination was regarded as a form of biopolitical tattoo (see, in another context, Agamben 2004). Ultimately the medical issue of the fight against smallpox grew into a political struggle about the government's right to intervene in the private domain of its citizens.

Supported by the antivaccination movement, Albert Pear, the son of a local Republican Party leader, appealed to his right not to be vaccinated. In the legal case *Commonwealth v. Pear*, which was tried in court on 13 November 1902, Pear claimed that his doctor had advised him not to allow himself to be vaccinated and that he had given him powders against smallpox. A similar case took place on 27 February 1903. Like Pear, Henning Jacobson, a Swedish immigrant who was living in Cambridge, Massachusetts, during an outbreak of smallpox in 1902, was supported by advocate James F. Pickering. The arguments in this case rested upon the core arguments of the antivaccination movement: vaccination leads to new diseases, isolation offers better protection against smallpox, citizens have a right to protection against the arbitrary exercise of governmental power. Ultimately, various cases were combined to form one single legal case that was held in the Supreme Judicial Court of Massachusetts in April 1903. The judge decided that "the rights of individuals must yield, if necessary, when the welfare of the whole community is at stake" (Willrich 2011: 320). After this verdict, Jacobson decided to continue his case and to fight out the dispute before the Supreme Court. This became *Jacobson v. Massachusetts* (197 U.S. 11). The Court issued a verdict on 20 February 1905, and Judge John Marshall Harlan decided that the American Constitution does not speak of an absolute individual freedom but rather that the

> government is instituted for the common good, for the protection, safety, prosperity and happiness of the people, and not for the profit, honor or private interests of any one man. [. . .] There are manifold restraints to which every person is necessarily subject for the common good. On any other basis, organized society could not exist with safety to its members. Society based on the rule that each one is a law unto himself would soon be confronted with disorder and anarchy.

A striking feature of the verdict by the Supreme Court is the relation that is made with societal order. The verdict declares that a society organized in a modern fashion needs new forms of social and economic governance. In modern times, writes Willrich, "the old freedom to be left alone was no freedom at all" (2011: 327). One could also say that an interfering state is necessary in order to enable individuals to be free. In this way, the obligation of the government to intervene leads to the paradoxical situation that freedom exists as a result of interference by the government. In other words, freedom is not a natural fact or a natural phenomenon but is, to a certain extent, something that must be generated. It is self-evident that this case involves not only public health but also the right to free speech, freedom to trade, the implementation of property rights, and political freedom. The interesting aspect is the fact that the government creates the preconditions under which a certain degree of freedom can be reached. The platonic or essential question as to whether humans are thus free or bound is thus no longer leading in the debate about the ordering of society. Instead, the debate is more concerned with organizing society in a way that allows for individual freedom. With this, the liberal slogan "the less politics, the more freedom" is also abandoned, as the concurrence of politics and freedom assumes increasing prominence. Freedom is not opposed to the power of the state, as an irreducible and absolute individual right, but has become a component of the same movement toward the securitization of society.

State of the state

The issue of securitization has little to do with the familiar literature on the political history of the modern state. Within this literature, an important place is assigned to Niccolò Machiavelli's *The Prince* (2008). According to Machiavelli, the goal of the exertion of power is to strengthen and protect the territory. For this purpose, the dangers that could threaten the territory have to be identified, and subsequently a technique needs to be developed with which to manipulate power relations for the purpose of protecting the territory. In that sense, Machiavelli's treatise is exemplary of a sovereign exertion of power oriented toward the territory or nation ruled over. However, Foucault wishes to show that modern forms of governance, in contrast to sovereignty, lie not in "divine, natural or human laws" (2000: 317) but at the level of the population itself. In that respect, we are dealing with numerous new regulating and empowering security techniques that manifest themselves at population level. They refine and supplement older forms of power, while increasingly defining problems relating to individual freedom and social order as social problems (see also Rose 1999; Neocleous and Rigakos 2011). It is in this context that security is increasingly switching from being a defensive concept—entailing the thwarting of invaders and the punishment of criminals—to becoming an offensive concept. Foucault does not deal with this topic in great detail, but whereas sovereign power once only came into action when a citizen violated the law or when the national territory was endangered, measures are now being taken at an increasingly early stage in order to eliminate all risks. In addition, it seems that the citizen is no longer only regarded as an object of control, as a part of the security problem, but also as a constituent of its solution.

Although Foucault was opposed to the idea of power solely exercised by the state and the totality of state institutions, it cannot be concluded from this that the state plays no role in the process of securitization. In Foucault's scheme, governance does not replace the political realm (*la politique*). The concern for the population is ultimately a concern for the state. The legal concepts of law, for example, still play an important role in the large-scale management of populations. This presupposes the presence of a government, in the sense that the state defines and delineates these concepts and punishes any violations of these rights by third parties. This conclusion is a logical sequel to the new analysis of power relations of which the central and systematic fight against smallpox is illustrative. This means that Foucault's rational analysis of power must be seen in conjunction with the political context within which security is managed. With regard to this last point, David Garland (1990: 167–68) points out that the way in which power techniques are used is also formed by the political forces in a state. In other words, the way in which the power relation receives concrete substantiation depends on the political choice to configure society in a certain way, thus determining whether or not certain social issues should be tackled.

Nonetheless, it is of little use to regard the securitization of society as a return to the sovereign power of the state, as if the security power relation only issued from the state and could only be localized in a state apparatus. The instance of the modern state is "not a universal nor in itself an autonomous source of power," writes Foucault (2008: 77). Thus, in the process of securitization, the government is never the source of all relations. It will never be able to occupy the entire field of current power relations in a society. In his monograph on Foucault, Deleuze points out that "if the 'State-form,' in our historical formations, has captured so many power relations, this is not because they are derived from it" (1986: 82). It is therefore more apt to speak of the state in the plural form, not as "a household, a church or an empire" but in the sense of "states" (Foucault 2008: 5). The reason for this is that the position of the government in each separate field (welfare, public order, health) will never be exactly the same.

To a certain extent, the above considerations generate a more qualified conclusion than reflections that refer to the reduced influence of the government on everyday life and Hayekian demands for a minimum of state involvement. Perhaps the opposite is truly the case. Apart from the state monopoly on violence and political decision making, the underlying thought is that the state has generally become weaker since the 1970s, partly due to the pressure of recent forms of political and economic neoliberalism. Nikolas Rose and Peter Miller (1992: 176) have written that "the state has no essential necessity or functionality." Eugene McLaughlin and Karim Murji (1995) predict the end of public policing. David Bayley and Clifford Shearing (1996; 2001) speak of the fragmentation of the state monopoly on the policing function. These authors are certainly right that there is mention of increasing disintegration of the policing function. But, in contrast to the belief that, with this, the power of the state would decline and that of the private sector would increase, it is possible to assume a completely different perspective. In my opinion, there is stronger interference by the government in everyday life, precisely because security is linked to problems of a social, economic, and cultural nature. Not only do many practices turn out to be impotent without governmental involvement, but the government also succeeds, within the boundaries of those practices, in making them supportive of the overarching general interest of security, which can be called "greedy governance" (Trommel 2009).

In an extension of this, I have already pointed out the fact that the government has nestled in a continuum of public-private partnerships in which social, economic, and cultural problems are governed (thus, the government has not actually retreated). Within these partnerships, it is able to jointly determine the agenda and influence the aims and starting points of the tasks to be implemented. In addition, it can draw the attention of citizens and policymakers in other organizations to new problems. It will be self-evident that this is not a homogeneous and unequivocal development—the role and influence of the government in each partnership will be too divergent for this, and will be accompanied by the inevitable tensions and problems. As a consequence, it will not pick up every security program in the same way and produce the same effects everywhere. However, there ought to be some qualification of the opinions of authors who speak of an erosion of the state function under neoliberal economics and politics. With all respect to these authors, I do believe that the government is reinventing itself in this process of securitization and is looking over the shoulders of new parties. The state, and the police, have not yet fallen into a "zombie category," to use a term coined by Ulrich Beck (Beck and Willms 2004: 51), referring to an organization that is dead but still sees itself as alive and kicking and still among us. But the fact that the securitization of society is also a fight in which the state does not wish to surrender its authority, and the confidence that the citizens invest in it, is difficult to deny.

The thesis that security is slowly but surely taking over more and more areas of life is being acknowledged by an increasing number of authors. In *Crime in an Insecure World*, Richard Ericson (2007) declares that we are living in an era of uncertainty and that security has come to be primarily oriented toward a precautionary thinking. Whereas prevention is a rational approach to a risk objectified and estimated by science, precautionary considerations cover doubt and uncertainty, the uncertainty of scientific knowledge itself (2007: 22–23; see also Ewald 2002). Another important contribution to this debate comes from Jonathan Simon, who describes, in *Governing through Crime* (2007), how the tackling of the problem of crime (or, being more precise, of risk and danger) is governed by, on the one hand, collaboration among various parties of whom the state is merely one (although a very influential one) and, on the other, the fact that fields such as housing, health, education, and employment/workfare are being reconfigured according to the logic of security thinking. In this way, tackling growing criminality among young people is leading to the situation in which schools, in coordination with the municipality, the police, and the Department of Justice, formulate regulations that allow teachers to frisk school pupils when they suspect that they are carrying drugs or weapons (Kupchik 2010). In short, not only is the notion of security used to motivate all kinds of measures that have different intentions, but the technologies and metaphors of security are also more present and actual in diverse fields than ever before.

This observation requires explicit substantiation because the securitization of society, as observed here, is regulated on a contractual basis in local partnerships in which parties other than the government have exceptional competencies and resources at their disposal to execute their tasks. Because I have reviewed this point in the two previous chapters, I shall now restrict my remarks to the Dutch example of the Collective Shop Ban, which aims at preventing unacceptable behavior in commercial areas (Wesselink et al. 2009). In this construction, shopkeepers themselves have developed measures to combat crime and disorder. One of these measures is the imposition of a shop ban on troublemakers, and this ban is enforced throughout the entire city center. In this structure,

parties such as shopkeepers and private security personnel are jointly responsible for tracing and punishing offenses such as theft, abuse, threats,
and vandalism. For an answer to the question concerning the rationality
that prevails in this security program, I shall first discuss the policy of
the Dutch government with regard to the organization of security management. I do not do so with the goal of putting the primacy of the government at the forefront, but rather to investigate how, within the Dutch
political discourse, different answers are being sought in the interaction
with crime and disorder. In my opinion, it is necessary to take this step
in order to stimulate systematic reflection on the situation in which parties other than the police and the Department of Justice have begun to
circle around the issue of security, in the broadest sense of the term.

Dutch security policy

Even into the 1970s, the concept of crime in the Netherlands was primarily associated with the control of classical (also called "communal")
crimes such as theft, fraud, and homicide. In such occurrences, the
emphasis lies on exerting power "in the name of the law." This means
that the enforcement of law has no other goal than the enforcement of
social order on the basis of the legal order. More specifically, the public
order practically coincides with the legal order. After the 1970s, crime
became more the focus of attention. The increased attention paid to
crime seemed to be legitimate in itself if one looks at the decrease in the
citizens' faith in the government, the gradual decline of social control,
and the strong rise of crime in the Netherlands: from 130,000 incidents in 1960 to more than a million registered crimes in 2001. At the
same time, crime gained a much wider embedding. A shift from crime
fighting to security promotion took place. For an understanding of the
support base for this development, it is interesting to examine the report
of the Dutch police (1977) entitled *Politie in verandering* (The Police in
Transition), in which it specifies its aim as "to make a positive societal
contribution, partly integrated in governing and legal functioning, in the
form of social management, which not only contributes to a protection
of social attainments but also creates, to an equal extent, the conditions
for social development and innovation, directed toward the essential
values in our democracy (Politie 1977: 53). The same report speaks of the

pursuit of "optimum integration in the community in which police care is exercised" (1977: 55). With this, the police wish to indicate that they want to do more than merely keep order. They also wish to be involved with the welfare of citizens and society. The promotion of welfare must occur on the basis of mutual "knowing and being known" (1977: 54). This means that the police apparatus must maintain close contact and also develop a permanent and personal relationship with the population. The police should no longer be above society, but rather a party between other parties, thus generating a socially integrated force that will have "social information" at its disposal and can attune its activities to the needs and opinions of the various communities in society.

Almost a decade after the Dutch police pleaded for an expansion of crime fighting into a broad social responsibility (thus, one that is no longer only the liability of the police), the government's policy plan *Samenleving en criminaliteit* (Society and Criminality, 1985) also connects the crime issue with the "mobilization of individual citizens and social organizations, including local governmental authorities and business circles" (Tweede Kamer der Staten-Generaal [TK] 1985: 37). To create more coherence in the approach, discussion is devoted to what is called "integral security." This new way of speaking is remarkable because (in)security is a much broader concept than crime. Crime may be a cause of insecurity, but these two do not always coincide. Insecurity involves more than crime alone. Insecurity may be caused by relatively minor occurrences and activities, such as noise, antisocial behavior, and traffic accidents, and also even by poverty, health problems, and extreme weather conditions. The difference between crime and insecurity is demonstrated by the double significance of the term "integral." First of all, security is now no longer defined solely in repressive terms. More and more attention is being paid to a preventative approach as well as to aftercare in the shape of victim support and the settling of damage claims. Second, various sections of society and policy areas within security management are brought together, such as those dealing with crime, traffic safety, environmental security, the fight against terrorism, and (natural) disasters.

Traditionally, crime fighting is directed toward the perpetrator. One of the most striking aspects of "Society and Criminality" is that not only the individual criminal or criminal group is made the object of security policy. The same security policy appears to be functional only when, as can be read in the policy plan, the "entire population is regarded as belonging to the target group" (TK 1985: 36). In this way, the population becomes the means *par excellence* to intervene in the politics of security. It becomes a goal and an instrument of governance at the same time. It is a well-known strategy. The best way to win the trust of the people, which gradually decreased with the ongoing processes of democratization and individualization from the early 1970s onward, is to stimulate them to undertake action themselves. One practical result of this is that the maintenance of the legal order is no longer the exclusive task of the government and the Department of Justice. Responsibility must be shared with the social commons. Parents, schools, youth centers, neighbors, housing corporations, local governmental authorities, and other organizations are also being mobilized. It is essential to create a network of functional supervision, "a progressive (re)introduction of an adequate level of person- or function-specific supervision of all areas of society in which many crimes are committed" (TK 1985: 36).

Foucault already demonstrated in *The Will to Knowledge* (1976) that, since the eighteenth century, the population has been subjected to a whole range of techniques and mechanisms devised for the purpose of governing people's lives. He refers to the growing field of political practices and economic studies with regard to issues of reproduction, life span, public health, housing, and migration. Although he does speak of the way in which the human body is inserted into an extremely complex discourse of knowledge and power, he forgets to emphasize that this issue goes deeper than passive integration in the techniques and mechanisms that govern and control life. In other words, Foucault opens his diagnosis of modernity with the convergence of disciplinary and regulatory mechanisms of security, but devotes little or no attention to the fact that, within the general problem, the issue is not only about making the individual and the population controllable and optimizable but also about involving the citizens in the direct function of state governance, and particularly in the policy of the police and the Department of Justice—that is, involving citizens in combating crime.

The way in which the government scuttles sideways like a crab in order to build up structurally a whole network of relations has been recently elaborated in the Dutch police report "Prevention Pays" (*Tegenhouden troef*, Politie 2003). In short, the concept of prevention or restraint amounts to influencing behavior and circumstances in such a way that crime is avoided or curtailed prematurely. For example, it is relatively easy to take measures that aim at preventing an uncertain future by installing chips or sensors in theft-prone goods such as laptops, GSM devices, and cars. This should be implemented across the entire breadth of society, from education to the layout of public space, and from catering facilities to employment policy. In the operationalization of prevention, the involvement of private parties is subsumed in two categories: supplier and customer. As the producer of goods and services, business corporations must give substance to new policy. Policy terms and conditions may be of assistance here, such as discount premiums from insurers if security measures are taken in the framework of Police Quality Labels for Secure Housing or Quality Label for Secure Entrepreneurship. Such discounts may enlarge the willingness of citizens and entrepreneurs to take concrete measures to combat crime. One step further is that the nonparticipation of entrepreneurs in accredited security projects will lead to the insurer refusing to pay out in cases of damage (Politie 2004: 47).

In this way, an appeal to what is called "local security networks" (Dupont 2004; Terpstra and Kouwenhoven 2004) leads to a strengthening of the general fight against crime, due to the fact that state responsibilities regarding the tackling of crime have been adopted or shared by private parties. To enable this supervision to function properly, structural links have been forged among all kinds of "digital archiving systems" (Schinkel 2011). With this, the private sphere of influence penetrates the public domain—just like the public domain initially penetrated the private realm. This kind of interlock of the state and society makes the classical manner of thinking about security rather unclear. While state and society were always more strongly linked than was acknowledged in classical liberal discussions, the securitization of society has led to the situation in which it is becoming increasingly difficult to draw a hard distinction between public and private. A gray zone or a hybrid area is arising between public and private. I shall return to this topic in the following chapters, but in the meantime it is important to establish that all kinds of developments in the field of security have generated problems with regard to the opposition of public and private, while it is not yet clear what has come to replace these.

Quasi-criminal law

In the previous sections, I have mentioned that two important elements have received little attention in Foucault's analysis of governmentality. On the one hand, he points out the growing field of practices and studies related to the problems of propagation, lifespan, public health, housing, and migration and, in these contexts, speaks of the way in which the individual and collective body of the population is inserted into a discourse of knowledge and power. But, remarkably, he devotes little attention to the political interests that help determine the nature and use of security techniques. On the other hand, Foucault opens his diagnosis of modernity with the convergence of disciplinary and security techniques. But, within the general problem, the fact that we are concerned not only with making the future controllable but also with an active yearning on the part of citizens and businesses to be involved in the issue of security management seems to have escaped his attention. In this way, it becomes clear that the rise of the concept of the population as a living body leads to concrete changes in the governance of society. But the issue of which techniques and truths the longing of the population itself is heading toward does remain vague.

In conjunction with the growing attention being paid to the security problem, certain sections of the population have seized the initiative to enlarge social control themselves. Citizens watch over their neighborhoods in so-called citizen or vigilante teams. Entrepreneurs hire in security personnel to fight and prevent crime and disorder. More generally, such activities require joint endeavor by the government, businesses, and citizens in order to tackle security problems adequately. The formalization of that responsibility takes place by means of covenants or similar written agreements. These contracts are characterized by a system of reciprocity or communality, where agreements are made about what parties should and should not do, about who bears the responsibility for the implementation of certain tasks, and about the use that is made of the resources available in that context. At the same time, they dovetail with "a desire to control the uncertainty of the future" (Crawford 2003: 490) by decreeing all kinds of measures to prevent unwelcome behavior. In this way, the future is placed in the present. Apparently, this contractual governance accommodates nothing more than a farther-reaching regulation of the social order. In reality, a new set of instruments besides criminal law is being created to keep a grip on the public and moral order of society. To give this exceptional aspect of securitization more profile, I shall now discuss in more detail the abovementioned collaboration among shopkeepers, the municipality, the police, and the public prosecutor to prevent unwanted behavior in the city center of The Hague. The measure applied is referred to as the "Collective Shop Ban" (CSB).

A remarkable feature of the CSB is that it is a concept devised by the shopkeepers themselves. Its introduction cannot really be regarded as something new: entrepreneurs always had the possibility of refusing a person access to their shops. The new element of the CSB is the fact that the ban applies not only to the enterprise where it is imposed but also to all the enterprises that participate in the measure. These enterprises vary from small, one-person businesses to large chain stores such as Zara and H&M. Although the term "shopping ban" suggests that the measure only covers shops and shopkeepers, other establishments such as theaters, studios, and galleries, hotels, banks, restaurants, and even drugstores apply the CSB policy. A ban on entering these enterprises is possible on the basis of rules that are valid at that particular place. A legal suspicion in the sense of a reasonable presumption of guilt is not required in such cases. In order to be able to impose a ban officially, the CSB form must be signed by one witness and by the person who committed the offense. If an offender refuses to sign the form, a second witness may sign the form so that the document is thus valid. This being the case, one can say that shopkeepers thus make use of classical means of power such as the arrest of an offender and his or her exclusion from the shops that participate in the project. In this framework we are referring to classical criminal acts such as theft, fraud, slander, threats, and destruction. Such offenses have been listed in the Penal Code for many years. The competencies of the CSB are not recorded in law, however, but in a covenant that has been locally agreed to by the participating parties. Moreover, the primary search for truth occurs without the aid of police and the Department of Justice, through shopkeepers, large-scale chain stores, and private security guards. For this reason, legal protection is organized via a complaints procedure, a regulation that not only gives the offender fewer guarantees than criminal law does but also requires the offender to undertake steps in order to win the case. The offender must submit a written complaint to the board of governors of the entrepreneurial association, objecting to the fact that a CSB or a caution has been imposed on him or her.

Because these differences with classical criminal law seem to go further than the similarities, I wish to speak of "quasi-criminal law" here: a new domain of regulations and prohibitions in which considerably fewer demands are imposed upon legal protection than in classical criminal law. With this new term, I build upon the relationship between security and law. Regarding the relationship of discipline to law, Foucault spoke of a "counter-law" (1975: 224–25). In his opinion, discipline generates a particular coercive relationship between individuals, one that differs in its basic principles from contractual obligation. For instance, law qualifies legal subjects according to universal norms, whereas discipline "compares, differentiates, hierarchizes, homogenizes, excludes" (1975: 185). Regardless of how universal discipline may be, declares Foucault, it consequently remains a counter-law in its mechanisms. In the case of security, quasi-criminal law does not function completely outside classical criminal law. In a certain sense, it actually operates within the regime of criminal law, because its execution presumes a system in which the police and public prosecutor participate and to which they have given their approval. Although the sphere of influence of criminal law (punitive measures, stricter and more extensive police action) has irrefutably increased in the last twenty years, it must be stated at the same time that a completely new instrument has appeared to reinforce norms and to exclude people from certain facilities and areas. As a result, quasi-criminal law cannot be regarded as being totally independent of the traditional style of prosecution, as executed by police and the Department of Justice. In that sense, it is more of an extension rather than a replacement of the way in which classical criminal law tackles disorder. Inasmuch as quasi-criminal law attaches an extension of meaning and fixation, it seems to fulfill a "supplementary function" in relation to criminal law, to use one of Jacques Derrida's terms (1994). A supplement is not merely a random addition, but a necessary appendage (similar to the white space between the lines of this text) of an existing reality or legal sphere. In this particular case, it concerns a supplement to criminal law that is enforced by the state.

The supplement does not have a neutral meaning in the sense that the offender is subjected to prevailing Dutch criminal law alone. At the core, the protective function of criminal law, as elaborated in the reform philosophy of Enlightenment thinkers such as Montesquieu and Beccaria—the legalization of power in the *trias politica* and the theory of the social contract, respectively—is eroded. In this philosophy, the legitimacy and integrity of a constitutional state are determined not only by the restriction of the government's power but also by the capability to protect citizens against legal aberrations. However, in quasi-criminal law, a different legal route for the same type of delict is in force, with fewer legal guarantees for the offender. This consists of an internal complaints procedure. The unification of the forces of criminal law and quasi-criminal law thus makes the corresponding legal protection vulnerable, because protective claims are now instrumentalized in the hands of all kinds of small sovereigns—in the case of the CSB, the shopkeepers. Viewed from this perspective, the danger is not that the introduction of quasi-criminal law would further help regulate or govern security issues but rather that this quasi-criminal law would increasingly function as a refinement of criminal law. The ultimate consequence of this is that criminal law will be incorporated into quasi-criminal law and that, with this, every mediation between concrete power forming and power exertion will vanish.

Politics and culture

We often feel that thinking about security in terms of prevention and risks is something that arose after the 1980s. But, remarkably, the transition to weighing up situations in terms of risk and prevention is the provisional result of a much longer development. I have demonstrated that the process of securitization began in the nineteenth century with problems related to public health. With the disappearance of the horsemen of the apocalypse (leprosy, plague, and smallpox) from the social scene, the securitization of society has increasingly come to stand in the light of the approach to crime and disorder. This provokes the question as to why this thinking in terms of prevention and risk has arisen in Dutch society at such a late date. For example, why is criminal law and legal policy—the political discourse, thus—only now, more than a century later, being seen in the light of prevention and the use of risk profiles, risk estimation, and the distinction between good and bad risks? What is the reason for the shift in criminal law at this particular moment from the importance of legal protection of the citizen against obtrusive governmental intervention toward the importance of protecting the citizens against all kinds of security risks?

Social and cultural processes play a major role in this development. A part of the explanation has already been articulated. Where objective security is concerned, a strong increase in registered crime, in both quality and degree of seriousness, has been visible in the Netherlands since the 1960s. In 1980, the police registered 24 violent crimes per 10,000 inhabitants. This had risen to 87 per 10,000 inhabitants by 2004. Over the same period, crime against property rose from 459 to 625 incidents per 10,000 inhabitants. And the number of instances of vandalism and destruction registered by the police also rose substantially: from 65 in 1980 to 132 in 2004, per 10,000 inhabitants (Eggen and van der Heide 2005; Wittebrood and Nieuwbeerta 2006). The past few years have witnessed an irrefutable decrease in crime, but in comparison to the 1960s and 1970s, one can still refer to a "high crime culture" (Garland 2001) in which the approach to crime is characterized by a strong emphasis on the protection and safety of the public.[5] As a result, it is becoming increasingly difficult to uphold the view of criminal law as being the *ultimum remedium*. The enormous growth of the number of penalizations in all kinds of fields and the extension of competences in the area of detection of crimes give the reach of criminal law a previously unknown scope.

This latest development is reinforced by the fact that, since the 1980s, the political discourse has been largely oriented toward the attempt to control risks. For example, Ulrich Beck (1992; 1999), to name the most important author from the large flow of literature on risk, believes that politics is no longer directed toward the production and distribution of wealth and not even toward the promotion of solidarity and equality. We have landed in a society obsessed with risk, which is ordered along the lines of security and insecurity. In this framework, a revolutionary agenda has made way for the ordering principle of risk limitation and regulation. Within this shift, security is defined in terms of the absence of risk or as an exorcism of experienced risks. The essential point here is that the coordination of "security" and "risk" makes it possible to establish links between public and private living areas. Security is something that occurs in all shapes and sizes. There is a security aspect to everything we say and do. Accordingly, it is becoming more and more evident that various forms of security are mutually connected and can be integrated in a wider security policy. For instance, care and repression go hand in hand with the approach to drugs, and the police and the Department of Justice are now placing increasing emphasis on public health (Korf 2010).

However, security as a political problem cannot be seen separately from its cultural dimension. Security is also a cultural issue involving notions of how secure or insecure we feel, and in which public support is determinative of the approach to certain problems and the introduction of new rules and punishments.[6] Political decisions are partly based on the feelings and emotions of citizens about the intensity of the insecurity and on ideas of what they can expect of the government. Two matters are of particular importance here. First, with the increase in the number of connections between security and other areas of life, there is a decline in the acceptance of risks among the population. The slogan has become "No More Misery." In the realization that we ourselves create the conditions under which we live, we now tend to look differently at risks than we do at the consequences of natural processes. The more we can personally do and decide, the greater our own responsibility. This probably explains why we are increasingly refusing to accept the remaining insecurity in our social environment, although this same environment, seen objectively, has become more and more secure in terms of enhanced lifespan, for example (Piret 2002). Second, citizens are increasingly expecting that the government should protect them against risks in society. Risks that used to be regarded as self-evident have now become a question of poor governance. It is of the utmost importance that the government demonstrate that it is taking insecurity seriously. In this context, one can refer to the populist tone of the political debate and also to the introduction of punitive approaches to law and order for which no hard evidence that they are effective is available (zero tolerance, street coaches, boot camps, etc.). In short, criminal law has progressively become an instrument in the hands of government, which uses it to fulfill its paternal obligations in the domain of security. The consequence of this is that criminal law is evolving into a more proactive tool, and prevention is playing a more central role in the governance of security.

One might comment that, to the police, prevention is nothing special. The writings of police commissioner Patrick Colquhoun (1745–1820) showed that the police were already strongly oriented toward the prevention of crime from the early nineteenth century onward. In *A Treatise on the Police of the Metropolis*, Colquhoun wrote that the essence of the police is "the prevention of crimes and misdemeanors" (1806: 540). In the opinion of Sir Robert Peel, who was responsible for the founding of the London Metropolitan Police in 1829, it is necessary for the police to maintain good relations with the population if they wish to make prevention the basis of the fight against crime, and to enter regularly into various neighborhoods and districts to guarantee the citizens' safety (Reiner 2010). In that respect, the Dutch report *"The Police in Transition"* (Politie 1977) formed the blueprint for a socially aware police force that wishes to generate the preconditions for social development and innovation. However, the point is not that prevention is something new but rather that the focus of judicial policy does not essentially concern the protection of life and property through subsequent action based on exclusive responsibility. Instead, it is more concerned with the aim of preventing crime and of reducing anxiety about crime (van Swaaningen 2005). One of the related effects has been the even earlier deployment of detection methods and techniques, as well as growth in the number of controls carried out without a magistrate supervising the process. In that respect, Matthias Borgers (2007) speaks of "the flight forward." Accordingly, detection investigations are expanding to people who are not suspected of having committed any crime—without the people in question having any knowledge of this situation. The instrumental exertion of this informal or proactive maintenance of order has far-reaching consequences for the citizens' sense of freedom, in view of the fact that formal legal reality seems scarcely to have altered despite all these changes. In that respect, the distinction between "normal citizen" and "suspect" is becoming increasingly vague. In the process of securitization, everyone has become a "risk citizen."

* * *

On the basis of the central issue of this book, I have shown that Foucault's work contains various points of address that enable us to proceed further than static structures such as "public-private." Clarifying the increased complexity of society by means of such schemes alone means not only selling societal manifestations short but also misunderstanding them. Indeed, the story becomes contradictory because a blurring of public and private fields occurs due to the fact that power relations traverse life areas such as health care, education, and welfare, and join one another in new entities. This development began in the nineteenth century on the basis of a medical model aimed at fighting smallpox. The application of Foucault's conceptual structure thus presents a picture of a society that has been primarily oriented toward security, with modalities such as prevention, population, normalization, and risk that make this power relation more regular, efficient, and constant.

With regard to the changes in security management, I have built three bridges. The first extends from the issue of public health to other risks related to the lives and living circumstances of people, such as the tackling of crime and disorder. Whereas the fight against smallpox was initially a medical problem, it became generalized as a result of its conceptual framework being shifted to a comprehensive way in which social issues can be governed.[7] I have allocated the term "securitization" to the epidemic spread of techniques that are aimed at making the future secure. Similar to a virus, security continually seeks contact with completely different life domains that are not related to one another in their nature, but thus become interconnected. In this way, the problem of crime is explained in a medical discourse of disease, infection, diagnosis, and recovery. This occurs with the common adage "prevention is better than cure."

The second bridge is the one between security and the role of government. The idea of governance is often associated with the image of modest government that relies upon costeering, corowing, coproduction, and cooperation with other parties to achieve security objectives. The limitations of the government in working in a problem-solving way form a central feature of this managerial perspective on governing security issues. In the process of securitization, however, the image of a retreating government ought to be revised. The influence of the state has not dissolved, in the sense of having vanished into thin air.

Public-private partnerships do not necessarily undermine or hollow out the role of the government. On the contrary, the partnerships can be a way of achieving goals of the national state. Accordingly, it seems incorrect to describe the government as a party that has lost its power in a fragmented security landscape. In fact, the government has managed to strengthen itself by nestling in old and new security domains.

The third bridge links security to quasi-criminal law, which is a striking supplement to the legal set of tools as recorded in the Penal Code. In quasi-criminal law, the rules are not laid down in a universal law that determines, a priori, all cases and situations, while investigation into offenses is not assigned to public instances such as the police and Department of Justice. In contrast, the offender has to fall back on a complaints procedure. In such a situation, he or she can appeal to his or her rights as a citizen, but this kind of procedure offers fewer legal guarantees than common criminal law does. Such development questions the legal protection of citizens in the process of securitization and the democratic control of the approach to crime and disorder.

These three bridges prompt further consideration, now that the securitization of society in general is leading to the disappearance of the differences between private and public. There is no longer mention of a simple choice for or against this development. Public and private have become so interwoven that there is little use in opting for only one of them as the starting point for (future) security policy. In that respect, we have landed in the unbounded space of the middle ground, where everything and everyone are becoming hybrid. The following chapter will cover this topic in more detail. The thinking of Gilles Deleuze will function as a conceptual framework for this angle of approach. Again, attention will be devoted to the forces that lie at the basis of the dynamics of social reality.

4

Assemblages

With the advent of the technology of security, the gate has been opened to the situation in which common life domains such as health care, education, and welfare, which are inherently very different in their nature and function, are being integrated into new wholes. This raises the question of how these wholes can be understood without our falling back upon general categories such as "public" and "private." Foucault's analysis seems to indicate that such orderings are not imposed from the outside, by an institution, person, or group that is legally authorized to do so or possesses the resources to perform this act. To obtain a good understanding of the current situation, it appears to be more logical to approach the issue from the other side and to request that attention be paid to the phenomenon of processes that are self-organizing and are thus not directly caused by external factors.[1] This is therefore not a classical, structural perspective on social reality, but rather one that involves the way in which changes can be derived from their own processes and conditions. In stating this relational approach, I take a second step toward a dynamic perspective on security, with the aim of being more able to clarify the changes in the governance of security. The thinking of Gilles Deleuze offers great assistance here, as his work supplies important concepts that can shed more light on the question of how changes in social reality are generated.

The middle

In the conclusion to the previous chapter, I tentatively pointed out "the middle" as a point of address to further open up the working of practices of security. It is in relation to this middle that Deleuze introduces a different type of thinking that can be summarized as an attempt to elude what he calls "dogmatic thinking." The problem with dogmatic thinking is that it is not capable of considering the dynamics that underlie the representation itself. We have already seen this in the opposition between public and private, discussed in the first chapter. Right from the start, this undertaking returns at various places in Deleuze's work. It is concerned with a dismantling of a modern logic that has exercised a firm grip on political and scientific thinking for more than two hundred years, and is locked in an antitheses whose poles, Deleuze claims, do not exhibit a lucid mutual relationship: "subject-object," "inside-outside," "private-public," "micro-macro." How does the dismantling of these antitheses take place?

The question is easier to ask than to answer. After all, what actually is this midpoint from which Deleuze wishes to set out? What is the middle that could put us on the track of connections among various elements in security that, in their strictly intrinsic nature, have nothing to do with one another? Wouldn't it be better to ask about the correspondences or similarities between the enforcing parties that are engaged on the security issue? What do they have in common? Do they share the same mentalities? Do they have the same goals? In Deleuze's opinion, one certainly does not find an adequate answer to such questions by making the middle an object of research and by seeking its essence. In his view, the middle does not lie encapsulated in the things themselves. If that is the case, it must coincide with a fixed property or a permanent essence of a form or sort. In this framework, matters have an underlying and authentic core ("meaning," "truth") that is waiting to be (re)discovered. In this way, the essence of a concept is localized in a general and unchangeable point from which something subsequently appears, such as in the old Aristotelian relation between potential and reality, within which the ultimate form is already present in potential in the original situation. However, according to Deleuze, people tend to forget that this kind of thinking is incarcerated in a representational logic that is incapable of conceiving reality as such, and has difficulty coping with changes and unexpected events. As Deleuze remarks, the essence of a concept of the world differs from the manifestations and occurrences that we experience on an everyday basis. This latter domain changes permanently and therefore can never form an origin in itself. Accordingly, instead of a train of thought that appeals to the distinction between essence and appearance, Deleuze wishes to take the step from essences to real or concrete circumstances. "The search is not for an eternal or universal," writes Deleuze, "but for the conditions under which something new is created" (2003: 284). In other words, what should be sought is the situation in which various elements are connected to one another, and this situation, as Deleuze never ceases to emphasize, is always contingent.

Not only does the middle not coincide with an essentialist view of reality; it also contains a rejection of possible reconciliation of divergent matters and of unification in new and overarching entities at a higher level. Often without any form of reticence, we use terms such as "fear," "precaution," and "risk" to refer to the whole of society, contextualizing numerous expressions. This principle of generalization covers concepts such as a "risk society" (Beck 1992), "culture of fear" (Furedi 1997), "exclusive society" (Young 1999), and the like. A remarkable feature of such all-embracing approaches is the shadow bookkeeping system that is used. The suggestion is evoked that one individual is capable of comprehending reality as a whole. Detached from reality, that person can oversee everything. It is also assumed that it is possible—in principle—to identify the forces that shape society, even if that turns out never to be the case in practice. In addition, such approaches presuppose that it is possible to have a generally valid, objective perception of something such as a "whole." A consequence of this is that one's own scientific position is seldom subjected to examination. But, despite these shortcomings, the picture of a more or less universal and largely homogeneous society continues to appeal to many. It is repeatedly proffered as a description and explanation of divergent phenomena in society.

In *Empirisme et subjectivité* (*Empiricism and Subjectivity*, 1953), Deleuze outlines, for the first time, his objections to this way of looking at social reality in which confirmation is sought by combining matters in a single and independent concept. He states that reality cannot be understood as a whole or totality, as a collection of loose elements, like components of a construction package that are going to form a fixed and immobile entity. This would entail that something would be able to function as a homogeneous or unifying whole and would work in the same way at all levels of that whole. Deleuze uses the word "artificial" (1953: 28) to describe the idea of a homogeneous unit that can only exist by means of the assumption of a shared order. The consequence of this is that one cannot appreciate the difference and disparity of things that do not correspond with this method of conceptualization. Contrasting with the interpretation of a fixed entity, he deploys, in *Critique et clinique* (*Essays Critical and Clinical*), the image of "a wall of loose, uncemented stones, where every element has a value in itself but also in relation to others" (1993: 110). Here, too, there is mention of a whole, but this whole consists entirely of "separate" stones that have much in common but are never 100 percent identical. An important consideration here is that with every stone one can ask about the molecules it contains, the sand layers that are constituent elements, the age of these layers, or the animal fossils that may lurk within. Something similar can be found in modern art, with the ordered white reliefs of the Dutch painter Jan Schoonhoven. These monochrome reliefs are made of cardboard, papier-mâché, and toilet rolls, and exhibit cardboard planes with a strict systemology as well as all kinds of subtle variations.

Trees and rhizomes

The key concept of "middle" cannot be reduced to the things themselves, and the things do not form constituent parts of a fixed and immobile whole. But how should we understand the concept of "middle"? Can something like this exist at all? In the last few sentences of the first chapter of *A Thousand Plateaus*, Deleuze and Guattari give an important clue to what can be understood under the term "middle":

> The middle [*milieu*] is by no means an average; on the contrary, it is where things pick up speed. *Between* things does not designate a localizable relation going from one thing to the other and back again, but a perpendicular direction, a transversal movement that sweeps one *and* the other away, a stream without beginning or end that undermines its banks and picks up speed in the middle. (1980: 37)

A few sentences before this passage, they give the concept a name by means of which this middle can be better understood: "A rhizome has no beginning or end; it is always in the middle, between things, interbeing [*inter-être*], *intermezzo*" (1980: 36). In his discussion of the middle, Deleuze assigns a significant position to the concept of the rhizome. For this reason, I shall first describe what the concept involves.

"Rhizome" is a term from botany and literally means a root branch that grows horizontally rather than vertically, and whose root bifurcations spread out over considerable distances underground in inextricable tangles. Deleuze contrasts the image of a rhizome with that of a tree structure. Whereas the latter expands from an "origin, seed or center" (Deleuze and Parnet 1991: 48), a rhizome has no beginning or end. It seems to begin at a random spot. With the structure of a tree, Deleuze has directly articulated the philosophical concept that he wishes to rebuff by means of the rhizome concept. In Western metaphysics, various movements have mirrored themselves on this tree image, ranging from Plato's parallel-worlds theory—ideas and the material reflections of these—to Descartes' ontological dualism—mind and body—via Hegel's dialectic thinking, on to twentieth-century structuralism with its tree diagrams. At the same time, these are also the most well-known philosophical traditions that start from representational thinking. All such trains of thought postulate "an identity—the one (1)—from which differences (n) develop" (Oosterling 2009a: 189–90).

Deleuze uses the rhizome to signify a different way of thinking that, outlined simply, does not rely upon a metaphysical concept of reality in which the changeable character of reality is consistently reduced to a unit or a new entity. Instead of an interpretation that falls back on a transcendental element or original signifier, Deleuze wishes to approach changes in social reality by starting in the middle, where radically opposite forces are active. In this way, rhizomatic thinking works on the basis of the tension between forces, a tension that cannot be determined and is therefore not representable. In accordance with a manner of thinking that is not hierarchic, and that starts from all kinds of associations, there is mention of a process (rather than a position) that produces diversity. But, to Deleuze, this does not mean that the middle is a principle that reallocates an unambiguous direction and unity to reality. It concerns an interstitial space or what I would wish to call, in conjunction with the author William Burroughs, an "interzone" (1959; 1990)[2] from which processes develop and new connections are created. In more general terms, the middle is thus connected to the changing circumstances under which something new can arise, and to everything that changes. The verb "to connect" is characteristic of this situation. This connecting principle may be physical, lingual, or conceptual, and is thematized by Deleuze through the term "rhizomatics."

If one imagines society as a rhizome, perspectives other than the classical logic of private-public become possible to explain the ordering of society. The essence and unity of categories such as public and private are replaced here by a dynamic "in-between," an "intermediate place," which continues to connect things mutually in an existing reality. This results in a society without fixed categories, a coexistence liberated from previously construed meanings and consisting of spontaneous connections, unexpected events, and identity-free moments. In this framework there is no central actor or underlying structure of significance that governs everything, as was the case, to a certain extent, with Marx (position in the production apparatus), Weber (position in the professional structure), or Durkheim (position in the labor division). Instead of that, components develop (as in root branches) independently of one another, and no fixed structure can be discovered with regard to the way in which the connections among the parts arise. The changeability and complexity of social reality are such that they cannot be organized and stored away with the introduction of new fixed structures.

This perspective on social reality led to many objections and criticisms. Whereas Foucault oriented his thoughts to concrete problems such as crime, madness, and sexuality, and was, in political terms, a radical who supported prisoners' rights and the gay movement and expressed enthusiasm for the Iranian revolution and the return of Ayatollah Khomeini, Deleuze is tied to the image of a philosopher who is primarily interested in concepts that have nothing to do with everyday reality. His thinking is referred to as "elusive," or as utopian, anarchistic, and even romantic. Whatever the case, it is unsuitable for chartering practical matters like the governance of security. After all, how can things be described when every fixed meaning is constantly being postponed? How can significance be given to circumstances that are, in principle, always variable? Thus, how can we cope with reality when it is fluid?

Machines

I believe that it is possible to approach Deleuze's work in a different way, one that is important for finding a response to the question of how the dynamics in security management can be understood. In *L'Anti-Œdipe* (*Anti-Oedipus*, 1972), Deleuze and Guattari analyze current power relations in light of the development of capitalism and, in doing so, they make use of a remarkable definition of the concept of "machine": "Everywhere it is machines—real ones, not figurative ones: machines driving other machines, machines being driven by other machines, with all the necessary couplings and connections. An organ-machine is plugged into an energy-source-machine: the one produces a flow that the other interrupts" (1972: 7). The examples that they give of machines—desire machine, organ machine, territorial machine, anus machine, barbarian machine—show that a machine must be understood in functional terms. A machine is a device that is connected to other devices. The function of a machine is then to link heterogeneous elements together. It becomes useful and productive by means of these temporary connections. And it can consistently generate something new.

Traditionally, two approaches have been taken in examining machines. First, the word "machine" refers to an item or object. In this meaning, a machine is viewed in a strictly technical sense. Then we are talking about a car or a pistol, invented to meet a human need or want. The word can also be used to refer to a way of thinking and acting that makes one more able to understand complicated relations in reality. In this sense, we can think of a model that applies to a household, for example, or a business organization. A good example is the representation of the penal law procedure as a factory. In this structure, the procedure, ranging from the tracing of crimes to the implementation of the punishment, is seen as a serial production line whose aim it is to combat crime (Steenhuis 1984). The same symmetry also lurks behind the notion of the police as a concern, with the paramount idea being that governing the police is the same, *grosso modo*, as governing a large corporation. Here, the police are described as a company that works on the basis of apparently neutral terms such as customers, effectiveness, efficiency, contracts, indicators, and yields. Both notions of a machine are tempting representations because they fit into a generally mechanistic model in which reality is regarded as having been constructed from mutually dovetailing components that convey movement to one another. The narrative at the basis of this is relatively simple: matters work in a causal and pattern-based way. Purposefulness, manipulability, and controllability are the leading features.

Mechanistic thinking developed in various periods. Well-known periods are those of chronometry (from roughly 1600 to 1790), the steam engine (from 1835 to 1950), and the computer (from 1950 to the present). In each of these periods, people attempted to obtain a grasp on the changeability of social reality by dissecting the workings of things and introducing the components thus obtained into standardized and controlled processes. An example of the first period is the mechanistic metaphor of the world as a clock, in which various entities, such as the solar system, the state, and the body, are compared to a large clock. This metaphor was recorded in *Leviathan* (1963) by Thomas Hobbes. The book begins with the famous comparison between the state, the human body, and the clock:

> Nature, the art whereby God has made and governs the world, is by the *art* of man, as in many other things, so in this also imitated, that it can make an artificial animal. For seeing life is but a motion of limbs, the beginning whereof is in some principal part within; why may we not say, that all *automata* (engines that move themselves by springs and wheels as does a watch) have an artificial life? For what is the *heart*, but a *spring*; and the *nerves*, but so many *strings*; and the *joints*, but so many *wheels*, giving motion to the whole body, such as was intended by the artificer? (1963: 59)

It is evident that, to Hobbes, the cold mechanism of the clock functions as the central concept for the ordering of society. It is used as a general representation of thought and action in reality. One turns it on and it goes. Individuals are seen as cogs in the wheels of a giant machine.

Again Deleuze argues that he does not find this way of viewing social reality very convincing. He also explains why. In contrast to closed-system thinking with fixed ordering, Deleuze wishes to understand a machine as an open system of unequal elements that "cannot be reduced in any way to mechanics" (Guattari 2009: 74). A machine, in contrast to a mechanism, has no organic unity and can be connected to everything else in principle. In this situation, productions are not previously determined and do not comply with strictly causal links. They are, as Deleuze and Guattari call it, diverse and heterogeneous. Strikingly, Deleuze does not adhere to the notion of machine for very long. In his books after *Anti-Oedipus*, the machine concept is replaced by the term "assemblage" (*agencement*). No reason is given for this change. This is probably related to the fact that the machine concept induces too many associations with a mechanical idea of reality and evokes too many preconceptions of strictly technical equipment with corresponding characteristics of causality, such as push, pressure, and thrust.

The connection principle

In *A Thousand Plateaus*, Deleuze and Guattari speak of the working of an assemblage, again without supplying a comprehensive elucidation of the term. Nevertheless, the concept recurs in all chapters, which are called "plateaus"—with reference to Gregory Bateson—where the procedural and changeable qualities of reality are examined. In an interview with *l'Arc* magazine in 1980, Deleuze responds to the question concerning what connects the various chapters in *A Thousand Plateaus*: "I think it is the idea of an assemblage (which replaces the idea of desiring machines)." Contradicting the dual and shifting meanings through the various chapters, the significance of the term "assemblage" is most clearly expressed as the whole of relations among heterogeneous elements in a specific environment, where every element can again be regarded as an assemblage, *ad infinitum*.

In the explanation of this concept, it is essential to consider the French word for "assemblage" because it contains the changeable character of social reality. "*Agencement*" is related to the Latin word "*agens*," which means "governing" or "setting in motion." This governing principle expresses a process of "arranging," "organizing," or "adding together." But the governing power of this process is never outside an assemblage. An assemblage has its own operational force, is self-organizing. This self-organizing activity cannot be reduced to its elements, but lies in the relations among the elements that are part of an assemblage. These elements may be people and tools, as well as images, moods, instruments, sounds, buildings, organs, or forms. After all, both people and things have the ability to exert force and, in doing so, are able to (help) change affairs in their environment. This means that elements are related to one another via a whole network of relations in such a way that a certain consistency exists with respect to one another. In his Dutch novel *Bezonken rood* (*Sunken Red*), Jeroen Brouwers articulated this insight concisely: "Nothing exists that does not touch something else" (1981: 7).

Deleuze uses the example of the stirrup to demonstrate the way in which relations consistently activate different connections among heterogeneous elements (Deleuze and Parnet 1991: 109; Guattari 2009: 91). The stirrup attached to the saddle, enabling the easy mounting of a horse, is an Asian invention dating from around 800 CE. Originally the horse was a domestic animal used to pull light carts, but the invention of the stirrup changed everything. As a result, the horse became part of a new method of waging war. Mongolian warriors used the invention to sit up straight on a horse and to control the gallop better. Due to the stirrup, the lightly armed horsemen could partly rotate in the saddle, allowing them to shoot arrows at targets to the rear. Later, in the feudal age of waging war, the significance of the stirrup changed due to the introduction of other weapons and a new battlefield. As an attribute of a horse, the stirrup worked as a footrest so that the horsemen could gain more grip when fighting with lance and shield in a seated position in a formation. Thus, the stirrup did not remain the same instrument when added to a different assemblage. When an element is mediated by relations that link it to other elements, it is no longer possible to speak of a fixed significance of an element. It can acquire a multitude of meanings. This means that all relations among stirrup, horse, weapon, and horseman determine the significance of the instrument, not vice versa.

The above text brings me to Deleuze's argument about the independence of relations. Just like Foucault, Deleuze states that relations are not subordinate or reducible to the elements they connect. Deleuze illustrates this by means of the example "Peter is smaller than Paul" (2001: 37). Peter's "being smaller" and Paul's "being larger" are not encapsulated in the idea of Peter or Paul. In addition, they do not jointly form a concept that lies at a deeper level so that the relation would be inherent to that concept. Therefore, relations are not a quality inherent to terms, impressions, or ideas, but are external to these. This aligns with the previous chapter, which dealt with various power relations. We saw that power should not be understood as something that is the property of an institution or person, but is rather a relational fact: "What characterizes the power we are analyzing is that it brings into play relations between individuals (or between groups)" (Foucault 1983: 217). This raises the question of how the elements behave in a whole, with regard to the relations involved. After all, an element can detach itself from an assemblage and can function further in a different assemblage. It can be extracted from an assemblage and incorporated into a different context (see also DeLanda 2006). In turn, this context is formed by other circumstances and other relations among the elements.

Content and expression

The connection principle is of crucial importance to the functioning of an assemblage. The example of the stirrup shows that the act of connecting forms a self-organizing process of an ongoing gathering or fragmentation of various elements that are only defined in and by this process. It is important that this process is constantly in motion and is not subjected to a unit-forming force. Much more than a realization of a deeply embedded essence, it is about processes of change that are active at various levels (chemical, physical, biological, or social) in which heterogeneous elements reach a critical point at which they begin to cooperate and generate a certain ordering. In this process, the relations and the elements permanently mediate one another. As a consequence, there is always mention of a unique constellation that changes its nature and composition as soon as new elements join in or old ones fall away. The emphasis on the open combination of elements in an assemblage leads, however, to questions concerning its consistency. In which way are heterogeneous elements in an assemblage held together? Or, more concisely, how can a system be stable and changeable at the same time?

Deleuze and Guattari discern two movements or dimensions in an assemblage that bring about stability and change. First of all, they speak of a horizontal dimension. This dimension is formed by the relation between content and expression. The content of an assemblage refers to the interactions of bodies in a concrete practice. This practice may be the police, Tax Department, or housing corporation, or political events such as the French Revolution, May 1968, or 9/11. The expression is the whole of signs or the semiotic system that links a system together (Deleuze and Guattari 1980: 629). In this framework, one can think of lingual (symbols, words) and nonlingual expressions, such as physical posture or clothes. The latter is more than something used to keep one's body warm. Clothes can express a certain function (judge, conductor, police officer), assign a social status (three-piece suit), or serve as a form of self-styling (Hell's Angels, punks, football fans).

For their distinction between expression and content, Deleuze and Guattari base their work partly on the research performed by the Danish linguist Louis Hjelmslev, who developed a "Spinozist lingual theory" in which content and expression do not rely on an omnipotent signifier (Deleuze 1986: 55; Guattari 1984: 73–81). Here, expression does not coincide with a signifier (*signifiant*), and content is not the same as the signified (*signifié*). There is no similarity or agreement between them in the sense of description or correspondence. In a critique of the work of Ferdinand de Saussure, who is regarded as the "father of structuralism," Deleuze and Guattari question the relation between content and expression. De Saussure (1986) defined a sign as being composed of a signified and a signifier. The signifier is the bearer or physical existence of the sign. This may be a letter, letter combination, sound, or diagrammatic representation. The signified is the referent in reality, or the "mental" concept that underlies the signifier. The common notion of the signified and the signifier is that they need one another. They cannot be separated from one another. Without a signifier and a signified, there is no sign. The sign only acquires genuine meaning in the connection between these. But the relationship between signifier and signified is actually completely arbitrary. The signified has no natural relation with a certain signifier. In addition, de Saussure's sign theory presumes that a whole system of rules (*langue*) lurks behind individual use of language— the spoken dimension (*parole*)—that functions independently of the use that any random individual makes of it.

In contrast to the relation between signifier and signified, content and expression function relatively independently of one another. I say "relatively" because they exist only through the relations that lie between them. Content and expression are in no way directly or absolutely dependent on one another. Both are stand-alone processes that operate independently of "the event" or "the case" to which they refer. In other words, the expression is related to the content without describing or representing the latter. Take, for example, the phrase "I swear." This phrase acquires different meanings when spoken by a pupil to a teacher, by a minister during his inauguration, or by a witness in a court of law. It is not enough to comment that only the environment (school, parliament, court of law) changes. That would suggest that the statement in fact remains the same. Not only do the elements or "nature" (Deleuze 1986: 20) differ from the various environments, but also the statement itself takes on a different expression. Deleuze and Guattari take this argument quite far here. Not only do they call content and expression two "independent formalizations," but they also have their own form and substance (which are again completely heterogeneous), and sometimes even several forms and substances. From this perspective, there is no ultimate form that ensures a link between content and expression. Between these two, there is only a process that mutually connects both forms, and this process itself has no form. Deleuze speaks of a play of forces and of a zone of indistinguishability. In this, he typifies this process as pure intensity.

Thus, expression and content are not related to one another as signifier and signified, but blend into one another and constantly activate one another. Accordingly, a fixed meaning is always absent. Deleuze explains this through the lingual philosophy of the Stoics in antiquity, where the emphasis on difference is the characteristic feature. In the philosophical thinking of the Stoics, difference must not be undone, but should be the central focus. In *Logique du sens* (*The Logic of Sense*), Deleuze discusses the example of the "greening of a tree" (1969: 33) in this context. It is important to realize that "green" is not a quality that is intrinsically associated with the object "tree." Before it can be a property of the tree—namely, for the tree to be "green"—there is mention of the event of the "greening" itself. To be more precise, the "greening" is an independent process, a stand-alone occurrence that combines two properties: that of the idea of "green" and that of the idea of "tree." For this reason it is better to speak of "the tree turns green." In this process, there is a change both of the tree toward green and of green to the tree. It is not solely about the encounter of the "greening of the tree," but the reverse is also just as important: the "treeing of the green."

This convergence of changes is far from exhaustive, but I shall curtail it here. It is evident that the dismantling of the relation between content and expression offers a possibility to avoid descriptions that represent reality as if there is mention of an object at rest. Instead, the accent comes to lie upon continuous change, articulated in each separate case, in every new situation, and consistently under different circumstances. It is relevant that each case can be approached as an event or as a process of becoming, as such. This indicates that its meaning is essentially never fixed but is always dependent on the relations that mutually connect people and things.

De- and Reterritorialization

There is another side to an assemblage. Deleuze and Guattari refer to this as the vertical dimension. In this context, they reason in terms of territory. Every assemblage is territorial (Deleuze and Guattari 1980: 629; Deleuze and Parnet 1991: 112). The discovery of the environment (in the sense of *Umwelt*: the surroundings in which we are situated) by the Baltic-German biologist Jakob Johann von Uexküll was of great significance in this field. Von Uexküll introduced the idea of *Umwelt* into theoretical biology in 1909. In *Umwelt und Innenwelt der Tiere* (*Environment and Inner World of Animals*), and in *Theoretische Biologie* (*Theoretical Biology*) a year later, he described animals in terms of their sensory structure and instinctive reactions. He elaborated the thesis that the environment worked upon and influenced the senses of an animal, on the one hand, and that the animal experienced its environment in a unique way, on the other. This means that our *Umwelt* is not a communal and unchangeable fact that is experienced by everyone (i.e., every living creature) in the same way, but rather depends on the person or animal itself. Every living creature experiences its world in a different way. Von Uexküll illustrated this by discussing the life of a tick. The tick reacts to three changes in its surroundings: light, smell, and temperature. If there is a change in light, the tick climbs onto a leaf or branch of a plant or tree. The smell of a mammal ensures that it lets itself fall onto its prey. Difference in temperature ensures that the tick nestles on the place on the skin where it can suck blood with the least effort. Seen in this way, the *Umwelt* of the tick is incomparable to that of the fish. And the *Umwelt* of the fish differs hugely from that of the heron. Humans also live in an *Umwelt*, but the absence of certain instincts causes humans to generate their own external reality. In this way, von Uexküll used the concept of *Umwelt* to demonstrate that it is a mistake to think that social reality provides a single shared ordering for all living creatures. In doing so, he took an important step in articulating a pluralistic notion of reality that postulates just as many worlds as there are possibilities to see and feel them.

The idea of an *Umwelt* was iconic of the previous century—note Henri Lefebvre's studies of everyday urban space, and Michel Foucault and Erving Goffman's work on the influence of totalitarian institutions on the individual: prisons, schools, psychiatric institutions. These studies are not concerned with the traditional question "What is the human being?" but rather with "Where is the human being?" It is self-evident that a territory can be a closed location or a part of a city, such as a police station, football stadium, shopping mall, and the like. But it is more than just firm ground under one's feet. A place is also where something occurs, where something takes place or is experienced between people. It is thus the issue of contextuality or, as Jeroen Brouwers (2007: 50) articulates it, "as a goldfish hates the cat, and the cat hates the water." What is unpleasant to one creature, what it fears and what it wishes to avoid at all costs, may be a life resource to another.

With regard to the problem of contextuality, Deleuze and Guattari consistently pose the question of how territorialization—that which defines the boundaries of a territory—actually works. Take a gated community, for example. In addition to the rules and regulations of the government, local arrangements are also in force in such areas. When someone purchases a house in a gated community, he or she signs a detailed contract that lists the rights and obligations concerning the lifestyle and culture of the relevant community that are valid at that location (Blandy et al. 2003). These rights and obligations may vary from a ban on drinking alcohol to the place where the washing ought to be hung out. In essence, one could speak here of local jurisprudence. With this, I have arrived at the most important aspect of the vertical characteristic of an assemblage. It perhaps looks as if territorialization only limits the mobility of an assemblage because the process of territorialization brings about a unification of a social space, a certain cohesion of place and identity of the people and things present. However, a territory cannot always retain its form; it does not remain a coherent ordering of a concrete social field forever. It is only conceivable against a background of an endless mobility of social reality. To thematize this, Deleuze speaks of "deterritorialization" or "line of flight," a movement that disjoins an assemblage. This kind of line eludes every assemblage, which means that it constantly undermines the existing field of orderings by supplying new openings and creating other connections. In this way, every assemblage can dissolve at any moment. However, this movement of consistent dissolution also continually morphs into its opposite. Deleuze and Guattari refer to this as "reterritorialization." Both movements presuppose the other. One does not exist without the other. Every reterritorialization entails a deterritorialization, and vice versa.

Thus, an assemblage consists of four aspects, namely, content, expression, territory, and deterritorialization. This last notion fulfills a central role in Deleuze's work and requires further elucidation. In *Dialogues*, Deleuze describes deterritorialization as follows: "It liberates a pure matter, it undoes codes, it carries expressions, contents, states of things and utterances along a zigzag broken line of flight, it raises time to the infinitive, it releases a becoming which no longer has any limit, because each term is a stop which must be jumped over" (Deleuze and Parnet 1991: 113). To Deleuze a line of flight has two features. First of all, it is abstract; one cannot understand it in terms of content or expression. But it goes even further. It is abstract because it not only ignores the difference between content and expression but also dismisses the distinction between form and substance. Second, a line of flight is immanent, which means that it always forms a part of the organization of an assemblage. To emphasize the openness of an assemblage and the changeability of reality, there must be something that breaches the nature and coherence of these and makes a connection with other elements. This does not happen by synthesizing new elements or by adding new elements, but by removing these from an assemblage and forming a new assemblage in the connection with other elements. In that respect, according to Deleuze and Guattari, the movement of deterritorialization is linked to new machinal production—in other words, to the forming of a different assemblage. It gives an impulse to the creation of a subsequent ordering. In a double movement, the territory is consistently reconfigured, as the recurring temporary effect of a deterritorializing movement. For this reason, the line of flight is of primary importance to Deleuze: it precedes everything. Territories are secondary in this matter.

Form and substance

In speaking of the change factor in social reality, it is vital to be aware that Deleuze does not restrict an assemblage to formations such as schools, hospitals, and workplaces. He also uses the term in biology ("the wasp and the orchid"), literature ("Kafka"), psychoanalysis ("little Hans") and processes of subjectivization.[3] An assemblage is therefore not necessarily a delineated place, but may also be an organism or individualized lifestyle. Graffiti may serve as a useful example here to help the social sciences understand the reach of the concept. For instance, under certain circumstances, graffiti can assume a certain meaning and become an element for new assemblages. The presence of graffiti in urban neighborhoods, for example, may indicate the degeneration and decline of the relevant zones. In that framework, the conservative criminologists James Wilson and George Kelling state in their "broken windows" theory (1982) that feelings of insecurity may rise in a poorly maintained neighborhood where there is much vandalism. Graffiti gives the residents the idea that they are living in an uncontrolled and uncontrollable part of town. But when spray cans are used to decorate the roller-shutters of hip stores such as Nike and Stüssy, graffiti works as advertising or branding. Here, graffiti performs the task of enticing people into that particular shop, of drawing them to that neighborhood. In turn, Banksy—the English artist renowned for his political and amusing murals—has proven that graffiti can function in public space as a political statement and as an art object. That the personnel of the anti-graffiti team of the Transport for London company painted over a work by Banksy on the wall of a transformer shed is a well-known fact. The value of the work was estimated by a museum director to be around half a million euros. Finally, graffiti signatures—also known as "tags"—can also give residents a feeling of security because they function as a form of demarcation of the edges of a territory ("my neighborhood" or "my street"). For example, street gangs such as MS-13 use graffiti as boundary marking and as a warning to other youth gangs not to transgress the boundaries of that area.

However, the force of the term "assemblage" is most prominent in the light of the previously described power analysis by Foucault. The concept of assemblage can be used to further consider Foucault's argument on the technology of security. In this framework, I think primarily of the explanation of the prison, the institution in which punishment is substantiated behind closed doors. In order to comprehend the concrete constellation of bodies and lingual expressions, and also to obtain insight into how the four aspects of assemblage influence one another, one must pose the question concerning the content of a prison. One could reply by mentioning the aims that are associated with a prison sentence, such as deterrence, resocialization, or incapacitation. But "content" refers to something other than the objective of punishment or the idea behind a prison sentence. The question concerning the content of a prison must be posed differently: Who goes to prison? The prisoners are then the content. Stated otherwise: it is all about human bodies that have performed a certain action (or have failed to perform an action) and have consequently been convicted of an offense by a legal institution. In addition to substance, content also has a form. Following Foucault, Deleuze speaks of a "prison-form" (Deleuze and Guattari 1980: 86). To describe the form of the prison in the eighteenth century, Foucault refers to the model of the Panopticon designed by Jeremy Bentham. This Panopticon was a circular building with large windows in the middle of the prison, which offered the guards a view of the cells on the inside of the ring. Although this optical power technique is accepted as an exemplary model of the disciplinary society, its form is not fixed. For instance, it need not be circular. According to Foucault (1975: 176), "a pyramid" can work just as effectively and is perhaps even more suitable for enabling the disciplinary power to function. In addition, the form does not coincide exclusively with the prison as an institution. The prison also enters into associations with other forms of content and expression—in schools, factories, and army camps, for example. Merely due to the fact that the disciplinary working of a school is equal to that of other institutions with which the individual is faced during his or her life, this institution can be compared to the factory that has, in turn, much in common with a prison.

The form of the disciplinary institution therefore does not refer to an all-embracing signifier, and not even to the concrete object of the prison, school, or factory. It refers to new concepts, to different ways of doing and saying—and, in this specific case, to different relations among breaches, punishments, and human beings. In this play of relations, the aim of the punishment is to produce specific and measurable effects on convicted bodies. For this reason, Foucault no longer speaks of prisoners in the last chapters of *Discipline and Punish*. It would be erroneous to adhere to the way in which legal-philosophical thinking was expressed in the sixteenth and seventeenth centuries. It is better to speak of "delinquents" and "delinquency," expressions that coincide with the entrance of the penitentiary, the "disciplinary addition to the juridical" (1975: 251). In the "penitentiary form" the delinquent assumes the place of the convicted law transgressor (previously the prisoner). In this way, a delinquent no longer coincides with a prisoner, because he or she forms the specific expression of a penitentiary complex in which humanities such as psychology and sociology play a decisive role. In this construction, the delinquent distinguishes himself or herself from the prisoner in two essential ways. On the one hand, the prisoner's life becomes an object of analysis: under the influence of all kinds of human studies, he or she increasingly becomes an object of knowledge and power. Taking the humanist insights of the Enlightenment, the prisoner is also subjected to a biographical study that accurately charts his or her life, motives, and behaviors. This biographical aspect ensures that the "criminal" already exists prior to the perpetration of a crime. He even becomes detached from it. On the other hand, various typologies or separate sorts of delinquents are discovered. Different kinds of delinquents arise, with diverse characteristics, motives, qualities, and backgrounds. Delinquents are divided into various classifications. These classifications contribute to a "positive" knowledge or new objectivity regarding the prisoners. In this penitentiary complex, it is no longer sufficient to ask if someone is guilty or not guilty. New questions are posed. What is the underlying cause of the misdemeanor? How did the offender get this far?

Diagram

Until now I have discussed small formations such as prisons, graffiti, and gated communities. More generally, I have demonstrated that assemblages are invariably dynamic structures, in which a provisional ordering arises from the relations among the elements in play. Although the term "structure" would seem to indicate otherwise, there is nothing unchangeable about an assemblage. An assemblage has a certain stability, and there can even be mention of a provisional unity. Nevertheless, it never involves a closed whole or a "causal infrastructure" (Deleuze and Guattari 1980: 347). For instance, a prison has its own internal dynamics: it receives its own specific expression (timetables, exercises, biography) and assumes a unique content (bodies, architecture, organization). This content and expression also have their own form and substance. On the content-related side, there is the Panopticon (form) and the delinquents (substance). On the expressive side, one can discern criminal justice (form) and the delinquency (substance). Thus, one can argue that criminal law is consistently expressed in new assemblages. In the vernacular, the institution is still called "prison," but in reality the assemblage has already been transformed into a "penitentiary complex." And that process is not yet finished. Punishment repeatedly finds new expressions. Recently, in the Netherlands, electronic monitoring (by means of ankle bands) has been introduced, while portraits of suspected rioters have been displayed on billboards in Rotterdam. Accordingly, the question has arisen as to what currently conditions the expression of criminal justice? Why did criminal justice previously express itself as a prison and now as a penitentiary institution? Why wasn't it the other way around, for example? Why is electronic monitoring now an expression of criminal justice and not something else? In other words, what conditions an assemblage?

To Deleuze, a certain logic forms the basis of an assemblage. He refers to this situation as a diagram or an abstract machine: "The abstract machine is like the diagram of an assemblage" (Deleuze and Guattari 1980: 126). The way in which Deleuze discusses this topic is rather complex. Diagram is a difficult concept that requires much more scope than is available in this book. In broad terms, his train of thought is as follows. Normally, a diagram is defined as a graphic representation of the structure of a phenomenon. It serves to clarify a certain situation. For this reason, many sciences—medical studies, natural physics, economics—use it as an aid to chart an objectified phenomenon. Diverse graphic resources (legends, graphics, lines, curves, signs, profiles) present an image of the way a phenomenon is structured. In other words, a diagram shows the components of the phenomenon and the relations that exist among the parts. The discoveries of Kepler, Galileo, Huygens, and Newton were expressed in kinematic diagrams in which the path of an object and the speed were set out in relation to one another (Krausse 1998). Although there are various basic types of diagrams (such as histogram, line diagram, pie chart), they all have in common that events and circumstances are ordered in a graphic figure and made comprehensible. Seen in this way, a diagram is a true-to-life visual translation of an existing situation. It functions as a representation of an objectified world.

To Deleuze, a diagram is something other than a reduction of findings or a representation of an objectified world. In his view, a diagram is not a blueprint of social reality. It represents nothing, but "constructs a new type of reality" (Deleuze and Guattari 1980: 177). In other words, it is not a systematizing unit but rather something that constantly (re)produces itself everywhere. In that respect, the diagram is already fully real or, as Deleuze says, virtual, even if it is not yet actual. The words of the author Marcel Proust are illustrative of this state: it is "real without being actual, ideal without being abstract" (Deleuze and Guattari 1991: 148). This being the case, the virtual is not something that lacks reality, but is rather something that can be actualized. In this way, Deleuze can pose the ontological question about the "basis" of our age without having to fall back on Aristotelian essences in which the real is a materialization of the preformed. For this purpose, he introduces the diagram and, in doing so, seeks to align his thinking with that of Immanuel Kant. At first sight, this would seem to be somewhat strange. After all, Kant had given an impulse to thinking in pure *a priori* forms that precede every empirical perception. In his philosophy, time and space fulfill a transcendental function, which means that they help constitute our perception of the things beyond us. Space and time, emphasized Kant in *The Critique of Pure Reason* (2010), do not really exist as such, but are ordering or perceptive forms by means of which we can experience things. In other words, we do not perceive space and time as such, but merely spatial and temporal things. What we experience in this way is nothing other than what has been ordered and reduced to an entity in a delineated part of space and in a well-defined part of time.

Whereas, to Kant, the ordering of space and time belongs to intuition—the subject's sensory knowing capacity—reasoning connects the material from sensory perception to categories or concepts. This occurs by means of what Kant calls "synthetic judgment": a connection among various capacities. On the one hand, Kant discerns the sensory capacity through which we perceive phenomena in time and space while, on the other, he recognizes the rational capacity that combines the sensory impressions into the unity of the concept. The mediation between these two separate capacities is performed by the imagination. This movement is closely related to the way in which Deleuze approaches the diagram. The role of the imagination is "to schematize," writes Deleuze (1963: 28) in *La philosophie critique de Kant* (*Kant's Critical Philosophy*). The problem for Deleuze, who thus largely shores up the position of Henri Bergson, as well as of post-Kantian philosophers such as Salomon Maïmon, Johann Fichte, and Friedrich Schelling and later empiricists such as William James and Alfred North Whitehead, is that this schematism remains incarcerated in strict dualism. It is wedged between two separate entities that differ in their nature: reason and sensibility. As a result, the heterogeneous and the mobile characteristics of social reality always remain external. They are located outside the schematic construction of reason and sensibility.

But this changes when space and time are no longer empty frames or formal borders whose only purpose is to enable our experience of reality. Imagine that reality in itself is already "a spatio-temporal dynamism," muses Deleuze (1968: 276); wouldn't a completely different perspective on reality arise? What Deleuze does is to carry schematism to reality itself. He adopts Kant's schema, but refuses to define it any longer as a mediation between concept and experience. In contrast, he regards it as the becoming of reality itself, as a genetic perspective in which the intelligible and the sensible cannot be distinguished. The schema or diagram is thus latent in the unity of reality, as the principle of multiplicity. In this way, reality itself is schematic or diagrammatic, writes Deleuze in *Différence et repetition* (*Difference and Repetition*).

To Deleuze, a diagram has nothing identifiable. It does not have at its disposal substance or form; neither can one speak of content and expression. The texture of the diagram consists of endless series of pure differences or, expressed in Nietzschean terms, unbridled and unformed forces that continually clash and vie with one another (here, Deleuze speaks of "differentiation," with a "t"). This means that the schema or diagram is radically different from that used by Kant. It functions as a precondition or background of speaking or seeing (the "strata" in Deleuze's terms, or "episteme" in Foucault's) in reality. The differences form a matrix on the basis of which current determinants can arise and vanish again. It is a virtuality that has its own consistent reality. In this way, the social space is always imbued with a presocial field, an interface that is present "under" the things that surround us, an intermediate area that Deleuze, following James Joyce, calls "chaosmosis" (between "chaos" and "cosmos") (Deleuze and Guattari 1991: 192).

With the diagram I have arrived at the core of Deleuze's philosophical notion of the process-based and changeable character of reality. The actualization of the technology of security, as described in the previous chapter, can finally be better understood. Although the terminology alters radically from book to book, the diagram plays a crucial role in *A Thousand Plateaus* (Deleuze and Guattari 1980), *Francis Bacon* (Deleuze 1981), and *Foucault* (Deleuze 1986). In each of these books, the idea that the diagram is a reality "that is yet to come" (Deleuze and Guattari 1980: 177) assumes pride of place. In *Foucault*, Deleuze approaches the diagram as the collection of possible relations among forces. The investigation of "the essence" of the diagram is performed on Nietzschean ground and, more specifically, as an outcome of Nietzsche's will-to-power. To understand relations among forces, it is necessary to comprehend that forces are always interlocked. There are no forces without relations, and it is also impossible for relations to develop without the question arising as to what causes these relations to turn around. This means that forces cannot work independently of one another. A force cannot exist without another force. Between forces there is a field of tension or a differentiating element that cannot be claimed or discarded. Only in their effects are these forces perceptible.

Actualization

Deleuze speaks of a "piloting" or "modulating role" (Deleuze and Guattari 1980: 177) when discussing the relation between a diagram and an assemblage. Here, he draws a parallel with the functions of an analogue synthesizer. In contrast to a digital synthesizer in which the links between the configurations of the modules are fixed, the configurations of the modules of an analogue synthesizer are influenced by differences in voltage. In principle, every module can influence a quality of a different module in the synthesizer. In other words, there are endless possible combinations among the modules. The connection of various modules gives a musician the ability to personally determine the sound and the timbre. But what does this have to do with the dynamics in social reality?

Whereas changes in reality were long believed to be based upon a dialectical clash (Hegel's master-servant relationship), a straight line of progress and betterment, or a realization of a deeply rooted essence, Deleuze argues that they ought to be understood on the basis of the structure of a diagram. The diagram does not bring the world together in a single harmonious vision, but regularly produces new social syntheses. In other words, on the basis of the relation between the diagram and concrete assemblages, it becomes clear that the relations among heterogeneous elements, everything that makes social reality so changeable, consistently experience their own actualization. This progression does not occur from point to point, as if something is steadily being added to an original situation, but begins somewhere in the middle, as I have previously outlined. It is located at the interface of what is "seen and spoken about" and everything that could have been "seen and spoken about." In this way, a diagram is the endless possibility of modulation, comparable to the simile of the analogue synthesizer. Or, as Deleuze puts it, it is the "immanent cause" (1986: 44) that is encapsulated in the analogue variant but is repeatedly given shape in various sound hues. This does not mean that the diagram is the explanation for the transformation of society in an abstract sense, like the shift from a disciplinary to a security society (in the work of Foucault) or a shift from a primitive to a modern society (in the work of Durkheim), but is a cause within the whole body of transformations in a local sense. The diagram is the pure relational element that supports the social synthesis, and can be given form in endless variation. In this framework, Deleuze and Foucault both follow the empirical slogan of Alfred North Whitehead that an abstract explains nothing, but instead must itself be explained. The security power relation that I analyzed earlier is therefore not "the" explanation of the current developments in society; it is indeed the question as to how security can repeatedly appear in all kinds of diverse formations while also receiving a different expression and content in these. After all, security relations are always actualized in local assemblages or, in the words of Foucault, "at a particular time, in a particular country, to satisfy certain needs" (2000: 292).

Deleuze provides further explanation of this in his monograph on Foucault, where he makes a sharp distinction between power relations and nondiscursive formations. As mentioned, Foucault characterized the eighteenth century as a disciplinary society in which power was exercised in a way different from that in a sovereign society. With the shift toward a disciplinary society, the features of what Foucault calls a sovereign power—expression, negativity, and a vertical structure—are replaced by anonymous and horizontal power relations. These spread out like a network and cover the entire social field. The exercise of power can therefore no longer be ascribed to a person (the "monarch") or to an object ("the law"). The most radical consequence of this power concept is that power in itself is no longer anything. Power has no essence. It is a pure relation among forces, in the sense that it has not been formalized. Power relations (virtual, unstable, unlocalizable, and molecular) define only possibilities or probabilities of genuine interactions in social reality. The actualization of these different relations takes place in the formations of society—in schools, prisons, hospitals, and factories.

This state of affairs does not involve an unambiguous process, but rather the provisional result of a whole series of mutually reinforcing effects in which every institution integrates the power relations of the diagram of the social field in its own way and in its own environment (here, Deleuze speaks of "differenciation," with a "c"). Without the elements of an assemblage, there are no power relations, and without the relations among the elements, there is no exercise of power. Power categories (attribution, classification, combination) hold the various elements in the institutions together, as a relational quality. They set certain relations within these same formations to work, with the consequence that these practices can function on their own. A good example of this is the working of the Panopticon, which I discussed earlier. The model of the Panopticon continues to exert its power even when no guard is present in the screened-off prison watchtower. So the delinquent continues to feel under scrutiny, as he or she cannot see whether or not a guard is present in the watchtower. In this way, the Panopticon needs nothing more than this to be able to function. It is self-organizing and uses no other energy than the bodies to which it devotes its attention. On this basis, François Ewald, Foucault's assistant at the Collège de France and one of Foucault's closest interlocutors, can state, "Where physicists dream about making the *perpetuum mobile*, politicians perhaps dream of a dispositive that functions unrestrictedly on its own merit, following the example of the Panopticon: self-regulating" (1986: 51).

Control

The notion of the diagram is not yet wholly satisfying. When it coincides with a societal form—a sovereign, disciplinary, or security society—it unavoidably provokes critical questions. What causes the transition between different diagrams at a certain moment? What lies at the bottom of this? As an objection to the diagram, one may comment that it does not explain how diagrams are related to one another, blend into one another, and ultimately partially replace one another. But to Deleuze, the issue of origin is of no importance. It serves no goal whatsoever: "When a new formation appears, with new rules and series, it never comes all at once, in a single phrase or act of creation, but emerges like a series of 'building blocks,' with gaps, traces and reactivations of former elements that survive under the new rules" (1986: 30). Deleuze connects this to the throwing of dice, which also plays such an important role in the work of Nietzsche. "The dice which are thrown once are the affirmation of *chance*, the combination which they form on falling is the affirmation of *necessity*. Necessity is affirmed of chance in exactly the sense that being is affirmed of becoming and unity is affirmed of multiplicity" (1962: 29). The affirmation of coincidence comprises the notion that things could have been different under other circumstances. But this does not answer all the questions. When every society has its diagrams, the issue of actuality becomes important. The problem of the diagram thus shifts to the present and, in the light of this book, to the dynamic character of present-day security management.

In "Post-scriptum sur les sociétés de contrôle" ("Postscript on Societies of Control"), one of his last articles, Deleuze analyzes how a different diagram slowly replaces the effects of the disciplinary society (1990: 240–47). He states that we are now at a point where the disciplinary society is slowly shifting toward a control society, a term he borrowed from William Burroughs, who mentioned this new power relation in an interview with *Penthouse* in 1972: "The point is that now the means of control are much more efficient. We have computers. [. . .] So the opportunities to control are much more potent now than they have ever been" (1999: 40). And in *Naked Lunch*, Burroughs wrote, "The logical extension of encephalographic research is biocontrol: that is, control of physical movement, mental processes, emotional reactions and apparent sensory impressions by means of bioelectric signals injected into the nervous system of the subject" (1959: 162). In an extension of Burroughs's remarks, Deleuze observes that everyone's lawful or unlawful position can be traced in a control society. All kinds of technologies, ranging from intelligent cameras to DNA banks, make it possible to follow and control people ceaselessly, regardless of whether they are at home or in public places such as streets and squares.

Whereas Foucault talks about an internalized disciplinary view, Deleuze prefers to speak of a flexible control that works on the basis of modulation. He observes that the disciplinary society, with its closed structures, is slowly losing its influence. There is mention of a general crisis in the field of imprisonment. Electronic monitoring, where the convict undergoes his punishment outside the walls of his cell, is an example of this. Through domestic care, the hospital also shifts its activities to the living environment of the patient. But the transition from school to work has also become diffuse. At work, one must constantly be engaged in further education by means of training courses and study. At the same time, employees take work home on the laptop so that they can work on the weekend. The significance of these transitions lies in the perspectives they offer on the relation between a diagram and concrete assemblages. At the same time, they make it clear that once-distinct life domains are now becoming increasingly interwoven. Or, as Deleuze remarked in a previous article, "You don't confine people with a highway. But by making highways, you multiply the means of control. I am not saying this is the only aim of highways, but people can travel infinitely and 'freely' without being confined while being perfectly controlled" (2003: 300).

What Deleuze describes on the basis of the control relation in "Postscript on Societies of Control" represents a reinforcement of the discipline that has already existed for some time. The most critical comment with respect to this is that it is still all about techniques that make individual bodies productive, efficient, and obedient. The methods that are applied on highways, for example, to indicate that drivers are breaking the law ("You're going too fast" or "Keep your distance") have no other goal than an immediate adjustment of the driver's behavior on the road. And also the processing of RFID chips in products intends to realize a similar internalization or normalization of conduct. Japanese manufacturers plant chips in the clothes of primary school pupils to help reduce truancy. Because the chip can be read at a distance, the physical location of a pupil can be discovered at a glance. But, at the same time, with the term "control," Deleuze comes close to the technology of security described in the previous chapter. With security, Foucault overtakes his previous analysis of discipline and describes the contours of a biopolitical framework of techniques that work centrifugally, and in which all kinds of different fields are mutually linked in new entities. With his description of security, Foucault not only foresaw these shifts; he also gave an impulse to a further analysis of these changes in the current approach to crime and disorder.

Nevertheless, Deleuze indisputably has an original point when he describes how new power relations ensure that demarcated and closed structures are making way for a different kind of space through which we are moving. Whether one defines the changes in society in terms of security (Foucault), control (Deleuze), risk (Beck), or IT (Castells), it is clear that the term "environment" has become a very wide concept. In "Postscript on Societies of Control," Deleuze writes, "The conception of a control mechanism, giving the position of any element within an open environment at any given instant (whether animal in a reserve or human in a corporation, as with an electronic collar), is not necessarily one of science fiction" (1990: 246). In his analysis of those changes, he exchanges dichotomies such as "inside-outside" for thinking in terms of "movement" and "real time." In a disciplinary society, the content of a space was still simple. It involved function-specific locations, where special spaces are assigned to special categories of people. Pupils attend school, patients lie in hospitals, and lawbreakers end up in prison. Accordingly, every separate space has its own way of doing and saying or, in other words, its own way of disciplining.

While the disciplinary society works via closed and fixed spaces (walls, boundaries, gates), each with its own specific function, the society of control functions through constantly changing networks. Mobility, flexibility, and acceleration are the qualities of these networks. The carved spaces of the disciplinary society thus make way for what Deleuze and Guattari call a "smooth space" (1980: 437). In a smooth space, the functional division of detached and separate places vanishes. Separate zones are connected to one another so that they can subsequently function once again. In this way, one can no longer speak of a fixed form with a separate "inside" and "outside." Notions such as "distance" or "opposite" lose their classical meaning here. The clearest example is again imprisonment. The environment of the prison is shifted, by means of electronic monitoring, to the direct living environment of the prisoner. But that relocation does not convert a smooth space into a homogeneous or unshared space, as if there were no segments or cracks in its middle. Several spaces can be present here, just as several languages are present in one language. In my opinion, one should only interpret this to mean that the cracks between the spaces are not absolute, as in a carved space in which one has to pass all kinds of physical barriers (gates, boom bars, guards) to enter into a prison or hospital. In contrast to a carved space, a smooth space is a hybrid place in which various spatialities fuse with one another without there being mention of a totalizing entity. There is thus a continual variation of form and content. In this way, it is possible to be private in a public space and public in a private space. I shall return to this topic in chapter 10.

Security assemblage

Elaborating on the concept of assemblage, I hope to give further substance to the working of the above-described security diagram. It is by means of the assemblage concept that Deleuze gives social reality, which has no intrinsic unity and is always fluid, a consistency. Assemblages are recurrently changing configurations of heterogeneous elements that somehow function together. This is also the insight that Kevin Haggerty and Richard Ericson (2000; 2006; Ericson 2007) place at the center of their notion of "surveillant assemblages." Appealing to the work of Deleuze, Haggerty and Ericson write that "surveillance is driven by the desire to bring systems together, to combine practices and technologies and integrate them into a larger whole" (2000: 610). In addition, they emphasize that surveillance techniques cannot be approached from a single viewpoint, which happens, for example, in pleas to the government to prohibit certain techniques, or to limit the use of these due to far-reaching breaches of privacy (think of the experiments with genetically modified organisms). The fact that techniques are combined with one another and consequently converge to form completely new applications makes it difficult to gain a clear overview of the consequences in advance.

In the light of a dynamic perspective on security, I regard the term "surveillant assemblage" as too descriptive to be discerning. In my opinion, the way in which this term can be helpful in understanding the dynamics in security management is not sufficiently clear. This being the case, the analysis of Haggerty and Ericson takes place at an epistemological level, and is not active in the ontological sense of the "becoming" of social reality. Haggerty and Ericson see primarily a becoming of the security issue rather than a becoming of social reality. The consequence of this is that the term is used as a tool to reorder the world. And ordering is something that I wish to avoid as much as possible, because it pins down thinking and makes it insensitive to the subtlety of a reality that is permanently in motion. It is precisely against this background that an assemblage must be understood. Otherwise one misses the fact that there are always forces in an assemblage that can elude everything and can ensure that the form and content of an assemblage constantly change. This may appear to be futile, but nevertheless the crucial distinction here plays with terms that are often named in the same breath with an assemblage, such as sociological terms like "network," "system," or "structure."

Therefore, a specific elucidation of the term "assemblage" is needed, one that dovetails better with the mixed collaborative efforts mentioned in the first part of this book and the technology of security that we encountered in the work of Foucault. In order to be able to explain these issues in conjunction, I speak of a "security assemblage." By combining the concepts of security and assemblage, I bring the focus clearly on the present day and the tangles of power relations that influence security management. I define a security assemblage as a short-lived or durable constellation of territories, rules, and authorities.[4] With this definition, I establish a direct relation with the previously described dimensions in an assemblage that ensure stability and change. I believe that a security assemblage, defined in this way, is also a usable concept with which to investigate the dynamics in the security issue more thoroughly. Various arguments in favor of this approach can be offered. I shall discuss three of these.

To start with, the point of departure of the investigation is no longer linked to a distinction such as "public-private." Thus, the investigation is no longer forced to formulate solutions and dilemmas against a background of such oppositions. The elements in a security assemblage receive significance in and through the relations that play a role there, between authorities with different interests, for example, which also have to cope with all kinds of considerations. This enables multiple interpretation and variations in significance. For instance, meanings may arise that not only are unforeseen or undesired but also contradict the fixed meanings that are attached to the poles of public and private. This means that one, as a researcher, does not need to be preoccupied with the question, What is it?—a question that always risks essentialism and functionalism. In fact, it is more concerned with questions involving the functioning of the security assemblage itself. Does it work? If so, how? Where? By posing these questions one obtains more insight into the network of relations that is active in an assemblage and into the way in which meanings may alter. In this way, something that is regarded as being risky, for example, can thus repeatedly acquire a different content depending on the assemblage within which it is expressed (see also O'Malley 2004: 27; Maurutto and Hannah-Moffat 2006).[5] Now this, and then that. . . .

But in other respects, too, the idea of a security assemblage forms a clear break with classical notions of security management. In general, security is defined as a way to achieve, to a greater or lesser extent, previously determined objectives of policy or detection. Behind this, one finds the idea that the actions of the authorities are decisive in the achievement—or otherwise—of these aims. In this matter, explanation of the outcomes is sought in rational capacities, and one assumes that the authorities know exactly how to distinguish between their personal and their formal roles. In contrast, the perpetually moving assemblages are the ordered opposites of an anthropocentric perspective (from the Greek "*anthropos*," "human/man") in which humankind is seen as the origin of and the fundament upon which matters are governed and adjusted. In an assemblage, a relation such as security, for example, must be considered as being external and primordial with regard to the elements that it connects. It is therefore no personal quality in the sense of a characteristic linked to a person or organization, but concerns an impersonal fact that, due to the lack of an inner dimension, is available for connection to other elements, such as objects like intelligent cameras, cars, and computers.

Finally, there is a third, perhaps the most stubborn, blind spot in the study of the governance of security. The idea that a certain phenomenon can be demarcated by assigning it hard boundaries and by separating it from the rest of reality is a dominant one. The result is that this kind of phenomenon is regarded as being quasi-homogeneous. This simplification allows a survey of internal patterns and, on this basis, the formulation of explanations of and possible solutions to problems that arise (Van Calster 2010). On this point I have already observed that a security assemblage never stands completely alone but always refers to other assemblages that are working or should start working, with, as a consequence, an almost unbridled explosion of completely different assemblages and productions of social syntheses in social reality. After all, a security assemblage is not a closed situation with a causal infrastructure, but is a ceaseless combining of detached elements in a unique consistency that changes its nature as soon as new elements are added or old elements disappear. This means that the attention of the research must be directed toward the open character of phenomena and the possibility that loose elements can always become the starting points of new assemblages.

In short, in anticipation of the more empirical analysis given in the third part of this book, I provisionally typify the importance of a security assemblage by means of the following characteristics: the indeterminacy of the elements, relations, and an open structure. These points sound attractive because they broach the subject that has fascinated people since time immemorial: How can social systems obtain form from the bottom-up? However, this point ought to be put into perspective. I cannot maintain that there are no top-down governing processes in security management. The idea still prevails that an adequate solution to numerous social problems can be found in the acquisition of as much information as possible. The central formation of specialized teams to cope with certain forms of crime fits in with this kind of approach. But a top-down approach also means that a certain degree of order will have to arise. After all, order also concerns shared values and norms, and these are difficult to impose in a top-down fashion. As a result, it is seldom possible to make a lucid distinction between a pure top-down and a pure bottom-up approach. Therefore, I believe that it is still meaningful to speak about security assemblages.

* * *

The second step toward a dynamic perspective on security began with the observation that the middle offers an exit from the dilemma of having to choose between alternative opposites such as public and private. The middle precedes such forms of ordering. In doing so, the middle forms the basis from which relations develop and elements from various practices attach themselves to one another to form new combinations. I have called the provisional result of this process a "security assemblage." I have observed that an assemblage provides a model that allows a better comprehension of the complexity of ongoing changes in reality. I define a security assemblage as a short-lived or durable constellation of territories, rules, and authorities. In this, the emphasis lies on the open structure and the indeterminacy of the elements that are components of a security assemblage.

In anticipation of the empirical research in the third part of this book, several presumptions can already be formulated. For example, the notion of a security assemblage provides a concrete point of address through which to devote more attention to the dynamic setting of the public-private partnerships to be examined. This setting cannot be reduced to a process that enables well-considered governance, in which the functions and goals of a partnership remain the same. The above-described perspective of security assemblages breaches the "aims-means relation." A security assemblage also entails that attention is requested for the presence of unexpected events that can provide an impetus for the creation of different assemblages and, with this, the production of new meanings. In this way, scope for unpredictability arises. Moreover, in a security assemblage, everything is, in principle, equally meaningful. Every coupling has the intrinsic possibility that something new will be created. Accordingly, the emphasis comes to lie on a series of endless changes in the security assemblages to be studied, even if these changes initially appear to have only marginal significance with regard to the reduction of crime and disorder and the improvement of safety.

In the following chapter I shall further examine the relations among elements in an assemblage that cannot fall back on a fixed meaning. These relations are exactly what makes an assemblage so interesting. They continue to function and constantly generate effects. In addition, they harbor the potential to allow things to occur differently from what has been ordained from above or has been officially determined. At this moment, I am not concerned with the specific content and expression the relations assume in a security assemblage. That question will be the focus of attention in the third part of this book. It is more important to know what these relations are, *in concreto*. To give an answer to this, I appeal to the long-forgotten but important work of the nineteenth-century sociologist Gabriel Tarde. The power relations and assemblages described up to this point are not yet quite sufficient to comprehend the dynamics in the governance of security. We have a skeleton and some flesh, but no spirit as yet.

5

Molar and Molecular

It is now necessary to take a third and final step toward a dynamic perspective on security and thus bridge the gap between theory and action. I do so by directing my attention to the actions of the authorities in a security assemblage, an approach that is almost entirely lacking in the work of Deleuze and Foucault.[1] For example, Foucault prefers to speak in abstractions such as "the bourgeoisie," "the judges," "the psychiatric experts," or "the administration" when he writes about people of flesh and blood. And Deleuze is also more interested in abstract processes of subjectivization or the conditions under which the subject arises than in the question of what a subject is or does. The result of this is that security seems to be completely unrelated to people and their emotions and feelings. The question dealt with in this chapter is, therefore, In which way can interactions among people ensure that changes occur in an assemblage? Here, I understand an interaction as an autonomous relation that can serve as a basis for the dynamics in an assemblage. Gabriel Tarde, a contemporary of Émile Durkheim, was someone who developed instruments with which to research this area. I shall now begin with a short introduction to his work.

Landmarks of sociology

Tarde was a magistrate in his hometown of Sarlat, head of the office for statistics of the Ministry of Justice, and the precursor of Henri Bergson as head of the Faculty of Philosophy at the Collège de France. Besides his activities as a lawyer and criminologist, he devoted effort to studying statistics and psychology. He also found time to write essays as well as the novel *Underground Man* (1905), which was a science-fiction story—with an introduction by H. G. Wells—about an ice-covered earth where people lived underground and busied themselves with creating art and music. Despite the fact that Tarde engaged himself extensively with all kinds of criminological questions, it would be an overstatement to name him among the most well-known and influential people in the history of criminology. Although it is difficult to give an exhaustive list of such figures, one encounters his name only very rarely among those of Cesare Beccaria, Adolphe Quetelet, and Cesare Lombroso, to mention only a few of the scientists whose work is regarded as standard in Western criminology. If one looks back at the impact of his work, in the words of Piers Beirne, one can only speak of "an uninfluential silence when the historical landmarks of sociology were later reconstituted" (1987: 814).

According to Beirne, the fact that Tarde's ideas are no more than "a footnote in intellectual history" (2001: xi) is due to the meager current value of his thinking. At most, one can claim that he gave an impetus to certain developments in criminology. These comments should not, however, detract from the fact that Beirne recognizes important lines of research in the work of Tarde. For instance, Tarde's research was directed toward escaping from the impasse in the nineteenth-century theoretical struggle between, on the one hand, voluntarism, which is expressed in autonomous determination by the free will of the individual, and, on the other, determinism, as outlined in the work of Cesare Lombroso, Enrico Ferri, and Raffaele Garofalo. In addition, Tarde wished to offer a sociological explanation of crime, based on the concepts of imitation and invention, and engaged himself in the development of new punishments without surrendering to the largely deterministic presuppositions of individual-positivist thinking in the second half of the nineteenth century.

However, I wish to call the scant interest in his criminological work "remarkable" for a number of reasons. First of all, Tarde, in conjunction with Alexandre Lacassagne and Léonce Manouvrier, belongs to the founders of the influential French Environmental School that devoted attention to the importance of the social environment in the genesis of criminal behavior. Second, his insights into imitation and invention in social processes at the end of the nineteenth and the beginning of the twentieth century have had a major influence on political philosophy, psychology, and social theory, with the American urban sociology of the Chicago School as the most renowned example. For example, *Introduction to the Science of Sociology* (1921), the manual written by the founders of the Chicago School, Robert Park and Ernest Burgess, contains more references to Tarde than to sociologists such as Comte and Durkheim (see also Hughes 1961). Also Edwin Sutherland's differential association theory of the 1930s was influenced by the work of Tarde. Third, the American Institute of Criminal Law and Criminology had Tarde's *La philosophie pénale* (*Penal Philosophy*, 1890) translated into English in 1912, as one of its first European works. And last, Tarde enjoyed much respect among other scientists and academics in his era. His reputation not only rested on his study *Penal Philosophy* and the previously published compilation of short texts *La criminalité comparée* (Comparative Criminality, 1886) but was also allied to the fact that he regularly published articles in scientific journals such as *Archives de l'Anthropologie Criminelle* and *Revue Philosophique*.

It will thus be clear that Tarde occupied a leading position in discussions in the social sciences in the nineteenth century. As a result, it is worthwhile from a historical point of view to examine the most important questions in which Tarde assumed a standpoint. For instance, he rejected the positivist thinking of the criminal-anthropological movement of which the Turin doctor Cesare Lombroso and his work *L'Uomo delinquente* (*Criminal Man*, 1876) are one of the most important representatives. In addition, Tarde criticized the proposals of the "moral statisticians," as personified in the nineteenth century by the Belgian astronomer and demographer Adolphe Quetelet. And last, but perhaps most important, Tarde disagrees with Durkheim with regard to the extent to which crime can be seen and studied as something that is "normal"—in other words, as a phenomenon that exists everywhere and will never disappear completely.

Theoretical debates

The first debate revolves around the issue of whether or not criminality is something that is innate in some people.[2] As is known, Lombroso sought the causes of crime in the character of the offender, in the physical and physiological qualities of a person. In his view, criminal behavior was an inherent deviation that could be identified by means of physiognomy, the art of reading someone's personality through his or her appearance. Terms such as "skull meters" were used mockingly at the time. Tarde, and a number of other scientists, attacked the evidence that was used to support Lombroso's findings. Tarde stated that it was impossible to reach scientific agreement on the qualities to be ascribed to the criminal. In addition, it is impossible to determine precisely whether crime is committed by "born criminals"—people who have not developed further than a primitive stage in the evolution of humankind—or whether crime is committed by persons as a result of changing circumstances in their lives. To reinforce his arguments, Tarde quotes, in *Penal Philosophy*, the work of Antonio Marro, who wrote in his report *Sui caratteri della donna criminale* (On the Character of the Criminal Woman, 1889) about Lombroso's conclusions that these "are sometimes divergent and even opposite" (qtd. in 1912: 65). Marro had performed a study of 507 male and 35 female criminals and, according to Tarde, no other conclusion could be drawn from this than the fact that a criminal type suffered from "a badly nourished brain, misfortune and poverty" (1912: 67).

To support his hypothesis that criminal and recidivist behavior could not be explained by biological factors, Tarde referred to the study *La sociologia criminale* (Criminal Sociology, 1889) by Napoleone Colajanni. This showed that the Italian provinces with the highest crime figures, the south of Italy, were characterized by "the fine health of their inhabitants" whereas the provinces with the lowest crime figures had "the greatest number of bodily illnesses and deformities" (1912: 237). Moreover, Tarde requested attention to other striking elements than merely physical properties that could have an effect on the genesis of criminal behavior. Again he made use of the work of Marro, this time speaking of a "spirit of imitation, vanity, and idleness" (1912: 66) among delinquents that leads to specific role patterns, exchange systems, and codes of conduct being developed and emulated. He points to the tattoos of many delinquents and compares prison to a tattoo booth. Finally he speaks of the striking difference in the number of registered crimes in the various French departments. These display differences in crime levels rather than in inborn qualities, writes Tarde in "Comparative Criminality" (1886); these are much more related to social and personal circumstances, such as poverty and alcoholism.

The second debate is about the scientific status of statistics, a discipline that arose in the nineteenth century and was largely directed toward the study of human populations. Tarde criticized the theory that statistics were capable of making credible statements about the future. Against Quetelet's "law of great numbers" Tarde (1912: 299) riposted that the more observations made, the greater the inconsistencies of the outcomes. This unavoidably leads to a decline in the predictive power of the presented results. In *Les lois de l'imitation* (*The Laws of Imitation*, 1962: 33), Tarde points to the large statistical swings that were taking place at that time with regard to the number of births, deaths, and marriages. Whereas Quetelet speaks of a certain degree of regularity, official French sources show that, toward the end of the nineteenth century, not only do the crime figures rise dramatically but the number of divorces, the use of alcohol, and the number of murders, manslaughters, and incarceration in institutions also rise substantially. What statistics cannot do is show the causal links with regard to the genesis and spread of crime. Accordingly, factors such as poor education and poverty need not be indicators of criminal conduct, in Tarde's view. Although Tarde does not deviate from what Quetelet claims in *Recherches sur le penchant au crime aux différents ages* (*Research on the Propensity for Crime at Different Ages*, 1831) on this point, Tarde does state in *Penal Philosophy* that some criminals have actually had better schooling than noncriminals: "all this [education] may supply crime with new resources, may modify its methods of proceeding, which become less violent and more crafty, and may sometimes strengthen its nature" (1912: 378).

Tarde engaged in the third debate with Durkheim, who became full professor in the Department of Pedagogy of the Sorbonne in 1906 and occupied the first chair in sociology at the Sorbonne in 1913. In his work, Durkheim devoted much attention to crime and particularly punishment. According to Durkheim, punishment is a moral issue that confirms the normative relations of a community. As such, punishment aims "to heal the wounds inflicted upon the collective sentiments" (1960: 77), as Durkheim wrote in *De la division du travail social* (*The Division of Labor in Society*, 1893). Thus, punishment is primarily directed toward reinforcing mutual solidarity among the population rather than toward the offender himself or herself. Tarde's argument with Durkheim is focused on whether or not crime is a social fact with its own individual character. As is known, Durkheim did not regard crime as a pathological phenomenon and did not seek psychological arguments to explain the behavior of criminals. Durkheim declares that crime is a normal social phenomenon that occurs in every society. It is even impossible to have a society without crime. Crime only becomes abnormal "when it reaches or goes beyond a certain level which it is perhaps not impossible to fix in conformity with the previous rules" (Durkheim 1968: 66).

First of all, Tarde poses the question as to what is "normal" and argues that the concept conceals a completely different significance than the one Durkheim assigns to it. In "Criminalité et santé sociale" (Criminality and Social Health, 1895) Tarde writes that crime is a "conflict between the great legion of honest men and the small battalion of criminals, and both act normally given the goal which each pursues." Tarde further combats Durkheim's notion that crime can be functional. Besides the fact that solidarity in society can be stimulated by making certain actions illegal, Durkheim also believes that deviant behavior is a necessary phenomenon for healthy social relations. An act is criminal, states Durkheim, "when it offends the strong, well-defined states of the collective consciousness" (1960: 43). And exactly because one can act against deviant behavior that has been deemed punishable, the norms can be reinforced. Tarde praises Durkheim for posing the question as to whether or not crime can have a positive significance, but in "Criminality and Social Health" (1895) he also asks Durkheim the rhetorical question as to how socially functional crime may be if it encourages other people to commit crime and gives them an example of how to do it.

Durkheim: social fact

Beirne must receive great praise as one of the few scholars to draw attention to the largely untranslated thinking of Gabriel Tarde. He emphasizes not only the prominent place occupied by Tarde in the nineteenth-century school debate but also the fact that Tarde covers various issues in criminology with regard to the study of criminal conduct, the offender, and the reaction of the government to that behavior and to the person exhibiting that behavior. Apart from the issue of whether or not Tarde solves all these issues, his style of examining social reality still provides valuable insights. In this context, I wish to demonstrate that Tarde laid the basis for a style of thinking in which order is not generalized into a phenomenon that is detached from the event of the action itself. The question is therefore whether or not he is making, in his work and debates, a much more fundamental point about the way in which one might regard social reality. One might also say that, in the discussion with Durkheim about whether crime is a social fact, Tarde declares that reality should not be understood as a stable whole, but rather as a continuous process of change and difference. To make this clear, further explanation of the object of Durkheim's sociology and of his ideas on morality must be given.

Summarizing Durkheim's ideas, one might say that social facts form the object of his sociology. A social fact or, in other words, the description of what the social exactly contains or delineates is characterized by the fact that it exercises external pressure on individual behavior and influences personal attitudes and needs. Examples of social facts include legal and moral rules, religious customs, ways of acting, practices, and the language in which we communicate. We become familiar with such matters from birth onward, and this being the case, they force themselves upon us in an unavoidable way. They possess an imperative and invisible force, as it were, from which we cannot retreat. No one is obliged to accept the rules of language or to use them, but if one does not use them, it is almost impossible to interact with other people in a natural and normal manner. Not only is a social fact characterized by its external shaping of the expressions and actions of individuals, but it also has an intrinsic reality that cannot be traced back to the qualities of separate individuals. It is an independent entity that imposes certain ways of seeing and doing upon individuals who would otherwise not act in this way. In *Les règles de la méthode sociologique* (*The Rules of Sociological Method*, 1895), Durkheim describes a social fact as that "which is general over the whole of a given society whilst having an existence of its own, independent of its individual manifestations" (1968: 14). From that perspective, a social fact is not only coercive and supra-individual; it can also be understood as objective (in the meaning of "thing"), as Rudi Laermans (1995) summarizes Durkheim's views.

The properties of a social fact are clearest in Durkheim's thesis of a collective consciousness (*conscience collective*), the largest common denominator of the content of the moral conscience of individuals in a society, which manifests itself as a separate entity and forms the foundation for cohesion in society. In terms of quality, the collective consciousness involves feelings that differ from those in individual perceptions. It also has specific characteristics and forms its own reality, according to Durkheim in *The Division of Labor in Society* (1960: 39). In more general terms, the collective consciousness thus has a double meaning, in the sense of a shared culture and its representation. Fundamentally, there is mention of a communal whole or closed system of collective convictions, norms, meanings, and customs that precede individual actions so that, in the most ideal case, these take place in a recognizable and predictable way. The notion of a collective consciousness is self-evidently an abstraction, a social fact that cannot be studied in a direct sense but only in reference to other, more tangible social facts. Durkheim sees crime, for example, as a breach of the collective consciousness, and thus of culturally based solidarity at the macro-level.

Nevertheless, one should not conclude from this that, to Durkheim, society leads a separate and eternal life, as if it functions separately from the individuals that are part of it. Durkheim rejects a transcendent notion of society that propagates a reality independent of its constituents. According to Durkheim, society itself ensures that, through associations of individuals, specific ways of acting and speaking arise that jointly form a collective entity. He further elaborates his theory of solidarity in various types of societies in *The Division of Labor in Society* (1960). In Durkheim's view, primitive society enjoyed a mechanical solidarity based on equality. In this situation, the moral and social concord among individuals is fashioned and dominated by a collective will. In contrast, modern society is typified by an organic solidarity that rests upon differences and inequality. Individuals are detached from one another, and the mutual link is formed by the complementarity of functions in the labor process. Factors such as a new division of labor and strong population growth are responsible here, as a result of which mutual interactions only increase. The transition from mechanical solidarity to organic is reflected in law and punishment. In the article "Deux lois de l'évolution pénale" ("Two Laws of Penal Evolution," 1900), Durkheim states that the transition from a primitive society to a more developed one will ensure that the severity of punishment will decrease and confidence in the function of prison will increase.[3]

In order to fully understand the discussion between Durkheim and Tarde, it is important to realize that both academics regard the interactions among people in a society as a social fact. In fact, as Durkheim would probably claim, they form the basis of the changes that occur at the level of moral solidarity in a certain type of society. But, as Durkheim would immediately add, those interactions primarily depend on the psychological characteristics of an individual and the particular circumstances in which they occur. In that respect, interactions among people are not phenomena that belong solely to sociology. In *The Rules of Sociological Method*, he writes that "social facts are more liable to be objectively represented the more completely they are detached from the individual facts by which they are manifested" (1968: 44). Durkheim speaks of "social-psychic phenomena"; they interest sociologists, without them being the immediate object of their study. According to Durkheim, "the determining cause of a social fact [must] be sought among antecedent social facts and not among the states of the individual consciousness" (1968: 109). For this reason he formulates the adage that the cause and function of social facts can only be explained by other social facts. For instance, psychological insights regarding the associations of individuals can be important in any attempt to understand changes in solidarity in a society. But it is up to sociology to subsequently study this solidarity as an independent social fact. This can be done through scientific methods and models, as Durkheim demonstrates in his work, by means of which matters such as the number of births, marriages, suicides, and the degree of criminality can be objectified and verified. Without delving into the individual circumstances that have played a role, the annual average of these occurrences, all of which are an expression of the collective consciousness or the morality of a society, can be calculated.

Tarde: interactions

Which criticism of Durkheim's relatively closed concept of reality does Tarde express? To obtain a good grip on his claim that Durkheim takes the social to such extremes that there is little space left for the contribution and significance of action itself, it is useful to pay more attention to, as Tarde articulated it, his "pure sociology" or "general sociology" (1962: ix–x). Whereas Durkheim believed that, stated simply, social facts should be analyzed as separate entities (as things in themselves), Tarde refers to the interactions among people that do not allow themselves to be bound to a single moment but continue to advance uninterruptedly in new series, thus ensuring ongoing changes in social reality. These positions need not be diagonally opposite one another, however. But they do find expression in different fields of research.

In contrast to Durkheim's functionalist concept, which is oriented to the study of the notions and behaviors that have been established by a group or collectivity as a whole, Tarde believes that interactions among individuals are themselves an element that should form a topic of scientific research. This means that, to Tarde, the metaphysical significance that Durkheim ascribes to a social fact has neither validity nor value. Tarde's interest lies, so to speak, in the dynamics of social reality itself. Regardless of how convincing and influential Durkheim's thinking may still be, his quest for and definition of a social fact rests upon the unproven assumption that something such as a shared conviction does actually exist. Despite the social status that Durkheim ascribes to this shared conviction, it remains vague as to how this can arise or is formed. Durkheim simply assumes its existence and makes no effort to research its genesis in detail or to study the way phenomena cease to exist. In other words, the collective consciousness functions as a starting point in the determination of research, but without having raised the fundamental question, How can we form a single entity with so many different individuals? Or, formulated otherwise, How can the similarity of thousands of different people be explained? (See also Deleuze 1968: 104–5; Deleuze and Guattari 1980: 267.)

Instead of attacking Durkheim's concept of social facts or questioning the results of his analyses of suicide and religion, Tarde does something essentially different. On the one hand, he questions the rigidity of Durkheim's assumption of a collective entity that underlies the shared solidarity and morality of a society. On the other, he asks how a social fact can exist outside the individual himself or herself. In doing so, Tarde does not reject the notion that solidarity or morality can exist among people, but shifts attention to the way in which similarities among people arise that entail a degree of solidarity or morality. Durkheim simply took for granted that similarities multiply and that these form their own reality that is relatively detached from the level of the individual. Moral action thus means nothing more than individuals subjecting themselves to the power of the entity that imposes—from above—rules, norms, and codes upon individuals. But, according to Tarde, this assumption is nothing more than an "ontological illusion" (1969: 115) that resembles a revaluation of Plato's theory of ideas. Similar to Durkheim's social facts, Plato's ideas stand for eternal and unchanging primal images of things, which can only be experienced by the intellect. The ideas themselves are not attached to matter, time, and place, but are located in a higher world that, according to Plato, is fixed forever and leads an autonomous existence, independent of thinking. This means that the truth of these ideas is transcendent. They are independent of everyday reality.

Tarde sees more value in a form of sociology in which the general character of interactions can be explained and that is applicable to every social fact. He speaks of "general laws" (1912: 326) when he deals with processes of interaction among individuals that continue to advance in consistently new series. Although terms such as "general laws" and "general sociology" seem to indicate otherwise, Tarde cannot be classified as a "modernist" (Henry and Milovanovic 1996: 132), nor can his contributions be considered as "structuralist" (see also Barry and Thrift 2007). Whereas in the work of Durkheim, attention is primarily paid to structures that are not directly perceptible, which form the basis of relations in social reality, Tarde's work shifts the focus to the relations "among" people in social reality. After all, prior to arriving at the question of whether or not there is an underlying structure and, if there is, how it might work in everyday activities, a study ought to be made of how similarity can arise in the actions and communication of all those different people that form part of social reality. Tarde locates this similarity in the notion of repetition. "All resemblance is due to repetition," he writes in *The Laws of Imitation* (1962: 14). Nevertheless, this does not mean that a linear process evolves in which people continue to reproduce one another's behavior endlessly and obsessively. Again in *The Laws of Imitation*, Tarde writes that repetition exists by the grace of variation: "Resemblances and repetitions [. . .] are the necessary themes of the differences and variations which exist in all phenomena" (1962: 6). He elaborates this idea further in *Les lois sociales* (*Social Laws*, 1898). For this purpose, he makes use of a more abstract and horizontal approach to interactions among people, and speaks of "repetition, opposition, and adaption."

In his work, Tarde seeks a middle course between the Scylla of an absolute relativism and the Charybdis of an absolute absolutism. Here, a society coincides with a "group of beings who are apt to possess common traits which are ancient copies of the same model" (1962: 68). In *The Laws of Imitation*, he studies those resemblances on the basis of various series of imitations that he connects with somnambulism and hypnosis, which were much-discussed concepts at the end of the nineteenth century. Somnambulism refers to a state of half-sleep or sleep-walking, in which the senses function normally and people do all kinds of things but retain no memory of their activities. Somnambulism may occur spontaneously or be induced by hypnosis. In line with Tarde's thinking, society thus becomes "imitation, and imitation is a kind of somnambulism" (1962: 87). The emphasis on somnambulism and hypnosis recurs in *Penal Philosophy*, where Tarde deals in more detail with the idea that hypnosis is "the experimental junction point of psychology and sociology; it shows us the most simplified sort of psychic life which can be conceived of under the form of the most elementary social relation" (1912: 193). On the basis of this kind of conditional formulation of action, Tarde continues to expand the notion of a society. He points out that even the smallest units, such as cells, molecules, and atoms, have a certain degree of organization and are minor societies. However, in the context of this chapter, it is more important that, from Tarde's view on interaction, the Durkheimian primacy of a collective entity is vigorously put into perspective. Seen from Tarde's position, change and difference have pride of place. Order and stability come later. They are formed on the basis of the process-driven or changeable character of social reality, as the temporary confluence of consistently ramifying series of interactions that never reach their ultimate significance.

Imitation and . . .

To obtain an answer to the issue of how interactions among people occur in general and how changes and differences happen in everyday activity and communication in particular, Tarde dismembers social reality with tweezers and a sharp knife, as it were. He makes a systematic distinction between processes of imitation and processes of invention, two series of interactions, each of which forms a reality in itself but also influences the other. Tarde defines imitation as the movement by which something is repeated and diffused, introducing it in lieu of concepts such as authority and obedience, terms that were common in social theory forming up to that time. In the foreword to the second edition of *The Laws of Imitation*, he speaks of "the action at a distance of one mind upon another" (1962: xiv) and of "every inter-psychical photography, so to speak, willed or not willed, passive or active" (1962: xiv). In tangible reality, this means that people consciously or unconsciously imitate one another's actions and words, by assuming a certain way of acting, varying from method of working (process or technique) to a style of clothing (fashion) or musical preference (taste). But imitation can also lie in extremely small movements, such as minute adjustments of behavior when young people copy one another's expressions or make the same physical movements. For instance, Jan Dirk de Jong (2007) shows how Moroccan youngsters in the Netherlands act in keeping with shared street values and the associated norms affecting the behavior that is good or bad under certain circumstances. More specifically, de Jong demonstrates that statements such as "typical Moroccan" are insufficient to explain delinquent group behavior among Moroccan youngsters. Arguments that refer to a Moroccan culture of confrontation, emphasizing male virtues such as courage, honor, and respect, do not demonstrate why Moroccan youngsters in particular often form groups that are perceived by the outside world as provocative and threatening. It is better to explain this, states de Jong, by looking at the dynamics of group processes and the extraordinary circumstances in which young people in certain neighborhoods grow up. In such cases, remarkable similarities arise through the imitation of one another's behavior and the sharing of significance ascribed to certain actions.

In this context, it is important to point out the branching character of imitative series. This means that, in the dissemination, all kinds of new series are formed. They may cross one another, so that new relations arise that, in turn, engender other imitative series. Through the addition of new series to existing series, the possibility of creation stays open and the sociocultural field remains in motion. Crime should also be approached in that way, Tarde writes in *Penal Philosophy*, as "a phenomenon of imitative propagation" (1912: 362). Forms of crime spread "like every industrial product, like every good or bad idea" (1912: 338). With this, he is not claiming that crime can be studied as a separate entity, one that is separate from other phenomena in society. The question is whether the many other phenomena of imitative propagation, which taken all together are called civilization [. . .] foster or impede the progress of the propagation of crime. Or rather, the aim is to discover, if that were possible, which among these various spreadings of example which are called instruction, religion, politics, commerce, industry, are the ones that foster, and which [are the] ones that impede, the expansion of crime. (1912: 362)

In order to clarify this process of differentiation, Tarde distinguishes between two laws (1962: 140 ff.). He speaks of a "logical law" when something is imitated on the basis of the idea that it may contribute to a higher goal, or because it is expected to solve a problem better than other inventions could. However, imitation more often takes place according to "extra-logical laws," rather than on the basis of rational or well-considered ideas. Such laws tend to be founded on culturally determined causes, although psychological and sociological influences also play a role here. With regard to the question of insecurity, Tarde shows that certain forms of crime and disorder occur increasingly frequently because the number of interactions among various people is rising, ranging from the countryside to the city and from the aristocracy to the citizenry. In that context, he mentions the notorious case of the nursemaid Henriette Cornier, who beheaded a nineteen-month-old child in Paris in 1825, and subsequently threw the head out the window. Not long after that, other nurses admitted that they also felt an "irresistible impulse to cut the throats of their employers' children" (1912: 340).[4]

. . . invention

With "general laws," Tarde refers to the fact that the process of imitation plays a role not only in social life but also in fields such as geology, astronomy, and chemistry. Although he calls the laws "general," the result is different in each individual field. In this framework, the phenomenon of invention assumes an exceptional position. Tarde defines an invention as "a combination of dissimilar imitations" (1969: 153). For inventions, too, branch into series, according to Tarde, like links in a chain with "highly variable intervals, sometimes of a few days or months, sometimes of several centuries" (1969: 160). They merge into series of imitations, as a result of which they expand like an oil stain, leading a social-cultural field to increasingly acquire sameness. In doing so, inventions spread out like ripples in water—to use one of Tarde's favorite analogies—moving toward the boundary of an area until they come into contact with another obstacle. In Tarde's view, this obstacle will be the imitation of a previous invention, and a new product will arise from the collision or conflict that occurs. It will be a new invention that can, in turn, be imitated until it again comes into contact with new obstacles. This analogy makes society "one large irrigation system: with currents, undercurrents and countercurrents in constant flux" (van Ginneken 1992: 200).

In this connection, an invention is only social, as Tarde writes in *Social Laws* (2000), when it is imitated in social life. Seen from a social standpoint, inventions that are not imitated are unimportant, Tarde believes. This means that an invention only produces results when it is incorporated into series of imitations "which have fallen one after another into the domain of the commonplace, the traditional, and the customary" (1912: 118). Only when it has been taken up into a powerful imitative flow can an invention break into social reality at a certain point. This involves small and large imitations, imitations that occur in the long and short term. To gain a better understanding of the idea that a small invention can have great social consequences, I wish to digress for a moment to the dance called "the twist." This dance appeared in the 1950s and brought a new rage to the dance floor. In the twist, the upper part of the body makes a revolving movement while the arms are lifted, and the lower part of the body makes a movement in the opposite direction. The exceptional feature of this dance is that it can be performed with little or no contact between the dance partners. Although the body's reaction to the beat of the music may be pretty small, the effect is large because this dance completely confuses the traditional relationship between a man and a woman. To do the twist, a woman does not need a dance partner— for the first time. The man is no longer the leader on the dance floor. In all its grandiose triviality, the twist is known as the dance of female emancipation: "It takes two to tango, but one to twist."

Although invention and imitation cannot be positioned opposite one another hierarchically—after all, they are powers that mutually influence each other—Tarde seems, in his approach, to hold on strongly to the classical notion of genius, as is outlined in Kant's *Critique of Judgement*, dating from 1790, among other places. According to Kant, a genius has at his or her disposal an autonomous designing capacity ("autonomy" literally means "self-legislating"). This person pays attention to something that is regarded by others as being merely coincidental or insignificant. In much the same way, Tarde attributes inventions to the capability of "truly great men" on several occasions. In *Penal Philosophy*, he declares that the genius can "reform the multitude and little by little makes it conform to himself" (1912: 164–65). At the same time, this rationalist vision only offers a partial explanation for the fact that "we are more imitative than innovative" (1962: 98). In contrast to Durkheim's rational approach and following Théodule Ribot's *Essai sur l'imagination créatrice* (*Essay on the Creative Imagination*, 1900), Tarde also speaks of other matters that may influence the genesis of new inventions, such as "fear or anger, sadness or joy, hate or love" (1969: 150). In *The Laws of Imitation*, he even refuses to draw a distinction between conscious and unconscious inventions:

> I have certainly applied this name [invention] to all individual initiatives, not only without considering the extent to which they are self-conscious—for the individual often innovates unconsciously, and, as a matter of fact, the most imitative man is an innovator on some side or another—but without paying the slightest attention in the world to the degree of difficulty or merit of the innovation in question. (1962: xiv)

Nevertheless, Tarde seems to propagate the idea that an invention is a strictly individual matter, whereas imitation is a situation involving two separate individuals. Consequently, in *The Rules of Sociological Method*, Durkheim rebukes Tarde for this approach, stating that "imitation never expresses what is essential and characteristic in the social fact. [. . .] If social facts were unique in bringing about this effect [expansion], imitation might serve, if not to explain them, at least to define them. But an individual state which impacts on others nonetheless remains individual" (1968: 12 nt.1).[5] In other words, to what extent is Tarde's approach anything other than a plea for the exercise of "psychologism" or "spiritualism"? In *Difference and Repetition*, Deleuze rejects Durkheim's criticism that an interpsychologism is skulking behind Tarde's sociology.

Deleuze declares that Tarde's analysis concerns a "*microsociology*, which is not necessarily concerned with what happens between individuals but with what happens within a single individual: for example, hesitation understood as 'infinitesimal social opposition,' or invention as 'infinitesimal social adaptation'" (1968: 105). This means that what happens at an individual level is always in relation to the social field of which that person is a component. Tarde's statement that "everything is a society and all things are societies" (1999: 58), which Bruno Latour (2002) described as "a flat society argument," demonstrates thus a profound philosophical insight: there is no intrinsic distinction between individuals, animals, bacteria, cells, or occurrences such as a flea market or crime. We need this reminder in order to be able to conceptualize the fact that interactions cannot be reduced to the qualities of the individual; in other words, they cannot be reduced to the qualities of the substance or the subject to which they refer or are ascribed. There are no purely internal psychological factors, apart from connections that stimulate thought and action. Just as is the case with Foucault and Deleuze, Tarde's basic principles and their capacity to explain are expressed in the way in which relations arise with other people and things. Accordingly, the decisive element of reality is, to Tarde, not the individual but rather a series of affective relations that produce difference, movements by means of which something qualitative and quantitative is activated. Imitation and innovation—and this is the crucial point—are middle terms, which bring other elements together and allow them to communicate.

It requires little argument to show that Tarde did not succeed in his efforts to formulate laws that could compete with scientific knowledge of people's behavior. In contrast to what he perhaps hoped, the concepts of imitation and invention are not capable of equaling current psychological and sociological insights and research methods in popularity. Nevertheless, the problem that Tarde is trying to deal with remains unabatedly topical. There is still much obscurity with regard to the way in which changes occur in reality and the way in which new orderings arise amid these changes. Whereas Durkheim placed the emphasis on macro-sociological factors that support and maintain the unity of a society for a long period, Tarde demonstrates that the social context is always less structured and less self-evident than we tend to believe. It is not unity but rather variation and movement that he sees as the quintessential feature of social reality (see also Alliez 2001). And it is exactly that last aspect that betrays Tarde's general conviction, namely, the idea that dynamics can be explained on the basis of the relations between people and things. These relations, the behavioral patterns that develop from these, and the orderings that subsequently arise in a social field are the central elements of his elucidation.

All this leads to the conclusion that the stability level, which I refer to as "molar" in this book, is only one part of the story. There is always a second level at work that we are all too keen to forget. At the same time, there is a "molecular" level with its own individual dynamics.[6] I regard these levels as two ways of looking at the same social reality. In the following sections, I shall further elaborate both levels in terms of their nature and function. In the third part of this book, I shall apply them to the empirical research on security assemblages.

Molar

For a tentative answer to the question concerning the nature and function of the molar, I stray for a moment to the science of thermodynamics, a branch of natural science that studies interactions among large gatherings of particles at the macroscopic level. In this framework, the term "molar" refers to a certain amount of a substance. Similar to a "dozen" or a "gross," the term "molar" refers to a certain quantity. A mole of a substance is the atomic or molecular mass of that substance, expressed in grams, and this mass is called the "molar mass" (Beavon and Jarvis 2003: 20–21). The volume of one mole of gas particles is called the molar volume of a gas and is represented by the abbreviation "Vm." To provide information on the number of molecules or formula units, use is made of "n," the amount of substance expressed in mole. In such expressions, the discoveries of the Italian natural physics and chemistry expert Amedeo Avogadro (1776–1856), a specialist in the domain of gas chemistry, played an important role.

In 1811, Avogadro demonstrated that, with equal pressure and temperature, the volume of an ideal gas is directly proportional to the number of particles it contains. His experiments showed that two equal volumes of different gases, with identical pressure and temperature, contain the same number of particles. These particles may be atoms or molecules, but also ions or subatomic particles such as electrons, for example. In this way, it can be determined that the number of molecules in a gas is independent of the magnitude of the mass of the gas molecules. In other words, one mole of any gas always occupies the same volume at any given pressure and temperature. On this basis, it is possible to deduce the molecular mass of a gas and, by allowing gases to react with one another, to say something about the composition of a molecule. Subsequently, it is only a small step to Avogadro's number that indicates the number of molecules in a mole of matter. The number of particles in one mole is approximately equal to 6.02214×10^{23} mol^{-1}. This number is known as "the Avogadro constant" and indicates the magnitude of the number of particles that constitute a system that satisfies the laws of classical dynamics. The magnitude of this number is difficult to imagine. Computer models have shown that the number is equal to the number of nuggets of popcorn that are needed to cover the whole of the United States to a depth of 14.4 kilometers (Bryson 2003: 93 nt.).

Right down to the present day, the Avogadro constant is used to estimate the amount of matter produced during a chemical reaction. On the basis of the premises provided by Avogadro, one can recognize overlaps with insights from the social sciences with regard to the issue of stability and change. One of the greatest advantages of inventions in other disciplines is that they offer new "thinking instruments" or a "toolkit" (Foucault 1980: 145) with which to approach other systems. Of course I am aware that the above outline gives only a drastic simplification of these inventions. However, this does not negate the fact that analogies can indeed be drawn between the natural sciences and the humanities, and that scientific functions can be converted to concepts that can be applied or transferred to other realms of knowledge, such as the social sciences in general and security issues in particular. Although the distinction between the natural sciences and the humanities has been institutionalized in separate faculties at universities for several centuries, this distinction is not entirely problem free. For instance, scientists such as Leibniz and Newton were also intensively engaged in philosophical issues, and it is also debatable how useful it actually is to study humankind in separate categories (mind, brain, DNA) instead of emphasizing their association.

In my opinion, the natural-scientific definition of the term "molar" fits in with a long tradition of expressions that are also used in the social sciences to describe and contextualize social reality. The term embraces concepts that express what I wish to call a "fixed state" in which the separate constituents are firmly linked to one another and form an inextricable entity. In this framework, one can think of the previously mentioned concepts of the clock and the body, in order to say that a social field (organization, society, person) works *as* a machine. There are countless examples in which a society or a people is regarded as an indivisible body with certain qualities and some kind of essence.[7] One of the most appealing examples is Hobbes's *Leviathan* (1963), in which he unfolds his political philosophy on organized society. The renowned image on the cover of the work illustrates the idea of a social body and its constituents. That body consists of numerous small bodies that represent the subjects of the sovereign. The social body is presented as a whole consisting of separate components that not only support the whole but also enable it to function in an optimum way. It is self-evident that that body can become ill and weak. A process of healing or purging is then required. Although this imagery is metaphorical in most cases, the dividing line between literal and metaphorical often turns out to be thinner than we originally think, as the history of humanity has shown.

Although there has never been an outright, lucid definition of molar thinking down through the centuries, four determining features of such thinking have made their presence clear. First, it is based upon the existence of a social whole that can be strictly demarcated. Second, it presumes that this whole consists of separate components. Depending on the whole that is described, these components may be individuals, families, or corporations. Third, the primacy in this thinking lies with the whole. The components are presumed to exist for the sake of the whole. This means that the whole has relative autonomy with regard to the components. Fourth, this thinking attaches great importance to a harmonious order. The whole can only function well when there is order and harmony among the components. There is no space for noise, the musical counterpart of chaos. Noise is regarded as an obstacle; it disturbs the order of the whole. For this reason, the whole is directed to exclude "friction"—a term that Manuel DeLanda (1991: 60–61) used for the "uncontrollable" and "unpredictable"—as much as possible.

A relevant aspect is that the molar tends to dominate modern social-scientific research. Just like most scientific researchers, those who study social reality have a tendency to break it down into separate pieces and to research these pieces by means of certain patterns. This method is characterized by the itemizing of reality and by "focusing attention on isolated and controllable matters" (Van Calster 2006: 20). The urge to divide, separate, fragment, and atomize leads to researchers studying the parts in terms of what they contribute to the whole. This means that the whole is studied as an independently functioning "thing" in which nothing can occur simply "out of the blue"—thus, as an autonomous force that has an intention and can be held responsible. If social reality is looked at in this way, attention is directed to the entity that initiates the activity of people. The entity can be stopped at any moment to make a snapshot in time. In this way, an action is enclosed in an entity that is always given in advance, and that partly determines the interactions of people themselves. After all, the interactions take place in a system that is extant prior to the actions of people themselves. The consequence of this is that actions can be isolated from the elements in that entity and occur in a recognizable and predictable way. They are implicitly presumed to be "the same." I wish to refer to this as the "they-all-look-alike syndrome." This syndrome ensures that actions always appear to have the reversible relationship of "if A, then B," and follow the linearity of one series, namely, the line that extends from a known past via the present to a certain future. Researchers who suffer from the "they-all-look-alike syndrome" trace interactions among people back to the functionality of the entity—in other words, to the degree to which the interactions contribute to the formulated goals—whether these have been explicitly stated or not—and their starting points.

Molecular

The molar rests on the metaphysical idea that human interactions can ultimately all be brought into harmony with one another to support the workings or objective of a whole. In this way, no account is taken of spontaneity, coincidence, heterogeneity, and unpredictability. Indeed, it is striking that the molar level cannot cope with this situation and omits such matters from the research framework. In doing so, it does not admit real changes and transformations, and refuses to acknowledge the many series of interactions among people of real flesh and blood who cannot be controlled or managed. The conclusion of all this is that the molar only gains a grip on part of the current problems in everyday reality. For this reason, it should actually try to put its own pretensions into perspective and should do more justice to a permanent and dynamic "becoming" that is not, or only scarcely allows itself to be, formalized or interpreted on the basis of previously construed categories or abstract concepts. Instead of regarding the uncontrollable and uncertain as an evil that should be neutralized to the greatest possible extent, one could perhaps better emphasize the creativity or productivity that is inherent in the uncontrollable and the uncertain.

With this observation, I have come to a level that complies, to a much lesser degree than the molar, with unambiguous laws or general principles. The molar cannot be understood without the molecular—which is also a concept drawn from natural physics—by means of which I wish to express a changeable or liquid state that is incomplete and can never be absolutized. In contrast to a fixed state, particles in a liquid state are detached from one another and are "constantly in motion" (Kubbinga 2003: 65). The explanation of this instability is to be found in the power relations among molecules. To concretize the dynamics among molecules (proteins, lipids, metabolites), chemists speak of "interactions." Although scientists agree that this involves one of the most fundamental levels of interaction, still not everything is known about the movements of molecules in relation to one another and about the interactions among various molecules. For instance, there is insufficient insight into the way in which molecules enter into interactions with one another and unexpectedly order themselves in what natural physics call "self-assemblages" (Sijbesma 2007). Thus, nature is an excellent example of a self-assemblage of molecules, but checking the form and structure of self-assembling systems has led to many questions in the exact sciences, at least up to the present.

In order to provide insight into the way in which molecules mutually communicate and apparently spontaneously order themselves, scientists distinguish three kinds of interactions. In essence, this distinction concerns the "senses" of molecules by means of which they establish mutual contact. These interactions, also called "noncovalent bonding," play a leading role in the most vital processes in nature, such as the binding of a substratum by an enzyme and the folding of the precise spatial form of DNA, RNA, and proteins. In a sequence of diminishing strength, this comprises electrostatic interactions, hydrogen bridges, and Van der Waals bonds. The most interesting feature of electrostatic interactions is that they involve a physical force among molecules with elementary charges (ions). In contrast to hydrogen bridges, these interactions are dependent on a direction. The power of attraction of the ions is the most important motivating force. The electrostatic binding is one of attraction when there are two electrically charged particles with opposite charges. Van der Waals interactions are weak to very weak interactions among molecules. These interactions were named after Dutchman Johannes Diderik van der Waals (1837–1923), and they contain, in principle, all the forces that are not the result of covalent bonds or electrostatic forces among ions. The existence of these mutually attracting forces can be deduced from the fact that all solid matter can become liquid. This even applies to gases that can be stored in liquid form with only a slight increase in pressure.

In philosophical terms, the natural sciences can illustrate that, at the molecular level, small complex relations are more important than large dialectic structures that should give unity and order to the whole. When one translates this insight into a general perspective on change, the molecular is formed by occurrences that have no reference at all to a center, standard, or norm. Seen from a molecular point of view, the world is made up of countless trivial details, interesting failures, events without beginning or end, loose ends that cannot be tied up anywhere. In short, it is a mass of apparently "small and extremely small maneuvers" (Sloterdijk 2004: 87) that do not underpin the agreed-upon rules but continuously lead to new exceptions. In contrast to the molar, the material or DNA from a social field is then found in a permanent "becoming" and not in a logical order detached from this. This is also what Zygmunt Bauman means when he writes that, in contrast to fixed or solid entities, fluids do not retain their shape. Fluids, as Bauman writes (2000: 2), have "no clear spatial dimensions." The moment in time is more important to fluids than the place they occupy. In this connection, Bauman speaks of a "liquid society," a notion that serves as a metaphor for the present stage of modernity in which once-so-fixed institutions are becoming dislodged from their former positions. Everything is constantly in motion in our world, ranging from the fleeting relationships that people enter into to their restless search for identity and happiness. Desires are being constantly satisfied only to be aroused once again. Borrowing from Bauman, Lucia Zedner (2006a) develops the notion of "liquid security," highlighting its endless, fluid, and dispersed character.

For a more precise elaboration of the molecular, I distinguish three particular qualities. First, the molecular is situated in the realm of the *immediate*, which involves expressions and desires that immediately make the world actual, and fall outside the framework in which actions are clarified on the basis of a rational-calculating view of humanity. The latter approach, as dealt with in the work of Hobbes and Beccaria among others, presumes that people are weighing the costs and benefits of potential actions, and choosing those actions that maximize their net benefits. One of the problems of this approach, in addition to the question concerning the decision-making talents of the individual and the amount of relevant information that he or she has available at that moment, is the limited time horizon. The consequences of such a choice only come into force in the long run. The *immediate* is primarily concerned with passions such as pride, frustration, pleasure, and anger that play out in real time—in other words, in the here and now. They are pushed aside as being abnormal or unimportant—seen from a molar perspective—because they fall outside the discussion on uniformity and a recognizable goal.

Second, the molecular is characterized by *dissimilar* series of interactions. This includes one long chain of connections between nonlinear associations that lead to an entity moving in a direction that was not agreed upon or determined in advance. "Nonlinear" is a broad concept that indicates that the coherence between variables need not have a fixed course. For example, a doubling of the number of police officers does not mean that the number of solved crimes will also become twice as large. In the case of nonlinearity, activities cannot be reduced to unilateral causal processes that determine all higher-order phenomena. There may be mention of nonlinear influence—and thus of processes from various directions where all kinds of factors influence one another in ongoing reciprocity. The irony of this is that the original meaning is often completely lacking. This makes it problematic to say exactly what causes what, or what is the result of what. There are always minor occurrences that put everything into disarray. These unexpected, disturbing events are often not taken into account in the formulation of legal rules and the formal establishment of agreements in covenants. This is indeed difficult. Nevertheless, no one will deny that these have always existed and will continue to exist.

Third, the molecular is concerned with a Nietzschean *perspectivism*—that is, the acceptance of the fact that truth can only be surveyed in the context of the perspectives that people employ and have of one another. For instance, a certain problem is always approached from a unique viewpoint, where it cannot be claimed that one perspective is worth more than another. In other words, there is no interpretation of social reality that is always complete or perfect, which indeed makes it an interpretation. It is important to realize that this perspectivism has nothing to do with a casual relativism in which every standard by means of which things can be assessed is lacking. The impossibility of resolving a problem in a single coherent explanation forces one to examine the relations between the occurrences and the circumstances under which a point of view is adopted. Formulated in this way, perspectivism is a source of renewal and vitality, if people are prepared to develop sensitivity toward other and divergent points of view and to put their own opinions up for discussion, regardless of how uncomfortable that may be. Absolute standpoints on a certain situation are thus undermined and room is created for new content.

Between rule and exception

It can be stated, on the basis of the issues covered above, that a security assemblage always unfolds at two levels at the same time: molar and molecular. However, the starting point that, in addition to the molar level, there is also a molecular level of direct and unequal processes of interaction is less self-evident than it appears to be at first sight. If one observes the attention social scientists pay to social practices, it seems as if they nurture structural distrust of the process-driven and changeable nature of reality. Sociologists or economists often file down interactions to the level of usefulness to a larger whole (profit, turnover). Criminologists who devote time and energy to processes of group dynamics often go searching for the characteristics of a group, such as rivalry, structure, and leadership, which actually give a static picture rather than a dynamic one. These scientists prefer to concentrate on molar patterns or expressions. In doing so, they build on a structure of fixed meanings that can be applied to separate elements. An explanation of this probably lies in the fact that the molecular is regarded as embodying minimal order or—even worse—as disarray or chaos. The term "molecular chaos" is used in the field of thermodynamics to outline the behavior of molecules before they collide: they are independent of one another (Prigogine and Stengers 1984). Or perhaps it may come from the assumption that the molecular may be capable of neutralizing the molar at any given moment, in which case the power of the molecular would effortlessly prevail over the molar. In my opinion, both assumptions rest upon a misunderstanding. The molecular should not be regarded as chaotic and revolutionary, and neither should the molar be conceived as dogmatic and conservative. The difference between the molar and the molecular is much more related to the angle of approach and the standpoint that the researcher adopts. Accordingly, it is advisable to purge a few misunderstandings about the difference between these two levels. There are at least four erroneous ways to understand the relation between molar and molecular in an assemblage.

Molar and molecular do not refer to "the collective" on the one hand and "the individual" on the other. In that case, molar would refer to the behavior of a group of people, whereas molecular would refer to the actions of an individual. But, contrasting with this classical image of social reality, the terms "molar" and "molecular" give an impulse to reflection *beyond* the collective and the individual. In reality, the levels cannot be distinguished in terms of size or scale. It is better to speak of a difference in composition, organization, and consistency between the elements at molar and molecular levels. After all, the molar and the molecular are not determined by the number of elements they connect, and therefore not by their multiple character, but rather by the nature of the relations among the elements. The difference is related to the manner of ordering that they impose upon everyday reality and to the system of reference by means of which each level can be described. In the case of the molecular, this involves previously mentioned concepts such as rhizomatic, multivocal, nonlinear, smooth, changeable, intensive, and indivisible. In contrast, the molar is associated with characteristics such as arboreous, univocal, linear, striated, static, extensive, and divisible.

Moreover, the distinction between molar and molecular does not coincide with the conceptual couple "form-substance." It has been previously stated that the molar is primarily concerned with wholes and with isolated and controllable elements. Although effects at the molar level will be visible sooner, simply because, for example, the interactions among people are fixed and framed to a certain extent on the basis of unequivocal and coercive prescriptions or everyday routines, the molar should not be reduced to merely an abstract or legal form, such as Durkheim's "collective consciousness" or the social contract of Hobbes and Beccaria, which is detached from action itself. For this reason, the molar is not a structure without interaction. In Tardian logic, it is even fundamental that new series of interactions consistently arise at the molar level too. In this context, one can think of the behavioral patterns that people gradually develop to make their work more pleasant, such as drinking coffee with colleagues, having a break for a smoke, sending e-mails to friends, or putting on music at work. And one should not forget the automation of actions, including formal use of the language that people use to address one another. A characteristic feature is that both levels enable a localization of actions that have, in the case of the molar, the function of binding or unifying the molecular, to put it simply. In that respect, molar forces can also be defined as forces that divide people on the basis of norms statistically derived from a larger group. For instance, people in baseball and basketball circles speak of "averages" of a batsman or point guard. In security domains, people use codes such as "white," "yellow," "orange," or "red," which refer to the frequency with which children younger than twelve years come into contact with the police, either as witness or as victim or offender. In turn, Foucault speaks of disciplining in order to visualize the application of human action in institutions such as prison, school, and workplace.

The levels do not differ in scale or magnitude. In this field, the same problem occurs as with the first misunderstanding. The danger is that the molar is regarded as one large entity, whereas the molecular is a minor phenomenon. If this is the case, there is the chance of becoming tangled up in a classical micro-macro debate in which the explanatory level of the microscopic or molecular is seen as "the real occurrence," while the macro-level refers to "fixed entities and systems" (Simmel 1968). In an assemblage, micro and macro are one and the same. In fact, molar and molecular must be defined as relative in relation to a certain scale or magnitude. For instance, it is possible to see someone as a molar identity when one studies the subjectivization processes that make a person an individual. At the same time, this person can be seen at a molecular level in relation to the environment of which he or she is a component.

Finally, there is no opposition between the levels. The difference between the molar and the molecular is not pure or absolute. In fact, they can never be completely separated from one another. There is no Great Wall of China between the molar and the molecular. Although both levels are usually dealt with separately, as if they represent two different sorts of social reality,[8] there is actually only one process operational. This means that there is no mention of "a dialectic 'and' that dissolves in a higher order, but rather of a differentiating 'and-and' that combines unequal things" (Oosterling 2009a: 200). In this way, everything always happens simultaneously and contiguously. The molecular thus never exists independently of a molar level. Instead of an absolute difference, the two levels continually blend into one another and are combined in a zone of indistinguishability.[9]

Social engineering

It will be evident that the approach sketched here is at odds with perspectives in which the possibilities and effects of policy, or the freedom of choice that authorities have in a security assemblage, are unquestioningly embraced. In that framework, a person is seen to appropriate the truth and act as the giver of meaning to his or her existence, a logic that finds its formulation in Descartes' magical maxim "I think, therefore I am." This evokes questions concerning the way in which existing practices and institutions can be changed, and the attitude to be adopted with regard to formulating policy in security management. Although many nuances are already being acknowledged in the approach to processes of governing and ordering, the classical administrative approach of rule by a government that formulates policy and sees the world as a design still remains valid. This raises the question of the malleability of security.

The Dutch term "malleability" ("*maakbaarheid*") first appeared toward the end of the 1970s and formed the impulse for a development in governance in which the formulation of policy became a central theme (van Oenen 2008). It is possible to change social reality with the aid of certain instruments. Anyone wishing to order a society formulates specific goals, makes use of policy tools, and creates the preconditions to make everything possible. In this way, policy and malleability presuppose one another. In this connection, Martin Terpstra (2002: 210–13) points out that the idea of malleability is based on a number of assumptions. A first assumption is that reality can be objectified. Reality is regarded as an object with certain properties that enable it to be influenced and formed. This entails that causal relations among certain things with properties are possible and produce a desired effect. With regard to the idea of malleability, it is necessary to know these properties but also to know how to intervene in order to achieve a desired result. In addition, this approach presumes that two realities are possible. The one pole is the world in which the problem occurs, and the other pole is the person or organization that can supply a solution. In other words, the person or organization that can supply a solution is situated outside the problem field and, as a kind of outsider, evaluates these dynamics, forges plans, and prescribes the proper policy, after which it can be applied (Van Calster and Schuilenburg 2010).

This is again a very mechanistic way of looking at reality. It presupposes that policy formulation functions according to the model of a technical machine. In this model, the properties of things are seen in the light of their working. The consequence of this is that change can only be explained when it is imposed from the outside; in other words, it is implemented from outside the whole ("the watchmaker"). In security management, this is visible in the rationality or the exceptional qualities and visions that are ascribed to relative outsiders such as scientists, legislators, politicians, and policymakers. They will often be the first to see that certain affairs are not running according to plan, and subsequently prescribe—outside the world and independent of the world—the correct remedies so that the problems can be tackled adequately. With this, they are expected to be free of the determining forces of a more or less closed whole. What happens at the moment one is faced with these solutions can perhaps best be described in the words of the French philosopher Alain Badiou (1993) as making "a hole in knowledge." The usual way one is accustomed to act, and the significances, values, opinions, and beliefs that belong to it, are then breached with such force that one is forced to (re)determine one's position in the light of those exceptional solutions.

But exactly because policymakers are outsiders, they are always in a weak position to rectify imperfections. The train of thought described here indicates that all knowledge, regardless of how detailed it may be, is not only relational but can also provoke all kinds of reactions in and from the professional field. Therefore policymakers cannot remain outside the reality and social dynamics that form the basis of new policy measures that they subsequently impose upon reality. With this, the boundaries of faith in malleability are exposed. After all, this faith neglects the changes that consistently occur in reality and exert influence on what takes place at a social level. In relation to the idea that effective changes in society can be generated, malleability should not be regarded as a strategy according to which well-considered decisions can be made and implemented (Schuilenburg 2008b). Instead of idealizing policy as an objective source of knowledge and thus remaining in line with many social-scientific studies that place emphasis on administrative or malleability thinking with regard to security issues, it is more important to accentuate the relative importance of policy with respect to universalizing or objectifying methods of description, so that primarily unequivocal and simple solution orientations will be submitted. In fact, there are constantly changing processes about which absolute statements or predictions can never be uttered with any certainty.

* * *

We have seen that Durkheimian thinking identifies the ordering of security with the way in which authorities attempt to gain a grip on an insecure and unknown future. This takes place through the formulation of rules, the making of agreements, and the denomination and establishment of objectives in covenants among parties in a security assemblage. This generates certainty and predictability. Once the rules have been committed to paper, they constitute the authorities' legitimacy to act. But this idealization distracts from the everyday commonness of action and from interactions in the here and now. In Tarde's view, it is exactly this commonness that echoes incessantly in social practices and that has the capacity to develop in unexpected and spontaneous ways. With this, Tarde draws attention to the fact that the Durkheimian approach ignores social reality's ongoing dynamics and possibility of transformation, and can explain change in no way other than that an exceptional occurrence or individual has imposed that change.

In response to the limitations of Durkheimian thinking, I have introduced the concepts of "molar" and "molecular." I have demonstrated how both levels are present in a security assemblage and continuously resound through one another. Molar and molecular are directed to human actions and create a clear picture of the dynamics in a security assemblage. One could also regard them as conceptual spectacles or magnifying glasses with which to describe and study stability and change in an assemblage. The first glass focuses upon fixed characteristics, such as the decisions made and the routine character of the activities in a collaborative venture. The second glass draws attention to deviating series of interactions among authorities charged with the implementation of numerous security measures. In this chapter, I have argued that both levels must be seen in mutual coherence and can consistently be studied at the same time.

The combination of the molar and the molecular has consequences for empirical research on the ordering of security. Rather than defining the molar in isolation, we should examine its coherence with a molecular level and the subsequent effects of interaction. The challenge is to investigate "what is happening" without reducing this in advance to fixed orderings or overarching structures. After all, even if everything seems at first sight to be running smoothly, the smallest actions and passions can ensure that things at the molar level occur in unforeseen ways. Accordingly, the empirical part of this book has the aim of examining which content and expression the interactions and behavioral patterns possess that could breach the formal order at a molar level in a security assemblage. Thus, I am not primarily concerned with predictable events such as meetings and routine actions that bring orderliness to everyday occurrences. I am much more interested in interactions that are scarcely visible or noticeable but that have the potential to open up an assemblage and realize a different order. The self-organizing processes at the molecular level of a security assemblage form the starting point here.

PART III

Among People

The issues we are now faced with concern the way in which the dynamics in security assemblages can be made visible, and the new social and institutional orders to which such dynamics may lead in the approach to crime and disorder. These issues are relevant because the current study of security is primarily oriented to whether or not a chosen approach actually works, rather than to "why and under which circumstances" (Nelen 2008: 70) that may be the case. One is mainly interested in the visible and concrete results of security policy. In that respect, the study of policy outcomes of security measures is well served, particularly with regard to the reduction of crime and the attainment of public trust. However, much investigation into security does a very poor job when describing the thoughts and actions of the authorities that (help) execute security policy—shopkeepers, insurers, commercial security officers, housing associations, energy suppliers, damage-claim firms, and other organizations—although it is very probable that the interactions and significances that these authorities ascribe to their own and one another's actions can have consequences for the results of a security program.

The molecular level of four security assemblages has been taken as the starting point of the empirical study that forms the basis of the third part of this book. The data collection has the aim of determining the content and expression that interactions and behavioral patterns have at this level. In the study of such dynamics I direct my attention to the Dutch security diagram. Since the 1980s, the Netherlands has witnessed an ongoing development in which an attempt is being made to find an answer to crime and disorder through cooperation between private and public parties at the local level. Research into the molecular level of these forms of collaboration is closely linked to the performance of ethnographic investigations such as interviews, participant observations, document study, and other qualitative methods. In this framework, the researcher must study a security assemblage for a longer period of time in order to obtain an adequate picture of the processes that are active in that setting, such as mechanisms of influence and conflicts. As a consequence, the researcher is more able to examine why and how processes operate as they do. Although this is an exceptionally time-consuming and labor-intensive exercise, this type of study can extract insights that cannot, or can only with great difficulty, be otherwise obtained.

I have already stated that little ethnographic research has been performed on security-related parties engaged in tackling crime and disorder. Various reasons lie at the bottom of this. Ethnographic research has a strong connection with cultural criminology, which tends to concentrate on crime or criminal patterns in relation to (youth) culture, subcultures, and lifestyles (Ferrell et al. 2008: 174–91). In addition, to criminologists, commercial organizations are difficult to penetrate (Verhage 2009). Researchers often do not receive permission to carry out participant observations or to interview members of staff or the managers of companies. Private enterprises, as well as municipalities, prefer not to be mentioned in connection with crime or criminological research. This is largely due to the reputation of a company and the good name it has among the general public. Finally, many parties in the realm of security do not regard crime and disorder as their most important area of concern. For instance, energy suppliers will be faced with unsafe situations in houses, but their primary task is to provide energy to their customers. Crime and disorder are seen as exceptions to the rule.

The research performed here is a multiple-case study. In such studies, the intention is to give an accurate description of the reasons, motives, attributions, and experiences of the authorities in contact with others. In this way, insight can be gained into the way in which viewpoints change and the way in which new behavioral patterns in security assemblages arise on the basis of such changes. The four case studies were carried out by means of interviews, observations at the locations, document research, and study of the literature. In total, 132 interviews were held with damage experts, police functionaries, municipal civil servants, insurers, members of staff of the Ministry of Social Affairs and Employment, energy suppliers, housing associations, policy staff, security guards, shopkeepers, and other authorities. The interviews varied in length from half an hour to three hours. The number of discussions depended upon the complexity of the case studied and the number of authorities active in that framework. That quantity varied from fifteen interviews related to the approach to road-transport crime to eighty-seven interviews with authorities involved in the Collective Shop Ban. Supplementary discussions of a more general nature were also held with people from ministries and municipalities.[1]

A number of simple questions were asked in every security assemblage. How do the authorities give substance to the agreements made? How do they interpret and evaluate official policy? Which interests do they attach to the governance of security? Do they feel supported or impeded by other authorities? Which emotions and feelings play a role in such interactions, and how are these elaborated in practice? Do they nurture opinions other than those agreed upon? Do these opinions have consequences for the execution of their responsibilities? Do individual interpretations of rules and initiatives arise that could influence official policy? Do new aims arise in the partnership over time? On the basis of such questions, I believe that this study can contribute to knowledge forming about partnerships between the government and other parties in the area of security.

The ethnographic research is not served up as proof of the previously formulated dynamic perspective on security. The two research methods occurred simultaneously, with continuous interaction between theory and practice. On the basis of the findings, I have consistently adjusted the theory forming in the second part of the book. Thus, the theory has also altered during the ethnographic study. This does not mean, however, that a number of remarks should not be made about the empirical part of the book, particularly with regard to the methodological handicaps that were difficult to overcome. Numerous practical obstacles arose during the data collection. Molecular research appears to be very simple, resembling the work of a good journalist: observing, noting, and elaborating. But much work still remains to be done before a coherent narrative has been generated. Interactions and occurrences vanish into thin air at the moment they have taken place. Moreover, the troublesome element of new behavioral patterns is that they only become conspicuous when they have disappeared. Therefore, in order to gain a precise picture of the molecular, it is necessary to set up a very extensive scientific battery. For instance, Tarde once suggested that fifty sociologists should document the succession of changes in their direct environments. In this line of thought, he was influenced by Abbé Rousselot, who had begun a study of the dialect in his home district in 1879. The film *Kitchen Stories* (2003) by director Bent Hamer is illustrative of this intensive working method. It deals with a small Norwegian village where a large-scale scientific study into the patterns of movement of the housewife in the kitchen is performed.

Another handicap is the fact that respondents are not overeager to admit to a third person that they cherish other views about the starting points and aims of a security assemblage, let alone that they have developed behavioral patterns that deviate from the agreed-upon working method. From Oscar Wilde we have learned that a man is least himself when he talks in his own person. The data presented have never been present in major narratives, but always in small clauses. Occasionally these clauses become leading statements but only after much prompting and gaining the trust of the interviewees. Finally, the duration of the research made it difficult to demonstrate how the play of molecular relations modifies the molar level of an assemblage or that the self-organizing processes exposed have themselves become molar, due to the genesis of new routines, for example, or a different use of language. This will generally be a question of years rather than of weeks or months. In that respect, I regard the data presented here primarily as micro-predictors (what would be called "circumstantial evidence" in law) of new molar orderings. The analysis in the third part of the book is therefore provisional and schematic by definition, inasmuch as it describes molecular effects that are ongoing and have not yet ended. The findings presented are a snapshot in time, without a definitive statement being made and without the described results leading to major or minor changes at the molar level in a more or less distant future.

6

Combating Marijuana Cultivation

The first chapter of the ethnographic study covers the approach to organized marijuana cultivation, which is an important theme within Dutch
crime fighting and a topic that has been on the front pages of newspapers regularly over the past five years. Marijuana cultivation brings
disorder, degradation, and risk situations to residential neighborhoods.
It may also entail welfare fraud, tax, and theft of energy (Bovenkerk and
Hogewind 2002; Spapens et al. 2007). In a follow-up to the "Cannabis
Letter" of 23 April 2004 sent by the Dutch government to the Second
Chamber of Parliament, a national intensification of the policy to eliminate illegal marijuana cultivation was initiated. An attempt is being
made to realize a more integral approach in which the government and
other aggrieved organizations act jointly against marijuana growers
(*Notitie Integrale Aanpak Hennepteelt* [Memo for the Integral Approach
to Hemp Cultivation], 2006). In this cooperative effort, the police and
the public prosecutor work with other authorities, mostly municipalities, housing associations, and energy suppliers.[1]

Here, too, we see that it is no longer possible to make a distinction between public and private parties. The possibilities of tackling the problem of marijuana cultivation in its entirety are enhanced when forces
are united in a new whole. The combination of means and instruments
makes the approach less dependent upon the possibilities, commitment,
and capacity of only one party. This can be understood in the light of
the legal and control possibilities that each individual party possesses
(Bergmans 2007). But the combination of forces also makes one inquisitive about interaction at the molecular level between the authorities in
the integral approach to marijuana cultivation. Because the molecular
level cannot be reduced to the formal features of the approach itself, and
a researcher therefore cannot know this level in advance, the actions of
the authorities have been studied on the basis of interviews and observations in two Dutch cities that apply an integral approach: Eindhoven and

Rotterdam.[2] In this way, it is possible to obtain insight into the everyday practice that the authorities undertake in the fight against illegal marijuana cultivation.

Administrative background

For a long time, the Dutch government gave little priority to the fight against marijuana cultivation. This was linked to the fact that the cultivation of marijuana had a relatively innocent image and was largely tolerated in society. It was only toward the end of the 1990s that people began to realize that a great deal of money could be made in marijuana cultivation. The image of small-scale cultivators who act on the basis of ideal motives, growing marijuana for themselves and at their own risk, began to alter. Studies showed that indoor marijuana cultivation had taken on a professional character. It is a lucrative trade by means of which much money can be earned. Serious profits can be made with relatively small investment. The retail price of Dutch marijuana ("*nederweed*") has risen considerably in the past few years. Whereas the average price was 5.80 euros a gram in 2000, this had become 9.59 euros by 2013. In addition, much of the production is meant for export. Criminal cooperation also plays an important role, with criminal networks buying hemp products on a large scale and processing and trading these products. These organizations often have large plantations at their disposal (Wouters et al. 2007; Fijnaut and de Ruyver 2008; Korf and Wouters 2008).

A significant feature of the new approach to marijuana cultivation is that it intensifies and reinforces detection by enabling public and private parties to cooperate more closely. According to the literature on security, the usual method for understanding this way of working is to see it as a somewhat complex variant of a simple collaboration. After all, most parties in the partnership already played a role prior to the implementation of the integral approach to marijuana cultivation. Their role is thus not a new one, although it is often modified by the new form of collaboration. While the partnership becomes more complex in its nature as a result, the new unit is still simple to govern and alter. In this way, the idea prevails that the differences among the parties are relatively easy to bridge and that everyone's working method can be ordered in such a way that it contributes to the functioning of the greater whole. Accordingly, more effort is required to fathom the whole configuration, but the effect remains the same as in a simple system (see also Teisman 2005).

To enable the new entity to function in an optimum way, all kinds of resources are deployed to achieve the aims of the integral approach. These aims are described in the "Model Covenant on the Integral Approach to Hemp Cultivation" (*Voorbeeldconvenant Integrale Aanpak Hennepteelt*):

> The joint taking of preventative and repressive measures, in mutual consensus, which lead to the elimination of dangerous situations, to the prevention and combating of criminal activities relating to hemp plantations, to the improvement of the livability in the relevant streets and neighborhoods, to the removal of feelings of insecurity, and to the termination of improper use of living space, the unlawful receipt of welfare benefits, the illegal tapping of electricity, and tax fraud in this framework, will lead to a broad palette of sanctions and measures against the grower. (2007: 2)

The diversity of the formulated goals is largely linked to the presumed advantages of the integral approach. This approach allegedly increases the chances of the marijuana growers being caught, and if they are caught, the offenders can be punished more severely and along various lines of attack. In this process, sanctions from the Penal Code may be applied, but measures based on administrative law and civil law may also be taken. In an extension of this, mention is occasionally made of the deterrent working of this approach. People are apparently less prepared to run the risks that are involved in marijuana cultivation (Bergmans 2007). In addition, there are the practical advantages of the cooperation itself. These mainly involve what are called "the learning processes of cooperation" (Reagans and McEvily 2003; Kane et al. 2005). This involves the transfer of knowledge among the participating parties as a result of which the cooperation can be reinforced and the aims achieved more quickly and effectively. By dismantling marijuana plantations, the parties learn a lot about the different aspects of the problem and about one another's tasks, interests, and expertise—about the technical facets of the work of an energy supplier, for example. This knowledge can subsequently be used again in an even more effective approach

(Bovenkerk 2008). At the same time, the work of the police is greatly alleviated by the municipality's (partially) administrative and juridical approach to organized crime, which is oriented to the hindrance and removal of opportunities and situations that facilitate crime (Huisman and Koemans 2008). As a result, the police can devote more attention to the detection of the criminal networks behind marijuana cultivation.

The covenant agreed upon among the participating parties forms an important means to achieve the aims of the approach to marijuana cultivation. To this end, working agreements have been made about the objectives and the acceptance of responsibility. Such covenants are being formulated to an increasing degree. In 2013, 65 percent of the municipalities in the Netherlands had established policy for the administrative approach and 70 percent had established specific policy in accordance with the Public Administration Act. The hemp manual, better known as the "script," is another tool that is used to reach the agreed-upon goals. It contains an explanation of the various steps in the work process of the integral approach, and fixed points of contact are defined in order to deal with questions from the participants. In this way, the progress of the cooperation can be monitored, and there is adequate control over the functioning of the whole. If one adds the formal structures of consultation among the authorities, the job performance interviews that the managers hold with team members at certain times, and the obligatory (often monthly) reports on the results of dismantling operations (the number of plantations eliminated, the quantity of plants found, the neutralized profit), a certain amount of structure and regularity can quickly be found in the tackling of marijuana cultivation. This image can be underpinned by scientific research on the dismantling of marijuana plantations in the Netherlands. This shows that the dismantling of marijuana plantations in the past few years "has increasingly assumed the character of a structured, streamlined and also more routine approach" (Wouters et al. 2007: 34).

Implementation in real-life practice

The fact that much research underpins the above-stated conclusions is due to the fact that criminological research is primarily directed toward the molar level of the governance of security. I have defined the molar level as the stable level of the integral approach. On the one hand, one can group the objectives, agreements, and control instruments of the security assemblages in this category. On the other, there are the work processes and actions with a high degree of regularity, such as technical routines, daily rituals, and the formal use of language by the authorities. Directly opposed to this is the notion expounded in this book that there are also processes that develop unpredictably and irregularly. After all, in the integral approach, actions and interactions will always occur, with their own dynamics, among the authorities. These actions will indeed often have a structured and routine character at the molar level, as is consistently acknowledged in scientific studies on the approach to marijuana cultivation, and will continue to develop in linear fashion. But, at the same time, interactions arise that are irregular and unexpected, which frequently also have a nonlinear character. These interactions are difficult to anticipate, and correlate to a large extent with the substantiation and significance the authorities give to their own and other people's actions. They can also occur as a result of sudden events during the dismantling process, and thus take place by surprise. In that respect, this is the same phenomenon as we previously encountered in the work of Deleuze and Tarde.

The question is whether or not, in the integral approach to marijuana cultivation, deviating processes occur that could influence the molar level and could engineer differences in the outcomes of the approach between the municipalities studied and the teams whose responsibility it is to detect and dismantle marijuana plantations. Before I deal with the recorded results in both security assemblages, it must be emphasized that the approaches in Eindhoven and Rotterdam are different from each other. The difference lies in the way the job is performed on the day of operations. In Eindhoven, the "positivization" is performed in advance. "Positivization" is the confirmation of suspicion by means of heat measurement at the location, ampère measurement, and data from other sources. Two or three "positive" results are sufficient to justify a request for admission to the premises. The Administrative Intervention Team of the Municipality of Eindhoven (BITE) and the police then set these "positivized" addresses on an agenda for one of the fortnightly action days. In contrast, Rotterdam deploys the "hemp train" system. The police, a civil servant, and a fraud expert from the energy supplier undertake joint action and visit, every week, a number of addresses that have been reported. In this way, the team collects the "positive" evidence needed to concretize the suspicion at the location itself. In some cases, certain verifications are already known. A municipality may have performed previous research, with an infrared camera, for example, on forms of irritation such as olfactory nuisance. In other cases, an (anonymous) complaint may have been received so that the remaining items of evidence must be gathered on the day of action itself.

Although the integral approach to marijuana cultivation is replete with administrative forcefulness of expression, such as "decisiveness," "persistence," and "clarity," reality turns out to be somewhat different. Practice has shown that imposition of the rules is faced with all kinds of obstacles and discord. It can be said that the approach used in Rotterdam has led to less discussion among the participants than that in Eindhoven. This may be related to the fact that work is carried out in a fixed formation in Rotterdam. In a national context, Rotterdam is also regarded as the guide and example of a successful integral approach. But the interviews also indicate that the mentality of the housing associations also has an influence on real-life practice and results. In Rotterdam, the housing associations receive a complete dossier from the hemp teams, containing the data that are needed to initiate a civil procedure against the offender. Moreover, in that municipality it is more an exception than the rule when a housing association does not ride on the hemp train. According to a Rotterdam housing association respondent, this approach enables a better view of the specific situation, and the contract of the tenant can be immediately canceled. In contrast to Rotterdam, the housing associations in Eindhoven have decided to no longer send members of staff to the action days. In addition to organizational reasons, the members of staff interviewed state that their presence at such actions brings no added value, and that the dismantling of marijuana plantations is not the task of a housing association. One respondent declared, "This is a criminal matter, and that is not our domain. We are not an organization engaged in the capture of villains. A senior client manager should not be involved in the dismantling of marijuana plantations. We are not cowboys." Another housing association respondent mentions the security aspect of dismantling. In the past, various threats have been uttered against housing associations. However, this argument is challenged by members of staff of energy suppliers because they too are at risk in their role as fraud inspectors during the action days, and find that the housing associations are "taking the easy way out."

Other parties share this opinion. They believe that the housing associations benefit very readily from the information they receive when action days have been held, after which they can initiate a civil procedure against the tenant. One respondent declared that the housing associations rely too much on other partners and take their own responsibilities too lightly. One respondent from the police pointed to the possible consequences of this type of conduct: "You notice among the police that some members of staff are not motivated to send information to a housing association because it assigns no priority to participating in our operations." The respondents from the housing associations respond to such remarks by stating that matters are being approached from the wrong direction. According to the respondents interviewed, the police only express criticism of the housing associations because they wish to prevent all kinds of problems in the cooperation being attributed to the police themselves. This provokes questions as to which problems actually occur within the cooperation, and to what extent these problems may be related to the attitudes and perceptions of the authorities and the interactions among them.

Conflicting interests

To obtain a sharp focus on the dynamics in the integral approach to marijuana cultivation, I shall first examine the developments in the makeup and hierarchy of the two partnerships. The makeup of the security assemblages studied displays great diversity in terms of the work experience of the authorities (ranging from police trainees to experienced fraud inspectors) and the presence of diverse parties (ranging from private dismantling organizations to energy suppliers). The previous section discussed the decision of the housing associations in Eindhoven not to participate in the dismantling operations. Discussions in the two municipalities reveal issues concerning two other parties: energy companies and the police. With regard to the energy companies, there is the recurring accusation that they show too little understanding and patience when it comes to the cooperation itself and the adaptations that are required to improve and streamline operational methods. One respondent articulated this as follows: "Only one thing is important to them [the energy companies], namely, that they can reclaim as much lost energy as possible from as many premises as possible. But when you're a part of an integral approach, you should also show understanding of the positions of other parties." Nevertheless, all parties see the energy companies as a serious and essential partner in the collaborative effort. In both Eindhoven and Rotterdam, the energy supplier is described as a party that does not need to be spurred on and that fulfills its task as thoroughly as possible. In addition, its technical knowledge and expertise with regard to dismantling equipment (such as the installation of a meter cupboard) is seen as indispensable in the collaboration.

With regard to the police, the accusation has been made that they assign too little capacity to tackling marijuana cultivation. Other parties have problems with the situation that the police do not devote sufficient personnel to the dismantling of marijuana plantations in houses. "The police do not account for this in their annual plans. No extra time is made available for such activities. They are claiming things they cannot realize," said one respondent. Although the parties do show an understanding of the police's capacity problems, they are nevertheless critical of the effort made. One respondent stated, "If marijuana really were a priority, they would do more about it. The police should do their duty. We have been talking for four years but I don't see any results. That makes it difficult. You then get vague meetings where everyone puts the onus on the others and gives them the blame." Other respondents have the feeling that the police tend to use the capacity problem as an excuse. "Marijuana is not always a popular topic. You can easily say that you have no available capacity and that you won't be doing anything in the near future."

In the extension of the abovementioned criticism, some respondents point to the individual preferences that police officers have. For example, one respondent said, "Among the police, I know who is interested and who isn't." Various reasons are given for the fact that not all police officers are equally motivated to participate in the action days in Eindhoven and in the Rotterdam hemp train. First of all, many of those involved mention the time-consuming nature of the dismantling operations. The police give a similar explanation and state that they spend more time on the integral approach than the other parties do. A respondent among the police stated, "Coordinating does not mean that you do most of the work [this is a reference to BITE]. The police will always carry out most of the work, in terms of time and capacity." Mention is also made of the administrative burden on the police. After a dismantling operation, police officers must spend much time at their desks to fulfill the administrative tasks around their duties, such as the formulation of a formal charge, the entry of data, and the delivery of a dossier to the public prosecutor. Although there is no clear picture of the magnitude of this burden, these tasks are certainly not the favorite activities of police officers, and are often regarded as rather stressful. In addition, it is said that the police often think that the approach is rather harsh and that marijuana is relatively harmless. For instance, one respondent stated, "The situation sometimes has a pretty pathetic side and I believe that this is why the police often think that they could be catching bigger fish. There's no rush. Crimes such as murder and armed robbery have priority."

The combination of these factors leads to the conclusion that the police fulfill less of a connecting role within the investigated assemblages than the theory might lead one to expect. After all, in the integral approach, they fulfill an important function for the public prosecutor with regard to the penal side of the problem. On the other hand, housing associations and energy suppliers depend on the police when conducting civil procedures against the offender. In both cases, a police report is necessary for further juridical steps. In addition, motivated police staff help boost cooperation. However, in real-life practice, it appears that none of the parties, not even the government, can directly command any of the other authorities. Almost everyone depends on everyone else and the cooperation of another player is always needed to achieve the desired final result. Moreover, all the players have at their disposal their own power instruments that they can apply to realize certain goals. Police functionaries who are closely associated with the approach to marijuana cultivation confirm these findings, and occasionally feel unhappy about their shortcomings. The following quotation illustrates this admirably: "Shame is a strong word, but I do sometimes feel uncomfortable as a member of the police. You make a gaffe now and again."

Self-organizing processes

In response to the question concerning the interactions and processes of meaning assignment to the anti-marijuana-cultivation approach at the molecular level, it is important not to reduce these interactions and processes to molar aspects of cooperation, such as composition, coordination of the style of approach, consensus on the aims, and mutual relationships, which should be self-evident in the optimization of the fight against marijuana cultivation. This also applies *mutatis mutandis* to a factor such as the trust the authorities ought to place in one another. Regardless of how necessary and useful these factors may be for the structure of the cooperation, the focus remains on characteristics that serve the effectiveness of the antimarijuana program and that fall back on forms of governing or malleability thinking with regard to security. Factors such as consensus and trust are, however, not static features that can be objectified, but rather the provisional result of the attitudes and perceptions of the authorities that implement official policy and of the relations that precede this situation. Accordingly, instead of a molar description, it is more important to expose the way in which consensus and trust among authorities arise, and to find out how, in concrete situations, the actions of the authorities before, during, and after the dismantling operations acquire a certain content and expression.

An answer to the above-stated issues can be given by seeking the self-organizing processes in the integral approach. By "self-organizing processes," I mean interactions that cannot be reduced to the properties of the whole or to one of the parties individually, and in which—or from which—new system properties can arise. The implication of this is that the integral approach can take on a functionality and target that differ from those for which it was originally devised. In theory, this can go so far that, with the passage of time, one no longer knows the original reason for setting up the approach. This question therefore becomes no longer important because the approach has taken on a completely different aim. This spontaneous generative dynamics strongly resembles the concept of autopoiesis (In Greek, "*autos*" means "self" and "*poiein*" means "to make.") that Francisco Maturana and Humberto Varela (1980) introduced into biology. Autopoiesis is a wholly new view of the nature of an organism and its relation with the environment in which it is situated. From this viewpoint, there is no longer any absolute distinction between a subject and an object. Organisms and environments are involved with one another in a never-ending process of co-creation, in which a biological entity is understood as a network of production and transformation processes that produce components and (re)generate these components on the basis of their interactions in the network of processes that form the foundation of their own productions and transformations. In this way, living creatures can be regarded as autopoietic systems that organize themselves in such a way that they constitute and (re)produce themselves.

At the risk of simplifying matters, I regard self-organizing processes as interactions without central governance by means of which authorities test a new form of conduct in the tackling of marijuana cultivation. However, use of the term "self-organizing processes" does not mean that one can also personally understand such processes. The relation between cause and effect is often very ambiguous and difficult to determine. In his book of that name, Nassim Taleb speaks of "black swans" (2007). With this he is referring to unexpected interactions and events with major consequences that only in retrospect turn out to be predictable. The explanation of this lies in the fact that these interactions will never be the exact realization of the preceding societal design. Only the repetition of this, in the words of Tarde, can lead to a collective, new assignation of meaning in the cooperation.

To elaborate further on this dynamic, I shall discuss two forms of self-organizing processes that have been encountered in the security assemblages studied. They are processes that provide insight into the problem of how consensus and trust arise among the authorities. In this context, I make a distinction between (1) motivation tactics and (2) relations of trust.

(1) Motivation tactics

To involve the police more closely in dismantling operations, the authorities have drawn up tactics that aim to motivate the police and encourage them to undertake more action. This is illustrated by the following quotation: "We are juggling with stimuli to persuade the police to do more against marijuana cultivation." Another respondent states, "It's about how you interact with the police, how you get them on your side. That determines what they can do for you." And yet another respondent says, "It is sometimes a matter of playing a higher form of the game Stratego." The following four motivation tactics can be distinguished in the framework of dismantling operations.

First of all, the motivation of the police can be piqued. This can be done by saying, "If those premises burst into flames this evening, many questions will be asked. I'll be pleased to pass them on to you." This tactic was used to convince a district head of the Rotterdam police to make personnel available for a dismantling. It was also used when an inspector refused a warrant to enter a house while there were concrete indications that a marijuana plantation was present in the building. A respondent from the municipality of Rotterdam applied a similar variant. When the police would not cooperate to the required extent, he stated, "I respect your decision. But I do not agree with it, and that means that I place the responsibility for any consequences regarding this location with you."

Parties also confront the police with the option that they themselves will undertake action. Although this may not comply with the agreements in the relevant covenant, some parties do actually have such possibilities. For example, a representative of one of the municipalities declared in a consultation, "Then we will do it ourselves, with an administrative ruling." Because of the pressure to display decisiveness in security operations, this strategy is often used by various authorities as a psychological lever. In reality, without the aid of the police, municipalities will not eagerly enter a building where they suspect a marijuana plantation is situated.

In addition, anecdotes are told in order to energize participants. The story of the member of staff of an energy supplier, about the fact that he regularly has to deal with apathetic police officers, is illustrative in this context. For this reason, on action days he recounts sensational stories of previous dismantling operations, such as the spectacular discovery of forty kilos of marijuana behind a specially bricked wall in a house. The same respondent also mentions the problem that the composition of the teams often changes: "Every time you have to persuade the officers. Things seem to be running smoothly and then the team members are transferred to other sections. Then you have to deal with a number of new police officers." During one of the observations it was conspicuous that the police officers became more motivated at the moment a plantation was discovered in a house. If nothing is discovered, the whole day is seen as time lost or wasted. The same attitude also manifests itself at the end of a dismantling operation. In response to a question from colleagues about how many plantations had been dismantled, a police officer was visibly elated and reported that several plantations had been taken apart.

In addition, the authorities in both municipalities engage in mutual competition about who can dismantle the most plantations. Verbal skirmishes such as, "Have you only dismantled three plantations this week?" are quite common. This motivation strategy demonstrates that dismantling should not be seen purely as a legal matter of detection and punishment and as an instrumental application of security measures, but is also related to experiences from the world of sports. For instance, one of the respondents declared, "I see it as a competition in fact—we have beaten the growers once again." In this framework, examples from the world of sports are instructive because sportspeople never describe their success or failure in terms of scientific and technical knowledge, despite all the scientific supervision and the medical and technical expertise that is available nowadays. The argument for this is the fact that it is "the occurrence of success or failure that sportspeople rely upon in their explanations rather than the use of knowledge" (Boomkens 2006: 78). The decisive moment cannot be objectified, not even by science. As a scientist or researcher, one can—at most—attempt to describe the occurrence, or clarify it through anecdotes, or compare it to other situations, without having the illusion that one can convey the exact moment at which everything happens differently from what was planned beforehand. The similarity between dismantling marijuana plantations and participating in sports is also confirmed in the following quotation: "When your suspicions turn out to be correct, you feel a kind of euphoria." It is at this point that one can expect more respect from other involved parties when several plantations are dismantled. The "common enemy" that the authorities evoke during dismantling operations is closely related to this. This image of the common enemy promotes team spirit and mutual collaboration. "We are there together to catch the offender. United we stand," declared one of the respondents.

(2) Relations of trust

Well-known features of a cooperative effort are the trust that authorities place in one another and the degree of certainty that they must have in their belief that the approach to the problem is the proper one. In the literature on this subject, which is indebted to the classical work by George Simmel, "Geheimnis und die geheime Gesellschaft" ("The Sociology of Secrecy and of Secret Societies," 1968), trust is regarded as one of the most important factors for the correct functioning of a security program. It is maintained that trust is the answer to the complexity of partnerships, and contributes to the success of the chosen approach (Smith et al. 1995; Terpstra and Kouwenhoven 2004; Edelenbos and Klijn 2007). The crucial point here is that hierarchical leadership and direct supervision are less suited to more horizontal cooperative associations such as the joint tackling of marijuana cultivation. Thus, trust has consequences for the mutual relations in a cooperative effort. But this does not answer the question as to how trust arises in the interactions among authorities and is embodied in the immediate presence of those who are involved in dismantling operations.

It is self-evident that trust is related to the fulfillment of agreements that have been made at a molar level and the promises that are made mutually within the work process itself. Most of the respondents regard the fulfillment of agreements as the most important aspect of trust. People point out that trust declines when agreements are not kept. It must be noted, however, that building trust must concern a pattern with a longer history. According to one respondent, trust decreases when ignorance is used as an excuse for not adhering to an agreement, as when one claims not to be aware of the fact that certain information ought to be passed on, whereas this is standard procedure. In the view of several respondents, such actions are seen as unreliable. Although there is a certain amount of understanding for people who cannot meet a deadline due to specific circumstances, or are unable to pass on information in good time, some kind of explanation is expected as to why things have not occurred as agreed.

Many respondents also connect the genesis of trust to a strong sense of integrity. This is shown by the following statement: "You see and hear things that may not be intended for you. You have to deal with such things appropriately. You must not misuse this information." Thus, private data should not be shared among too many people, such as the addresses visited on an action day, for instance. In addition, respondents insist that no personal property of a tenant may be removed from a house. Not satisfying such norms may have a devastating effect on the cooperation. Such incidents did not occur in the security assemblages studied. A respondent from an energy supplier did state that he had experienced incidents like this in other regions.

Apart from this, trust is also named in relation to the expertise and competence of the authorities with whom cooperation has been set up. This came to the forefront on an action day in one of the municipalities studied. When walking through a street in the city, a municipal member of staff became convinced that there was a plantation in one of the houses nearby. He believed he could smell the aroma of marijuana and saw on the rear of the building in question several clues that could indicate that there was a plantation inside. However, the police officer in the team had his doubts. In contrast to the municipal worker, he did not smell the marijuana. In the integral approach, the police officer is often the person who organizes the warrant to enter the house. Because he trusted the expertise and capacity of his colleague, he decided to request the warrant after all. In this context, his words are rather illustrative: "I know you well and I know that you are mostly right." Nevertheless, he was visibly nervous when entering the building and showed signs of relief when a plantation was indeed discovered there. After all, danger may lurk in placing too much trust in one another's expertise and competence. One respondent stated that action is sometimes too quickly undertaken on the basis of the judgment of others. This occurs in the determination of the number of harvests, for instance. Based on the evidence available, various opinions may exist with respect to the number of harvests that have already been gathered. In such cases, the involved parties must reach a compromise. Another respondent pointed to the fact that people can begin to doubt their own expertise and competence when their estimation deviates substantially from that of others.

Finally, it is also plain that trust arises when authorities are able to articulate criticism of one another. When people trust one another, they can address each other about the errors that have been made in the work process. For instance, one respondent always makes an agreement with his colleagues: "If there is something about my actions that you don't like, please tell me. Then I can explain why I do or don't do something." It is important that the criticism be addressed directly to the person in question and not reach him or her via a roundabout route. It will be self-evident that articulating criticism is not always beneficial to mutual collaboration. One respondent remarked, "Ultimately you get to be known as a whine." The counterpart to expressing criticism is gossiping, according to the respondents. In normal vernacular, "gossiping" has a negative significance, involving a negative or even reproachful exchange of information about someone who is not present. If, in the assemblages studied, someone gets the impression that gossiping is taking place, this is regarded as mood manipulation, and trust in one another is reduced. But the study also shows that gossip can have a positive side. Gossiping can lead to the rapid distribution of information about a colleague with whom someone may or may not identify himself or herself and, in consequence, informal social control can be exercised in the cooperative effort. For instance, gossiping appears to be linked to the fact that someone is known as a person who is not always equally enthusiastic about performing his or her duties. One respondent stated, "Sometimes you hear remarks such as: 'It's no use relying on him, he's never interested.'" Accordingly, one could claim that the gossip can actually reinforce the group process (see also Gluckman 1963). In this way, gossip contributes to the stability of the security assemblage.[3] In criticism of this opinion, it is said that gossip is a form of communication by means of which an individual wishes to gain an advantage and therefore promotes his or her own interests (Paine 1967). From this perspective, gossip does not necessarily lead to further stabilization of an assemblage. It can also help shatter it.

Resistance

Whether or not a security assemblage works as a well-oiled machine depends on many factors. Occasionally, so little work is required that the parties regard the cooperation as self-evident. In other cases, more is demanded of the parties and the feeling may arise that control is being lost. The latter is also the case here. Various respondents indicated that some organizations and people displayed much resistance to working with other parties. More particularly, there is resistance to the controlling role that the municipality fulfills in the integral approach to marijuana cultivation. The "Memo for the Integral Approach to Hemp Cultivation" (*Notitie Integrale Aanpak Hennepteelt*) of 2006 states that the municipality has control over and has a pivotal function in the integral approach to hemp cultivation. The observed resistance does not manifest itself in a large-scale crisis of governance in the assemblages studied. It is not characterized by activism and protest, aspects that are often mentioned as specific forms of political resistance (Hayward and Schuilenburg 2014). In this context, resistance has assumed different forms—not the form of a radical refusal to participate in the new structure, but rather the form of local and fleeting counterforces that arise in diffused configurations and lurk just under the surface of the partnerships. In this framework, two discoveries play an important role.

First of all, there is a sense of power loss. Respondents indicate that police officers have the idea that something has been taken from them. One respondent declares, "Some police officers get a kick from walking around as district police agent and having many contacts in the neighborhood and with the local people. They are used to doing their own thing. Now you only go as a police officer when everybody is ready for it." Another respondent refers to what he calls "typical police blood." District officers often feel closely connected to the ups and downs in their neighborhood and see it as their personal responsibility to keep an eye on what is happening in their quarter. According to a respondent from the municipality, "the police have most difficulty with relinquishing that element of power and control." More specifically, he states, "the police would like to say: 'we are the initiators of their approach.' In contrast, we [the municipality] always emphasize the cooperation itself."

There is also a sense of unfamiliarity with the new situation, which is primarily related to the possibilities that other parties have. We also see this aspect in the approach to road transport crime. For instance, it may be unclear to the police how they should deal with the administrative competencies of the municipality. This became apparent in a discussion with a respondent from the municipality:

> I am continually having to explain what our competencies are. The police sometimes have the idea that we are a kind of neighborhood team

working on their behalf, and we should be doing what the police tell us to do. And we often do just that, because of the covenant we agreed to. But when I outline what our administrative competencies are, they are sometimes surprised. Only then do they realize that we can do a great deal ourselves. That is also a degree of veiled frustration. I sometimes tease them about it.

The police do not deny the assertion that they are not easily led by other authorities and prefer to act in accordance with their own ideas. Interviews show that some police officers think it is a pity that they cannot operate more independently when they suspect that a plantation is present in a building. One respondent from the police remarked, "At first we could do everything ourselves and we had direct links. Now we have to do everything jointly, and we regard this more as an obligation." The same person also refers to the fact that police functionaries are traditionally skeptical about changes in the organization and the introduction of a new way of working, such as the integral cooperation in the fight against marijuana cultivation. "Many things change with great regularity within police operations. This leads to a feeling of 'they impose it on us and we simply have to accept it time after time.'"

* * *

I began this chapter with the observation based on scientific research that there is a structured, streamlined, and routine approach to the fight against marijuana cultivation. This conclusion is valid for the molar level of the approach and the results of the working method. In this context, the integral approach is regarded as a somewhat more complex variant of a simple system. The idea behind this is that there are a great many components that are mutually connected to one another like separate cogs in a machine, and contribute to the functioning of the larger whole. Every "thing," in the sense of a manageable element, has its own place in a demarcated whole. In this construction, the various parts of the system are easily controlled. However, this is a complexity-reducing or rational-mechanical approach to the issue at stake. I declared that attention to the molecular gives a better picture of the various aspects that play a role in a security assemblage, with a focus on self-organizing processes among the authorities in the cooperative endeavors studied.

These more or less irregular processes are indeed difficult to foresee, so that the outcomes or results of the work processes are less predictable than they appear to be.

The self-organizing processes that were discovered do not come to expression as a single entity in any of the security assemblages studied, but nonetheless they can still cast a shadow on the approach to marijuana cultivation. For instance, the study shows that the participants have to be motivated to undertake action, and that winning trust is a constant point of concern. These aspects correlate with findings from other studies, where it has been established that the functioning of cooperative efforts is strongly influenced by the motivation of the participants as well as their mutual trust. However, this study has gone further and shows the way in which relations of trust arise in the context of the approach to marijuana cultivation, and the way in which authorities influence one another on the work floor. Aspects such as spreading rumors and narrating sensational stories also come to the forefront here. The conclusion from all this is that not only is the official working method of the approach of major importance, but the narrative and the motivating arguments among the participants also play a significant role.

7

Tackling Road Transport Crime

The Dutch Parliamentary Inquiry Committee into Criminal Investigation Methods examined various sectors of the Dutch economy to check whether trade and industry have been infiltrated by organized crime, or perhaps have maintained close contact with criminals in another way. The committee concluded that, in various sectors, criminogenic situational factors are present that could facilitate criminal behavior. Such factors have been exposed in the road transport sector, the insurance sector, and the waste-disposal sector. With regard to the first sector, companies occasionally lend a "helping hand" to organized crime. Transport companies are set up by smugglers to carry drugs to Europe, and drivers of existing transport firms are also engaged in drug running (Bruinsma and Bovenkerk 1996: 54). Small enterprises are particularly vulnerable, especially if they get into financial difficulties. If a company has to cope with setbacks as a result of theft and robbery, the chance that it will cooperate with organized crime increases.

The committee also focused on the question concerning the extent to which the road transport branch itself is the victim of crime. With respect to the theft of trucks, the committee observed that no reliable figures are available on the quantity of stolen vehicles. There are only rough estimates by organizations, such as Transport and Logistics Netherlands, for example, which estimates that 80 percent of the cases involve freight theft. The insurance sector is an important disadvantaged party in such situations. In most cases, the insurance company will have to pay damages when a truck or freight is stolen. As a consequence, considerations of cost and benefit play a major role in the decision of insurers to trace and arrest offenders themselves through self-established investigative units.

In this chapter, I cover the collaboration between insurance companies and the police that is aimed at generating more effective detection of road transport crime.[1] What makes this security assemblage so interesting is the fact that all kinds of strategies for tackling organized crime, varying from preventative means such as report systems to the tracing of stolen loads and vehicles, are followed. It is striking just how little is known "about the implementation of these strategies and the experiences that the parties have of such strategies" (Terpstra 2010: 114). For this reason, it is useful to pay serious attention to the molecular effects in the approach to road transport crime—in this case: the various images that the parties have of one another and the way in which strategically deviating behavior is developed on the work floor.

Damages and covenants

In Europe, around 72 percent of freight transport takes place over land. The Netherlands is an important transit land with hubs such as Schiphol airport, the ports of Rotterdam and Amsterdam, and good water and road connections to other countries. With regard to crime in the road transport sector, merchandise such as computers, audiovisual devices, and household appliances are the main targets. Apart from these, cosmetics, tobacco products, alcoholic drinks, brand clothing, and metals are also desired articles. In the Netherlands, the damage incurred due to the theft of merchandise between 2003 and 2006 amounted to more than 15.5 million euros, according to reports by the European Union (European Parliament [EP] 2007: 77). Other researchers state that the damage can vary from eleven million euros to hundreds of millions (Kuppens et al. 2006: 25). The great difference is related to the fact that damage indices are often exclusively based on registered direct damage, such as the value of the stolen freight or truck. The indirect damage is frequently much higher due to the late delivery of goods, the costs of a delayed production process, and the erosion of a company's image. Estimates indicate that this indirect damage can amount to double the amount pertaining to direct damage (EP 2007: 15).

To improve the detection of road transport crime, the government and private organizations have decided to enter into more intensive collaboration. The contribution by private parties ranges from participating in various consultation structures to the exchange of data on movable and immovable goods in the framework of a legal investigation. One of the most remarkable parties in this whole is the Dutch Association of

Insurers, the overarching organization of Dutch insurance companies that champions the interests of private insurers on the Dutch market. The association is an organization governed and paid for by the member companies, and represents around 95 percent of the insurance market in the Netherlands.

The cooperation between the government and private organizations is formally recorded in three covenants. In the document "Tackling Crime in the Road Transport Sector" (2005), the Transport Logistics Netherlands, Organization of Private Transporters, Association of Insurers, Ministry of Economic Affairs, Ministry of Justice, Foundation for Tackling Road Transport Crime, and Royal Netherlands Transport Bond have stated their intent to reduce road transport crime by at least 25 percent. In addition, the document refers to the availability of training, crime prevention, and information for transporters and the layout of secure parking places with the aim of realizing safe overnight parking. In the document "Public Prosecution Service and the Transport Sector," also dating from 2005, agreements have been made on improving communications, registration, expertise, and the tackling of transport crime. The participants in the covenant are the Public Prosecution Service, the Organization of Private Transporters, Transport and Logistics Netherlands, and the Royal Netherlands Transport Bond. Finally, there is also the "Information and Registration of Freight Theft" covenant, dating from 2007, in which the parties have defined their goal as an attempt to obtain a more complete picture of the nature and magnitude of criminal damage in the road transport sector. The registration of this type of crime has become the responsibility of one institution: the Insurance Agency for Transport Crime Foundation. In that connection, the website www.isgestolen.nl has been established. The parties in this cooperative effort are the Association of Insurers, the National Police Services Agency, and the Agency for Traffic Enforcement of the Public Prosecution Service.

At the initiative of the supra-regional investigation unit of the South Netherlands, the Freight Theft Team was set up. This team directs its attention to the tackling of transport crime in the regions of Brabant, Zeeland, and Limburg—border areas with transport routes to other European countries. The team concentrates on the tackling of fences (traders in stolen goods) and the network of thieves around them, under the slogan "no receivers, no thievers." The team also initiates information exchanges between police and insurers to improve the tackling of crime in the road transport sector. For instance, the team can make relevant information available when the insurer, as the disadvantaged party, initiates a civil procedure. In that case, the public prosecutor determines which information is exchanged. It is remarkable that the covenant is only concluded for each individual concrete case, thus for each insurer. There is no framework agreement under which all insurers are accommodated. In addition to the Freight Theft Team, there is the National Team for Transport Crime, an auxiliary service for regional police services, special investigative departments and research teams, and part of the National Police Services Agency. The area of concern for this team is crime that affects heavy transport, such as theft of freight, trailers, and trucks. The team receives information from police sections but also maintains contact with branch organizations, damage assessors, insurers, and the public prosecutor. It links data from various police systems and signals when a truck is stolen in a certain region and is found elsewhere. The further settling of the case is then assigned to the police region responsible.

Preconditions

To ensure that the tackling of crime in the road transport sector runs smoothly and effectively, the above-described security assemblages will have to satisfy a number of preconditions. Rather than displaying features of a security program from the nodal-governance story I analyzed in chapter 2, these preconditions are more administrative in their nature. They primarily aim at enabling a coordinated reaction to crime and disorder and to the problems that are caused by these. The preconditions to be applied in this context are central in the "multi-agency approach." This approach is used to combat degeneration and petty crime in underprivileged districts (Sampson et al. 1988; Gilling 1994b). Although the approach is applied at the local level in most initiatives, and is seen by some as a top-down strategy coming from central and local governing bodies, the preconditions formulated in such initiatives are also used in other areas to guide matters in the right direction.

First of all, agreements have to be made about the division of tasks and the responsibilities of the parties that make a contribution to the chosen approach. This is called the "structure and coordination of the cooperation." A good structure provides a means to coordinate the activities in a cooperative endeavor (Liddle and Gelsthorpe 1994). The lack of mutual agreements may lead to a shortage of knowledge and information about the policy of other partners and confusion about the division of tasks and the position of the parties. In that framework, cooperation is enhanced by regular consultation, structured mutual communication, and clarity with regard to leadership (Rosenbaum 2002). The structure of a cooperation may be in the hands of one party that has the governing role, but it may be beneficial to aim at a division of tasks, coordination, and decision making that are as equal as possible.

A second precondition is a clearly defined goal. Parties may have their own objectives and interests that are decisive for collaborating on a certain approach. Contradictory aims and interests may weaken a cooperative effort. But differences in perspectives do not necessarily obstruct good cooperation, as long as there is agreement about the joint target. It must be emphasized, however, that the goals of a cooperative effort must be challenging and feasible. The third precondition is clarity about financial resources. Financial resources may play a role in various ways in the agreed-upon approach. A good financial basis is especially important for the duration of the cooperation. This offers projects scope to develop further. In addition, it is essential to make the costs of the cooperation transparent and to restrict overexpenditure (Clarke and Eck 2003). Parties will be less reserved about taking part and there is a greater chance that parties will be willing to invest in the cooperation. Besides costing money, a cooperative effort can also yield financial benefits. A negative side effect may arise in this framework. Organizations that are only persuaded to participate because of the extra income may actually have little interest in the aims and interests of the cooperative effort (Gilling 1994a). Finally, a cooperative effort may be influenced by dissimilar financial resources (Walters 1996). If one party has more financial resources than another, this may lead to power differences and mutual tension. Such affairs come to the fore in the operations of urban intervention teams, a topic covered in the next chapter.

A fourth precondition is optimum information exchange. The sharing of information is essential in enabling parties to work together (Wastell et al. 2004). Mutual trust is of great importance here. Trust not only brings about less anxiety about sharing information with one another, but parties will also make more effort to supply the desired information to the appropriate party (Ekblom 1995). Just as with the previous precondition, the situation may arise that small organizations have fewer resources at their disposal and often have less information that can contribute meaningfully to the collaboration. As a consequence, there is a chance that they will be less inclined to share the information they have.

The situations sketched above give rise to questions concerning the way these preconditions are realized in the tackling of road transport crime by insurers and police. Which substantiation in the security assemblages is given to the objectives? How does the exchange of information among the parties take place? Are there mutual frictions and, if so, how do these affect the goals of the partnerships? To answer these questions, each of the above-described preconditions will be examined more closely, except that the precondition of possessing a solid financial basis is replaced by the precondition of trust. The argument for this is that the financial precondition is difficult to investigate at the molecular level. Moreover, I have already indicated that trust is seen as one of the most important binding elements in a security assemblage.

Structure and coordination

If a security program wishes to be successful, the necessary first step is to bring the most important parties together—in this case, the police and the insurers. But the question as to which insurers could be eligible for cooperation with the government is more easily posed than answered. The police have difficulty finding their way in the insurance world. The interviews show that the insurance field is too diverse and too wide to get a good overview of all the parties. "I'm making a more in-depth study of the insurance world. But it is a real jungle," says one of the police respondents. This person claims to be seeking "furiously" in order to find the "right insurer." Another respondent states, "The police think that *the* insurers actually exist. But they don't exist at all," he adds, "no more than *the* Dutch police exist." The fact that these same insurers have no regular point of address for the police means that the latter have to invest great effort in order to connect a penal court case to the right insurer. Added to this is the fact that not all transport insurers have signed up to the agreed-upon covenants. Moreover, the situation occasionally arises that one insurer has more possibilities for and better access to the police and the public prosecutor than another. "This can lead to skewed relations and unhappy faces in the insurance world," declared a respondent from an insurance company.

It is important that the tackling of road transport crime is not restricted to the police and the insurers alone. The interviews show that damage experts are also an important element in the partnerships. Here, one speaks of the "eyes and ears" of an insurer. Insurers make use of their resources, knowledge, and services as a supplement to what they do not have themselves or to what they themselves cannot do. Some damage experts are specialized in vehicle damage, whereas others are authorities in the field of physical harm. When the damage is serious, the insurer calls in a damage expert in order to investigate the nature and cause of the damage. On the basis of his findings, the insurer subsequently assesses whether or not the damages are covered. During their investigation, damage experts actively approach the police and maintain intensive contact with individual police staff members. For example, in major cases a damage expert always establishes contact with the police before starting his or her own research. After all, it may be the case that both parties wish to speak to the same person. "First of all, I want to discuss what I can and cannot do," remarks the respondent. "Sometimes that works excellently. Then you get a signal from the police stating when I can interview the person myself."

To a damage expert, networking and maintaining informal contacts with the police are of utmost importance. Documenting contacts can be an effective means to build up a network. In this way, the expert can fall back on people with whom contact has already been established in a certain case. Moreover, the building up of personal contacts is necessary because there is no regular collaboration between the police and the damage experts. Not only are they not party to the agreed-upon covenants, but the damage experts also speak of police hesitancy to work with them. In a penal investigation, this frequently leads to no concrete agreements being made regarding everyone's role and possibilities, and ultimately to the expert following his own inclinations. "I'm not going to wait until the police has rounded off the research," says one of the damage experts. "Generally we begin our own investigation or have completed our investigation before the police have begun theirs." In a figurative sense, the same person then advances like "a bull in a china shop." At the insurers' own initiative and without their taking into account the research interests of the police, "reward advertisements are spread, videotapes are requested, photos or images are placed on the Internet."

I have already declared that covenants are agreed upon in order to enable the police and insurers to collaborate more closely. But the interviews show that it is primarily the damage experts who play a crucial role in the investigation into the issue of liability. This occurs not only because they perform independent research parallel to the police research but also because they have invented all kinds of tactics to stimulate the police to undertake action sooner. These inventions, to recall the ideas of Tarde, elude the molar level at which agreements are made with the aim of preventing conflicting actions. They are passageways or lines of flight that deterritorialize the current structure and reterritorialize in a new structure. The consequence is that new assemblages arise that themselves have the tendency to expand or become larger. In the public-private partnerships studied here, the inventions of the damage experts assume rather extraordinary forms. For instance, they make use of the following tactics to stimulate the police to undertake more action.

A damage expert may personally attempt to intercept the criminals involved in freight theft. When these people are caught red-handed, they can be handed over to a police officer. In addition, the interviews show that damage experts attempt to buy stolen goods on Internet sites such as Ebay.com. The next step is to pick up the goods and to confront the seller with the fact that they have been stolen. Then the police are informed of the situation so that the goods can be confiscated. Another way to allow the police to "discover" the stolen freight is to personally break into a storage shed. After the "burglary," the police are informed of the discovery. Finally, a respondent stated that a small fire is occasionally started to get the police to visit the location in question. When the shed is broken open by the firefighters and the stolen goods are discovered, the police are forced to initiate a criminal investigation.

The tactics discussed here lead to a decontextualization of the molar order in the security program dealing with road transport crime. With each invention, other wholes are accessed and coupled to one another in new, usually temporary associations. This makes a clear delineation of the original security assemblage between insurers and police problematic. For example, the abovementioned small fire functions as a "switch point," as Foucault would call it (2009: 215), to activate completely different assemblages. It is an occurrence that blows up an assemblage, and simultaneously makes a new association with other "authorities [firefighters], rules and territories" so that a new entity arises. In more philosophical terms, there is mention of an interassemblage, which guides the transition from one assemblage to another. At the same time, the fire proves that everything and everyone can play a role in an assemblage. Despite the widespread attention in the security literature to the executors of policy, an assemblage is actually determined by the principle of neighborhood, by the fact that subjects (people) and objects (things) coexist on a basis of equality. We have seen this in my treatment of the work of Deleuze, in which I declared that people and things are mutually interwoven. Significance and representation in our everyday experience, and also in economic, juridical, and social practices, arise from relations that mutually bind people and things. However, right down to the present day, security thinking has turned out to be exceptionally anthropological, and "nonhuman actors" are scarcely mentioned in security thinking. And if they come into the picture, they do so primarily as passive instruments by means of which people shape their mutual relations or wish to achieve certain goals. But this type of reduction does not do justice to the fact that "things" themselves also enter into associations and create new relations among the authorities. Thus, people and things do not have a negative and mutually subordinate relation, but rather one of positive combinability and cumulability. In the simultaneous presence of everything and everyone, both people and things exert a certain influence on "what happens" in a security assemblage. As a result, they have significance and therefore must be investigated in relation to one another.

Aims and interests

Effective policy seems to be based on a simple formula: formulate, in general terms, an aim that all parties can agree to support. This can also be done in the fight against road transport crime, where the aim to reduce crime by at least 25 percent has been expressed. Nevertheless, the interviews indicate that the practice is more intractable than the theory. This is partly due to the fact that the police, insurers, and damage experts have divergent goals and therefore do not always share the same interests. As described in Article 2 of the Dutch Police Act, the core task of the police is to ensure maintenance of legal order. On the basis of that article, the police have a responsibility toward society. In contrast, a damage expert or insurer "only" has a responsibility toward his or her client or company. In this framework, he or she must primarily take into account costs and benefits, which should not be limited to financial significance alone. Another concern is the avoidance of negative publicity with regard to the name and reputation of a company. Insurers and damage experts serve no social interest, as a police respondent states, but instead serve primarily an economic interest.

I have previously mentioned the fact that, in the nodal perspective advanced by Clifford Shearing and his colleagues, the problem that conflicts, hostility, and distrust may exist between parties is all too easily circumnavigated. In the interviews, the respondents from insurers and damage expert firms emphasize that the worlds of the insurers and of the police are often at odds with one another. Each party's style of thinking and acting is functional within its own domain, but does not automatically dovetail with that of the other party. The most crucial point of contention concerns the balance between the financial interest and the importance of detection. In this context, the issue of finding the truth recedes into the background. To begin with the first point: the interviews indicate that the police do not regard the recovery of every stolen truck or freight as their primary goal. In most cases, no investigation is set up on the basis of one single report. One respondent declared that if it increases the chance of arresting the offenders, the police prefer to allow a transport to be taken. The importance of neutralizing the organization behind the theft is greater than that of recovering the stolen goods. Or, as one respondent expressed it, "The police wait for occurrences that are interrelated in order to chart the criminal network." When the criminal organization has come into view, the suspects are trailed for a longer period to gain more information and to ultimately arrest the offenders. Police officers call this style of working "rocking and rolling."

The interviews also show that the police are largely offender oriented, whereas insurers and particularly damage experts are more interested in recovering the stolen goods (see also Levi and Maguire 2004). The idea that the police do not concentrate on individual cases leads to perplexity among the insurers. The following quotation from an insurer makes this clear:

> The moment the police adopt this kind of attitude, there is the chance that they will become lax and will not undertake any action at all, with all the resulting consequences. The police forget that they can save a complete transport company from going under. If they do nothing, the criminals remain at large and the entrepreneur is held responsible [for the damage resulting from the goods being stolen]. The company can then close down.

At the same time, the police action encourages the damage experts to behave as police officers in their parallel investigations. "Our interviews with suspects feel like police interrogations," says a damage expert. "This is because we often play the role of police officer during this kind of interview. The people being questioned also experience it in this way. Recently somebody remarked: 'I seem to be a suspect.' Of course that person is not a suspect, but we do ask more detailed questions that the police do." In addition, damage experts claim to act sooner in order to limit the damage. "A stolen freight is rapidly distributed. To enhance our chances of recovering the freight, an investigation has to be started up quickly." Accordingly, in contrast to the police, they propose a more, as they call it, "incidental approach." After all, every incidence of damage costs money. Exactly how the incidental approach works is indicated by a remark by a damage expert. At the moment a road transport crime is reported, the power game between the interested parties bursts loose. The freight may be insured by a company other than the transporter in question, so that these companies may therefore make use of different damage experts. "The first thing you do as a damage expert is to send a fax to the other insurer in which you make him liable."

With regard to the quest for truth, a complicating factor is that former police officers are increasingly taking up employment with private parties. Moreover, the police are increasingly hiring in expertise from companies such as accounting and insurance organizations. David Bayley and Clifford Shearing (2001: 14) point out that, in the current security diagram, police officers are allowed to wear their official uniforms when they are working for a private firm. What exactly are the effects of this metamorphosis? Although the Netherlands does not experience the same practices as other countries do, people in the Netherlands also switch from the police to insurance companies and damage agencies, and *vice versa*. In doing so, they take their acquired knowledge, networks, and informal know-how from their former job with them. Nevertheless, one respondent points out the differences between the public and the private sector. He states that as a policeman he was able to do more than he can as a damage expert: "As a policeman, if you wanted something, you got it. Now I have to tackle things differently." Former colleagues who have gone to work for private firms feel frustrated when the police adopt a reticent attitude: "All at once you cannot ask for anything from your former colleagues." Another respondent remarks, "While you are working for the police, the police is your best friend. If you leave, and come back a day later to the reception desk where you used to stand, they hardly know you."

With their monopoly on violence and the legal authorization to perform investigation, the police have many possibilities at their disposal. They are treated with fitting respect by the other authorities. However, in everyday affairs, damage experts have little or no trouble from legal restrictions. In contrast, they find it agreeable that their activities are subject to fewer rules than those of the police. "You come to understand that much can be done without special authority, more than you think anyway," says a damage expert. Damage experts refer to their work as "creative." In their own words, "We show audacity and don't do everything according to the book." Two respondents from an insurance firm confirmed that this enhances their possibilities, and reinforces their position in the security assemblage of road transport crime. In the interviews, the insurers referred to the damage experts as "cowboys," people who maneuver between "being not quite correct and the official approach."

Damage experts try to achieve their aims and interests by making smart use of all kinds of resources. Again, the molecular associations arise outside the "original" assemblage. Not only do Internet sites such as LinkedIn and Facebook provide much information about the identity of a person; it is also quite easy for damage experts to ascertain whether or not someone has been previously involved in punishable offenses. A damage expert can call the public prosecutor with a request to copy a person's dossier. If that is not successful, other means are deployed to obtain insight into the dossier: "For example, when we are not permitted to make a copy, we simply copy everything in writing." In addition, one respondent says that he always submits a request to the Judicial Documentation System to see the content of a person's criminal record: "I just call to ask if I can see it." Another interviewee says that calling a court is an easy way to find out if a suspect has been involved in other punishable offenses. "The court gives you the District Attorney case number when you say that you want to write a letter in a certain case, but unfortunately do not have the number," declares one respondent. "The fact that the offense is not known is not very important," states a respondent from an insurance firm. "After that, the suspect only has to be confronted with the findings." Finally, help-desk personnel of companies that deal with disruptions and outages of services often release customer data quite easily. "A telephone number is often sufficient to find out the personal details and address of a person."

Trust

The previous chapter illustrated that trust is not a static given—something that is self-evident—but arises gradually and hesitantly. It is built up in relations among authorities in an assemblage, on the work floor, via recommended contacts, at receptions, and during joint dinners. Ultimately, trust is either generated or simply fails to appear. And when it does appear, it is difficult to describe. In fact, it is impossible to define it entirely. Because trust is such a diffuse and fluid precondition, covenants are agreed upon in order to remove mutual suspicion among the parties as much as possible. For example, the covenants between the police and the insurers state that the parties must deal confidentially with the information they receive. "This provides a good basis for a working relationship," according to two respondents in the police force. Nevertheless, not everyone shares this opinion. The interviews with insurers show that insurance companies usually regard covenants with the government as positive advertising for their core business. In this way they can manifest themselves as solid and trustworthy firms, and this reinforces their image as a party that feels responsible for social affairs. Moreover, concluding a covenant does not mean that all parties invest an equal amount of effort in complying with the agreements made.

Although covenants can have a positive influence on the relation of trust among the parties—because work agreements and objectives have been specifically recorded and the parties can be tackled on these—they do not remove all suspicion. The insurers interviewed declare that a covenant can never ensure that insurers and police will trust one another totally. The problem of trust will never vanish completely. It is inherent in the measures that are taken to resolve a problem. Although insurers are convinced that the police will be careful with the information given, they have less trust in the way the police settle issues. An important cause of this is the fact that the evidence that is put forward in a certain case may become public knowledge or may become fodder for the gutter press as the result of a trial or a transaction put forward by the public prosecutor. "The police can do little about this," state insurers and damage experts, "but it does have an influence on mutual relations." This even goes so far that damage experts sometimes only provide "half-information." One respondent says that it is often about "what is not written down rather than about what is written down." This particularly applies to insurers and damage experts who have insured and investigated the accountability of the transporter. Sharing all the information in an investigation with the police is often unrewarding. There is a chance that evidence may be found for the accountability of the transporter himself.

The fact that mutual trust is very fragile is shown by the traditional views that the authorities have of one another. On the one hand, the police believe that the insurers will ultimately compensate the damage. If they do not do so immediately, they will eventually do so "indirectly by raising the premiums." Moreover, according to the opinion of the police respondents, the insurance sector itself will have to accept more responsibility in order to prevent criminal damage in the road transport branch. For example, the Dutch police mention in their report "Prevention Pays" (*Tegenhouden troef,* Politie 2003: 52) the possibility that, in cases of damage, insurance companies should not pay up if the entrepreneur has not participated in an accredited security project. The terms and conditions of insurance policies can also be an important lever, states the report. The insurers could give a premium discount when transporters impose security measures. On the other hand, insurers and damage experts claim that the police deploy too little capacity and give too little priority to combating road transport crime. This kind of criticism back and forth is not mild. At the same time, however, it is not new. A more important feature is that the criticism is nourished by all kinds of frustrations that determine the outcome of the partnerships just as much as the molar aims do, as articulated in the covenants.

Nevertheless, one should not conclude that the security program to combat road transport crime has fallen short or failed. The insurers and damage experts speak positively of the commitment and results of the Freight Theft Team in the South Netherlands. To expose the dynamics of an assemblage, however, not only the results achieved but also effects such as pride, shame, and anger, which the authorities experience during contact with others, should be taken into consideration. After all, they fulfill their own reality-constituting role, and keep an assemblage alive. I have previously observed that agreements are mainly made on the basis of informal contacts with the right people. This picture is confirmed by the way in which the authorities exhibit trust. Although the covenants enable a more flexible exchange of data, there are still all kinds of formal restrictions. The police are not permitted to give information to private parties in all cases, and making use of information on private companies is not always legal. To avoid such problems, information is passed on clandestinely, under the table as it were. The interviews indicate that this happens by means of exceptional language. When a detective says, "I have trouble with my ears," a damage expert understands that the suspect is being bugged. Not only do the police make use of a strange language—"*une sorte de langue étrangère*," to quote the words of Marcel Proust—but damage experts also copy all kinds of specific expressions from one another in order to inform other parties without harming anyone's interests or putting people in another organization in difficulty. One of the interviewees supplied the following example. In some cases, damage experts often have at their disposal more information than they actually report. They often have an idea of the criminal before the police manage to latch on. To inform a police officer of the identity of a criminal, the damage expert will say, "Mr. X may not come to my birthday party." This style of information exchange only works when there is already substantial trust between the damage expert and the police officer in question. "Knowing and trusting one another," says one respondent, quoting the motto of the Dutch police, "is the basis of cooperation."

Information exchange

On the basis of covenants between the police and the insurance companies, an exchange of information occurs when a punishable act has been reported. The public prosecutor then determines which dossiers and which information will be made available to the insurer. Information from insurers can help the police in a judicial financial investigation. For instance, insurers are asked to find out serial numbers of objects in order to provide information on a subject's property, such as houses or boats. At the same time, in a civil procedure, insurers can use information from the police about a current investigation. But the problem of information exchange is that people always expect something from the other party in return, namely, that the information supplied will be answered with a fitting repayment. In this way, the information exchange has features similar to those of a gift, as studied by anthropologist Marcel Mauss in his *Essai sur le don* (*Essay on the Gift*, 2004). According to Mauss, a contemporary and a nephew of Émile Durkheim, the mechanism of gift exchange forms the basis of culture and society. Whereas Durkheim seeks the unity of a society in collective consciousness and the structure of labor division, Mauss states that the dimension of giving ensures that individual interests are reconciled, and that a form of social order is shaped. Giving to others makes it possible to communicate with one another and to enter into social relations. The principle of reciprocity is the basis of the gift, according to Mauss, an idea that is further elaborated by Claude Lévi-Strauss in *Les structures élémentaires de la parenté* (*Elementary Structures of Kinship*, 1949). The reciprocal obligation is threefold: there is the obligation to give, the obligation to receive, and the obligation to present a gift in return. The discussions with the authorities involved, on the exchange of information, illustrate just how difficult it is to find equilibrium between giving and receiving in real-life practice.

Regardless of how well everything seems to be arranged, various circumstances obstruct information exchange between the police and the insurers and between the police and damage experts on the work floor. First of all, the poor registration of road transport crime is conspicuous. The report of a crime is registered by an administrative member of staff or reception desk worker of the police. That such people often lack adequate knowledge is a claim regularly heard from damage experts and insurers. "They don't know what a vehicle identification number is, or a trailer or a container. The difference between a tarp truck, a box truck or a container is nowhere to be found in the charge," remarked one of the respondents. In addition, it appears that placing an offense in a certain category can lead to problems: "A stolen freight is sometimes registered under 'freight,' or under 'burglary' or even 'social security.'" A respondent from an insurance company illustrates the fact that reports are registered by people who are not familiar with the issues at stake: "If you say that the name of the truck is 'Max Load,' they simply write it down." At the same time, the respondents refer to the consequences of a shortage of capacity and to insufficient prioritization by the police. The former occasionally leads to amateurish scenes, as the following quotation shows: "Then a driver is asked if he can come back at another time to report the event. This is usually impossible because he is somewhere else in Europe, on another delivery route." Apart from this, the police sometimes hide behind other priorities: "Road transport crime is still a blind spot."

Second, the respondents mention a lack of knowledge and expertise among the police. The following quotation is illustrative of this state of affairs. "Officers enter a truck that has been found and they make use of exactly the same handles that the thieves used to enter the truck. All the fingerprints are immediately obliterated. In addition, they do not check whether or not the alarm signal is still working and if the original keys have been used." For this reason, damage experts sometimes propose carrying out these actions themselves. According to several respondents, the absence of knowledge and expertise is due to the circulation of functions within the police organization. Not only insurance personnel but also damage experts remain longer in the service of one firm, or are employed in the same sector for a longer period of time, than the average police officer. "Experts and insurers become incrementally smarter, whereas a police officer will change teams after a couple of years and therefore has to start all over again." As a result, the knowledge available in the organization is insufficiently guaranteed, according to the same respondents. One respondent explains this problem as follows: "It's not about gathering and storing knowledge. Knowledge gathering is no problem, it's the storage that is more difficult. If someone leaves the force, he takes his knowledge with him. If that were a computer, you would simply connect the hard disks. But unfortunately, that is not the way humans work." This picture is confirmed by a respondent from the police. In the gathering of information, police culture turns out to be strongly dependent upon personal contacts. The police work with what he calls "camping contacts." Information gathering takes place "generally on the basis of coincidental contacts who are acquainted with a certain subject." This works in the short term and in a regional structure, in the opinion of the respondent, but in the long run there are only disadvantages.

Third, feelings of anxiety play a role in the sharing of information with other parties. For instance, private firms are not keen on allowing rivals to look into their *modus operandi*. "It's not always beneficial to share all information," says one respondent. In this framework, damage experts have to consider first and foremost the interests of their client. Only with permission from the insurer are they allowed to exchange information. Due to the financial interests in the road transport sector, this permission is often refused. Not only do the damage expert's priorities lie primarily with his or her client—the information that the damage expert reports will be in line with the assignment to gain as much (financial) advantage for the insurer as possible—but an insurer may also give the instruction not to release any information at all or perhaps only a minimum amount, due to reasons of competitiveness with other insurers. "The art is to be selective with the sharing of information," outlines an expert. In reality, damage experts frequently know more than they report. "That is the game as it is played," says a damage expert. "Everyone knows that that is how it goes."

Police officers are also plagued by feelings of uncertainty and reticence, but these turn out to be based on completely different circumstances than the feelings that occur among damage experts and insurers. On the one hand, the police have a limited view of the relations between insurers and damage experts and of the agreements that are made between the two authorities. As a result, a police officer will often have the feeling that he or she is walking on thin ice. On the other hand, many police functionaries have the idea that they are living in a glass house. The actions of police officers are recorded in increasing detail in the police system. "The notion that they are being closely scrutinized leads to the situation that the police tend to choose the 'safe rather than sorry' option, and release less information." This reticence is reinforced by the container concept of "privacy-sensitive information." One respondent from an insurance firm remarks, "Much is classified under the heading of 'privacy,' whereas the average policeman has no idea of what the Privacy Act covers."

The contribution of the business world to the issue of security is not only a technical issue. It also leads to ethical questions about legal responsibility and democratic control over the organization and implementation of security. The interviews indicate that the legal denominator of "privacy" generates contradictory effects. The most complicated aspect of cooperation and, with this, the most interesting one, is the difference among what I call, for reasons of brevity, the unknowing, the pragmatists, and the principled. Some police functionaries are not well versed in the content of privacy legislation. They normally articulate phrases such as, "Sorry, I can't say anything about that for privacy reasons." These people lack—in the words of several interviewees—"nerve and creativity." Other police functionaries do understand the problems, says one respondent. "It is indeed possible to have an exchange of information without this necessarily involving sensitive information." This group thinks that one should not cause too much fuss about privacy and, in the interests of society, one can sidestep the law if doing so leads to a better result for all parties. The danger with these pragmatists is that they sometimes go too far in their well-intended proposals. They often include police functionaries who are so eager to cooperate that they even extend detailed information on the investigation to other parties. Damage experts and insurers state that they "have to offer these people protection" to prevent them "going to pieces." Finally, there is the group of principled police functionaries who adhere very strictly to the rules of law and believe that the issue of privacy should not be taken too lightly. As an argument in favor of their views, they say that the law has been formulated for a reason. Although these people do acknowledge the importance of sharing information with other parties, "they often collide with the restrictions of privacy legislation," concludes one respondent.

* * *

I began this chapter by mentioning the official covenants drawn up to tackle crime in the road transport sector and the preconditions of successful cooperation in this domain. In real-life practice, cooperation turns out to be more complex than merely ratifying agreements on information exchange, arranging consultation structures, and forming a team that is primarily engaged in the investigation of road transport crime. The substantiation of responsibilities also takes place at a molecular level and is thus determined by processes other than routine work, everyday rituals, and formal use of language by the authorities. Within the official language of the security assemblage, a new language arises—a specific way of speaking involving terms such as "rocking and rolling," "camping contacts," and "invitations to birthdays"—in which rather advanced tactics have been invented to compel other parties to undertake action, such as starting fires and making trial purchases to force the police to initiate action. Moreover, personal preferences, frustrations, and tensions qualify the idea that the parties are all aiming at the same goal and aspire to the promotion of the same interests. Whereas the partnership between the police and the insurers is regarded as a rational arrangement of people and resources designed to achieve formulated goals, account must be taken of diverging interests and visions that frequently turn out to be contradictory. For instance, we have seen that police and insurers employ different perspectives in similar situations and, in their activities, appeal to different interests. The police set-up, in particular, appears not to accommodate the direct interests of the insurers, although these may concur in some cases. If the police wish to implement a different security policy with parties that work on the basis of other structures and other mentalities, they will have to organize their interests differently and formulate their goals differently too. This is not by definition good or bad, but it will lead to a tense relation with constitutional principles such as proportionality and legitimacy. I return to this topic in the final chapter.

8

Urban Intervention Teams

Nowadays intervention teams spring into action to deal with families if there are suspicions that things are going seriously wrong. This approach has various names. "Behind-the-front-door" is an expression that appeals to the imagination. But the approach entails more than merely stepping across the threshold and entering into people's private domain. The house visit is "a component of a chain of actions that must eventually lead to improvement in the living circumstances of households and whole neighborhoods" (Lupi and Schelling 2010: 4). Depending on the nature and aims of a project, the parties involved will include municipal departments, housing associations, welfare organizations, the police, health-care institutions, labor-mediation organizations, debt-relief institutions, community workers, welfare benefit services, schools, and youth-care associations. During these house visits, which may or may not be announced in advance, the teams check circumstances such as potential illegal occupation, welfare-benefit fraud, fire risk, and inadequate maintenance of the building. Because the teams do not restrict their activities to merely one or two areas, all concerns and problems of the families can be charted at once.

The key term here is "integral," which refers to completeness, taking into consideration all underlying causes of insecurity and livability. In chapter 3, I mentioned the advantages of an integral approach. In the ideal situation, authorities no longer work separately and independently of one another while they are dealing with the same subject. Another advantage is that administrative-legal measures can be aligned with one another to a greater degree. But there is also a ripple of criticism. People mention the vagueness of the concept of "integral" and question the validity of the argument that a coherent approach is essential in all those areas (de Haan 1995; Ombudsman Rotterdam 2007). For example, the authorities may hold differing opinions about the precise nature of the problem and about the solution orientations that are applicable there.

Moreover, strong horizontalization may bring the risk of too much or too little governance and coercion, both of which lead to a reduction of the content (Raad voor Maatschappelijke Ontwikkeling [RMO] 2008; Prins and Cachet 2011).

Despite the criticism, the relevant literature displays a relatively large degree of confidence that an integral approach will lead to the disappearance of the barriers between organizations, and to a better approach to the problem: so-called decompartmentalization. The underlying train of thought is that the participating parties will be inspired and motivated to collaborate more, which should lead to a more effective approach to security and livability. In short, "integral" produces only winners. But is this actually true in real-life practice? To answer this question, I examine the power game currently playing out in the Social Investment Plan (SIP), a project team that tries to regulate livability and insecurity in Amsterdam neighborhoods, in conjunction with housing associations, relief workers, and welfare-benefit institutions.[1]

Mission creep

Urban intervention teams come in all shapes and sizes, ranging from teams that direct their efforts to punishable offenses such as illegal employment and welfare-benefit fraud to teams that are engaged in providing care to families, as discussed in this chapter. In the latter case, there are also major disparities in the staffing and operational methods of intervention teams in the Dutch security diagram. In Rotterdam, for example, intervention teams combine the tackling of social problems with actions against rule-breaking behavior. The idea is that preventative measures and assistance do not help much on their own, but the deployment of repressive resources is also necessary in order to rectify the complex problems of residents and housing districts. In Rotterdam, around thirty-eight thousand visits are made annually, to control data in the domains of living, working, income, health, education, and security (Ombudsman Rotterdam 2011). This is done by both municipal and submunicipal intervention teams. Municipal teams wear a uniform; submunicipal teams wear normal civilian clothes. In contrast to the municipal teams, the latter almost always visit without prior announcement.

The Rotterdam approach originated in the Strevelsweg in the Feijenoord neighborhood. In 2001, to combat degeneration and disorder, an intervention team checked the structural state and the fire-safety situation of 675 houses. On the basis of the findings, the team assessed whether or not an incident should be referred to the case management team. An important element here was the fact that positive pressure (education, work, social assistance) could be applied, while the authorities also had the option of imposing repressive measures such as fines. The Rotterdam intervention method received major endorsement when it was soon adopted by other submunicipalities and officially anchored in the urban policy program. Although the teams have often changed in composition since 2001, the core is formed by the (sub)municipality, the Department of Employment and Social Affairs, the Department of Housing and Urban Planning, and the police.

Whereas the pivotal function of the intervention teams in Rotterdam can be partly explained by the unique combination of parties and broad objectives, other cities have teams that prefer to concentrate upon the social issues. The Social Investment Plan (SIP) in Amsterdam is an example of the latter. The SIP was started up in 2001 as a project in the Overtoomse Veld neighborhood of the Slotervaart district. The initiators were the erstwhile housing association and the Slotervaart district authorities. The impulse for the project came from the major problems facing the neighborhood and the residents in the field of livability and security (Wetenschappelijke Raad voor het Regeringsbeleid [WRR] 2005: 113–14). One of the goals of the SIP is to raise the socioeconomic status of inhabitants so that they can contribute to the livability, security, and social cohesion of the neighborhood. The SIP also wishes to provide insight into the questions and problems that exist in a neighborhood, with the aim of better realizing a mutual alignment of the aspects of welfare organizations and housing associations that are related to supply and demand. In this way, it can contribute to the livability, security, and social cohesion of a neighborhood.

Despite the fact that house visits in various cities do not entail the same procedures and objectives, a number of elements do recur (Metaal et al. 2006: 149; Cornelissen and Brandsen 2007: 7). First of all, there is the idea that the authorities no longer have to wait until people bring their problems to social assistance organizations. Social workers are encouraged to emerge from their offices and visit clients in their own surroundings, instead of the other way around. This outreaching style of working is connected to the realization that, certainly in the more harrowing cases, people appear to be unable to reach the official institutions for numerous reasons. As a consequence, a large group of people receive no help or support with their problems. A second element is the large scale of the approach. Eefke Cornelissen and Taco Brandsen (2007) have examined seven behind-the-front-door projects and conclude that urban intervention teams select a large number of households to visit. They ring the bells of all inhabitants of certain streets or of a whole neighborhood. The reason for this is that this gives a clear picture of the problems within a street or neighborhood, while unknown appeals for help also become tangible. At the same time, this helps prevent people feeling stigmatized. The third element concerns the promotion of self-sufficiency. Inhabitants are stimulated to solve their own problems. In this respect, the intervention teams fulfill a supporting and referral function, in such a way that the responsibility lies with the inhabitants. Despite the emphasis on self-sufficiency, there is always a latent danger that inhabitants with problems will be coerced into a care procedure. The fourth element is the previously mentioned integral approach, in which various organizations combine a range of measures, and implement them jointly.

One thing is evident: the composition and objectives of intervention teams have not remained identical in the various cities that deploy them. The approach in Rotterdam has been consistently adjusted, and other parties, such as the energy company and the Tax Department, have also been recruited. An expansion of the original target group has also taken place with regard to the objectives of the intervention teams. Whereas the method of intervention was initially only applied to a specific street, now the whole city has become the work field of the intervention teams, and a whole assortment of goals and functions has been added. Nowadays, social care, the Tax Department, and youth and health care organizations are all pushing their noses around the door to examine the complete lifestyle of the inhabitants. The consequence of this expansion of both subject and object is that the intervention teams have acquired a different functionality than the one for which they were originally founded. In the IT world, this is referred to as "function creep": unintended shifts in technical function. My earlier analysis demonstrated that something similar is going on in security (see also Chun and Rainey 2005; Haggerty and Ericson 2006: 18–19). Accordingly, I wish to speak of "mission creep" in this context. Laws, regulations, measures, programs, and policy can all take on a completely different significance than originally intended, occasionally even in a totally different field. With the addition of new goals and the appearance of new security risks, the initial objectives surreptitiously shift to cover new areas.

Differences in vision

Intervention teams are one of the most frequently discussed instruments in the process of securitization. The teams provoke negative as well as positive reactions. In this framework, the discussion switches among three extremes. A first group of authors accentuates the classic issue of constitutionality or rule of law, and believes that the visits must satisfy fundamental legal principles, such as the fair-trial principle (Art. 6 EVRM) and a resident's right to privacy (Art. 10 Constitution; Art. 8 EVRM) (Ombudsman Rotterdam 2007; 2011; van den Berg 2008). This group bases its views on the notion of "rules are rules." With regard to the fair-trial principle, for example, a citizen may not have the opportunity to exercise his or her rights because there is no clarity about the reason why, and for which fact, an intervention team gathers data on that citizen. The most explicit document on this topic was the report by the Ombudsman Rotterdam (2007) about the approach of Rotterdam intervention teams. The subtitle of this report, "Yes, we come for everything in fact . . ." covers the content admirably. The conclusion of the report was that "the apparent mixture of aims (repression, help, control) and the mingling of competencies have led to a multifaceted and too-vague instrument that leads to confusion in the mind of the citizen" (2007: 8). In addition, the report states that the organizational forms and structures of responsibility are too diverse and consequently obscure, so that control over operations is not possible. In a later report, the Ombudsman Rotterdam (2011) points out that much, although not everything, has changed for the better. For instance, the number of people in a team has been reduced from five to three, and the municipality has formulated a separate House Visit Protocol for the intervention teams. Nevertheless, the Ombudsman Rotterdam observes that a well-grounded reason for a house visit is often lacking. Residents are also often inadequately informed about the nature and magnitude of the investigation, with regard to aspects that are dealt with during the house visit.

The second group of authors approaches intervention teams as a successful means to effectively promote the security and livability of neighborhoods. Aware that too few lateral links are being forged in the supervision of security and livability, this group believes that intervention teams form an appropriate model for governmental innovation in general and for an effective tackling of neighborhood disorder in particular. It is especially the combination of law enforcement and care that makes the approach so successful. One much-used argument is that the integral approach is the only way to do something about the tunnel vision of (local) government and other institutions. In this context, the disadvantages of an integral approach are not as counterproductive as those arising from tunnel vision. Pieter Tops writes that the intervention teams "constitute an effective executory practice in which care and prevention can be linked in a natural way" (2007: 298). Cornelissen and Brandsen (2008) champion the standpoint that, to reach problem households, "you have to get a foot over the threshold in the implementation of policy." These authors, too, point to the importance of constitutional principles, although the argument is more practical in its nature. Here, the starting point is, "What works is what's important."

The last group focuses primarily on the moral side of the interventions and attributes the government's meddling in social life to a "new paternalism" (Schinkel and van den Berg 2011) or sees it as an attempt to "remoralize" society (Boutellier 2011: 72). According to this group, intervention teams form a component of a renewed call for a civilization offensive in which the government wishes to educate the population and therefore strongly emphasizes social values and norms. This offensive evokes recollections of the paternalism of experts in the 1950s and 1960s who, on the basis of their knowledge and position, had the opportunity to express and impose their vision of a good life (and had also been assigned the responsibility to do so), with the mitigating factor that pure coercion seldom occurred in those days (Tonkens et al. 2006: 16). However, the third group believes that it is difficult to establish precisely when the actions of intervention teams are effective and proportional. Evelien Tonkens (2003) and Marc Räkers (2008) state that the "behind-the-front-door" approach is only justified when the interests and needs of the clients are the focus of attention and the approach is used for social revival. That makes the rule of thumb for this group, "Only when really needed."

It is difficult to bridge the gap among these three groups. There is a clear difference of perception of the formulation and implementation of policy, and this difference will probably also give rise to tension in real-life practice. That makes it interesting to examine the context in which the position of the authorities could possibly change. When a large number of organizations are represented in an intervention team, numerous obscurities can arise with regard to individual responsibilities and competencies. For example, the police may appeal to a formal regulation in a certain case, whereas a housing association may wish, in good consultation, to allow a tenant time to reduce his or her rent arrears. In another case, the roles and expectations may be reversed. Although molecular research ought to determine which position should enjoy priority when, it can already be observed that the separate visions on intervention teams have roots that reach back to the orientation struggle in the fight against smallpox in the nineteenth century, which I analyzed previously in my outline of the technology of security.

At that time, a furious struggle raged between proponents and opponents of governmental supervision of personal lifestyles aimed at preventing risks to public health. It was a public and political debate about the relation between the actual substantiation of the *bonum commune*, the general interest of society, and individual freedom. It is self-evident that this debate about these potentially mutually conflicting values cannot be seen independently of the institution and competencies of the police in those days. But although the norms of the nineteenth century appear to be incompatible with those of our times, it would seem useful, nonetheless, to gain more insight into the continuity between the activities and operations of the police then and the actions of intervention teams now. I believe that this is an unjustly neglected theme in present-day security research.

Continuity

In the nineteenth century, people gradually began to acknowledge that a human being is not only what he or she eats but also a part of the environment in which he or she lives. Changing notions about security and certainty contributed to the situation that biopolitical techniques were being deployed, directed toward the conditions under which people were living as well as the fields in which they were active. These techniques are not primarily repressive but are aimed at making a society stronger and healthier through the introduction of detailed supervision of life domains such as work and urban hygiene. Foucault analyzed this political technology in terms of the German and French words "*Polizei*" and "*police*," which are both derived from the Greek words "*politeia*" ("citizenship") and "*polis*" ("city"). "Everything that serves to preserve the good order of society is a matter for police," is how Foucault (2009: 329, nt. 2) summarizes the techniques, resources, goals, and domains that the police supervise. At first sight, the contrast with the modern meaning of "police" seems considerable. If one asks citizens what police work consists of and what police officers do all day, explanations such as "they are a body of people patrolling public places in blue uniforms, with a broad mandate of crime control, order maintenance and some negotiable social service functions" (Reiner 2010: 3) are soon given. In contrast to Foucault's usage, popular vernacular does not refer to a comprehensive way of governing but to a rather narrow image of police work. If one looks closely at the operations of urban intervention teams, the similarity with the concept of police as Foucault describes it is the most conspicuous feature.

Let us return to the approach deployed by urban intervention teams in which a connection is made among repression, care, and prevention. The aim of this is to "recapture the city in social terms" (Engbersen 2009: 180; WRR 2005: 19) from people who cause disorder and crime ("risk citizens"). More generally, this policy is characterized by interventions that are directed toward (1) the enhancement of livability and security in public space, (2) the realization of a more balanced social structure, and (3) the formulation of shared competencies and rules of conduct to improve everyday social traffic among the residents. A noticeable feature of this broad organizational approach to metropolitan problems is that the authorities do not recoil from entering the private living environment of citizens, and that very diverse life domains, such as health, education, and welfare, are mutually linked. In that sense, the urban intervention teams are a clear example of biopolitics or, even better, of life politics.

Rotterdam, in particular, has made large-scale investment in population control in order to improve livability and security in various neighborhoods. In this context, people speak of "an innovative implementation practice" (Tops 2007: 213). However, the question arises as to just how new the phenomenon of intervention teams actually is. In the long term, many changes with regard to security can be viewed in a completely different perspective (see also Garland 2003; Zedner 2006b). What this might mean comes to the fore in the work of the sociologist Stanley Cohen (1979; 1985). Cohen, who was strongly influenced by Foucault, states that the center of control over unwanted behavior has not been the prerogative of the government since the second half of the nineteenth century. Cohen speaks of a "correctional continuum" or "correctional spectrum" that is thrown over the population like a control net whose mesh is drawn increasingly tight ("thinning the mesh and widening the net"). In this process, there is a mingling of private and public control ("merging public and private") and a "penetration" of the personal life sphere by all kinds of social relief workers, welfare workers, and pedagogues. According to Jacques Donzelot (1977), the family environment increasingly becomes the object of "moralising" (providence, order) and "normalising" (medicalization of the family) interventions. In this way, a form of behavioral regulation takes place on the forecourt of penal law, where the classical idea of punishment now scarcely plays a role. In this framework, the nature and reach of the intervention-team approach display many similarities with the activities and working methods of the police in the nineteenth century. What the phenomena mainly have in common is the scale and level of detail of the supervision. In both cases, a direct relationship is established between interventions and defined risk populations, on the basis of statistical techniques, with the aims of removing specific risks and of reinforcing protective factors. In addition, the supervision is not limited to the criminal circuit but involves an integral governing power that permanently monitors and examines the life domains of all citizens, and intervenes where necessary. Thus, the concepts of Foucault and Cohen readily lend themselves to placing the intervention teams in the biopolitical framework of the nineteenth-century police. Seen in this light, the intervention teams are less unique than they might appear to be at first sight, but reach back to the governing techniques of the police, supplementing these in accordance with their own approach.

The SIP and its partners

The SIP started up in the Overtoomse Veld neighborhood of Amsterdam in 2001. This is a district with around ten thousand inhabitants, wedged between the A10 urban circular road and a railway track. The neighborhood consists largely of housing blocks, four stories high, owned by housing associations. These are mostly rented houses; there are scarcely any private homes in the area. Another feature of the neighborhood is that two-thirds of the inhabitants belong to ethnic minorities, including a relatively large proportion of people with Moroccan roots (30 percent here against 8 percent average for Amsterdam) (WRR 2005: 43–45). Problems in the fields of livability (housing, rubbish on the streets) and security (theft, violence, burglary) formed the impulse for the establishment of the SIP. In the meantime, the SIP has become one of the so-called pillars of urban renewal, and is recognized as a successful example of the integral approach (Cornelissen and Brandsen 2007: 13–15). Nevertheless, the working method of the SIP is not the same as that of the Rotterdam intervention teams. Not only are the aims and measures of the SIP less extensive, but the SIP also primarily aspires to a demand-oriented approach in which inhabitants are offered a package of support and assistance that is tailored to their own situation. In contrast to the Rotterdam variant, the SIP also makes use of a network-like approach, in which four phases can be discerned.

In the first phase of the approach, the SIP gathers information on the situation in the neighborhood. It checks to see if a demolition or renovation of a housing complex is scheduled to take place. In addition, it obtains input from discussions on the streets and in doorways. Network partners such as the police can also provide information on households that are earmarked for a visit. Close cooperation with housing associations is most relevant in the first phase. In the next phase, the SIP begins to carry out door-to-door visits. Although the SIP does not make appointments to visit people, the visits are not entirely unannounced: folders proclaiming the visits are distributed before the SIP's resident advisors start on their rounds. The door-to-door visits are carried out by a team of two people, consisting of a resident advisor and a resident assistant. The team is put together on the basis of ethnicity and the mastery of languages. If a resident is not at home, or refuses to open the door, the SIP will pay a maximum of three visits to check if he or she is at home. After the third attempt, the SIP leaves its contact information so that the resident can seek contact at his or her own initiative. During the house visits, the team pays attention to seven fields, also referred to as "dimensions": language, education and upbringing, social participation, view of life, work and income, security and health, and welfare and housing.

In the third phase of the door-to-door approach, the back office continues where the SIP begins to leave off. The back office consists of network partners such as housing associations, schools, and sports clubs, the Youth Care Agency, the Impulse Foundation, the Municipal Work and Income Department, the Mental Health Department, and the Neighborhood Foundation. In this structure, short lines of communication must prevent long waiting lists. Social relief projects involving residents are evaluated in this phase. If multiple problems are observed in one family, a report is made to the coordinator of Families at Risk and to the registration point of the Care and Nuisance Agency. The SIP also accompanies residents to interviews with such organizations. In this context, people refer to "warm transfers."

The fourth and last phase is directed toward the monitoring of the process. The SIP checks to see if the resident has been registered with the proper organization and if the care prescribed dovetails with the problems observed. If the resident is dissatisfied, the SIP gives feedback to the organization in question. It must also be noted that the feedback may also occur at an earlier moment in the process: during a house visit, for example, if the resident makes remarks or lodges a complaint about an allegedly inadequate approach by certain authorities.

Molar robustness

The question is how, in view of the complexity of the problems in metropolitan districts such as Overtoomse Veld, the SIP and its partners can jointly succeed in achieving results. After all, the issue concerns not only the conception and documentation of policy but also the real-life implementation of interventions in problem areas. On the basis of interview and observation material, I wish to demonstrate the way in which various authorities, each in its own particular way, give substance to the formulated policy. In fact, the case study delivers a picture that differs from the decompartmentalization that is discussed in the literature. At the molar level, there are mechanisms that ensure that old structures remain intact in the new situation. Spontaneously occurring behavior that cannot be traced back to the old structures occurs much less frequently than one might expect on the basis of the information supplied in the previous chapters. To make the effects of these molar barriers more transparent, I distinguish three mechanisms with a certain "robustness," which is a well-known concept from the world of product designers. A robust product is a product whose performance is insensitive to undesired and unexpected variations in the composition of the material. Variations and imperfections are regarded as "noise" or turbulence. For this reason, the design is configured in such a way that it can accommodate disturbances, and can maintain its original function, structure, and goals. The variation in quality in a robust design can therefore remain as small as possible. Despite imperfections or changes in the material, the product always works in the same way. In this context, people speak of "making systems robust." To a certain extent, a robust system is therefore also insensitive to unpredictable variations, such as those that can be caused by human interactions or by external political and economic circumstances. In that respect, it diverges from a fragile system. In contrast to a robust system, a fragile system is damaged by volatility or uncertain events. In addition, there is an antifragile system that does thrive on change, uncertainty, and variation. This kind of system works even better in times of uncertainty and coincidental variation (Taleb 2012).

I now discuss three forms of molar robustness that came to the fore during the study. The interesting aspect of these forms is that they strongly restrict the desired synergy among the authorities in the SIP. In concrete terms, these forms of molar robustness are (1) methodological, (2) institutional, and (3) financial.

(1) Methodological robustness

The approach of the intervention teams is conspicuous because very diverse fields such as upbringing, work, and health should provide, in mutual coherence, an optimum picture of the way in which a family's household is run. A member of staff of a participating housing association talks about the "seven sides of life." The combined attention devoted to the various fields strongly determines the way in which an intervention team assesses the specific circumstances of a family. Because every separate field is too large to be entirely overseen, it is first translated to the concrete local situation by means of questionnaires. With this approach, the quality of the interventions can be increased. An important aspect here is the fact that the way in which a field is concretized in a specific case may lead to a change in the significance of a field in the long term, or new fields may be added to existing ones. In that way, the working method of the intervention team remains a dynamic whole of mutually influential molar and molecular processes.

Against the background of the major social, cultural, and economic problems in various Amsterdam neighborhoods, the interviewees articulate the necessary skepticism about the way in which the chosen methodology is applied. The enthusiasm of politicians and policymakers about the methodology is not shared by everyone. One of the staff members of a housing association remarked,

> Behind-the-front-door was very much directed toward trust and visiting those in need. In other words, it was totally geared to that. Now everything has become generic. As a result, you miss the specific side of the problem. And you need that specific side. The method applied in Overtoom Noord is now being rolled out to other districts. But every district has its own points of concern.

In this statement, there is implicit criticism of the large scale of the approach. This effort is directed toward acquiring a good picture of the problems in a street or neighborhood and toward avoiding stigmatization. This is why the decision has been made to visit all the houses in the street instead of selecting only a few families.

In a response to this, some of the interviewees declare that the concrete problems of a family are no longer being taken as the starting point of interventions. In the words of a participant, the geographically tinted approach of the intervention teams leads to "a dogmatic system." A staff member of one of the participating housing associations adds, "It's all about quality. Quantity says nothing at all." The negative image that some respondents have of the methodology used also turns out to be related to dissatisfaction with container concepts such as "security" and "livability." The fact that house visits are performed in the framework of security and livability, where the emphasis of the SIP lies on support and social assistance, is a sensitive matter for some of the interviewees, and cannot count on support from all the authorities. For instance, various authorities have problems with the leading role of the municipality. A respondent from the Registration Point of Care and Nuisance states that he "is not happy with this and has difficulty with the fact that every house is visited." The self-sufficiency of the residents is not stimulated by such activities. Another respondent mentions the example of teams that visit people with rent arrears: "I couldn't accept that! It's my responsibility. They treat you as if you're a small child. I think you have to be careful with such things. It belittles people in a certain way." A staff member of a housing association even thinks that security should not be the objective of the interventions, but people should be offered a personal perspective instead: "If the people's situation improves, the neighborhood situation will also improve."

In short, the interviews with the respondents show a certain sense of discomfort with having to cooperate in an approach that does not fully gratify them, although they do not see any clear alternative in this case at this time. In the absence of a better alternative, the applied methodology forms not only the official framework for the integral approach but also the straitjacket in which the authorities themselves feel confined.

(2) Institutional robustness

Methodological robustness clearly demonstrates how the applied methodology can lead to a degree of incomprehension among the authorities. Analysis of the data has shown that this feeling is reinforced by the institutional habitus that forms the basis of each participant's operations. This practice influences the thinking, perception, and actions of people who are active in a certain field. For instance, the actions of the authorities in the case studied appear to be primarily oriented toward the structure of their own organization, which I wish to call "institutional robustness" in this connection. The authorities identify with their own organization rather than with the objectives of the intervention team. This comes to the fore in interviews in which people talk about one another in terms of "the culture" of an organization. Many remarks can be made about the hardness of an organizational culture. For instance, in real-life practice an organization cannot really be characterized on the basis of one shared and uniform culture. There may be mention of several (sub)cultures within an organization. Moreover, as we saw previously, a culture is not a static but a dynamic concept. Nevertheless, the empirical study shows that authorities mostly act on the basis of familiar interests and the adopted customs in their own organization, and do not easily take on forms of expression from other fields.

What is troublesome in the cooperation, as the research demonstrates, is that the authorities have to act in areas with which they are not particularly familiar. We also encountered a similar situation in the approach to marijuana cultivation in Eindhoven. In this case, not everyone in the assemblage can identify with the accent on care. A staff member from a housing association stated, "We are a housing association and our social context is of the utmost importance to us. But we are not social relief workers or welfare workers." The same vision on cooperation is articulated by a respondent from the submunicipal council of Slotervaart:

> We are a service-provision organization, not a relief organization. A relief organization tends to exude an attitude of "can't you just turn a blind eye?" They look at things from a social point of view and are primarily oriented toward the individual interest of the client. A service-provision

organization works according to the book, regardless of how irksome that may be for the clients. We look at the interests of the whole, as in the case of the client who engages in fraud.

At the moment an authority enters a field in which the game is played under different rules, conflicts may arise between the newcomers and the parties that have been active on that field for a longer period of time. Such conflicts occur around the issue of, for example, who is to have ultimate control of a newly institutionalized power structure. For instance, a special project has been set up in the framework of urban renewal to tackle the social problems of inhabitants whose house is to be renovated or demolished. In such a setting, the SIP will make a house visit at the request of a housing association in order to help the tenants relocate quickly and smoothly to a new or temporary home. The managing role in this process does not rest with the SIP but with both parties. This being the case, the SIP *de facto* transfers a part of the control to a private party. "We have formulated an action plan in which you see that we exercise more governance. We do not want people to be left to their own devices and we want to see results," says a respondent from a housing association. At the same time, the respondent states that the SIP wrestled with the new action plan: "They had difficulty with the fact that they had to realize their ambitions. I could see that they found this a bit frightening." The utterance of another respondent illustrates the fact that the SIP is regarded primarily as someone who does the job rather than as an equal partner. "There's no document stating that the SIP is the appropriate body to coordinate a social welfare process."

In short, the study shows that the SIP can lose overall control to another partner when the latter is better at defending its own interests. These shifts may indicate the complexity of the neighborhood problems that the SIP has to deal with, and may be seen as a fitting answer to the various possible approaches in a concrete case. What seems to play a role in the background is that some parties nurture a preference for a certain solution whose selection is primarily the outcome of the accepted interests of one's own organization, and is therefore not sparked by the issue at stake.[2] For instance, one respondent remarked, "The submunicipal council wanted it to be the residents of one specific street. That's not relevant to us. They want to pay attention to the neighborhood because they have certain priorities in terms of politics. But it makes no difference to us. That zone or maybe three streets further." Here, too, it is the case that the institutional robustness of each of the parties casts a different light on the idea that an integral approach ensures cohesion and coherence. Whereas the integral approach is regarded as the means to combat compartmentalization, the interviews indicate that a certain qualification can be applied to the notion that authorities influence and react to one another and that, without external organization, a working method can thus arise that cannot be traced back to the approach of one of the parties. In the case studied, differences in organizational culture often turned out to be difficult to overcome. This is closely related to the priorities of the organizations and the importance the authorities attach to this, which Anthony Downs (1967) calls "the economy of organizations." The dominance of one practice in relation to another also contributes to the fact that various authorities soon fall back upon their own tried and trusted methods, so that the intended integral approach receives too little impetus to get off the ground.

(3) Financial robustness

A third and last form of robustness that ensures that interaction processes among authorities are framed by interests other than those of the intervention team as a whole is the financial recompense that parties receive when certain measures are taken. I previously referred to the fact that organizations may receive money if they participate in a specific project. This may work in a motivating way (see also Gilling 1994a; Rosenbaum 2002). Particularly the receipt of subsidy appears to have a strong power of attraction on the decision (not) to cooperate in the integral approach. This is illustrated by a quotation from a member of staff from a job agency: "I am interested in good candidates that I can send to work. At the moment someone is hired, I can send an invoice." Accordingly, various organizations express the desire to have their specific area of concern classified under the objectives of the integral approach to the neighborhood. One respondent from a housing corporation articulated this as follows: "The subsidy junk plays an important role; everyone is fighting for the continuation of his job."

Because organizations are in a situation of mutual rivalry, and the competition is great, this leads to further demarcation of everyone's areas of duty: "In New West [district of Amsterdam] there is much competition between the various organizations. Everybody gets his own little piece of subsidy and does not want anyone else to share in it. Everyone is trying to make a show of themselves in the current economic climate." Another respondent expresses the same viewpoint in other words: "There is too much supply so that organizations have to compete. I would prefer it not to be that way. Whatever the case, you should be happy that people are being helped." The member of staff of a housing association also points out that one organization receives a subsidy whereas another one does not, which leads to a constant, although often hidden, struggle to secure a large piece of the pie as the tension increases. "Everyone receives his own part of the subsidy and is determined that nobody is going to pilfer any of it."

The fact that considerable financial sums are involved in subsidy distribution also seems to have an influence on the working method of the SIP and its partners for other reasons. The opinions on work must also be seen in this light. It is assumed that parties in the integral approach have a horizontal relationship to one another. According to the literature, the relationship is not about "who has the power" but rather about "the question as to how a collective capacity to act can be developed in a world in which power is limited and diffuse" (Tops 2007: 23). Horizontal work connections facilitate the coordination of the tasks and can breach compartmentalization, or an island structure. Horizontalization also provides an opportunity to work in a more customer-oriented way, and to develop tailor-made services and products more quickly in order to enhance the livability and security of streets and neighborhoods. In addition, the effectiveness can be enlarged because a faster response to occurrences in the city becomes possible. But the interviews show that the possession of financial resources may disrupt the horizontal relationships or even seriously obstruct the approach. A respondent from a housing association commented, "If we pay, we also want to be part of the decision making process. Otherwise, if we can't alter anything, we are only functioning as a cash dispenser." This means that parties may tend to follow their own agenda, which increases the compartmentalization of the approach while restricting the mutual dynamics.

Finally, financial robustness can develop in the work processes of the intervention team in another way. A member of the Slotervaart submunicipal council stated, "Our great handicap is that the policy makers do the subsidies. If we say that the organizations are not delivering high-quality work, the policymakers do nothing with this information. On the contrary, they give the organizations even more money." To escape from this dilemma, the respondent advises resident advisors to no longer pass on signals to the department that issues the subsidies.

* * *

Urban intervention teams are regarded as an important means to enhance the livability and security of problem neighborhoods. As policy concept, the phenomenon of these teams, composed on an interdisciplinary basis, seems to be relatively new. However, real-life practice has shown that many continuities are inherent in the implementation of security. For instance, the approach of the intervention teams correlates closely with the biopolitical administrative activities of the nineteenth-century police, in their aim to make society stronger and healthier. In that sense, the phenomenon is less unique than supposed. As a component of the securitization process, the approach is about a changing degree of social control, of more and less. In addition, the aspect of decompartmentalization cannot remain unchallenged. On the basis of the research material presented here, it appears that the integral approach of intervention teams should combat compartmentalization but is not successful in its aim: compartmentalization is actually reinforced. This is striking because compartmentalization is seen as a major obstacle to integral action.

All this provokes the question as to whether the stories about decompartmentalization as the answer to viscous bureaucracy and a lack of coherence in policy and implementation do not actually obscure the facts. The picture sketched in the literature of the disappearance of partitions in intervention teams seems too good to be true. And it is indeed so, as this chapter shows. Anyone who believes that the differences among the participating authorities can be readily solved is heading for deception. Contradictory operational practices, each of which has strong molar robustness, are latent in the intervention team. This robustness plays a role at various levels in the integral approach, ranging from relative institutional hardness to the magnetic force of subsidies. With this, the most important findings have been named: to a certain extent, the diverse forms of robustness are successful in controlling the molecular processes in the assemblage. In the case studied, the aim of decompartmentalization appears to be difficult to realize and awkward to use as establishing legitimacy for an integral approach.

9

The Collective Shop Ban

The Collective Shop Ban (CSB) was introduced to the center of The Hague in 2005 with the aim of preventing antisocial behavior, defined in terms of punishable acts and undesirable conduct. In the latter case, the "offense" is relatively mild, such as when someone behaves in an ill-mannered way to shop personnel, for example. In this framework, the entrepreneurs themselves can impose a shop ban on the offenders, and this ban is subsequently enforced throughout the entire city center. Anyone displaying undesired behavior in a shop or business that espouses the CSB policy can thus be refused admission to all enterprises that uphold the policy. For example, if someone steals a Mars bar from the newspaper kiosk, he or she will not be granted admission to the H&M store further down the street. Such bans may be imposed for a period of six months or a year. During this period, the banned person may not enter the shop that imposed the ban or any other of the 454 businesses in The Hague that apply the CSB. Shops that participate in the CSB can be recognized by the red sticker on the door or shop window, bearing the text, "Admission will be refused to shoplifters and others causing nuisance." With this, the sticker realizes a demarcation of a part of the city center where the security assemblage is in force.

With the CSB, entrepreneurs and security personnel have become responsible for the detection and punishment of classic criminal offenses such as theft and fraud. From this book's angle of approach, the CSB has consequently become an interesting focus of study, all the more so because the measure leans heavily on quasi-criminal law, which I introduced earlier in my treatment of the work of Foucault. It thus becomes interesting to investigate the practices of shopkeepers in The Hague who implement this measure.[1]

The city center

The CSB measure arose as a reaction to increasing concern in Dutch business circles about the security of public space and the damage incurred as a result of criminal activity. For this reason, entrepreneurs in The Hague developed their own security measures to ban trouble-makers from shops, and to extend this measure to the whole of the city center. This being the case, the CSB is a typical example of a bottom-up initiative in which local parties, with the aid of the government, design their own security program and prescribe certain behavior for people in public space. According to the entrepreneurs, the classical reactions—detection and punishment—of the police and the public prosecutor provide an inadequate response to the problems of crime and disorder. In consultations with the municipality, the police, and the Public Prosecutor's Office, three categories of behavior have been formulated for which a CSB can be imposed. These categories are registered on the Notification of Collective Shop Ban form and range from offenses such as the theft of (goods worth) up to fifty euros to more serious forms of misconduct, such as threatening with violence and molesting shop staff. The last two offenses can lead to an immediate ban for twelve months.

If a security guard, the shop personnel, or a customer observes punishable behavior, consultation of a database will indicate whether or not the offender has previously incurred a CSB or official warning. Subsequently, the security guard or a manager from the shop will decide whether or not the offender is to be given a CSB. In addition to the shop ban, any punishable offense is reported to the police. This occurs with a first infringement and with any subsequent violation of the code of behavior, which is a punishable offense according to Article 138 of the Dutch Penal Code. In the latter case, a new CSB is generally imposed, so that the period of the ban is extended. There is no maximum on the number of possible prolongations.

Currently, a third of the businesses in the city center of The Hague make use of CSB policy. These enterprises have been brought together in business associations that, in turn, almost all belong to the Federation of City Center Entrepreneurs (FCCE). This is the overarching entrepreneurial association in which fourteen of the nineteen business associations participate. Every business that is a member of one of the fourteen business associations automatically participates in the CSB policy. Membership in an entrepreneurial association is not only a precondition of participation in the policy measure but also entails that the affiliated shopkeeper actively supports the measure. Collaboration is thus not without engagement. The shopkeepers must comply with the agreed-upon protocol that aims to improve security in the city center, combat shoplifting and nuisance, radiate a preventative ambience, and discourage troublemakers. Not everyone has entered into this agreement voluntarily. The head of CSB Registration of the FCCE explains that certain shops in shopping centers are compulsory members of a business association and are thus automatically tied to the corresponding CSB regulation. In this way, the economic problem of free riders is avoided.

To a shopkeeper, the most important advantage of being a member of a shopkeepers' association is that his or her losses decrease due to a reduction in theft, which is one of the effects of the policy, according to all parties involved. But the partnership also offers other benefits. First of all, private security can be hired on a larger scale, often bringing discounts when a complete shopping area participates in the Hallmark of Secure Enterprise structure. Second, on its website, the Center for Crime Prevention and Community Safety presents insurance discounts to those who apply this policy. This has never been granted, however, stated the vice-chairman of the FCCE during the meeting of The Hague City Center Board. But the Association of Insurers has declared that it will remit a one-time sum if the Hallmark of Secure Enterprise initiative is prolonged, with the provision that this sum must be spent on security. Third, the government offers subsidy opportunities, while fiscal benefits may also be granted on the basis of participation. Fourth, in the event of antisocial behaviour, the efforts of the city and the police are guaranteed. By not being a member of the shopkeepers' association, a number of shopkeepers exclude themselves from these benefits, and that is a great pity, emphasizes the head of the city center shopkeepers' association. "I just can't understand that they might not want to participate."

Beyond the Penal Code

Traditionally, offenses such as theft, vandalism, threatening behavior, and serious forms of disorder are tackled by means of classic criminal law. I previously mentioned that the roots of this law lie in the work of Enlightenment thinkers such as Beccaria and Montesquieu. In retrospect, a distinction can be made between two important features of this law. On the one hand, criminal law enables the state to exercise control, and guarantees the legal position of the citizens in relation to the state. It is precisely this conflict of interest between the state and the citizen that is the structural principle of criminal law (Peters 1972). In the distance between the state and the citizen, i.e., the space of this conflict, the legitimacy of the actions of the state can be tested on the basis of procedural norms and legal principles, such as the legality principle (no act is punishable except according to the law) and the reasonable assumption of guilt. On the other hand, the enforcement of order through criminal law is directed toward the protection of individual legal goods, such as life and property, by means of fitting actions, such as the deliberate threat and application of punishment in cases of violation. Both features harmonize with a penal mentality in which criminal law serves as a kind of psychic deterrent, and the state guarantees the security of the citizen by imposing a juridically established punishment or measure in cases of proven violation of the law. However, the CSB measure breaches the repressive toolkit of criminal law in a remarkable way.

First of all, the CSB is a civil measure and is separate from the criminal law system. The legislative status of the measure has its foundation in the binding declaration of agreement. With this, in the field of private law, property and contract form the basis of the CSB. The denial of access to a shop is possible on the basis of the protocol that has been locally agreed upon among the participating parties. This means that the entrepreneurs are primarily responsible for the imposition of a CSB. A shopkeeper or a hired private security guard decides whether or not someone should be refused entrance. A legislative ground, in the sense of "a reasonable assumption of guilt," is not required to enforce the denial. Although criminal law remains present in the background in the CSB structure—as a result of the legal authorization of the shopkeeper to arrest someone who is caught red-handed—the established penal process is largely skipped when a CSB is imposed. The police are only involved incidentally; mainly, discussions take place between witnesses and the person who issues the CSB.

In addition, the CSB is not accompanied by an indictment. The offender is not officially accused of committing a punishable offense. The CSB form reports what has happened. This form displays a number of different categories of conduct, one of which can be checked off. No extra information specifying the offender's misbehavior needs to be recorded. In contrast, in criminal law, the precise details of an offender's behavior must always be registered in order for it to be considered a punishable offense. However, when a CSB is imposed, a categorization of the behavior is sufficient, and the actual details of the behavior itself can be omitted.

The imposition of a CSB also requires less evidence than a settlement under the auspices of criminal law. The concept of "unlawful action" in civil law is wider than the concept of a "punishable act" in criminal law. Moreover, in criminal law, the minimum rule of evidence—there must be two pieces of evidence—is always required for a conviction. A single piece of evidence is sufficient when an authorized investigator catches the offender in the act. With a CSB, it is enough if a member of the shop staff or a security guard (neither of whom are authorized investigators) catches someone red-handed. In order to officially impose a denial of access, it is sufficient to have the form signed by one witness and by the person who has violated the rules. The latter does this on a voluntary basis. If the offender refuses to sign the CSB form, a second witness is needed. In this case, the second witness signs for the offender, thus making the document valid. Supplementary evidence for the imposition of the ban is not necessary. At the moment the CSB is signed, the status of the offender becomes that of a "perpetrator." After the signatures have been placed, the ban immediately comes into force.

In short, to make the city center of The Hague more attractive and to achieve the goal of realizing more security, new instruments in which criminal law only obliquely comes into the picture are now being applied. This disqualifies the image of criminal law as "an urgent agency for establishing the social order" (Boutellier 2004: 97). Besides the sphere of influence of criminal law, other techniques in the security diagram have arisen to substantiate certain norms. An important driving force includes ideas that have arrived from the UK and are known under the name of the "Antisocial Behavior Order" (ASBO). In this framework, measures are implemented to combat troublesome behavior such as vandalism, rubbish on the streets, public drunkenness, noise nuisance, and neighbor abuse. The related measures involve a ban on entering certain areas or associating with certain people. Although a number of critical comments have been made on the effects of ASBOs (e.g. Burney 2002; Bullock and Jones 2004), policymakers and politicians still assume that these ideas are effective and could also be applied in the Netherlands.

The practice in The Hague

For a good understanding of the CSB security technique, it is essential to know the differences from and similarities to criminal law. I return to this topic shortly. However, it can already be stated that, in the case of the CSB, the FCCE has not only received the support of the municipality of The Hague; two public prosecutors have also reviewed the project. They have stated that everything is in good legal order. In the framework of the project, the Public Prosecutor's Office has also declared that it will prosecute every charge of entering premises illegally, as well as shoplifting. In addition, the Dutch Data Protection Authority and the police have approved the shopkeepers' policy. Three times a week, the police hold a collective briefing in which security agents are informed about people with a CSB. At these meetings, photographs of the troublemakers are shown to security guards to enable future recognition. Although the FCCE would like to work with photos, the Dutch Data Protection Authority has indicated that this is not allowed. As a result, only accredited security guards are permitted to view the visual material. The coordinator of the CSB project states that the briefings are primarily for the benefit of enterprises with security staff. The businesses that have not hired in any security services cannot make use of the briefings. Nevertheless, it is clear that the government is willing to transfer an important part of its power to other parties and, with this, to another form of regulation, in exchange for order and safety in the city center.

Because the CSB measure is a relatively new phenomenon that is supported by the government, this research was applied at the molecular level in order to discover the way in which entrepreneurs deal with the CSB. After all, the CSB measure does not have to be imposed by the shopkeepers. This could explain why space for one's own substantiation of the measure—and for new initiatives—arises at the molecular level. In turn, this could potentially influence the official policy formulated in conjunction with the municipality, the police, and the Public Prosecutor's Office. The field study involved (1) the extent of familiarity with the measure, (2) the arbitrariness of imposition of the measure, and (3) whether or not changes in the measure arise—in other words, whether or not forms of settlement develop, other than those described in the agreed-upon protocol.

(1) Familiarity with the measure

It is irrefutably the case that the CSB serves a public interest. This means, therefore, that public interests are also managed by private parties. In the light of the previously described strategy of responsibilization, this is not strange or unusual. However, for the good implementation of these public interests, it is necessary to have the competencies of the authorities clearly specified and public liability accepted. The formulation of the competencies of the participating parties at a molar level is clearly given in the CSB in The Hague. Accordingly, for a proper implementation of the measure, it is important that the entrepreneurs be aware of the procedures to be followed, so that they can be applied correctly.

The research shows that the coordinator of the CSB, who is responsible for informing the businesses about the procedure they should follow, has a great deal of difficulty in executing this task. It is not uncommon for enterprises to go bankrupt and for new ones to take their place. Moreover, business associations become members of the FCCE relatively easily, but also cancel their membership just as effortlessly. The result of this is that the coordinator has a fragmented picture of what is going on in the professional field. Nevertheless, the incompleteness of the list of participants is not the only cause of problems with the provision of information. The businesses themselves play a major role in the situation. CSB policy is often regulated through the head office of a chain store, but the feedback to the individual shops is not always optimal. On the one hand, while a great many shops have indeed placed a red sticker on their doors, the salespeople hardly know what the sticker stands for. The system of rotation of business managers probably has an important influence here. In many cases, they do not remain in one branch for any noteworthy period of time and move on to the next one after a relatively short spell. Moreover, they often forget to communicate to their successor the relevant information on denials of access. Furthermore, some shops refuse to put the participation sticker on their door or window because "it can detract from the image of a chain of stores," as a police member of staff articulated it.

What also comes to the fore is that the various shopkeepers are largely unacquainted with the way the CSB forms ought to be used. They often do not know where they can request the forms, and consequently do not have them readily available. Those who do have the forms at hand are often unsure about how to fill them in. The police remark that a great many forms are submitted incorrectly. This means that the bans cannot come into force immediately and they first have to be rectified before they become valid. At the same time, it is striking that the companies that do fill in the forms properly often comment upon the blunt nature of the form. For instance, the security staff of a large commercial chain on the Grote Marktstraat state that they always have the form already filled in because the business wishes to impose a twelve-month ban in all cases of nuisance. Another large chain states that the forms provide too little space for their own comments. The staff therefore always supplement the form with their own report.

Another feature that emerges from the interviews is that many entrepreneurs do not know that there is a list of names of people who are banned. The database with bans is managed by the FCCE and can be consulted on the Internet. As a result, entrepreneurs cannot check whether or not troublemakers have been given a ban, so that the troublemakers cannot be accused of entering the premises illegally. According to the FCCE, the Internet provides an excellent opportunity to update the list on a daily basis, but the businesses must then have an Internet connection on the premises, and that is not always the case. It is interesting that the FCCE indicates that the enterprises themselves bear the responsibility to consult the list in other ways, via the computer of a shop in the vicinity, for example. The FCCE also allows the enterprises plenty of scope to personally determine whether or not they wish to impose a CSB. The FCCE has no objections to businesses formulating and applying their own criteria. This means that one business will be much stricter in the imposition of a CSB than another.

(2) Arbitrariness in the execution

Right at the start of the CSB project in 2005, in order to ensure the smooth operation of the project, agreements were made among the municipality, the police, and the Public Prosecutor's Office about the competencies and possibilities of the shopkeepers. The agreements cover not only the working method and its application with regard to a first offense or a repetition of this, but they also determine the duties of the police and the public prosecutor in the security assemblage. Although the CSB procedure specifies a uniform working method to settle cases of nuisance and shoplifting, real-life practice indicates that shopkeepers have difficulty in adhering to this setup. They make all kinds of exceptions to the written agreements and, partly as a consequence of this, the enforcement of order in real-life practice has acquired a more arbitrary character. Although these deviations from the rule frequently have a strongly individual motivation, they are generally based on the same practical considerations.

Various shopkeepers mention the lack of time to impose a CSB. This shortage of time mainly comes to the fore during busy evening shopping hours. Because there are many customers in the shop at such times, it is almost impossible for the staff to take a troublemaker to the back office to fill in the necessary forms. "I simply can't spare any of my salespeople," says a manager of a shoe shop. Instead of settling the formal procedure with the troublemaker, this manager opts merely to eject the offender from the shop on such evenings. Several businesses regard this option as easier and faster. Calling the police and making a formal charge are both very time-consuming. According to the manager of a chemist's shop, he "loses too much time." "I'm not going to get involved in all that red tape," he stated when prompted.

Shopkeepers also tend to make financial calculations when pondering a CSB. Various people indicate that the severity of the offense and the value of the stolen goods influence their decision whether or not to impose a CSB. During interviews with security personnel, one guard mentioned a concrete example of someone caught in the act of stealing a magazine. In this case, the theft was reported to the police, but no CSB was imposed because the security guard in question thought that this reaction would be disproportionate. Not only can the relative severity of the offense lead to exceptions, but, in concrete situations, shopkeepers also weigh up the difference between their hourly wage and the value of the stolen goods. Especially in cases of relatively light offenses, a CSB is not regarded as cost effective. A shopkeeper recounted, "I'm not going to start up a whole process with the police for an earplug worth five euros." The manager of a pharmacy on the Turfmarkt stated that her "hourly wage is more than a pack of diapers costing twelve euro." For this reason, she does not impose a CSB in all cases.

In addition, many shops have insufficient staff at their disposal to effectively uphold the CSB. Such cases mostly involve one-person businesses and small shops, and do not apply to large commercial chains such as Zara and the H&M. They hire in their own private security firm, so that the staff do not have to engage in filling in forms and pressing charges. However, hiring in a security firm is not profitable for all enterprises. The consideration here is again a cost-benefit one. The manager of a chemist's shop declared, "There was security, but I got rid of it because it was so terribly expensive." Without security guards, it turns out to be more difficult to uphold the CSB. Not only must there be sufficient personnel in the shop to take the offender into the office, but small shops are often concerned about safety when filling in the form along with the offender. The comments made by the manager of a clothing shop on the Haagsche Bluf are illustrative of this: "You do not isolate a thief to ask him politely if he would be good enough to fill in this form." "Moreover, it is quite odd," continues the manager, "to ask him to wait until the police arrive." In many cases, small shops simply eject the offenders without reporting any violations.

Occasionally, the staff may request assistance from other shopkeepers. This situation most resembles the idea of finely painted Russian matryoshka dolls—each doll containing a smaller doll. In this way, partnerships within partnerships, ever decreasing in size, arise in the security diagram of The Hague. Here, I speak of intra-assemblages: subsystems in larger entities that form a relation with their environment in their own way. A characteristic feature of these assemblages is that they bring further division to a predefined space. Regardless of how well-intentioned such a structure may be, from the standpoint of mutual cooperation this can lead to mission creep in the official public-private partnership and thus to a different content and expression of the security assemblage. A new, secure area is created with other authorities. Although the CSB may be applicable to the whole city center of The Hague, numerous intra-assemblages are cropping up in shopping precincts and other parts of The Hague in real-life practice. This kind of assemblage among the entrepreneurs is evident in the Passage shopping center. One shopkeeper declared, "If there are problems and aggression, we phone the neighbors. They then come to us. We have no security-related contact with other entrepreneurs outside our neighborhood."

Finally, some shopkeepers seem to display a double loyalty to certain people. For example, one shopping chain has even employed someone with a CSB. A security guard of an electronics business made this remarkable discovery. The reaction of the shop to this information was, "Yes, but the theft was from your premises. That doesn't mean he will steal from us." So here there is a unique situation of a shoplifter checking on shoplifters. This qualifies the presumption that a CSB always leads to the exclusion of the troublemaker from shops in the city center. "As long as they do their work well" was the sober response of the interviewees to the fact that people with a CSB are actually employed by some entrepreneurs. Shopkeepers also mention that they would not like to do without some of their customers. Many customers who have incurred a CSB in another shop are therefore not denied access to some other shops. As long as these people behave properly in these shops, they will be allowed entry. Here, too, the entrepreneur's financial considerations form an important motivation for the choices made. With this, the sense of responsibility for what is happening in the city center appears to be linked to the interests of one's own business.

(3) Individual forms of settlement

In general, it can be stated that, in classical criminal law, the punishment must comply with all kinds of rules pertaining to material and formal penal law. This is necessary because punishment involves penalties that are imposed by the state for the violation of previously defined norms. With a view to legal security and equality before the law, the Public Prosecutor's Office has formulated specific directives, and magistrates make use of normative lists of sanctions in order to realize a certain degree of uniformity in the imposition of punishment, regarding the nature and severity of the penalty. Moreover, with respect to the imposition of punishment, it is common practice for the judge to explain his or her deliberations when coming to a specific verdict. This requirement of motivation serves to protect the accused against arbitrariness and inequality, especially if prison sentences are involved. However, the whole structure of the CSB, which can only be accommodated under quasi-criminal law, indicates that, due to the quantity of participating parties—varying from one-person businesses to international commercial chains with their own security services—individual considerations have a major effect on the way in which the CSB is applied and observed.

It can be observed that quasi-criminal law works with assessments within loose margins regarding the sanctions to be imposed. In the case of the CSB, the formal framework presents a number of categories of behavior, one of which can be selected. Nevertheless, the simple opposition of what is permitted and what is forbidden requires some qualification here. Recourse to all kinds of personal initiatives regarding the settlement of violations has led to a proliferation of particular inventions that appear to have no relation to the fixed arsenal of sanctions that the CSB has at its disposal. For instance, the interviews with the entrepreneurs indicate that almost half of the shopkeepers interviewed have their own particular style of settlement, which is superimposed upon the approach championed by quasi-criminal law and ranges from escorting offenders out of the shop to intimidation of the offender. Although such settlements have varying manifestations, they all rely upon shared sentiments and motivations, and hark back to the alleged ineffectiveness of the CSB. "The next day they're back again," says one shopkeeper about people who have been given a CSB. Four alternative forms of settlement are used regularly.

First of all, shopkeepers personally phone the parents of offenders, underage thieves, or troublemakers. Various entrepreneurs experience this as very effective. With youngsters, the problem often concerns a one-time incident, they explain. According to the shopkeepers, a phone call to the parents makes sufficient impression on the youngsters, so that the police do not need to be called in. This works in a remedial and normative way, according to the interviewees. This style of chastisement, as a reaction to deviation from the social norm, thus contributes to the validation of the norm. In line with Foucault, one could say that the shopkeepers uphold the norm by educating and improving the offenders, at it were. In this way, the normal manifests itself as a coercive principle by means of which order is created in the city center of The Hague. This partly explains why the shopkeepers deviate from the official sanction, and take measures that promise more yield in the future.

Some entrepreneurs also make use of the pillory method or—perhaps more appropriate in the field of quasi-criminal law—"naming and shaming." This method can be linked to established criminological concepts and theories. For example, John Braithwaite (1989) stated that the process of shaming is an important means to tackle deviant conduct. In this connection, Braithwaite discerns two forms of shaming: stigmatizing shaming and reintegrative shaming. The former places the emphasis on the criminal activities of the offender, and both the behavior and the person of the offender are rejected. According to Braithwaite, this form of shaming is risky because it significantly and permanently destroys the link between the offender and society. The result is that the offender identifies with the "criminal" label that is attached to him or her, so that there is the possibility that the criminal will continue to play this role his or her whole life long and will develop a criminal career. In contrast, reintegrative shaming is a much more positive approach, placing the accent on attempts to rehabilitate the offender rather than on the undesirable facets of the person in question. This approach wishes to heal the link between the offender and society. The empirical study seems to suggest that, in the enforcement of the CSB, it is primarily stigmatizing shaming that is used with regard to people who deviate from the norm (see also Goffman 1968). A businesswoman in the Haagsche Bluf said that she deliberately opts for negative attention for the offender: "Eventually, together with the police, we printed out his photo and hung it in large format on the window with the word 'Wanted.'" Another way of stigmatizing shaming consists of publicly arresting the offender in order to have him or her led away by the police via the front door of the shop, in full view of everyone. The public pillorying of people encourages Jock Young (2007: 5–6) to speak of "conservative othering," where a person is defined in terms of "evil" and is ascribed qualities that are invariable.

In addition, shopkeepers impose their own fines as an alternative to the penal measure specified in the protocol. Since Beccaria's *On Crimes and Punishments* (1963) it has been generally accepted that, in addition to the punishment, the deterrent effect of a sanction depends on the chance of getting caught, the speed of sentencing, and the certainty that an imposed sanction will genuinely be carried out. But whereas the generalization is mostly related to sanctions that are imposed by the government, shopkeepers have translated the framework into new measures to reduce crime. For instance, the owner of a discount store explains that he always gives the thief a choice: "You pay double the price for the item, otherwise I will call the police." Such incidents mainly involve petty offenses, for example, stealing sweets. In other cases, the troublemaker is only addressed with regard to his behavior. In cases of theft, the person is requested to return the stolen item and to leave the shop.[2]

Finally, there is the "mug-shot folder" initiative. This was created to cope with the problem of recognizing people who have been given a CSB. After all, the shopkeepers' list of banned persons only contains names, without faces. The problem is, therefore, how can the shopkeepers recognize banned visitors? "We make photos of certain people who steal," states the head of security of a shop on the Grote Marktstraat. "Our control room is full of photos." All pictures are kept in the "mugshot folder." This more or less private registration is intended for the security guards, so that they can recognize shoplifters. Various large chain stores, with their own security, work with a similar system. Within the company, photos of banned people are available to the security guards, but not to the shop staff. Although the authorities claim that the infrequent charges of entering the premises illegally prove that the CSB policy is working, the shopkeepers themselves believe that this low figure demonstrates that the policy is unable to keep recidivists in check.

Legal position

What does the CSB measure, which must be classified under quasi-criminal law rather than criminal law, signify in terms of an offender's legal rights? To what extent is there mention of an infringement of his or her legal status? The disparity between quasi-criminal law and classical criminal law would be only theoretical (in both cases it involves the protection of interests such as security and protection against public misdemeanors), if there were not a number of striking differences between the practices. In reviewing these, I am aware that an ideal image of criminal law is being presented. Especially in cases concerning "petty" crime, even settlements under classical criminal law contain an element of arbitrariness. In this way, differences can easily arise regarding those facts that should be prosecuted and those that should not, while an eventual trial often takes place in communal hearings before an overworked judge. The accused often receives an oral verdict that is noted down only very succinctly. Unfortunately, it is beyond the scope of this book to study criminal law in terms of molecular processes and effects.

Criminal law offers legal protection by providing possibilities to appeal against the court's decision. However, legal protection for someone with a CSB turns out to be very limited. To start with, it is difficult to extract oneself from a CSB once it has been imposed. The measure cannot be contested straightforwardly, although a complaints procedure has been set up. If someone objects to the imposition of a ban, a complaint can be lodged with the board of the FCCE. However, the board actively supports the CSB measure and cannot really be regarded as an independent entity. In the case of a complaint, the board examines the details of the case and, if it sees fit, interviews the parties involved. If the person receiving the ban does not agree with the decision of the board, there is always the possibility of appealing to the Dutch Data Protection Agency (DDPA). "However, the Agency cannot make a binding decision on the matter," declared a legal expert from the communications section of the DDPA. The DDPA can only initiate a mediation procedure between the parties concerned.

In order to realize an annulment of the ban without engaging the involvement of the shopkeeper, a civil magistrate can be approached. This is something that has not yet happened, according to the same legal expert of the DDPA. Although there is no explicit criminal-legislative procedure to contest the ban, it must be possible, according to the prevention advisor of the local police, to obtain an annulment by a magistrate in a legal procedure in which the punishable fact for which the ban was imposed is further evaluated. This, too, has never occurred. The complaints procedure that was introduced along with the CSB measure has only been followed in two cases. According to the head of CSB registration, this is not an exceptionally small number: "Those who are involved know exactly what they have done."

A possible explanation of the fact that only two people have ever initiated a complaints procedure may lie in the fact that the procedure is no longer presented in various languages on the CSB form. With the introduction of the CSB policy, the DDPA insisted that those involved must be informed of the complaints procedure they could follow. Although this does happen, it happens to a much lesser degree than was the case immediately after the introduction of the measure. Despite the fact that an increasing number of East European names are appearing on the list of offenders, recounts the head of CSB Registration, the decision has been made to report the possibility of a complaints procedure in Dutch alone. Moreover, to some shopkeepers, that form looked too difficult to fill in, according to this respondent, so that they sometimes just abandoned any effort to do so. In addition, the explanation on the form does not state that an objection to the ban must be made within two weeks of the ban being imposed. If the objection is not lodged within this period, the objection is not valid. With which entity the objection must be lodged is also not immediately clear: both the FCCE and the DDPA are mentioned without any clarification of the difference between these bodies.

A CSB is often accompanied by a report to the police, after which the public prosecutor can decide whether or not to charge the troublemaker. The association of shopkeepers receives no feedback whatsoever about the further legal settlement of the case. If the charge does not lead to a conviction, because there is too little evidence, for example, or the witnesses turn out to be unreliable, or the offense is regarded as being too petty, or there is no real mention of punishable facts, the CSB still remains in force until the entrepreneur decides otherwise. The prevention advisor of the local police admits that "a situation that was dubious to say the least" has indeed occurred. In one specific case, it was unclear whether or not something had really been stolen. Someone appeared to have tucked something in her bag without paying for it, but had not yet passed the cashpoint. According to this advisor, "a yes/no dialogue" took place between the customer and the security guard. Moreover, the procedure for a ban had "not been properly followed." The customer was not only addressed impolitely and firmly held, but the camera pictures and the account given by the security guard did not match. Despite intercession by the police, the ban remained in force in this case—the entrepreneur had no desire to undo the ban.

The restriction of legal protection also takes place by means of disadvantaging the defense to a certain extent. This occurs in various ways. With prosecution under criminal law, a lawyer is assigned to the accused if necessary. However, in the case of a CSB, a sanction is applied that comes into force immediately. As mentioned above, a language barrier can cause uncertainty about the possibilities of fighting a decision made under quasi-criminal law. Another factor that has an obstructive effect is that relatively many people with a CSB have no permanent place of residence. This is a reason for the FCCE not to send a copy of the ban to the address given by the offender. Not only does this cloud the procedure even more, but any correspondence on the course of the complaints procedure also becomes more difficult.

In addition, the imposition of a CSB does not take into account the character of the offender. Under criminal law, an appeal to exculpation can be made if it can be plausibly argued that the perpetrator did not perform an action reprehensibly. General exculpation can be granted on the grounds of one not being accountable, circumstances beyond one's control, and emergency. These grounds apply to various misdemeanors, including the theft discussed here, as well as to molestation and fraud. A CSB measure does not take the accountability of a troublemaker into consideration. Undesired behavior is always punished in the same way. The head of CSB Registration referred to a boy with a shopping ban, whose memory did not work properly and was under social supervision as a result. The request submitted by one of his caregivers to allow him to go shopping under supervision was rejected by the FCCE.

Finally, if a complaints procedure is initiated, it is difficult for the FCCE to discover what precisely has occurred. The CSB form gives only a general report of the fact that led to the ban. In the imposition of a CSB, a categorization of the behavior is sufficient, and the factual details can be omitted. No explanation of the actions of the person in question is given. According to the head of a private security firm working for a chain store in the city center of The Hague, the police report is often a literal copy of the CSB form: "The police blindly accept what the shopkeeper has written." As a result, the refutation of the accusation becomes problematic for the defense. The ban does not need to be based on any evidence other than the statement of a single witness. To escape the ban, the defense has to supply evidence that the accusation is unfounded. This means that the burden of proof lies on the defense, which ultimately means that the issue frequently comes down to the word of the defense against the word of the witness.

* * *

With the advent of the CSB, a new domain in the Dutch security diagram has come to the fore. Fact and law are becoming increasingly difficult to distinguish, although some kind of decision has to be made in each case. Exactly the divergent nature of these two realms stimulates shopkeepers to point to all kinds of official regulations and outcomes that are aimed at justifying their own actions. Private security can be hired at a discount when the businesses in one shopping street do so collectively. Success is claimed by policymakers on the basis of the fact that entrepreneurs in The Hague have imposed almost nineteen hundred bans. Recently, the Main Commodity and Industrial Board announced that the CSB measure could reduce shoplifting by up to 60 percent. An increasing number of cities are introducing the measure and further extensions to it, such as the cinema ban and exclusion from public transport. Amsterdam, Apeldoorn, Arnhem, Beverwijk, Den Helder, Deventer, Eindhoven, Gouda, Heerlen, Helmond, Leeuwarden, Leiden, Leidschendam, Rotterdam, and Utrecht also apply a similar policy or have well-developed plans to do so.

However, molecular processes that cannot be understood from, or reduced to, a molar point of view also play a role here. I have demonstrated that, within certain margins, the official starting points of the protocol are disrupted. We have also seen something similar in the approach to road transport crime. In this context I have pointed to the generation of behavioral patterns that seem self-evident to some participants, although they entail the necessary arbitrariness in the implementation and enforcement of the CSB. The personal attitudes of the shopkeeper in question play a principal role here. For instance, where one shopkeeper may impose the strictest possible version of the CSB, others may be prepared to ignore much of the nuisance. This leads to an uneven treatment of the troublemakers. I also quoted the statements of shopkeepers that show that many alternatives to the official measure have come into being since the introduction of the measure. Some shopkeepers behave like petty dictators by imposing their own fines for violations, while other businesspeople may phone the parents of the troublemakers to confirm and underline the behavioral norm at hand. A general consequence of this policy is that, to an offender, there is great uncertainty about the way his or her case will be treated.

This poses questions as to the wisdom of the state in uncritically setting a responsibilization process in motion. It makes relevant the question of whether or not dealing with offenses like theft, fraud, intimidation, and vandalism can be left so easily to private actors such as shopkeepers. After all, not only has the CSB been devised by shopkeepers; it is also these very same people who carry it out. This makes the borderline between the individual private realm and the public realm a very diffuse one.

PART IV

The Era of Invisible Fissures

In the second part of this book, I defined a security assemblage as a short-lived or long-lasting constellation of territories, rules, and authorities. The relation between the elements of "rules" and of "authorities" was covered in the previous part of the book, where we examined the expression and content of the interactions among the authorities in four security assemblages. But the dynamics in the current security diagram can be thematized in yet another way. Accordingly, this last part of the book deals with the third element of a security assemblage: the process of territorialization.

Territorialization refers to that which defines the boundaries of a location. This process has two aspects that are inherently connected to one another. Reterritorialization involves the unification of a space—in other words, a coding of the place and identity of the people present. Deterritorialization refers to the disappearance of the coding that binds people to a certain place. The important point here is a spatial orientation toward the inclusion and exclusion (reterritorialization and deterritorialization) of people. This spatial process is articulated here and there and is occasionally studied, but it has not yet received the attention it deserves. The literature on security refers to the spatial concentration of crime (in certain neighborhoods, for example) and the role of the environment in the genesis of crime, which gave rise to situational crime prevention approaches, but, in contrast to many other social sciences, the physical and social setting is not wholly integrated into many studies on security. The spatial context (here regarded as "the city") appears as a "side show," states Keith Hayward (2004: 87; 2012), as something that must be added to the research in retrospect.

Life in the city is currently typified by areas that can no longer be understood on the basis of the classic "public-private" distinction. We have seen, in the chapter on nodal governance, that this concerns shopping malls, amusement parks, sports stadiums, and business estates.

The exceptional feature of these mass properties is that they are privately owned yet serve the public interest. Since the 1980s, the growth of these semi-public locations has increased enormously. This means that a previously mentioned problem again rears its querulous head. Anyone looking open-mindedly at the changes in the urban landscape sees that the categories of public and private into which territories are traditionally divided are no longer sufficient. To an increasing extent, the terms fall short as a designation of the spatial context in which we live. If one limits his or her perspective to the categories and characteristics that are attributed to these terms, one could well end up looking in the wrong places, with the wrong spectacles. The combination of activities and the reallocation of tasks in security entail new spatial orders, and again place old, often ignored, problems under scrutiny.

In French philosophy, the theme of the city belongs to a lengthy phenomenological tradition. Initially, the chief focus of attention was the experience and representation of the realm of dwelling: of the exterior and interior of being housed. The work of Heidegger played a prominent role in theoretical and ideological debates on this topic, as well as in French philosophy. In the shadow of Heidegger, his French contemporary Gaston Bachelard also wrote on the subject of the experience of dwelling. In *La poétique de l'espace* (*The Poetics of Space*, 1958), he emphasized the fact that the house itself is a specific experiential world, while seeking rapprochement to poetry to describe the very experience of dwelling. After May 1968, the theme of city and citizen assumed more political significance in French thinking. Changes in social and cultural life have been responsible for this, such as the rise of feminism and the squatters' movement. Although these groups have different starting points and are directed toward different goals, they share a criticism of the ideological starting points of the modern infrastructure of the city. They question the alleged value neutrality of public space.

The fight for the public domain and the idea that space is a social product return in Henri Lefebvre's studies on everyday urban space. Along with the sociologist Loïc Wacquant, who is perhaps the most important intellectual heir to Pierre Bourdieu, the issue of the city is also linked to the current problem of citizenship: being a part of a city.

Which boundaries can be drawn within a city? Which rights do the citizens have? Understanding the security diagram as a way of managing the poor in disadvantaged neighborhoods and ghettos in big cities, Wacquant sees risk management and penal powers emerging under the auspices of a "neoliberal project that can be indifferently embraced by politicians of the Right or the Left" (2010: 209). In that connection, he also mentions the exceptional role of prison. As he sees it, increasingly severe punishments are being meted out in order to respond more forcefully to all kinds of misbehavior, and prison sentences are being imposed for offenses that previously never warranted a restriction of personal liberty. In addition, in countries such as the United States, an increase in the number of people behind bars is taking place in a period in which a reduction in crime figures is actually occurring. In this way, Wacquant criticizes the idea that the prison has the single aim of locking up prisoners after conviction of a punishable offense. More than any other institution, prison participates, according to Wacquant, in the state's aim to enhance its power. It is deployed as a means to restore economic, racial, and moral order and to tackle social problems that are the result of the increased amount of freedom accorded to citizens since the 1960s. In doing so, prison directs its efforts to what Nils Christie calls the "control of the dangerous classes" in his book *Crime Control as Industry* (1993: 59–80; see also Garland 1985).

Besides being a matter of ordering, security is also a matter of normalization. The changes in security exert further influence in the spatial environment and have normative consequences that can, in my opinion, scarcely be overestimated. They lead to a different view on the theme of the city and the citizen, and also put pressure on classical legal principles and social ideals. In terms of legitimacy and justice, this leads to numerous new questions and problems. For instance, there is the question concerning the extent to which the previously discussed security assemblages introduce other divisions into the city and whether this is accompanied by processes of social exclusion—by the denial of access to the public domain to certain groups (see also Young 1999; Becket and Herbert 2008). Other questions relate to the democratic control over the performance of security tasks by parties other than the government. These are questions that generally attract less attention in the literature on security, although they are certainly not less important. It is precisely because of the far-reaching normative implications of security that the angle of approach of the next chapter will be of a more critical nature. Moreover, I apply a broader perspective than I have done in the previous part, by looking beyond the Dutch borders to similar developments abroad.

10

City and Citizenship

The urban infrastructure and the rights that can be borrowed from the use of locations in the city form the subject matter of this chapter. Ordering always concerns the allocation of places. More specifically, security is about the determination of boundaries. A typical element of this is the design of, and access to, public space. Much public space is designed in such a way that unexpected occurrences can be largely neutralized. This is called a "zero-friction" environment. Moreover, a whole body of regulators is often on call to ensure that social friction is precluded. In that respect, public space increasingly resembles a closed space with a strict admission policy. Not only is there mention of strong regulation of public space, but people are also progressively retreating into areas fenced off from the outside world, moving into guarded urban neighborhoods and luxury housing complexes. These developments toward partitioning and exclusion are articulated in terms of "splintering" and "capsularization" (Graham and Marvin 2001; De Cauter 2004). With this development, the question concerning the way in which these changes work and what they mean to security becomes very relevant. Which need do they fulfill and what are the consequences for the concept of "citizenship"?

Splintering

One of the most well-known contributions to the discussions on spatial changes that are currently occurring in and with respect to cities is that of the geographers Stephen Graham and Simon Marvin in their impressively thorough work *Splintering Urbanism* (2001). They propose the view that, from the first half of the nineteenth century onward, cities and infrastructural networks—street, transportation, telecommunications, energy, water—were always collectively realized. They developed simultaneously. Accordingly, infrastructural networks are inextricably connected to the physical and social fabric of cities, while the latter also consist of an interplay of infrastructural constructions. In this way, one can regard the city as an assemblage, a dynamic entity of highways, fiberglass cables, water pipes, and public transportation. The central notion in the argument presented by Graham and Marvin is that networks hold cities together and tie them to the hinterland. In that connection, they emphasize the fact that infrastructure is regarded as the glue of the city.

In historical terms, infrastructures were used to link urban functions and parts of the population to one another. Since the 1960s, the opposite tendency has been gaining ground. Infrastructures are being deployed to keep people apart. Graham and Marvin denote this process with the overarching term "splintering urbanism." The splintering or fragmentation of urban space goes hand in hand with policy through which national states have relinquished the monopoly on the delivery of public services and goods. We have previously seen that the state is increasingly retreating from the area of public amenities, and has transferred the onus to private investors and parties. The disintegration of infrastructural networks, which were largely nationally structured up until the 1960s, has thus led to the demise of a certain uniformity in public space. In numerous ways, the modern ideal of an open and neutral meeting place, a place where a collective world is constructed, has been abandoned. In response to the question as to what has caused the crumbling of the traditional image of the city in general and of public space in particular, Graham and Marvin discern five global trends. All of them are developments that make urban space less coherent and less collective.

First of all, they ascertain that there has been physical deterioration of the urban infrastructure. The degeneration of public space is painfully visible in old industrial cities in particular. In places such as Glasgow, roll shutters in front of shops, graffiti in the streets, and rising crime figures convey a grim criminal ambience. In addition, the economic crisis of the 1970s allowed governments little scope to invest in new facilities, but instead led to a reduction in expenditure on existing public amenities. As a result, many cities are still struggling with maintenance backlogs related to public space and the distribution and production of public services such as drinking water and public transportation. At the same time, a large section of the middle class have gone to live further from their place of work, so that the center of town has been left with an excess of poor housing. Complaints about social insecurity, high unemployment, poorly educated immigrants, and potential ethnic conflicts dominate everyday conversation. The media write about broken bridges, run-down highways, and polluted drinking water. The same themes are expressed in pop music. Think about "Motor City Is Burning" by the Detroit "noise" band MC5. The band sings about a city that changed from a prosperous working city into a moon landscape of asphalt deserts and abandoned factory yards after the major race riots of 1967 and the departure of the car industry in the same period: "My home town is burning down to the ground, worser than Vietnam."

The authors also point to the changing political economy. Partly due to pressure from economic actors such as the IMF, the World Bank, and the WTO, free-market thinking has come more to the fore. Whereas the provision of a broad palette of public services at standard rates once fitted into the tradition of the welfare state, this tradition has long made way for the increasing "privatization of urban infrastructural facilities" (Graham and Marvin 2001: 95). In this framework, it is notable that cities have entered into mutual competition. The competitive capacity of the city as a potential place of business location has suddenly become extremely important. Reacting to the fact that the world is becoming ever smaller and people can travel increasingly easily and cheaply, cities are now competing fiercely for more inhabitants and tourists. In addition, they vie to accommodate the headquarters of multinationals, to promote sea- and airports, and to attract international organizations, knowledge institutes, and laboratories. On the one hand, this international city mêlée has an economic aspect—having more inhabitants means greater income—but, on the other, it also entails an end to collective consumption. Custom-made infrastructure harmonizes better with the specific wishes and needs of new target groups than a diversified and large-scale public infrastructure for all inhabitants of the city. Brainports, knowledge clusters, and media parks give concrete substance to this trend.

In addition, Graham and Marvin describe the forces that have led to the demise of the modern ideal of urban planning. The welfare state enjoyed a self-conscious government that believed in malleability and governance. Political parties engaged in mutual ideological combat about the best way to structure society. However, toward the end of the previous century, people began to pay more attention to the limited possibilities of governments to realize effective changes in society. Large-scale strategic plans were regarded as inflexible and inefficient, while a businesslike approach to the layout of urban space received more interest. As a consequence, there was a shift from mega-projects that aimed to hold the city together as a unit toward "pragmatic attempts to address perceived local problems" (Graham and Marvin 2001: 103). Instead of a territorial entity that ensures unity and cohesion, policymakers began to see the city as a combination of various and separate zones that are connected by "nonspaces" (Augé 1992) or interstitial spaces, a concept referring to highways, private corridors, railroad tracks, and pedestrian bridges. Urban planners no longer attempt to understand urban space in terms of definitions that claim to have universal validity. Instead, they have become accustomed to the idea of a fragmented space, a space that even forms an "archipelago of enclaves" in its most macabre form (Graham and Marvin 2001: 112; Hajer and Reijndorp 2001: 53).

Another urban landscape progressively unfolded. Fragmentation, the physical spread of cities, regions, and districts, became a normal course of events. All this was linked to the rise of the automobile and the extensive network of highways that allowed a growing number of people to live farther from their place of work, on the edge of the city, for example. There was an exodus from the inner city, creating ghettos where clusters of poor families lived in zones with almost no public amenities or social facilities such as shops, transportation, and work. Although there were still major differences with the circumstances in the United States, for example, the number of underprivileged and run-down European neighborhoods and slums without running water and sewerage also rose substantially. With an increasing number of people exchanging the inner city for the suburbs, the vacuity of the city center became a clear social issue. As a result of decentralization and the growth of the urban periphery, the classical concept of "the city as a whole" began to come under great pressure. It is almost impossible to make a concrete representation of cities such as Los Angeles, where any self-recognition seems only to occur via the Hollywood sign on the slopes just outside the city.

As the latest trend, Graham and Marvin point to processes of social change and the rise of a broad assortment of political movements, such as feminism, environmental groups, and postcolonial disparagement of the West. Despite the different starting points and the aims these movements assign themselves, they adopt a critical attitude to the ideological principles of modern infrastructure. They criticize the idea of public space as an ethically neutral fact. In the struggle for equal rights, the feminist movement speaks of modern urban planning in terms of "a poem of male desires" (Graham and Marvin 2001: 124). Allegedly, the dominance of male over female is expressed in the architectural and urban planning layout of the city and the strict division between public and private domains. On the basis of this idea, feminism criticizes the exile of the woman to the private sphere and the association of the man with public life. To indicate the size of the fissures in the modern dream of urban openness, one can also point to the success of the squatters' movement in the West, the physical division between a small, powerful elite and the poor majority in developing African cities, and the growth of informal economies in the metropolises of highly developed countries (Sassen 1999).

Not on my island

The sociospatial deterritorialization of cities described in the previous section is a good point at which to begin to analyze the way in which the traditional image of public space is changing, but no more than that. It is also necessary to look at how the deterritorialization of functions and locations is connected to a reterritorialization of urban space, whether this concerns streets and squares, landscape structures, or hubs in a network. The dynamic perspective developed in the previous parts of the book is helpful in performing this kind of research on urban space. It draws attention away from a static urban vision and focuses it on self-organizing forces that enable new spatial orders (see also Farrías and Bedner 2010). In this angle of approach, I place the accent on the formation of guarded neighborhoods within which all kinds of infrastructural facilities needed to form a separate city are present. It is important to study the way in which the reterritorialization of such urban spaces entails changes in security, and how it influences the civil meeting function. In contrast to developments that occur independently of one another, the issues of ordering concerning territory, security, and citizenship are actually closely linked to one another.

A mosaic of separate units and screened-off environments with a rich concentration of infrastructural services and facilities at their disposal has arisen in countless cities. In that context, people speak of "enclaves" or "gated communities." Successful attempts at forming these variants of luxury containment can be found particularly in Asia, Africa, Latin America, and cities in the United States. An excellent example of this kind of location is Star Island, an island situated in the waters of the city of Miami. The island, which is accessible via a single safeguarded driveway, is home to film stars and famous sportspeople. The piece of land accommodates forty luxury houses, all of which border on the water. In the case of a move away or a forced sale, the house may only be sold to another superstar. Other well-known examples are Sao Paulo and Johannesburg, where wealthy population groups dissociate from the poorer districts. In this way, those with the most means have access to the best facilities. The outside world is dominated by the traffic chaos, fierce heat, crime, and noise pollution of the densely populated city. Inside, all conceivable facilities for a "city within a city" are present. It is a complex that is relatively independent of its position and direct environment. Whereas the poor districts suffer from a lack of infrastructural facilities such as running water and electricity, the residents of luxury enclaves have every conceivable "club good" (Crawford 2006b) at their disposal twenty-four hours a day. There are babysitters, servants, a laundry service, a newspaper and magazine delivery service, clubhouses, car parks, car maintenance facilities, shuttle bus transport, and the like. The normal relation between inside and outside is thus reversed, a phenomenon that the German philosopher Peter Sloterdijk calls "environmental reversal" ("*Umwelt-Umkehrung*") (2004: 331). The consequence of this is that the world outside this area ceases to exist. The world unfolds itself within the complex.

As a result of the great emphasis on isolation and the concentration of services and facilities, residents no longer have to leave their screened-off model city. On this point, the reterritorialization is accompanied by a reinforcement of the boundary between "inside" and "outside." Mike Davis (1992) was one of the first authors to point to this circumstance in his analysis of the militarization of public space in Los Angeles. Since the riots of 1992, there has been mention of increasing recession and flight of capital, severe cutbacks have been imposed, a vertiginous number of murders have been committed (despite the ceasefire agreed upon among the gangs), and the arms trade in the suburbs of Los Angeles has grown to enormous proportions. These four factors taken together have instigated a social dichotomy that has come to expression in architectonic terms in a series of inner spaces—gated communities, financial districts, cultural zones, senior neighborhoods—that are protected from the outside world.

City Walk in downtown Los Angeles is one of the most well-known expressions of this kind of structure. The complex is built around the idea of an American main street and reaches back to the period in which cars appeared only sporadically, and citizens could participate in public life in the city in a carefree way. This wide shopping street, designed by the Jerde Partnership architectural office in Los Angeles, is situated in the center of an area that is surrounded by car parks where visitors can leave their cars. According to the office, a unique area would be created in this way. "The only things kept out of this simulation are real poverty, crime and unplanned spontaneity," according to Jon Jerde. Cameras monitor all entrances to the obligatory car parks, and visitors must pay their parking fees in advance. Davis speaks of "Fortress L.A.": a city full of cameras, virtual moats, security gates, boom barriers, security services, fences, and walls that are designed to protect the residents of luxury complexes against an outside world with which they do not wish to interact. According to the Belgian philosopher Lieven De Cauter, this type of architecture works as "a space capsule, which creates an artificial ambience, which minimizes communication with the 'outside' by forming its own time-space" (2004: 29). In his view, airports, shopping malls ("no mall without a wall"), and theme parks are expressions of capsular architecture. An important change that goes along with this development is the restriction of access and free encounters among citizens.

Community forming is all about unity and difference, strangeness and familiarity. In view of the fact that community forming is only possible if boundaries have been determined, it manifests itself by creating an "inside" and an "outside" and by maintaining this difference. Reinforcement of security and mutual control then become of the utmost importance. In addition to the laws and regulations of the national state, contracts or similar legal arrangements come into operation in the demarcated inner spaces in order to guarantee the difference between inside and outside.

These instruments mark the transition to rules and prescriptions other than those that prevail in the rest of society. I have previously referred to the fact that, when someone buys a house in a gated community, he or she must also sign a detailed contract that outlines the local rules and regulations. These rules are linked to the lifestyle of the community and express the communal values and norms. They aim to enforce the correct behavior of residents and visitors. People entering these demarcated zones are expected to adapt their behavior to the regulations that apply within this community. In the shadow of the law, these regulations thus produce their own normality. In that respect, I wish to speak of a specific code of citizenship that prescribes a certain form of conduct.

Business Improvement districts

Growing feelings of insecurity and decreasing faith in the capacity of the national state to resolve problems currently play a major role in the changing way in which citizens wish to be protected against others in their direct vicinity. For instance, the police have at their disposal the authority to enter enclaves and gated communities that are partitioned off from the outside world, but the residents generally regard security as being much too important to be left to the police alone. They organize their own security under the slogan, "He who pays the piper calls the tune." Accordingly, commercial security services are hired in to enhance the feeling of security, in the broadest sense of the term. At first sight, such tendencies to create isolated, guarded zones scarcely exist in the Netherlands. To a certain extent, the welfare state still forms an important counterforce against the fragmentation of urban space. As yet, there are no hermetically sealed gated communities with high fences, thick walls, and monitored gates to repel unwanted visitors. Dutch private housing complexes tend to make use of soft edges and gentle transitions, in the form of a park or golf course, for example. Another difference with the situation abroad is the fact that Dutch screened-off complexes, inasmuch as they exist, are much smaller and normally comprise few facilities that cater to functions other than dwelling (Hamers et al. 2007: 96–101). With regard to the broader development toward the deterritorialization of the urban space, a remark must be made about the phenomenon of the Business Improvement District ("a mall without a wall"), a typical example of a place where it is difficult to create a concrete partition between public and private domains.

The Bloor West Village in the west of Toronto, with its twenty-five thousand inhabitants, was the first shopping area allowed to adopt radical measures to prevent further loss of customers and turnover. The result was a Business Improvement Area (BIA). In the literature, the BIA has become known under the name used in the United States, Business Improvement District (BID) (Williams 1996; Mitchell 2001; Brown 2008). A BID is preferably a private organization, authorized by the government, that provides collective services that supplement tasks normally performed by the national state. Entrepreneurs and real estate owners who wish to make their shopping area or business park more attractive to customers (and consequently enlarge their turnover) can set up a cooperative venture quite easily by means of a BID regulation. To do so, a majority of the entrepreneurs and real estate owners (thus, 50 percent plus one) must agree with the plans of the initiator. The great advantage of a BID is that all entrepreneurs in a district can be obliged to contribute to the costs of the measure when a majority of the entrepreneurs have agreed to the levy (Brooks 2008). In this way, the problem of free riders, which we also encountered in the chapter on the Collective Shop Ban, can be avoided. With respect to the measures that a BID can take, one can consider hiring private security firms, cleaning teams, and other staff that keep the area secure and clean to organize festivities and theme days to make the location attractive to visitors, and also take specific security measures such as the installation of surveillance cameras and lighting. These measures surpass the direct interests of the individual entrepreneur or real estate owner, and are directed toward the benefit of the collective.

Originally, BIDs arose mainly in American states. There are now more than sixty BIDs active in New York alone. They have a budget of eighty million dollars to spend annually. Small shopping streets have a budget of fifty thousand dollars, while larger chain stores have eleven million at their disposal. Following the American example, various BIDs have been established in the UK and Germany since the 1990s (Grail and Dawkins 2008). Anticipating a possible national introduction of BIDs, Rotterdam introduced the Business Improvement Zone (BIZ) regulation in 2007. Just as in a BID, this BIZ can levy a collective charge on the entrepreneurs so that it becomes financially possible to take measures aimed at promoting the attractiveness of the zone. Of the various projects started up, the Alexandrium BIZ is currently the largest and most well-known area. Alexandrium is a shopping zone in the Rotterdam submunicipality of Prins Alexander and covers an area of around 150,000 square meters. This is approximately equal to the size of twenty-five football fields and makes Alexandrium one of the largest shopping areas in Europe. The introduction of the BIZ has led to an expansion of the tasks and responsibilities of the security services in the shopping zone. The supervisory function, which was previously largely executed by the police, is now almost completely in the hands of private security guards who have also largely assumed the task of enforcing law and order.

Research into the enforcement of security in BIDs shows that the number of arrests by private guards is relatively small in comparison to the number of arrests by the police (Vindevogel 2005). An explanation of this can partly be found in the fact that private guards have fewer legal competencies than the regular police. At the same time, more attention is paid to the prevention of crime and the reduction of feelings of insecurity among the visitors. The emphasis lies on "neat and complete." Graffiti is removed within twenty-four hours and action is immediately taken against minor offenses such as noise nuisance, urination at unauthorized places, and public drunkenness. Cameras have been installed in most BIDs, security advice is given to companies and organizations, and the government and business circles exchange information on crime. More intensive supervision is directed toward "folk devils" such as beggars, tramps, drug or alcohol addicts, and loiterers. Where necessary, access to the zone is refused. Thus, here too, there is the tendency toward isolation and the desire to exclude undesired persons.

Sparta Rotterdam

Mike Davis is one of the most famous authors to point out that the city is not a homogeneous space but rather a place that consists of separate territories over which various groups exert some kind of control. In his *Ecology of Fear* (1998), building on the renowned urban diagram generated by Ernest Burgess from the Chicago School, he displays how the obsession with absolute security is reflected in capsular architecture that has NIMBY ("not in my backyard") as its slogan. On the basis of a classical Marxist vision, he describes the way in which the militarization of the city leads to sharp social polarization and spatial segregation. The rich people and the prosperous white people live in the fortified heart of the city. The ghettos and barrios, the quarters of the immigrant families and workers, surround this core. Both groups screen off their territories from one another with the technologies they have at their disposal, ranging from digital camera supervision in exclusive residences to barbed wire in front of broken windows in the underprivileged areas.

Over the past few years, much has been written about the spatial segregation in the security diagram and, in almost all cases, this concerns the anxious and insecure citizen, with much attention being paid to gated communities and controlled "public" domains (Blakely and Snyder 1997; Low 2003; Graham 2010). With regard to the elements of anxiety and insecurity, Setha Low studied the motives of people who bought a house in a gated community. In *Behind the Gates* (2003), she refers to the role of anxiety about becoming a victim of crime and to the residents' aversion to the strange, coincidental, and unknown. The wish to exclude undesired activity or undesired people from the community is well illustrated in the interviews with the residents: "I really like knowing who's coming and going" (2003: 147). Dutch studies show that the security motive to relocate to a protected neighborhood plays a much less significant role there than it does elsewhere (Lohof and Reijndorp 2006; Hamers and Tennekes 2008). In the Netherlands, families relocate mainly to private living domains such as country estates and recreational living parks in order to ensure a pleasant living environment and more transparency and predictability in their environment. However, recent research into privately managed living domains indicates that the new residents do seem to have a greater desire for security (Eshuis et al. 2011).

The above text indicates that various claims are being made upon public space. In addition, there is a strong tendency to screen off areas from the outside world, to a greater or lesser extent. By configuring these areas in a certain way, ranging from "defensible space" to "environmental design" and from "target hardening" to the "Secure Housing Quality Label" issued by the police, there is the expectation that the behavior of those present and their visitors can be positively influenced.

A consequence of this is that parts of the city take on the character of guarded fortresses as residents entrench themselves behind fences and boom barriers. It is tempting to regard the city as a strict dichotomy between luxury enclaves (for the wealthy) and impoverished locations (for the rest), but this ignores the way in which the previously described security assemblages demand their own place in the city. In other words, the territorial dichotomy discussed in the literature is too wide-meshed and too static. We need to adopt a more dynamic perspective in the study of governance of spatial security. A personal example can make this clear.

On Sunday afternoon, at 1:31 p.m., I close the door behind me to go to a soccer game featuring my favorite club, Sparta Rotterdam. In the doorway my neighbor informs me that she has registered for Civilian Net, an initiative of the police to enhance security in the neighborhood by deploying civilians to help in the investigation and detection of punishable offenses. The evening before, the police had left a message on her voice mail with the description of a man who had broken into a car in the street. If my neighbor were to see that person, she should call a certain number, after which the registration desk would send a police presence to the location. The walk from my house to the local shop, where I want to buy a bar of chocolate, is monitored by the security cameras of the submunicipality of Kralingen-Crooswijk, which link my face to a databank with photos of recidivists so that my face is compared to the faces of thousands of others within a period of sixty seconds. In more advanced forms, the cameras can recognize the emotions on my face. These may show that I am about to display aggressive behavior. It is now 1:35. I enter the local shop. This shop participates in the Collective Shop Ban project. Anyone displaying undesired behavior in the shop is denied access to all the shops in Rotterdam that are part of the same project. It is now 1:41. With the bar of chocolate firmly in my possession, I press my Public Transport chip pass against the scanner of the turnstile in the Oostplein subway station. According to the RET transport company, the chip pass is "easy, fast, and safe." With the approval of the municipality, the police, and the public prosecutor, all my travel movements are stored in a central database under a unique identification code. In this way, a complete overview is generated of the distances I travel with the subway, bus, tram, and train. Having finally arrived at the stadium, I show my season ticket to the stewards of Sparta football club, who are responsible for the order and security in and around the stadium. It is now 1:56.

What is immediately striking—at least, if one pays attention, because it is not absolutely apparent—is that one is consistently moving from one secured territory to the next. One checks in with one's Public Transport pass; one's face is recognized in the local shop. The consequence is that one has passed through five completely different security assemblages within no more than twenty-five minutes. And even then I am not speaking about the numerous smaller assemblages between my house and the Sparta stadium where it is prohibited to smoke or let one's dog out. In this way, there is a continuous space in which diverse upholders of the rules, sometimes in conjunction with the municipality and the police, are responsible for the security of a part of the route from my front door to the stadium. But regardless of whether one speaks of a carnival of detectives and security guards or of "little sisters" (Castells 1997: 301), what this example primarily shows is that the chance that one will be watched during one's everyday itinerary through the city has drastically increased over the past few years. The liberal application of security instruments such as cameras, radars, and other control and detection devices contributes to the situation that more people and objects can be monitored in real time. The fact that the less visible forms of security and the most visible security techniques cannot be physically or mentally removed from our living environment makes one curious about their effects on urban space. It evokes the question as to how urban patterns change as a result of the previously analyzed security assemblages. Which boundaries are shifting, and which new borderlines are being drawn?

Bird's-eye view

To enable a better understanding of the way security assemblages stimulate and impede movements in the city, it is first necessary to examine the ordering of the city from a bird's-eye view. Then it becomes evident that three molar lines give shape to urban life. These lines embrace the citizens and have their own history. As a result of their introduction into the city, the inhabitants are divided into demarcated areas where collective activities arise. These strict divisions are frequently determined by politico-economic factors and are grounded in ideology. Once they have been drawn, they produce specific effects and serve a certain purpose.

There are molar oppositions such as "city-countryside" and "nature-culture." Long ago such divisions ensured that citizens felt sheltered and protected against dangers that lay beyond their sphere of influence. In the city one was safe from the perils of nature. Advancing urbanization has meant a weakening of both oppositions. Whereas there were eleven cities in the world with more than one million inhabitants in 1900, the number of cities worldwide with more than three million inhabitants amounted to more than a hundred at the start of the twenty-first century. According to estimates, the vast majority of the "world population will be living in cities or urban areas within twenty years" (de Jong and Schuilenburg 2006: 45). Dual categories such as "center" as opposed to "periphery" and "nature" as opposed to "city" will then be obsolete. An urban life will even be possible in the countryside. Other oppositions have replaced the old ones. The subdivision into public and private is a good example of this development. The discussion about where "private" begins and "public" ends has a lengthy history, going back at least to the French Revolution. The end of the *ancien régime*, symbolized by the beheading of Louis XVI in 1793, ensured that the sovereignty of the monarch made way for the will of the people. No one had the exclusive right to rule over the people in his or her own name. In this context, the political philosopher Claude Lefort (1983) speaks of the "empty place of power." Two spheres are created to express what "life" entails. In the private domain, the government ought to leave the individual alone, as much as possible. Over the threshold of the dwelling, everyone can follow his or her own personal yearnings and opinions, and should not be troubled by others. In contrast, public space, the *agora* of the city, is a place where people can meet one another freely and where a common world exists. The free activities of thinking, speaking, judging, and persuading take place in this space, and every individual sets his or her longings and opinions aside for the common interest.

In addition, the city is divided into ever-expanding circles. This begins with the bed, the room, the house, the street, the neighborhood, the submunicipality, the city, and so on. This is the second molar line. This circular rationale continues to expand, and consequently wholly occupies the environment in which one lives and moves. Every circle accommodates one or more circles within. Expansion occurs when a circle is enveloped by a larger circle that, in turn, is embraced by a following circle. The larger the circle, the more complex the social structure and relations between the citizens and this inner world. The Czech author Vilém Flusser articulated this insight when he wrote,

> I built myself a house in Robion, so that I could live there. My usual writing desk stands in the middle of the house with the usual disorder of books and papers. I have gotten used to the village surrounding my house. There is the usual post office and the usual weather. Things become more and more unusual the further I get away: Provence, France, Europe, the earth, the ever-expanding universe. (2002: 100)

Finally, there are also linear divisions. In this case, there is mention of different periods or stages that follow one another chronologically: womb, family, school, work, pension, cemetery. In his or her life, the individual sweeps uninterruptedly from one stage to the next. What people call "growing up, growing old" are the shifts in these stages. On the one hand, this third line is characterized by the fact that every stage has its own function-specific place. Every place—house, school, office, old people's home—has its own physical, social, and symbolic features. On the other hand, each stage is rounded off as soon as a following stage makes an appearance. With this, there is a continuous series of separate spaces in which organizations consistently refer to one another. Each time, the individual begins at the beginning of every new stage. At school one hears that "you are no longer at home." At the office they say, "You are no longer at school" (Deleuze 1990: 240). In this way, a series of stages and spaces arises, in which one moves from point to point as if something new can always be added to life.

Much has been thought and written about these three hard lines. Historical study shows that every line has its own dynamics and does not always dovetail perfectly with the other two lines. Although these classical divisions are valuable as such, they do little justice to the security assemblages through which we move on an everyday basis. These rhizomatic structures break with the classical oppositions and modernist ideas of urban space. They run perpendicular to the molar divisions described here. Deleuze's notion of a smooth space is applicable in this connection, because the functional divisions of the three hard lines are dissolved in this configuration, as it were. In order to make the effects of a smooth space clear, it is necessary to devote more thought to the spatial effect of a security assemblage. But, before I come to that, I wish to conclude my review of the spatial division of the city with the introduction of the concept of the "bubble."

Security bubbles

Many people are proud of the city they live in. In the best scenario, the layout of the city harmonizes with the culture of the citizens. But the city is also a meeting place for people of very diverse backgrounds and cultures. Rules must enable coexistence and prevent conflict. Without regulations, many parts of the city would turn into a jungle governed by the will of the strongest. But if several parties impose regulations, a whole forest of rules will arise: a new form of jungle. In this connection, I have indicated that the urban space is populated by security assemblages that are expanding their sphere of influence through projects such as Civilian Net and the Collective Shop Ban. Whether or not these assemblages actually do increase security is a question that is not posed in this book. It can be stated, however, that external effects do occur with regard to use of urban space. One of the consequences is that new spatial orderings are produced.

In his *Sferen* (*Spheres*) cycle, which begins with *Blasen* (*Bubbles*, 1998) and *Globen* (*Globes*, 1999) and concludes with *Schäume* (*Foam*, 2004), Peter Sloterdijk declares that the oldest and most efficient means to create a space is to produce sound. In this way, prehistoric people could set up a division between the group and the surroundings by murmuring, talking, singing, and clapping, where the size of the inner world was determined by the reach of the voices. These microspheres screen off the interior from the exterior and provide the inhabitants with protection against the surrounding outside world. At the same time, the sealed-off surroundings form a reason to accept daily problems and challenges. Sloterdijk expressed the combination of both significances with the aid of the concept of the bubble. In our present-day society, the apartment is the bubble *par excellence*, according to Sloterdijk. The dwelling offers the resident an area of comfort, and screens him or her off from all kinds of harbingers of distress. In an original way, Sloterdijk thus demonstrates that even a dwelling can function as a security technique.

Sloterdijk's analysis is not only important for gaining a better understanding of living, of feeling at home, and of the strictly private atmosphere of the house itself. Sloterdijk also wishes to point out that there is a tendency to lay out the rest of our living environment as if it were screened off from the outside world. In that connection, George Rigakos and David Greener (2000) speak of "bubbles of governance." With this, they are referring to semi-public places such as airports and shopping malls, whose design now correlates with their controllability. It is of the essence that these bubbles can be clearly cordoned off to create a clear and predictable context, and therefore certainty and security, especially for visitors who are not accustomed to the environment. To enable these bubbles to function in an optimum way, the supervision relies upon permanent and all-embracing registration. In this way, the behavior and movements of the people and objects present can be closely monitored by means of computerized tracking techniques and systems. This means that a secure space can be realized by the techniques deployed. Thus, technology creates a certain spatiality, and also alters that concept. It is due to this spatial dynamics that I speak of security bubbles in this chapter.

In order to explain precisely what I mean by a security bubble, it is necessary to understand that the discussion on the city involves more than the classical philosophical theme of dwelling. The need for housing is only one side of the urban narrative. Besides the significance of dwelling for social and cultural life in the city, the process of spatial securitization also exerts an influence on everyday life that should not be underestimated. Although both themes concern security and protection, the impression that they coincide is incorrect. The dwelling as such is a clear example of the first molar line. It is a part of the opposition between public and private. In contrast to a house, security bubbles have much less of a fixed scope; in other words, they do not need to coincide with a demarcated piece of ground or location. Their boundaries are less attached to one place but are in every place where the movements of people and goods occur and are controlled. The new security techniques are all about traceability and algorithmic profiling, instead of imprisonment of individuals and normative consciousness of subjects.

For instance, with an Internet connection, one can view a database with information on shoplifters from anywhere in the world. The effect of this is that the urban space is continuously reproduced time and again, and repeatedly configured.

Gabriel Tarde, in his paper entitled "The Public and the Crowd" (1969a), supplied one of the first confirmations of the idea that techniques can create space. His hypothesis is that a third entity nestles between the individual and the population. He discusses "a public," and distinguishes this phenomenon from what Gustave Le Bon called "the age of the crowd." In new media, Tarde finds the most important explanation of the genesis of a public, first with the invention of printing, after which came the railway and the telegraph. Long before Marshall McLuhan's famous thesis (1964) that the printing press is more important than every book that was ever printed, Tarde declared that the art of printing brought about a completely new form of human organization that continued to increase with the spread of script. Technological endeavor and sociocultural standardization go hand in hand here. However, within a media theory frame, it would be incorrect to understand the term "public" as a sum of detached individuals in the way the term "audience" is often used. In contrast to a mass, a public is much more of a dynamic and specific concept. It refers to the way in which people with certain common qualities are grouped together, which Tarde calls "contagion without contact." It may concern a group of people with a shared experience or a common interest. This may be a spatial experience, as is the case with visitors to a shopping mall, for instance. But it may also involve a mediated experience in which the group of people are not physically present. The concept of "public" combines both elements. This means that security bubbles such as Civilian Net and the Collective Shop Ban are not passive casings but rather active processes that create their own public. The question is only, which public?

Not only can security bubbles be defined as space-generating techniques; it is also necessary to establish the way in which they actually lead to a specific use of urban space. The implementation of new technologies in combination with one's own formulated rules and punishments—regardless of the fact that these are often driven by the best intentions ("doing good")—can give rise to unforeseen social divisions. In that sense, the word "bubble" makes it possible to explain the ordering of the city in spatio-critical terms. Business Improvement Districts, where the shopping public has to comply with the regulations of the local authorities and from which youngsters are banned during school breaks, are illustrative of this situation. These regulations cover the visitors' clothes ("no shorts"), and private security guards are keeping lists of people who are denied access or may only enter the zone under supervision (Flint 2006: 60–61). In the urge to combat crime and disorder as early as possible, certain people can be banned from these spaces and the corresponding facilities. The consequence of this is that one is consistently forced to ask whether or not one is allowed access. I return to this topic in the final chapter.

Positive security

In this book, most attention is devoted to the significance of security in the sense of protection against crime and disorder. In this approach, the emphasis lies on the law and on breaches of the law by citizens. This connotation of security, justified by a "tough on crime" rhetoric and peppered with negative terms like "fighting," "combating," "tackling," "controlling," "punishing," and "preventing," is also explicitly present in the reconfiguration and revitalization of the urban space. Accordingly, in the fight against crime and disorder, the design of the Dutch post-1980 city center has been unequivocally oriented toward controllability. This is expressed, on the one hand, in a broad package of new measures and instruments, such as stop-and-frisk, bans on congregation, and the application of stricter rules against dubious entrepreneurs and firms. On the other hand, the quality of the urban environment should be enhanced by making parties other than just the government responsible for the security problem. These parties also apply various forms of control.

Although application of the notion of security in the sense of combating crime and disorder is not incorrect, the definition used does require extension. Paying attention to crime fighting alone leads to a situation in which little thought is devoted to aspects of meaning that designate other substantiations of security. My reading of Foucault's work showed that security also has other aspects of significance. In this context, one can think of the etymological fact that the word "security" in the Latin form also refers to an ethic of "care ("*cura*") without which no one can be secure ("*se-cura*") (Hamilton 2013: 284). In the Dutch language, "security" ("*veiligheid*") is closely related to the Middle Low German "*velich*" and the old Frisian "*felig*," words that mean "loyal," "dear," and "friendly" (van Zuijlen 2008: 12). Regardless of how obvious it may appear to be, academics seem to have forgotten that the idea of security not only refers to "crime," "punishment," and "control" but is also determined by notions of "trust," "care," and "belonging." Security is, in other words, "the producer and the product of forms of trust and solidarity" (Loader and Walker 2007: 8). As a consequence, security should not only be understood in a narrow or negative way, in the sense of us having to protect ourselves *against* something, but also allows leeway for a substantiation with more attention to the compassionate aspect of the concept, focusing on human connections and local capacity building as sources of security ("power to"). In the framework of this chapter, one could say that security has not only a negative meaning but can also be understood in a positive way. In that respect, an "antisecurity" standpoint (see, for example, Neocleous and Rigakos 2011) falls short because it offers no clear point of address for a new way of discussing the concept of security.

Security is a double concept. Security must not only be oriented toward the exclusion of risk and jeopardy, including antisocial and aggravating behavior, but must also be embedded holistically in more universal insights into the development of stable forms of coexistence. Focusing only on fighting or preventing crime and disorder results in little attention for aspects of security that point to connotations like trust, care, or belonging. In addition to a negative significance, the accent can also be placed on the fact that people always want to be included in social structures. They want to feel connected with things. They want to bond with people or things and feel at home somewhere. Walter Goldschmidt referred to this as "affect hunger"—in other words, "the urge to get expressions of affection from others" (2006: 47). With this, he emphasized that the pursuit of affective associations is just as strong as the urge to fill one's stomach. Such affective associations do not have to be, by definition, very robust. A defining precondition for feelings of security is that people feel at home somewhere and experience recognition. In that respect, people yearn for what one might call a "sense of belonging": "a feeling that members matter to one another and to the group, and the faith that members' needs will be met through their commitment to be together" (Chavis et al. 1986: 25–26). An interesting additional facet is that such an affective association is expressed in a forward approach—adopting an open attitude, directing oneself to a community (the neighborhood), and establishing social contacts. In this way, a spatial environment can become personal—with shelter and a feeling of security as potential results (Schuilenburg and van Steden 2014).

Anyone looking at security in this way does not narrow the concept to merely a protection against danger in the sense of combating crime and disorder, but actually supplements it with a positive sense of connection with the environment in which one lives. Concepts that often recur in this context are shelter, intimacy, familiarity, and hospitality. It is self-evident that the meanings of security, certainty, and shelter are mutually related. A loss of certainty and shelter can lead to a greater need for security. But an exaggerated emphasis on only a negative substantiation of the term "security" may produce insufficient understanding of how these other meanings acquire substantiation in the process of spatial securitization. For this reason, it is vital to develop a broader and more positive view of the process of securitization, based on the determination that security is an "essentially contested concept" (Gallie 1962); in other words, it is a fluid and dynamic concept. I begin my exploration of this situation with the previously described sociospatial fragmentation of the city. On the basis of the process of the deterritorialization and reterritorialization of urban space, I discuss two typical examples of the modern-day struggle for place and identity: the gated community and the "terrain vague." Which communality is present here? Which positive conception of security occurs in these spaces?

Gated community and terrain vague

The gated community lies in the extension of a series of protected environments that have a rich concentration of infrastructural services and facilities at their disposal. Edward Blakely and Mary Snyder (1997; see also Grant and Mittelsteadt 2004) reduce the differences among gated communities to three variants: lifestyle, prestige, and security communities. In the lifestyle community, protection comes in the form of fences and guards, but security is not the most important reason to move to such places. It is primarily pensioners and people with the same leisure-time interests who live here. The prestige community is intended for the rich and famous, the prosperous class that opts for a living environment with lots of privacy. The arguments of the residents who live in a security community are mainly founded on anxiety about crime. The idea is that everything that appears to offer a threat can be kept beyond the pale. Accordingly, streets are closed off at the initiative of the residents, and fences and barriers such as flower tubs are placed at strategic spots to prevent nuisance and minor irritations.

I wish to assign the name "*terrain vague*" to the reverse side of the gated community. The term comes from the Spanish architect and critic Ignasi de Solà-Morales (1996), and refers to an area that does not yet have a fixed identity, a kind of interzone or residual space. The interesting aspect of this term is that the word "*terrain*" refers to an enclosed space, whereas "*vague*" is related to the dissolution of that same space. This double meaning builds on the idea of temporary autonomous zones, places that are intended for short-term use before the local authorities, with their appetite for legislation, can sink their teeth into them. In his essay entitled "The Temporary Autonomous Zone," Hakim Bey (1991) demonstrates that such places offer an openness of which various groups can make unlimited and uninterrupted use. In this context, Bey—who was strongly influenced by the rhizome thinking of Deleuze and Guattari, as was Solà-Morales—spoke of "a temporary but actual location in time and a temporary but actual location in space" (1991: 109). The term concerns a vaguely defined location that has not yet been appropriated officially or definitively, and is allocated a provisional function. Here, one can think of empty, unused urban sites on the outskirts of the city and in desolate industrial zones. An important function of these empty grounds is that they provide space for collective activities and offer accommodation to vulnerable groups in society. Excellent examples of such zones exist in East Berlin and the free state of Christiania in Copenhagen. But virtual environments such as World of Warcraft can also fulfill the functions of a *terrain vague*. Without claiming that such practices are invariably effective, one can state that such structures involve a special relation between place and identity that differs from that in a gated community.

For a long time, the rationale of place and identity was derived from the symbols and rituals of the nation-state. The values and norms of the state provided significance at the level of identity. In the last few decades of the twentieth century, critiques of this modernist train of thought avidly praised the rhizomatic character of mobility. A world without boundaries would arise in which one wall after another— ideological, physical, mental—would crumble. With this evolution, the idea of a global identity that was no longer determined by nation, family, language, or religion took hold. The citizen was a "world burgher" and trade was global trade. Nowadays, people hold the opinion that matters are a bit more complicated than that. Not only does this apply at economic and political levels, but globalization also seems to have an individual and emotional price. For instance, the idea of a world citizen can easily be associated with a "McDonaldization" of our culture and, as such, with an increased lack of identity and a displaced existence. In my opinion, a discussion about place and identity will have to maneuver carefully between both positions. How is it possible in a rhizomatic world, to use Deleuze's terminology, to give substance to the longing for community and identity without retreating into a naïve world citizenship on the one hand and a conservative debate on national values and norms on the other?

It will be apparent that a gated community has little to do with what was called the "common interest" in the eighteenth century. It is not a sufficient answer to a public problem such as insecurity, but rather bunches together the self-interest of the residents. Characteristic features of such contractual communities are the physical traces that separation entails: fences, boom barriers, moats, monitored gates, and identity checks. Within the secure and controlled inner worlds, the outside world is defined as treacherous. "It's a dangerous world out there." At the same time, the *terrain vague* seems closely related to a utopian-nostalgic conception of premodern dwelling forms, and presupposes an authentic yearning for pirate hideaways and free states. Whatever the case, it is evident that what applies to the gated community also applies to the *terrain vague*: people claim a place and identity by taking their fate into their own hands. The most eminent effect of this, and this is the central notion in this chapter, is that a positive conception of security arises in those places. For instance, coexisting in an area screened off from the

outside world, such as a protected urban quarter or luxury housing project, can be reduced to a private need. But it is also determined by a sense
of community and the desire to build up a collective lifestyle. In the case
of the *terrain vague*, there is also mention of common interests and a
process of self-organization that, regardless of how brief they may be,
result in the genesis of a new collectivism. This provokes the question
as to which spatial concept can be applied to understand these dynamic
processes. For this purpose I introduce the term "*terroir*." *Terroir* has
to do with the specific qualities of a location, in much the same way as
stones can assume the color of the earth.

Terroir

Everyone who has immersed himself or herself in the domain of wine
will have encountered the concept of "*terroir*" at some point. Wine con-
noisseurs regard *terroir* as the most important characteristic of good
wine. In principle, the unique qualities of *terroir* have a major impact on
the quality of wine from a certain region. In that respect, people speak
of the identity of a wine when they taste the ground in which the wine
ranks are rooted. In this way, *terroir* gives wine a unique personality.
Plots that are only a few dozen meters away from one another can give a
completely different taste to the wine. The same grape sort can generate
a completely different wine according to the differences in the soil. But
not only does the wine taste different; the wine from one plot is regarded
as a different product from the wine originating from the adjoining plot.
Nowadays, the word "*terroir*" is used to indicate the unique character of
several products, such as fruit, tea, coffee, cheese, and tequila.

Although *terroir* has been an object of study among culinary gour-
mets in the past few decades, it remains one of the most complex terms
in the world of wine. The term arose in the French Bourgogne, where
each vineyard differs in *terroir*. Remarkably, there is no adequate translation for the concept. Sometimes the word "terrain" is used, and words
such as "soil," "land," and "ground" also crop up, although none of these
terms is quite specific enough to fully describe all the characteristics of
terroir (Barham 2003). To gain a better grasp of the meaning, it is best
to take the original French term. In the *Dictionnaire de l'Académie Fran-
çoise, dédié au Roy*, dating from 1694, "*terroir*" is defined as the typical

aspect or the specificity (*odeur, goût*) of wine that is related to the quality of a location. In etymological terms, the word "*terroir*" is a conjugation of "*tioroer*" and "*tieroir*," both of which are derived from the Latin "*terratorium*," which is a variant of "*territorium*." The Latin "*terra*" means "earth" or "ground." But what exactly contributes to a good *terroir*?

First of all, *terroir* is related to geographic and geological processes. In this respect, it primarily concerns the region in which a vineyard is situated. More specifically, it is related to the soil (clay, slate, sandstone, rock, chalk, marl) on which the vines grow. For example, how quickly can the soil soak up rainwater? Does the soil accept sunlight easily, and does it absorb heat? In this connection, one could speak of the natural capital of a location. Nevertheless, it is important to exercise a certain flexibility in localizing a specific *terroir*. The features of a soil on the west side of a plot may differ completely from those of the ground on the south side of the same vineyard. The color may be different there, and this plays an important role in the absorption of sunshine. Dark soils absorb more sunshine than lighter soils do, and are therefore more suitable for grape sorts that are intended for red wine.

In addition, *terroir* also refers to climatic factors: the climate of a country and the weather in a certain region, besides the average amount of sunshine and rain that fall on a plot. *Terroir* is also related to biological processes such as the quality of the vines and the specific grape sort. For instance, grapevines must be able to withstand drought, and white grapes require less sun than red ones. Searching for water and nutrients, the roots of old vines will grow deeper than those of young plants. And there is also the mystical aspect. Many peoples regard wine and its consumption as a mystic symbol. For instance, the Persian mystic Abû Yazîd wrote in the ninth century, "I am the wine that I drink, and the cupbearer." And in relation to the characteristics of *terroir*, the American geologist James Wilson refers to a spiritual component that he describes as "the joys, the heartbreak, the pride, the sweat, and the frustrations of its history" (1998: 55). People even speak of the spirit of the location.

Finally, it is also about human processes. The craftsmanship—the body of knowledge and expertise and passion for the work, to speak in Richard Sennett's terms (2008)—plays an important role in the stimulation of the right conditions for the growth of the vines. For example, the way in which a vineyard is laid out also has a great influence on the whole complex of conditions that promote the growth of the plants. The construction of terraces on steep slopes in order to capture more sunlight and the way in which the soil is treated to fight weeds and mildew are also of the utmost consequence. It is difficult to reproduce a total summary of the required human activity in this framework, but it is evident that *terroir* cannot exist without cultural and social capital: something that was recognized as far back as the seventeenth century by Sébastien Le Prestre de Vauban, the military strategist of Louis XIV: "The best *terroir* differs in no way from the worst if it is not cultivated."

In short, *terroir* is more than the ground alone. It refers to social, mental, and ecological processes, which Félix Guattari, in *Chaosmose* (1992), calls an "ecosophy." These processes always act simultaneously and work in and through one another. Regardless of how different these dynamic processes appear to be at first sight, they converge in the idea that a specific location acquires meaning and direction under certain circumstances, and that these circumstances can be altered to a certain degree so that the whole takes on a different significance. Take, for example, the winemaking tradition. In technical terms, plots that are adjacent can produce completely different tastes. This being the case, the wine from one plot is a totally different product from the one originating from an adjoining plot.

From territory to *terroir*

Despite the compactness of the allusions, there is sufficient reason to pick up on the characteristics of *terroir*, and thus give, in the process of spatial securitization, the issue of place and identity a positive input. It is a small step to translate the social, mental, and ecological processes of *terroir* into an urban context and the myriad of meaningful places and groups of people in the city that often brush against one another but never overlap. The interesting aspect of places such as gated communities and *terrains vagues* is that, first of all, there is a common basis, a social cohesion or alliance among people that is expressed in locally applicable values and norms. I have demonstrated that this can be enforced by legal means such as a contract or by physical protection through private security and boom barriers. This is the case in sealed-off dwelling domains where people choose to meet kindred spirits. All the same, feelings of insecurity appear not to be the sole reason for living in such situations. Many people cannot cope with the anonymity of the modern city. The yearning for "hospitableness" (Bijlsma et al. 2010) thus nurtures an environment in which social contact and neighborhood solidarity can arise.[1]

A second reason why *terroir* is interesting in this framework is related to the fact that a location does not need to be stabilized by means of defensive resources such as security cameras, boom barriers, and contracts. To keep a *terroir* intact, other processes that could be described in terms of "subjectification" and "the communal" ("*le commun*") are also possible. Keeping a living environment intact is not restricted to the configuration of surveillance techniques and defensive measures, but may also occur through other, more self-organizing processes, which range from feelings of solidarity to an active involvement in the neighborhood. Here, Tarde would speak of a mimetic contagion through which a certain method would arise to configure and demarcate a living space. In this context, the communal is that which a community makes or produces, and not just a trait that members of a community happen to share. It arises somewhere in the relations among social, mental, and ecological processes, and must be consistently produced in order to be able to survive.[2] This can be seen in the temporary use of areas to be restructured, which are used for gardening and recreation. Here, the production of the communal is generated via social connections and encounters. Thus, communality is not enclosed in an order that transcends the individual, such as politics or the nation-state, but is realized in the interactions among individuals and in the way in which this communality is expressed to the outside world. The communal is the provisional "outcome" of a local group process that enables new subjectification, such as in the form of collective signification among residents.

To avoid any misunderstanding: *terroir* does not coincide with the concept of territory. A quick glance at the conceptual history of "territory" shows that a form of governmental power is linked to this concept, which is exerted from a central point. Foucault calls this "sovereign power." The rule over a certain area is coupled with the protection of all subjects and the obligation to maintain peace. What we see today is that there is no easy way to exercise power based on a monopoly on security. In fact, there is an abundance of such powers and rational structures.

Terroir is also unrelated to Blood and Land (*Blut und Boden*), which refers to the connection between descent (blood) and the land that feeds a people. At the end of the eighteenth century, this kind of essentialist view of the historical links between a territory and a shared culture was anything but a strange notion, and was used by national elites to recruit the support of the people for the nation-state (Anderson 1983). From a romantic perspective, the nation is presented as a natural fact within which the internal differences fade away as the image of the community comes to the fore. In this way, the whole is superior to local group forming. Although this romantic vision strongly determined the discussion on place and identity around a century and a half ago, it will require little effort nowadays to persuade people that present-day social reality demands a new concept. For example, the vast majority of the world population has become much too mobile to accept this kind of static and often extremely nationalist view of place and identity. In this framework, not only is mobility related to social developments such as immigration and globalization, but telemobilization and automobilization have also enabled the virtual and physical scale enlargement of social life.

The right to *terroir*

The question now is whether or not it is possible to make a claim upon the configuration of local forms of ordering and identification in our urban environment. The plea of the French philosopher Henri Lefebvre for the "right to the city" (1972; 1996) can serve as a starting point here. The key element is the idea that the city is a project of all citizens. In this context, Lefebvre speaks of the city as "oeuvre," a collective process in which new ways to live are invented. The problem is, however, that an increasing number of places are being created *for* the citizen instead of *by* the citizen. As a consequence, residents need their own "right to the city"; in other words, they must lodge a claim to quality places where there is time for encounters and contact without commercial motives playing a role and without immediate assumption of property rights. It is interesting that Lefebvre wished to add the right to the city to the right to education, to work, and to a minimum living standard. More specifically, he formulated this right in response to the urbanization that was taking place all around him, basing it on the desire to reconfigure the social, economic, and political relations in the city. The right to the city is thus not a neutral observation. On the contrary, it has become a political ideal due to the fact that, to an increasing extent, an urbanity is being produced from which the citizens feel alienated and in which the production and consumption of urban space is made subordinate to economic interests. Authors such as Don Mitchell (2003) and David Harvey (2008) harmonize perfectly with Lefebvre's analysis when they demonstrate that nowadays it is a small political and economic elite that decides what the city ought to look like.

I have demonstrated that the present-day city is being increasingly splintered and fragmented. The idea of a city as a unit, as a freely accessible public sphere, has lost much of its expressiveness. The mutual cognizance of one another's activities and the mobilizing capacity based on sharing one's opinion with others in public space have become extremely constrained. However, the fact that the urban space is deterritorializing and the vitality of public space is coming under pressure does not mean that the need for a configuration of meaningful places has vanished. The plea for the right to the city, from authors such as Lefebvre and Harvey, is probably a little too optimistic, but does demand attention to the right "to change ourselves." What now comes to the fore is the way in which individuals can claim their own substantiation of *terroir*—thus, their own creation of specific social relations and life forms.

A claim to this is made possible, in my opinion, by translating Lefebvre's plea from the 1970s into a "right to *terroir.*" With the "right to *terroir*" I request attention to the productive side of *terroir*, to the social, mental, and ecological processes that play a role in that framework, and more specifically to new actualizations of collective subjectivity. With the terminology of *terroir*, I wish to emphasize the self-organizing capacity of contact with others and the way in which an identity is attached to this or that association of membership. On the other hand, I wish to refer to the fact that this identity, regardless of how provisional and short-lived it may be, can function as justification for the individual's demand for his or her own place in public space. The right to *terroir* can accommodate rights such as the right to community (the design of life in small and meaningful places), the right to differ (tolerance of practices that differ from one another), the right to openness (not determining how places will look several decades from now), and the right to citizenship (linking rights and responsibilities to local practices). It is not my objective to scrutinize all four rights. I limit my discussion to an elaboration of the right to citizenship. Here, the focus lies on the issue of the extent to which the classical concept of citizenship is still relevant to the current security landscape. Are other substantiations of citizenship possible, and if so, which ones are significant?

Citizens, denizens, and . . .

There is a plethora of ideas about what citizenship actually means. A distinction is often made between a formal notion of citizenship, which refers to citizens as members of a national state, and an informal definition, which refers to participation by citizens in diverse activities such as work, school, and sports. Another point of contention concerns the historical background of the notion of citizenship. According to some theorists, its origin lies in the ancient Greek city (*polis*), whereas others claim that citizenship is actually a modern invention—in other words, the outcome of the French Revolution. Within this modern idea, a liberal perspective shapes the rights of individual citizens, a perspective that can be distinguished from a republican viewpoint that lays the accent on the political debate and the influence of citizens on collective decision making. In this latter approach, the common opinion is that the public domain has more goals than merely efficiency and effectiveness. Conflicts among various citizens are resolved in the public domain by means of open discussions, and identity is given a profile at both individual and collective levels.

It will be self-evident that, in the above-outlined jumble of opinions, there are many overlaps and recurring elements in all kinds of standpoints. Nevertheless, one exclusive angle of approach is frequently chosen to examine and define citizenship. This element, such as the national state, individual rights, or decision making, for example, has a strong constitutive effect and helps determine the way in which citizenship is interpreted. Stated simply, one single element ensures coherence and cohesion. With the reflections presented below, I wish to make it clear that citizenship cannot be reduced to an ultimate essence of fixed significance. To gain a good understanding of the term, we must approach it in a different manner. I handle the benchmarking of the concept on the basis of a political vision of citizenship. The political significance of citizenship is expressed in the French word for citizen: "*citoyen*." On the one hand, this word is derived from the "*civis Romanus*," the free citizen in ancient Rome who had a number of rights, certainly in comparison to a slave. On the other hand, "*citoyen*" refers to the etymologies and wording of the city as a community ("*cité*"). Characteristic of the *citoyen* is that he or she does not retreat into the private domestic domain. Exercising the full expanse of his or her citizenship, he or she appears in the streets and squares of towns and cities. That is where the freedom of speech, thought, judgment, and persuasion occurs. The public domain is thus crucial to the concept.

I have previously discussed the fact that life no longer takes place in an undifferentiated urban space. Instead, there is life that assumes shape in numerous significant places, all of which mutually differ in character and magnitude, ranging from shopping malls to Business Improvement Districts, and from *terrains vagues* to gated communities. The question is then whether or not there is a form of citizenship that has a relation with the spatial changes involved in the process of securitization, as described above. A first clue to answering this question is offered by judicial theories about citizenship that establish a relation with the presence of immigrants in highly developed countries. In many countries, there are people who have a close relation with that country without actually being citizens. Not only do they live there; they also speak the language, have given birth to and/or raised children there, have a job, and go to school. In this case, we are speaking of immigrants who can be characterized as neither citizens nor aliens. These seminaturalized aliens can be called "denizens." This is an old English word that was used up until the nineteenth century for an alien who had been assigned the status of British subject by the sovereign by means of so-called letters of patent (Hammar 1990: 14). The longer they stayed in a country, the more rights these semicitizens or denizens were allocated. Ultimately they had fewer rights than national citizens, but they did have more rights than aliens. In many cases, these were civil rights that were closely akin to those of national citizenship.

The above-outlined category of denizens can be understood as an intentional collection of people. This categorization embraces the notion that a shared quality forms the backbone of a collection, and a collection constitutes a separate entity. This idea reaches back to the widespread but isolating practice of resorts and gated communities. Scientific research increasingly shows that the status of the residents of these units does not meet the criteria of classic citizenship but is somewhat similar to the position of a seminaturalized alien. These people are referred to as temporary subjects or "new denizens" (Shearing and Wood 2003b), thus elaborating on the idea of the congregation of citizens consistently changing in terms of size, place, and character. In this way, the term "denizen" refers to relations between citizens and governing bodies or certain mentality-forming practices, and the corresponding rights and responsibilities. These relations may be temporary (the visit to a shopping mall, for example), may cover a longer stay (engaging in a course of study at a university campus), or may even have a permanent character (living in a gated community).

As a result, two implications are important. First, citizenship does not coincide exclusively with the primary territory of a national state. In view of the fact that there are also other power forms and authoritative structures, it is better to speak of a patchwork of *terroirs* within a national state. Sovereignty and territorial association remain important features, but these are perhaps easier to find in places that can no longer be defined as completely public or unequivocally private. Second, citizenship is repeatedly discovered. This means that citizenship is rooted in the factual splintering of the urban space. The national state provides the framework, while the social practices provide the options for this development. In contrast to the political space that is normally envisaged in terms of a social contract and civil rights, the forming of rights and responsibilities depends on the specific practices in which a person participates. In this way, citizenship is detached from community and, instead, connected to the notion of the communal. In other words, the essence of the concept is sacrificed in favor of a more dynamic understanding of citizenship. One of the consequences of this is that a person may have more "denizenships" at his or her disposal. A person can go shopping in a shopping mall, and study on the campus, and reside in a gated community.

. . . margizens

The distinction between citizens and denizens does not bring us to the finishing line. There are people who fall outside these categories and therefore tend to remain out of sight. I refer to the people in this group as "margizens" (Schuilenburg 2008a). They are individuals and groups that are excluded from collective goods and services, which used to be called "public amenities." I wish to devote serious attention to this third group. After all, there is a growing number of groups in a situation where they have little or no access to certain places and the facilities available there. This being the case, the question is raised as to whether or not security is still a democratic good that unites society. Does security connect us? And to whom does security apply?

In response to these questions, an argument covering the substantiation of the concept of security is again relevant. It is clear that developments are taking place that can be interpreted as the genesis of exclusive locations to which only select groups are granted access and from which others are rebuffed. This occasionally happens on the basis of the law, but in many cases private initiative is the motivating force. Although these developments do not manifest themselves in all countries in the same way, the consequences of such development are widely distributed in the forms of separation and protection. Parts of the city are reconfigured under the guise of livability and security, and are screened off from people whom Loïc Wacquant (2009) defines as "discardable categories": the unemployed, beggars, the homeless, drug addicts, immigrants without papers. From the various examples of the way in which this occurs, it appears that it is quite conceivable that a situation might arise in which, on the one hand, commercial security services will be deployed for the areas that are in private hands (such as gated communities and shopping malls) and, on the other, there will be public police that direct their efforts toward the underclass regions for those who are not capable of purchasing security on the market (Shearing and Stenning 1981). In this way, margizens are subject to a punishment program, while denizens buy a security program. The primary effect of this kind of schism is that certain people are excluded from the facilities outside the underprivileged areas in which they live, and end up in a subordinate and dependent relation to other groups in society. They are temporarily (referring to short periods of time) and, in other cases, permanently excluded from participation in the life that goes on in other parts of the city. In that case, they suffer "civil death," to use an expression of Erving Goffman (1961: 16), as they lose many of the freedoms that they had taken for granted.

In my opinion, an important cause of this development lies in the "depoliticization" of democracy, a process with which a long-lasting and tenacious process of "desolidarization" of the security question can be associated. With the former term, I refer to the fact that all kinds of fundamental issues in our society have been stripped of their ideological aspects, ranging from the environment to public transportation and from education to security. With this development, these issues have been depoliticized. This has the administrative advantage that no ideological struggle need be undertaken with regard to the substantiation of these topics. In this kind of politics, it is necessary to exercise a far-reaching relativism that, as Alain Badiou articulates in his *Second manifeste pour la philosophie* (*Second Manifesto for Philosophy*, 2009), only acknowledges "the principle that there are no principles." The situation in which numerous fundamental issues are sacrificed to apparently neutral and widely supported "solutions," which are attained though negotiation and advocacy and which are presented to the citizens as universal consensus, is called "post-politics" (Rancière 1995; Mouffe 2005). The conflict between ideological visions of political parties that aspire to power and endeavor to win the favor of the electorate has been replaced by the collaboration of an army of spin doctors, PR figures, and opinion pollers. The consequence is that political parties scarcely differ from one another. Truly content-related differences seem to have disappeared; everyone speaks roughly the same language.

The depoliticization of democracy brings with it a desolidarization of the security issue. At the political level, there is consensual vision on security without a fundamental discussion having to be opened on the theme of underlying social, economic, or cultural causes such as exclusion and poverty. The prevailing ideology is one involving forceful action against isolated problems of specific groups in society, such as street crime, illegal habitation, welfare benefit fraud, and drug-related felonies. This desolidarization of security fits uncomfortably with sociologically oriented criminological research, in which the convergence of social arrears, poor economic circumstances, and insufficient access to the labor market is designated as one of the key causes of crime. In this sociocriminological research tradition, social and economic reforms are regarded as a means to reduce crime. That such insights are currently seen as rather uninteresting and unattractive in policymaking circles is shown by the fact that present-day security policy is scarcely linked to social issues such as work and education.

It cannot be denied that crime is a reality, or that it is largely committed by specific groups of people. But it is indeed the case that less and less political responsibility is being accepted for vulnerable groups in society. For instance, it is conspicuous that almost nobody nowadays defends the interests of an underclass. Traditionally, this concept has a socioeconomic meaning. Until the mid-1980s, it was much used in discussions on poverty, ethnicity, and social inequality (Engbersen 2006). The term "underclass" refers to the existence of a group that is characterized by high unemployment and low income, and has few or no means to realize the goals it has set itself. In the current security discussion, however, "underclass" has become a term that is solely associated with crime. As a consequence, ethnicity and income have become important factors in the security diagram. For instance, the registration of ethnicity is now being promoted in the Netherlands in order to achieve certain security aims. Examples of this strategy include the Polish people registration desk (*Polenmeldpunt*), where citizens can submit complaints about nuisance caused by Middle and Eastern Europeans, and the ongoing debate around the so-called Moroccan street terrorists. At the same time, inhabitants of some underprivileged neighborhoods or streets have to have a certain level of income before they can live there. The "Rotterdam law" makes it possible to impose income criteria on house seekers from outside the Rotterdam region, with the aim of discouraging people with lower incomes from coming to live in the city.

The depoliticization of democracy and the desolidarization of security are "sold" with the message that security is measurable and controllable and therefore can be managed. The execution of security policy is reduced to a cluster of technical decisions and seemingly neutral procedures. Security is problem management. As a consequence, efficient solutions are confused with good solutions, whereas the issue really involves difficult and long-term processes that do not lend themselves to short-term measures. Does one wish to tackle urban problems by offering inhabitants more opportunities and by giving them the chance to improve their living circumstances structurally, or is one merely seeking short-term success by fighting crime heavy-handedly in certain neighborhoods?

* * *

Security has an influence on institutional shifts between public and private organizations. Moreover, security is also connected to making spatial distinctions and the promotion and obstruction of movements in the city. Accordingly, the spatial infrastructure of the city has long been based on the idea of connection. Parts of the city and the surrounding countryside were once coupled to one another via networks and infrastructures and combined into larger entities. Nowadays, urban infrastructure has much more of a separating function. Security techniques are applied to create spaces of immunity that function as closed spheres, ranging from screened-off communes to shopping malls. These are short-lived or durable chrono-spatial orderings with their own forms of access, information, identity control, exclusion, management, and surveillance. The postulate that the use of public space thus comes under pressure not only says something about our interaction with security but also demonstrates that a different relation between people and their surroundings has come into being. This means that the established presupposition regarding the modern trinity of territory, security, and citizenship must be revised. Other terms are needed to designate the redrawing of boundaries and the concentrations of collective activities in the security diagram.

For a long time, issues of ordering concerning territory, security, and citizenship were associated with a clear political function. Whereas the old meaning of citizenship, as in "*citoyen*," referred to the political debate and participation in collective decision making, the public space was the place where citizens could freely meet one another and where a collective world was created. Besides the protection of life and property within the national state, security was primarily oriented toward streets and markets. People had to be safe and secure in such locations; they had to feel protected by the government against citizens who leaned toward malevolent activity. I have demonstrated that the three issues of ordering classified under social, economic, and cultural circumstances are now spoken of in other terms that, in turn, are part of other assemblages. With regard to the urban space, I have enunciated a positive conception of security that enables communality in diverse *terroirs*. In relation to citizenship, I have made a distinction between margizens and denizens. To the former group of citizens, security is primarily a product that can be purchased.

Ultimately, the aim is to comprehend the current coherence of the various security assemblages. Which sociability determines the relations in the assemblages described? Reflection on the mutual relations among the elements not only provokes questions about the splintering of public space but also obliges consideration of the practice of security in our society. What these questions have in common, both individually and in conjunction, is that they are no longer based on the pursuit of equality. The principle of equality—once one of the mainstays of the democratic constitutional state—is no longer a leading principle. Seen in this way, it is no more than logical that infrastructural networks disintegrate and certain groups are denied access to collective facilities and protected environments. The old alliance among territory, security, and citizenship has been broken. One day, the word "citizenship" will have disappeared from our vocabulary.

11

A Dynamic Perspective

As we come to the end of this book, let us look back and consider the implications from the previous chapters. In the past few years, the ordering of society has come to be seen primarily in the light of security. The fact that security has assumed the character of a societal project is related to social developments that have been taking place over a longer period, such as individualization, the rise of new information and communication technologies, and the increase in the magnitude and severity of crime since the 1980s. In this changing context, the call for more, harder, and earlier intervention has become louder and shriller. The effects of such developments have become visible in the nature and reach of the themes and activities that are currently being elaborated in security. In addition to the traditional investigation of crime, a more wide-ranging arsenal of measures is being applied to tackle insecurity. Parties other than government and modern risk management instruments now play an important role in this approach. As a consequence, a completely different situation has arisen, "with new actors, visions, relations, and a dynamism of its own" (Terpstra 2010: 44).

Responding to the plea to combat insecurity in an adequate manner, the new situation appears to be positive and hopeful: a lucid story in which security is less and less a governmental problem, and where work is collectively executed to ensure a safer future. At the same time, the changing context also induces numerous questions. To a significant degree, these questions relate to the necessity to obtain a better view of the changes that are currently taking place in the Western security diagram. This brings me to the objective of this book: to develop a new and, in many respects, critical perspective by means of which the dynamic character of security can be investigated as a whole. Moreover, I regard it as important to obtain knowledge and more insight into the way parties with various backgrounds collaborate in the tackling of security issues. Few scientific facts are known about the dynamics of, and within, public-private partnerships.

From a theoretical standpoint, the work of Michel Foucault, Gabriel Tarde, and Gilles Deleuze has formed a useful guideline. Studies of their concepts of security, interactions, and assemblage have led to a dynamic perspective that promotes a better understanding of changes in general, as well as specific effects on security. At the same time, such concepts encourage more discerning empirical and normative analysis and description. Subsequently, four case studies investigated the actions of the authorities participating in a security program, with the aim of making visible specific outcomes in concrete situations. The role distribution of the authorities in these partnerships was consistently different, ranging from support from the police in the Collective Shop Ban to the implementation of control measures by energy companies in the combating of marijuana cultivation. The theoretical and empirical studies touched upon the social issues of inclusion and exclusion, and led to questions about the legal equality of citizens. For this reason, I discussed the changes in urban space and recent developments with regard to the question of citizenship.

What and wherefore

Attempting to give a full overview of the social developments that have led to the current situation in security is a tricky business. Various developments have already been comprehensively discussed in the literature on security. Accordingly, I limit this review to the reiteration of a few conclusions that contribute to a better understanding of the context that forms the basis of this book. A generally accepted starting point is that, to an ever-increasing degree, the police are being surrounded by numerous police-like organizations of which private security firms and civil initiatives are the most conspicuous. As a result, the responsibility for security is spread across several parties, with the government being merely one of these. These facts do not harmonize with the (partly assumed) monopoly of the government on security as a public good, as summarized in the political philosophies of Hobbes and Beccaria on the topic of the government's responsibility to enforce order. On the basis of the social contract, a government "which is great enough for our security" (Hobbes 1963: 173) is installed.

I have demonstrated that this alteration can be clarified on the basis of the nodal orientation, as described by Clifford Shearing and his colleagues. They point to the fact that security, as a public good, has not been exclusively in the hands of the government since the 1980s, and is no longer reserved for specialized state agencies. The rise of the network society is an important reference point here. In *The Information Age*, Manuel Castells describes the way in which the position of the government is organized in a different way than used to be the case, due to IT usage and the genesis of global networks. The nodalists also refer to Foucault's ideas on power with the argument that the power to configure security is no longer exclusively in the hands of the state and police. Modern society does not have one unique center from which power is exerted, but rather several centers of power. This means that the governance of security is the result of consistently changing alliances between public and private parties and is not the outcome of a government monopoly on the implementation of security. In that context, I speak of a "hybrid security model."

The movement from monopoly model to hybrid security model fundamentally changes the relations between public and private parties. In the criticism of the nodal orientation, however, we have seen that the literature pays little attention to the dynamics between public and private parties. There is insufficient consideration of the interactions and significances that the authorities ascribe to their own and one another's actions in the execution of security tasks. As a consequence, it remains unclear whether and to what extent variations occur in the execution of a security program. On this point, nodal literature lacks reality. The issue of how the reality content of the study on security can be enhanced now becomes very apposite. My hypothesis is that this is made possible by taking change itself as the basis of deliberation—thus, without attaching fixed outcomes to change. This may sound somewhat abstract, but the issue becomes clear when its theoretical consequences are examined in more detail. Thinking on the basis of change implies that static representations of security no longer form the starting point of research. In this framework, I am primarily referring to divisions that confine reality to logical and fixed compartments, partitioning it into dualisms such as "public-private," "micro-macro," and "subject-object," for example. Making use of such conceptual pairs makes it difficult to fully come to terms with the dynamics involved in security. The dynamics are rendered harmless, as it were, before they can be considered. In *Götzen-Dämmerung* (*Twilight of the Idols*), Nietzsche spoke of "concept-mummies" (1994: 298), notions that give social reality a firmness that it does not inherently possess. Accordingly, it is not enough to approach the current organization and execution of security from a strict division or a simple sum of private and public characteristics, as long as it has not yet been empirically demonstrated which meanings are produced in the security diagram, and a comprehensible account can be given of how that actually happens.

The relational

The leitmotiv of this book is the work of Foucault, Tarde, and Deleuze: three thinkers who tell one story accompanied by various kinds of music. Their work makes use of a conceptual vocabulary by means of which the dynamic character of security can be understood in a much more precise way than through the terms used in the work of Beccaria ("law"), Hobbes ("the police"), or Durkheim ("culture"). As my analysis showed, these French authors begin with relations that are always situated in the middle and have their own autonomy. This is a common concept in their work, but it is given a different elaboration each time. Foucault summarizes the relational under the denomination of "power relations." In his view, power should not be regarded as a self-evident concept but preferably in a relational way in which power itself is an object of continual change. In the interview entitled "The Ethic of Care for the Self as a Practice of Freedom," he explains in a polemic way never to use the word "power": "[A]nd if I do sometimes, it is always a shortcut to the expression I always use: the relationships of power" (2004b: 196). The confrontation with Foucault's thinking demonstrates that power works from a basis of a multitude of relations that are always unstable and fluid. These relations are inherent in society and permeate all societal levels. In this context, I have referred to the security power relation, which Foucault introduced in his lectures at the Collège de France in 1978 and 1979. With this concept, his analysis of power in *Discipline and Punish* and *The Will to Knowledge* takes a different turn. In contrast to discipline, security does not create clear segments or lines of fracture in society, but actually has the tendency to integrate various fields in new wholes.

The security power relation made its mark in the nineteenth century with the problem of public health and the fight against smallpox. The tackling of smallpox involved preventative measures that affected the entire population. Statistical data formed the basis of the norm, and groups that formed a potential risk to one another or to society as a whole were charted ("a medical model"). With the term "securitization," I refer to the gradual occupation of society, from the nineteenth century onward, by techniques that are mobilized by a multiplicity of authorities with the intention of making the future secure and certain. In this process, the general features of prevention, population, normalization, and risk impose themselves upon society. Security works like a virus in this type of framework. It invades aspects of life such as spatial planning, welfare, housing, and education, and connects these domains with one another in ever-increasing entities—in organizational, spatial, programmatic, or other senses. A characteristic feature of this byzantine process is the fact that security is changing from a defensive concept—the rebuttal of intruders from outside and the punishment of offenders—to an offensive one. Despite the fact that Foucault demonstrates that, with security, the individual and collective body of the population is being thrust into a new discourse on knowledge and power, he pays no attention to the political discussion that helps dictate the character and use of security techniques. In my study of Foucault's power analysis, I have observed that he displays little interest in the fact that citizens and organizations wish to be actively involved in the security issue and therefore see themselves as a part of the solution to insecurity in society. Moreover, I have pointed out that the notion of security in the work of Foucault has nothing to do with people of real flesh and blood and their corresponding emotions and feelings.

We have seen that the relational also plays a major role in the work of Tarde. Just as Foucault introduces power relations into his work without making them subordinate to a law or organization, Tarde devotes attention to human interactions without reducing them to a fixed order or underlying structure of significance. In his criticism of the functionalist approach of his contemporary Durkheim, which dismissed rebellious behavior and the exercise of power, Tarde demonstrates that actions can come into conflict with one another and can breach fixed patterns. With this, he directs attention to the ordinariness or banality of action and interaction in the immediate present. A most relevant aspect here is that this banality redirects ideas on change to the countless ways in which we orient ourselves in local situations, and to the way in which differences of opinion and conflicts with other people arise and are settled.

In my interpretation of Tarde's ideas, I have argued that he approaches the relational (here understood as "social relations" or "interactions") as an independent entity that serves as a foundation for the dynamics in social reality. The relational possesses an autonomy that is not inherent in the people who bind it together. According to Tarde, human interactions do not allow themselves to be tied to one single moment, but rather continue to advance uninterruptedly in various new series and thus ensure ongoing change in social reality. We have recognized this in processes of imitation and invention, two self-explanatory series of relations, each of which forms a reality in itself but also influences the other. This means that, in the spread, all kinds of new series are formed that fertilize one another so that new relations arise that, in turn, generate yet other series of imitations and inventions. With new series being added to the existing ones, the possibility for creation remains open and social reality continues to move, and to exist.

Of the three authors, Deleuze focuses most explicitly on the relational in his thinking. In this connection, I referred to an important difference between Foucault and Deleuze. Instead of the use that Foucault makes of power relations, Deleuze makes a plea in favor of the productive character of desire (*désir*). "Desire causes the current to flow, itself flows in turn, and breaks the flows," write Deleuze and Guattari (1972: 11) in *Anti-Oedipus*. Whether or not Deleuze has been successful in surpassing Foucault's analysis of power is less important in this study than the question of how the above-described power relations and social relations manage to relate to one another in such a way that a certain consistency arises with respect to one another. In this field, use has been made of the concept of assemblage, as covered briefly and schematically by Deleuze. Although he never explicitly says so, the idea of an assemblage implies that change and stability are inherently connected. One can also state that an assemblage is something that is "relatively fixed." In this connection, I have elaborated an assemblage as a cross-linkage of power relations and interactions in a specific environment, where every element of an assemblage can be regarded as a new assemblage, *ad infinitum*. In an assemblage, heterogeneous elements attach themselves to one another and form new combinations that do not fall back upon and cannot be reduced to general categories such as "private-public," "micro-macro," and "subject-object." More specifically, I have demonstrated that an assemblage has its own operational power. An assemblage is self-organizing. This self-organizing activity lies in the relations that enable the elements of an assembly to function, as in the rattling and sputtering machines of the Swiss artist Jean Tinguely, in which the construction of coincidence due to the imperfections of technology is a constant theme. The steering power of this relational process is therefore never outside the assemblage. As a consequence, the effect of an assemblage can never be declared in advance, but can only be analyzed retrospectively in its subsequent given order.

Dynamic concepts

The lack of accessibility that can be ascribed to the three French authors vanishes when their thinking is used as a tool to obtain a better understanding of the dynamic character of security. What is needed are analytical and investigative instruments that one can use to distance oneself from a static representation of security. One could also say that more dynamic concepts are required in order to acquire a better understanding of the complexity of security. Dynamic concepts encompass the process-based character of reality. In doing so, they are more related to processes of change than to fixed structures. They also leave the outcome of processes open, and therefore do not fossilize those processes in the rocks of previously given significances.

Remarkably, it is not easy to find such concepts in the literature on security. Security thinking is strongly controlled by a "constant process-reduction" (Elias 1978: 112). The stability of entities is given pride of place, with a static situation being assumed to be the normal state of affairs. Despite the fact that there is mention of a growing, albeit still limited, interest in network-like organizational structures and the increasingly complex problems of security, more account could be taken, in my opinion, of the way things are related to one another. The inclination toward situation reduction also plays a role in another way, one of its consequences being that thinking about security is primarily directed toward order and harmony, at the cost of conflict and competition. Retention of the existing order is regarded as the most important goal. Conflict is interpreted as being oriented toward disturbing the order, without actual acknowledgment of the possibility that a qualitatively new order can arise from the conflict.

The security assemblage introduced in this book is the most important example of a dynamic concept in which elements are related in a mutually dependent way. I have defined a security assemblage as a short-lived or durable constellation of territories, rules, and authorities. It is important to realize that a security assemblage refers to other assemblages that already work or should begin to work, and change character as soon as new elements are added or old elements slip away. The security assemblages, which are always in motion, therefore cannot be demarcated by assigning them hard boundaries and separating them from the rest of social reality. This implies that the starting point of research on security is no longer tied to traditional parceling such as "micro-macro" or "public- private." The study is therefore not obliged to formulate solutions and dilemmas against a background of such antitheses.

At various points, this approach is absolutely up to date, such as in the way the issue of security is currently governed in countries such as the Netherlands. Because security is too important to leave exclusively to the police, its approach is no longer regarded as a matter for the penal system alone. Energy companies, health-care institutions, insurance firms, citizens, and shopkeepers for whom the tackling of security is often merely a secondary function have also become responsible. The new distribution of responsibility is most lucidly characterized by an integral approach to security. Typical of this integral approach is that, on the one side, account is taken of all factors that could threaten or promote security and, on the other, the concern for security is a responsibility shared by public and private parties. The behind-the-front-door approach of urban intervention teams, whose goal is both preventive and repressive ("prepression"), forms a good example in this context. The teams change in terms of composition, but mostly consist of police officers, members of staff of the municipality, and representatives from relief and care institutions. Through the tracking of punishable offenses and the application of preventative interventions in fields such as education and housing, attempts are being made to improve livability and security in local neighborhoods.

To apply a security assemblage as a practical concept to study the dynamics in security, I have distinguished two levels. There is the molar level of the aims and the agreements that are made to reduce insecurity. But I have also defined as "molar" actions with a large degree of predictability, such as technical routines, daily rituals, and the formal use of language by the authorities. Attention in security is generally devoted to the molar level of an assemblage and the results attained by the specific way of working. However, the molar is merely one descriptive level from which to deduce hypotheses about the way changes in security work. At the same time, there is a molecular level that cannot be envisaged within the "usual" constellations of representation. The conclusion that a security program is an ordered entity with a clear preparation, decision, and execution is therefore too simple. There will always be activities and interactions that collide with and tumble over one another without the authorities having much grip on them. It is this ordinariness or banality that is continually active in security, I believe, and can develop unexpectedly and in unforeseen ways. On this point I have referred to molecular processes that govern themselves and have their own dynamics, and that are at odds with the structure that has been imposed top-down. This means that security measures are always taken at the molar level, but they are simultaneously determined by molecular processes.

Thinking the consequences through

It is tempting to regard the molar and the molecular as two different levels in which knowledge-theoretical claims are reserved for the molar level and ontological claims for the molecular. The danger of this reduction is that the hybrid character of the molar and the molecular may vanish from the analysis of security. "Hybrid" means that the tension between the molecular and the molar is permanent, due to both levels being simultaneously active and consistently reciprocally interlocked. The distinction between both levels in a security assemblage is therefore primarily useful as an analytical tool. To avoid confusion, I prefer to speak of "sensitizing devices"—a term applied by Anthony Giddens (1984: 326)—that make a researcher receptive to phenomena that previously escaped him or her and that can help in the interpretation of his or her findings. In view of the conceptual apparatus I have developed in this book, I wish to conclude this study by discussing the consequences of this development with regard to three themes: (1) the implementation of security, (2) the effects of the new measures for certain groups in society, and (3) the democratic control of the activities of the participating parties.

(1) Recurring problems

When the molecular is taken as the leitmotiv or descriptive level of the study on security, one sees that a world gradually unfolds that is completely different from the one that politicians and policymakers refer to. In real-life practice, the world of security turns out to be muddier and messier than the molar perspective wishes to or could reveal. In the tackling of road transport crime, there were the inventions, to quote Tarde, of damage experts to stimulate the police to undertake action more rapidly, by breaking into a shed themselves where they know that stolen goods are stored, for example. In the combating of marijuana cultivation, the narrative and the motivating statements of the participants illustrate that the dismantling of plantations is more than merely an instrumental application of enforcement measures. The partnership is more a matter of trundling forward than of a streamlined strategy in which the participants work purposefully toward the dismantling of a plantation. And with the Collective Shop Ban, the alternative sanctions imposed by shopkeepers to punish unacceptable behavior—ranging from making the offenders pay double for the goods in question to the application of naming and shaming—refer also to something that radically disregards what has been legally organized or has been formally specified in the covenant with the local government.

If the goal is to demonstrate how these cases are representative of the dynamic perspective on security, it is not necessary to gather more empirical data. Rather, the research must show regularities that can provide insight into what is unimportant in a case and what is elementary. A difficulty here is that occurrences and interactions at the molecular level are often scarcely visible or noticeable. On the other hand, they do have the potential to disrupt a security assemblage, which means that an existing order is broken open and dispersed in directions that have not been agreed to in advance or specified in official documents. The most important conclusion that can be drawn from this is that security assemblages are primarily unstable entities that undermine malleability thinking. And it is exactly this malleability thinking, which relies upon an anthropocentric vision in which the human being is the measure of all things, that is directive in much security policy. I have demonstrated that this train of thought is a rational-mechanical approach to the problem at hand. The consequence of this is that the complexity of reality is calibrated at a low level. Many of the results obtained in the empirical research actually do not come from the presence of strong molar tools, but from the presence of strong molecular processes. Accordingly, one has to be constantly aware of the uncertain processes over which one has little or no external control, and that work differently from the approach to security at a molar level.

Due to the fact that interactions and occurrences never fully crystallize, and continue to branch out in all directions, it is inevitable that certain matters have been amplified. A good example here is the ignition of a fire to ensure that the police will come to a shed full of stolen goods. This kind of conduct can lead to an (over)simplification of the molecular, and give an erroneous picture of cooperation in the security assemblages studied. In the vast majority of cases, there is mention of a good reciprocal team spirit, and the authorities are positive about the input of their colleagues and the results attained. Nevertheless, it is conspicuous that, in the assemblages studied, numerous problems arose for which classic state law enforcement aims to provide the solution. For example, the classic state aims to solve problems resulting from conflicts of interest, coordination problems, abuse of power, and arbitrariness when citizens have to protect their own interests in their own way. I have previously shown that the approach to road transport crime is characterized by conflicting interests between insurers and the police. This is the reason why damage experts tend to behave as police officers when carrying out their investigations. At the same time, the approach of the urban intervention teams illustrates that collaboration can in no way be taken for granted. Accordingly, the intended integral approach has difficulty getting off the ground because the authorities identify more strongly with their own organization than with the common goal of the intervention team. In this case, the molar level has acquired a degree of robustness that ensures that it can absorb any deviating actions. Regardless of how different the case studies may be, they have in common the fact that, when security is no longer enforced by the state, the same problems that the state wished to resolve actually appear to return.

(2) Selective exclusion

New security assemblages have opened up the city and made it controllable. At the same time, these assemblages bring citizens together in new entities. As Foucault remarked, "to police and to urbanize is the same thing" (2009: 337). This spatial revolution is perhaps one of the most striking aspects of the securitization process. As I mentioned earlier, in that process, an increasing number of areas are being approached with security in mind, and security techniques are being applied on an ever-expanding scale. In conjunction, these changes seem to tell the story of a society gravitating toward the safest point. But they are also accompanied by an increasing loss of democratic control and by processes of exclusion. With this, the question arises as to how security can facilitate inequality and play a role in moral issues concerning who is granted or denied access to certain parts of the city. Which citizens count and which do not?

Immunity and screening-off are playing an increasingly extensive role in urban space. A good example of this development is given by the conspicuous markings in the landscape that serve as physical evidence of a separate lifestyle, such as the high fences, thick walls, and guarded gateways of gated communities. Besides the physical architecture of these demarcated locations, I have also pointed to a more complex phenomenon. Security assemblages such as urban intervention teams and the Collective Shop Ban make it clear that security as a social problem cannot be independent of its spatial dimension. These assemblages demand their own place in the city, and have the capacity to draw and control new boundaries in this context. A relevant aspect here is that these boundaries present a different reality to different groups in society. This is shown by the Collective Shop Ban through which offenders can be denied access to large parts of the city center for a period of a year. In this way, certain people are excluded from the inner city and the corresponding local facilities. I have referred to such people as "margizens."

The situation that an increasing number of people are being denied access to certain places and the corresponding facilities occurs in several countries. For instance, Katherine Beckett and Steve Herbert (2009) investigated the way in which undesired people were refused access to various areas in Seattle and the way they reacted to this refusal. They concluded that it is mainly poor people who are banished, with the black population being the greatest victim of the new security policy. The aim of the banishment is to improve the quality of the location in question. Another aim that should justify the ban, it is claimed, is that people who are excluded "are encouraged to desist from any deviant behaviors in which they may engage" (Beckett and Herbert 2009: 105). The authors provide various arguments for why they give preference to the term "banishment" rather than "exclusion." With banishment they wish to emphasize the coercive power of the government to refuse people access to certain places by means of an official decree. Moreover, they wish to draw attention to the punitive character of the measure. The problems of the people in question, often homeless and addicted, are generally seen as criminal issues. In addition, the term closely connects to the experience of the people who are banished. In the Dutch case, Henk van de Bunt and René van Swaaningen have used the same term to point to "the temporary or permanent denial of access to offenders or potential offenders to certain places or functions" (2004: 674; see also Boone and van Swaaningen 2013).

Although no term is perfect, it seems obvious that "banishment" is too general and has too little relevance to the security diagram in which this technique is exercised. In previous chapters, I have demonstrated that the inclusion and exclusion of people always depends on a specific assemblage, each of which has its own rules and punishments. In this study, we have come to realize that an assemblage is not sharply delineated and changes continually: in form, reach, content, goal. Accordingly, I prefer the term "selective exclusion" due to its more specific meaning. "Selective exclusion" reaches further than the term "banishment," which is associated with the state and which Foucault called "classic power" or "the power of law." In this latter usage, the emphasis lies on the monopoly of the state to implement rules and sanctions by means of the tools of public legislation. In addition, banishment is more related to the removal of people from a community. People are literally expelled from the common case—sent away from a village or town—such as in the case of the banished lepers in early modern Europe. In contrast, selective exclusion is a much more dynamic concept because it refers to the fact that there are all kinds of social divisions in the city that entail their own public and particular rules of behavior—creating fragmented security at the micro-level. In this construction, offenders are no longer welcome in distinct parts of the city in which separate social regulations apply and that are under the supervision of varying assemblages of police, private security firms, and related professionals. These are developments of which we are seldom conscious, although they exert a determining influence on everyday life.

(3) Diminishing legal protection

I have indicated that security and the means of control have a strong territorial thrust. The regulation of urban space takes effect via the security assemblages described. In this framework, the need for control is reinforced by individual forms of access, information, management, rules, and sanctions. This provokes questions concerning the democratic control of various circumstances. Often, changes that are regarded as innovations in security and changes that are regarded as problematic turn out to be two sides of the same coin. For instance, the interests of parties such as shopkeepers and insurers may be at odds with a solid affirmation of public interests such as universal access and equal treatment. The problem is, therefore, what happens when the government and the public interest are uncoupled as a result of the fact that optimum security can no longer be effectively organized on the basis of the national state.

There appeared to be numerous difficult cases among the assemblages studied. This was evident in the coverage of the Collective Shop Ban, and we saw something similar in the information sharing between the police and insurers in the field of road transport crime. In these contexts, I quoted various respondents, who often spoke of exceptional ways to store information and share it with one another in order to improve the detection and prevention of crime and disorder. We discussed the case of the "mug-shot folder," and I also mentioned the way police and damage experts furtively pass on information to one another by means of a "strange language" in order to convey relevant facts unearthed in parallel investigations. This consistently involves inventions that strongly differ from the code of law, even if they do rest upon certain judicial rules and prohibitions here and there. It was also apparent that legal protection in security assemblages is not always regulated identically. For instance, people who have been given a Collective Shop Ban can appeal to the local entrepreneurs' association to have the ban lifted. But I have also pointed out that this is a somewhat second-rate opportunity to claim their rights. Although offenders have the opportunity to appeal, this legal path offers fewer judicial guarantees than the Penal Code does. Measures starting out with positive intentions can thus work out negatively for some citizens. On this point I have spoken of a new area of decrees and prohibitions in which many fewer claims are made on legal protection than occur in classical criminal law. I refer to this as "quasi-criminal law."

Participation in security entails not only being part of the cooperative set-up but also accepting public accountability for one's actions. Regardless of how justified and convincing the measures may be in the view of the parties involved, security does benefit from more clarity about the nature and reach of the measures taken. After all, the instrumental function of security seems to be of greater consequence than the protective function. How can the behind-the-scenes sharing of information in the tackling of road transport crime, for example, be reconciled with someone's right to privacy? With the Collective Shop Ban, is the denial of access to offenders for a period of one year a proportional sanction for which the police and the public prosecutor must lend their approval? I realize that it is easier to pose such questions than to answer them, but answers will have to be found. One response could be that more clarity can be obtained when parties accept responsibility, in a systematic and transparent way, for the substantiation and execution of security measures. This can be done through a more reliable and functional substantiation of the system of conditioned self-regulation (instead of classic regulation)—in other words, self-regulation within the limits imposed by the government. The government imposes clear preconditions on the envisioned outcomes. These preconditions may be content related in their nature, but may also refer to the procedure to be followed. In this, there is mention of a specified minimum of preconditions and, simultaneously, real space for self-regulation (cf. Loader and Walker 2007). At this moment, it is striking how little interest the government is displaying in the issue of what the new parties are doing with the responsibility in security. Not only do the parties scarcely accept public accountability at all, but the government is also doing nothing to prevent abuse of responsibilities.

The part in the book where a part becomes a part of something else

The aim of this book is to develop a dynamic perspective on security. For this I have sought answers in the French philosophy of difference, although I have also made use of insights from other disciplines. On the basis of the work of Foucault, Deleuze, and Tarde, I have developed a conceptual system that enables thinking based on the process of change itself, in relation to ordering by security. In this way, numerous concepts that are oriented toward fixed representations of security, and that strongly influence our ideas and notions of security, have been critically examined. The ordering of society through security can hardly be described as an exact science. Regardless of how well security policy is conceived and prepared beforehand, it seems inevitable that incongruities and coincidences will play a significant role. Self-organizing processes occur that cannot be traced back to the properties of the whole or to the elements individually. This makes it difficult—actually impossible—for government officials and policymakers, as well as for scientists, to get a grip on the matter. One might hope that this is self-evident, but anyone reading the literature on security will recognize that it is not. The dynamic character of security cannot be molded into a state of inertia, but is actively present in the fight against crime and disorder.

ACKNOWLEDGMENTS

This book was originally written in Dutch under the title *Orde in veiligheid: Een dynamisch perspectief* (Order in Security: A Dynamic Perspective). With a view to publication in English, large parts of that book have been thoroughly modified and updated. In this process, various—primarily Dutch—literary references that were in the original publication have now been forsaken. The reason for this is that I wished to make the discussion in this book more accessible to an English-speaking public. The acknowledgments have also undergone change. In that context, I wish to thank Ilene Kalish, Emily Wright, David Garland, and Jeff Ferrell for their efforts to ensure that this book would be published by New York University Press. Without their support, I would have achieved very little. I performed a large part of the rewriting of my book during my stay at John Jay College in 2013. My analysis benefited greatly from the discussions with David Brotherton, Louis Kontos, and Barry Spunt on what "constitutes good science." On the Dutch side, I offer my gratitude to Hans Boutellier and Klaas Rozemond, who were always willing to contribute to the thinking and writing processes. Thanks to them, the book has improved in terms of lucidity and consistency. Various people were gracious enough to comment on the first versions of the chapters. For this, I wish to thank in particular Jan Terpstra, Joris van Wijk, Richard Staring, Ed Romein, Henk Elffers, and Willem de Haan. The empirical research would have been impossible without the effort of Annerieke Coenraads, Catharina Dijkstra, Freek van den Engel, Sophie Mommers, Desiré Peters, Lara van Roon, Wytske van der Wagen, and Moniek Weerts. Wise advice and assistance came from Patrick Van Calster, Sjoerd van Tuinen, Onne Schuilenburg, and Alex de Jong. Without the interest and support of my parents and my girlfriend, Loes Wesselink ("Never mind the Buzzcocks"), it would have been a different book. During the writing process, I was sustained by musical inspiration from Burial, John Coltrane, Radiohead, Four Tet, Scratch Lee Perry, Burning Spear, Caribou, Pharoah Sanders, and The Smiths.

CHAPTER 1. THE PROBLEM

1. Change as a constant factor of social reality has been articulated by many people in many different ways. It is not my intention to offer complete insight into the authors who have referred to this phenomenon. Nonetheless, I would like to mention the sociologist Norbert Elias, who points out that the social sciences will have to devote more attention to change as a universal feature of human communities. According to Elias, there are insufficient conceptual and investigative resources to express the factor of change. He writes that we have the tendency to base our ideas to an exaggerated extent on the qualities of solidity and stability. Concepts such as norm, individual, structure, or society have the character of an isolated object in a stable state. According to Elias, this results "in the changeless aspects of all phenomena being interpreted as most real and significant" (1978: 112).

2. In a sociological context, I refer the reader to the actor-network theory (ANT) of the French sociologist Bruno Latour (1991; 2005), in which the relationships and interactions among people, objects, and living environments are examined. When Latour focuses on relations and interactions in order to investigate the conditions of possibility of phenomena, he does so because common "modern" opposites, such as "subject-object," "culture-nature," and "politics-science" are insufficiently suited to understanding the hybrid nature of problems. With this, he advances a form of empirical philosophy in which the conditions of possibility of phenomena are not investigated in a transcendental way but rather by studying the interaction among scientists, journals, theories, instruments, and political opinions. A disadvantage of Latour's nonmodern approach to science, technology, and politics is that he pays too little attention to existing power structures (Williams and Edge 1996; Elder-Vass 2008; Levi and Valverde 2008). Latour also places too much emphasis on the standpoint that entities should primarily be studied in terms of their effects on other entities. As a result, it is difficult to take full account of the experiences and intentions behind people's actions.

3. In comparison to the Netherlands, the strategy of making citizens jointly responsible for their safety has been applied abroad for a much longer period. For example the first area-based projects were set up in the United States in the seventies under the name of "neighborhood watch" where citizens organized themselves in various ways in order to tackle lack of security in their own neighborhoods. In the course of the eighties, the project caught on in the UK, where it now has more than

155,000 networks and around six million participating households (Crawford 1999: 50–51; Bennett et al. 2003).

PART II. FROM PANOPTICON TO PATCHWORK QUILT

1. Foucault and Deleuze differ from each other on a number of points. For example, they hold different ideas about the character of a society. In an interview, Deleuze remarked,

> For me, a society is something that is constantly escaping in every direction. It flows monetarily; it flows ideologically. It is really made of lines of flight. So much so that the problem for a society is how to stop it from flowing. For me, the powers come later. What surprised Foucault was that faced with all these powers, all of their deviousness and hypocrisy, we can still resist. My surprise is the opposite. It is flowing everywhere and governments are able to block it. (2003: 261)

In addition, Deleuze attaches a different significance to the nature of the relations that are part of social reality than Foucault does. In contrast to the power relations of Foucault, Deleuze speaks of "desire" (*désir*). First of all, according to Deleuze, desire assembles social reality (Deleuze and Guattari 1980: 175–76). And in *L'Anti-Œdipe* (*Anti-Oedipus*), he writes, with Guattari, "There is only desire and the social, and nothing else" (1972: 36). Foucault disagrees with Deleuze and advocates replacing "desire" with the term "pleasure" (*plaisir*).

2. In his third period, Foucault turns away from his analytics of knowledge and power, and directs his interest to the theme of ethics. Accordingly, in *L'usage des plaisirs* (*The Use of Pleasure*, 1984a) and *Le souci de soi* (*The Care of the Self*, 1984b) he shifts attention to the Greek-Roman "art of living" and adds a third theme, the so-called technologies of the self, to his analytics of knowledge and power. Instead of a universal system of codes and behavioral rules, moral thought in Greek-Roman culture is primarily oriented toward behavioral stylization, in Foucault's opinion. This style of conduct enables the individual to recognize himself or herself as subject of a moral code.

3. A significant exception to this is the "constitutive criminology" of Stuart Henry and Dragan Milovanovic (1996; 1999), which displays major correspondences with the thoughts of French philosophers such as Lacan, Baudrillard, Derrida, Foucault, and Deleuze. In addition, in the fields of critical security studies and international political sociology, various analyses inspired by Deleuze have been published (Haggerty and Ericson 2000; Levi and Wall 2004; Muller 2008; Salter 2008; Abrahamsen and Williams 2009).

CHAPTER 3. SECURITIZATION

1. Michael Welch (2010) speaks of a "third Foucault effect." The first effect is the period between 1980 and the early 1990s, in which criminology paid great attention to Foucault's analysis of prison in *Surveiller et punir* (*Discipline and Punish*). The second wave of attention arose as a result of Foucault's lecture on the issue of governmentality,

which was included in *The Foucault Effect* (Burchell et al. 1991). This lecture, given on 1 February 1978, led to new interest in Foucault's work, especially on the part of Anglo-Saxon authors such as Pat O'Malley (1996; 2004), David Garland (1997), and Nikolas Rose (1999; 2000). The recent publications of his lectures at the Collège de France now form a third point of address for scientists to reassess the work of Foucault. It is striking that Shearing and his colleagues do not refer to the series of lectures entitled *Sécurité, territoire, population* (*Security, Territory, Population*) and *Naissance de la biopolitique* (*The Birth of Biopolitics*). In contrast to authors such as O'Malley, Garland, and Rose, they have had the posthumous publications of Foucault's lectures at their disposal.

2. There are various ways to conceptualize the process of securitization. A well-known strategy is to do so through the work of the Copenhagen School, which aims to understand "securitization" as a "speech act"—and deals with the problem of how security issues emerge, evolve, and dissolve. Securitization is then the formulation and placement of a threat on the political or public agenda (Buzan et al. 1998; Balzacq 2011). The other strategy is to use Michel Foucault's notion of "governmentality," in which security is studied in concrete practices and is seen as a power relation. The backbone of this book will be the latter approach, as important new aspects of the notion of "governmentality" have come to light in the posthumous publications of Foucault's series of lectures at the Collège de France.

3. There is little agreement about the nature of risk thinking. For instance, Pat O'Malley and Steven Hutchinson (2007) state that the basis of this can be found in nineteenth-century firefighting and the imposition of fire precautions in the UK and the United States. For an overview of the various standpoints in this debate, see Kemshall (2003: 28 ff.).

4. Surprisingly, Adam Smith did not use the term "invisible hand" in this sense. In *An Inquiry into the Nature and Causes of the Wealth of Nations* (1976), he merely stated that, if a shortage of a product occurred, the price of this product would rise, which would create a stimulus to manufacture the product. More particularly, he refers to the fact that people work in order to earn an income by means of which they can buy commodities. In doing so, they are concerned with their own security and benefit. But there is nothing wrong with this, states Smith (1976: 456), because—without this being their intention—this usually serves the public interest at the same time.

5. Explanations for the decrease in crime in the Netherlands are being sought in the security policy of the government, the imposition of preventative measures, and a reduction in the number of heroin addicts (Vollaard et al. 2009).

6. A clear example of this is the approach to pedophilia. Whereas it was possible in the Netherlands to declare one's sexual preferences without too much difficulty until around 1970, and there were even people in favor of relieving pedophilia of its negative label, the mood changed drastically after affairs with children in the village of Oude Pekela in the Netherlands and the Dutroux affair in Belgium came to light. Social norms changed to the extent that sexual relations between adults and minors again came to be seen as immoral and criminal behavior.

7. The reaction of British prime minister David Cameron to the street riots of 2011 forms an excellent example of this. England is a "sick society," Cameron informed the journalists at a busy press conference. He was referring to the young people in London and other cities who believed they could simply take what they think they are entitled to, flushed with anger about their lack of social prospects, growing up in a society that continually encourages them to buy the latest sneakers, clothes, jewelry, and cars. Cameron said that "society would fight back" and, in doing so, would deploy all available means to make English society healthy once again.

CHAPTER 4. ASSEMBLAGES

1. Complexity theories have created furor in the natural sciences in particular, where system development issues from all kinds of self-organizing processes. Reasonably accessible books in this field include *Order out of Chaos* (1984) and *Entre le temps et l'éternité* (*Between Time and Eternity*, 1988) by Ilya Prigogine and Isabelle Stengers. In these books, the authors speak of dissipative systems, which are systems that are somewhat off-balance and are extremely sensitive to environmental influences. Under certain influences, it may happen that order emerges from disorder, which is also referred to as the "possibility of self-organization."

2. In *Naked Lunch* (1959), William Burroughs describes the interzone as a free zone where people and alien beings engage excessively with sex and drugs. The term was used again later as the title of a collection of short stories (1990) that formed the experimental exercise ground for *Naked Lunch*.

3. The significance of music and the history of film can be explained by means of the concept of assemblage. Not only are films such as *Paranoid Park* (2007) by Gus Van Sant and *Psycho* (1960) by Alfred Hitchcock full of mosaic-like structures; interviews with the makers also provide much information on how an assemblage works. The murder of the woman played by Janet Leigh in the famous shower scene in *Psycho* is an excellent example of that here. What is immediately striking is that the spectator never sees the knife penetrate the woman's body. Neither are there total shots of the woman under the shower. The only thing Hitchcock presents to the viewer is pictures of the murderer raising the knife and plunging it downward, mixed with images of the expressive face of the terrified woman. All this is supplemented with shots of the blood that runs down the walls into the drain. By means of the editing and the music, Hitchcock manages to create the impression that the woman is murdered with the knife. In a delightful interview, Hitchcock explained his way of working as follows:

You could not take the camera and just show you the woman being stabbed to death. It had to be done impressionistically. So, it was done with little pieces of film: the head, the feet, the hand, parts of the torso, shadow on the curtain, the shower itself. I think in that scene there were 78 pieces of film in about 45 seconds.

This means that Hitchcock assembled short segments of film consecutively at high speed, in order to create a certain image. Professor Hitchcock once again: "You have two kinds of what we might call montage. We call it cutting. It isn't exactly that. Cutting implies severing something. It really should be called assembling." (Available at www.openculture.com/2013/04/alfred_hitchcocks_seven-minute_editing_master_ class.html, date of consultation: 7 September 2014).

4. This definition lies in the extension of the one Saskia Sassen gives in *Territory, Authority, Rights* (2006). In this work, Sassen describes how globalization processes are nestling in the national state. She, too, speaks of an assemblage where her attention is exclusively oriented to the process of de- and reterritorialization.

5. The extent to which certain concepts are unilaterally used in literature on security is quite striking. For instance, a specific concept such as "risk" has acquired a standard meaning and is applied as an organizing principle in each situation in which security is a point of concern. One could say that it thus works as a perfect slogan that can be easily supplemented as new dangers and developments arise. Nowadays we talk about young people at risk, risk statistics, risk justice, places of risk, risk groups, risk-signaling systems, risk assessment, and even "risk-free risks" (Hannigan 1998: 67). Accordingly, everything seems to form a risk. And therefore nothing does.

CHAPTER 5. MOLAR AND MOLECULAR

1. Among French philosophers such as Deleuze, Derrida, and Foucault, the subject ("the human being") is a troublesome and rarely used concept. For instance, in *Les mots et les choses* (*The Order of Things*), Foucault announced the death of the subject by stating that "one can certainly wager that man would be erased, like a face drawn in the sand at the edge of the sea" (1966: 398). According to many commentators, this prediction was a reaction to a long philosophical tradition in which the autonomous human being is the giver of meaning. This is not the whole story, however. Although Foucault's famous words are a variant of Nietzsche's "death of God," they do not mean that a definitive farewell should be said to the concept of subject. Looking back on his oeuvre, Foucault (1983: 208–9) emphasized that his entire body of research was really oriented to "the general theme of how a human being turns into a subject." And Derrida also states that the subject is absolutely irreplaceable: "I don't destroy the subject; I situate it" (1970: 271). Thus, the French philosophy of difference is not primarily concerned with "subjecticide" but rather with the problem of how someone becomes a subject in general, and with the development of new forms of subjectivity in particular. Although the term continues to exist, albeit in modified form, it can be stated that the concrete activities of people are not a focus of attention in the philosophy of difference. Deleuze declared in an interview with Catherine Clément, included in the collection entitled *Deux régimes de fous* (*Two Regimes of Madness*, 2003), that, with the concept of assemblage, he wished to replace the idea of behavior. Instead of focusing on behavior attached to the subject, he focuses on the interaction with the environment by means of which affects arise that are impersonal and meaningless, in contrast to emotions (as social interaction) and feelings (as personal).

2. For a reproduction of the debates, I largely follow Piers Beirne's article "Between Classicism and Positivism" (1987; 1993: 143–85).

3. In *Punishment and Modern Society* (1990) David Garland formulates a macro-sociological criticism of the ideas of Marx, Foucault, and Durkheim. With respect to

Durkheim's notions of crime and punishment, Garland points out that Durkheim is not interested in the underlying dynamics of the changes throughout history, but instead is mainly interested in the characteristics that can be ascribed to a separate form of moral order. This being the case, the notion that "'the moral order' or 'legal system' of any society is in fact the outcome of historical struggles and a continuing process of negotiation and contestation" (1990: 49) remains unexamined. This criticism must be taken into account, and I believe that Tarde's insights offer the possibility to do so. In contrast to Durkheim's functionalist approach, Tarde emphasizes the way in which actions can come into conflict with one another and breach established patterns.

4. In his lectures of 5 and 12 February 1975, Foucault (2003) also covered the case of Cornier, without making any reference to Tarde. In this series of lectures, he studied the genesis of the concept of "abnormality." In the case of Cornier, according to Foucault, there was no mention of any interest in or clear motive for killing the child. At the same time, Cornier showed no signs of madness. With the absence of a rational explanation for her behavior, the starting points of law and the implementation of a penal power ("the Beccarian dynamic") are "questioned, challenged, disturbed, put back in play, cracked, and undermined" (Foucault 2003: 129).

5. In *Le suicide* (*On Suicide*), Durkheim continues his criticism of Tarde's concept of imitation by stating that "imitation is a purely psychological phenomenon" (1979: 107). According to Durkheim, Tarde also applies the term in an uncritical and too-general way:

> It is one thing to share a common feeling, another to yield to the authority of opinion, and a third to repeat automatically what others have done. [. . .] The name of imitation must then be reserved solely *when the immediate antecedent of an act is the representation of a like act, previously performed by someone else; with no explicit or implicit mental operation which bears upon the intrinsic nature of the act reproduced intervening between representation and execution.* (1897: 115)

6. The terms have been borrowed from the work of Deleuze, to which I have given my own substantiation. To Deleuze, "the molar" refers to a fixed state (*état solide*), in which molecules are not free to move about, and "the molecular" refers to a liquid state (*état liquide*), in which molecules can move freely and merge into one another. In addition, Deleuze speaks of a gaseous state (*état gazeux*) in which all molecules have free movement (1983: 121; 2003: 280). In his film books, Deleuze recognizes a gas-shaped image in the French film school (Jean Renoir, Marcel L'Herbier, Jean Epstein), the pictures of Dziga Vertov, and the American experimental film (Michael Snow). In talking about the "French School," Deleuze is referring to French impressionism and surrealism (1918–1930) and poetic realism (1930–1945).

7. Plato used it in his *Politeia* (*The Republic*) to describe the city-state: reasoning was placed at the head, the guardians formed the noble heart or disposition, and the people occupied the lower parts of the social body. It also stands at the basis of Christian social thinking, with the work *Policraticus* from 1159 by John of Salisbury as an example. Here, as God's representative on earth, the king is the head of the social body,

and the farmers and peasants are the personification of his feet. Something similar occurred at the end of the Middle Ages with the advent of the absolute state and subsequently the social order after the *ancien régime*, symbolized by the beheading of Louis XVI in 1793, and ultimately in the work of sociologists such as Spencer, Comte, and Durkheim, who regard reality as a single large organism (Schinkel 2007: 47 ff.).

8. This differentiation arises in the book *Street-Level Bureaucracy* by Michael Lipsky (1980), about the execution of policy. It concerns the freedom of street-level bureaucrats to make choices within specified parameters. This freedom (or autonomy) evolves because the distance to the managers is generally rather large. Compelled (or not) by local circumstances, they can relatively easily develop their own routines and personally tailored working methods.

9. With the distinction between the molar and the molecular, I do not argue that other authors have not made all kinds of attempts to analyze the relation between stability and change in a systematic way. In addition to taking place in literary studies, it also happens in the social sciences, in symbolic interactionism, and in ethnography. It is also present in psychology and can be found in the work of authors who have been explicitly engaged with the theme of action and the result or formalization of action in structures or institutions. This group includes people such as Erving Goffman, who belongs to an interactionist movement, Pierre Bourdieu, with his distinction between habitus and field, and the British sociologist Anthony Giddens and his theory of structuration. Because it is impossible to review all these approached within the scope of this book, I shall limit myself to a discussion of the work of Giddens. In *The Constitution of Society* (1984), Giddens wishes to transcend the dichotomy between objectivist or determinist approaches (in movements such as functionalism and structuralism) and subjectivist or actor-centric approaches (in movements such as phenomenology and hermeneutics). However, the dynamic perspective presented here deviates subtly but fundamentally from his reasoning. First of all, one may ask if Giddens is actually more engaged with describing stability than with describing change. It is certainly the case that Giddens positions his theory of structuration opposite a constricted functionalism in which social phenomena are explained on the basis of their consequences or the functions they fulfill for other phenomena. But, with equal justification, it is possible to read his theory of structuration as a late representative of a functionalism that is primarily researching what gives reality its orderly character, and pays less attention to interactions that play out in a less orderly or tranquil manner. Take, for instance, the routines that Giddens regards as being of "vital importance" (1984: 60) to his theory of structuration. These patterns of action, which repeat themselves in space and time, have a large degree of predictability within organizations and will often be allied to precisely formulated work processes and the specific use of language that is common in this field. The same patterns of behavior may also lead to the situation in which people are reluctant to veer off the beaten track and in which a kind of organizational petrifaction will occur. This ensures that dynamics—to summarize the situation in one word—are less determinative in Giddens's analysis of social practices than they are in the approach to security

assemblages proposed here. In addition, Giddens speaks of a "dialectical relation" (1979: 53) between action and structure. Seen from a Hegelian standpoint, this articulates the notion that a positive conclusion of a social system is possible, where the accent lies on the general and identical. It is clear that this starting point is also contrary to the fact that an assemblage itself can never absolutize and round matters off. It is exactly the open character of an assemblage that ensures that new elements can be incorporated into a whole or that old elements can disappear at any moment. The conclusion that can be drawn here is that one can support Giddens's analysis of social practices, but not the dialectics he attaches to the relation between action and structure, or the emphasis he places upon routine actions or order-maintaining mechanisms.

PART III. AMONG PEOPLE

1. In the data collection, use was made of research assistants recruited from the Criminology section of the VU University of Amsterdam. To keep the research on one track as much as possible, regular meetings were held during the research period (2008–2001I) in which the progress of the research, the provisional results, and the possibilities during fieldwork were discussed.

CHAPTER 6. COMBATING MARIJUANA CULTIVATION

1. In the meantime, a trial has been set up in The Hague and Rotterdam with the aim of involving the citizens in the detection of marijuana plantations in their city. To this end, each of the municipalities has spread fifteen thousand cards carrying the aroma of marijuana, to help in the detection of plantations. This initiative was taken by gas supplier Eneco, which also distributed a so-called gas card among 1.8 million customers, in order to make them aware of the smell of gas.

2. Although other parties are also involved in the integral approach, only the authorities that actually have a share in the dismantling of plantations—and thus, in collaboration at the operational level—were interviewed. For this reason, the Social Welfare Department, which only subsequently receives information on premises where a plantation has been dismantled, was not interviewed. The same applied to the public prosecutor, who primarily plays a role in the procedure that may lead to a court case. In Eindhoven, nine respondents who were involved in the dismantling practice were interviewed: a hemp coordinator from the police, a network inspector from the municipality, two project leaders of the Administrative Intervention Team Eindhoven, a team manager and a fraud inspector from the energy supplier, the project manager for the "thematic approach to the cannabis sector" from the Tax Department in the region of East-Brabant, a project manager, and a senior member of staff for the customers of housing associations. In Rotterdam, six people were interviewed: a sergeant from the regional police and a neighborhood police officer, the project manager of the hemp team of the municipality (dS+V), a social director of a housing association, the team leader of the antifraud squad, and a fraud inspector of an energy supplier. In addition, meetings in the context of the Program for the Tackling of

Organized Hemp Cultivation were attended and observations were made during two dismantling operations.

3. In their study *The Established and the Outsiders*, Norbert Elias and John Scotson refer to a working-class neighborhood in an English industrial town. They state that "the better integrated group is likely to gossip more freely than the less well-integrated group and [. . .] in the former case the gossiping of people reinforces the already existing cohesion" (1994: 100).

CHAPTER 7. TACKLING ROAD TRANSPORT CRIME

1. Seventeen interviews were held in this case study. The selection of respondents took place on the basis of discussions with people familiar with the professional field. Five interviews were held with police functionaries: three (financial) investigators, one concerned with tactical investigation, and one team leader. These people work at regional, supra-regional, and national levels. There were four representatives of two major transport insurers: two work for a freight insurer; the other two work for a liability insurer. There were discussions with a policy advisor from the Ministry of Justice and with a senior policy specialist from the office of the public prosecutor. Furthermore, there were two damage experts from expertise agencies who were not employed by a specific insurer, and supplementary discussions were held with two advisors from the Dutch Association of Insurers and the Foundation for Tackling Road Transport. Finally, discussions were also held with a policy member of staff from the Transport Crime project group and a legal policy member of staff from Transport and Logistics Netherlands.

CHAPTER 8. URBAN INTERVENTION TEAMS

1. The SIP approach is characterized by the performance of collective house visits in order to gain insight into the problems in the neighborhood. On the basis of discussions with the SIP's resident advisors, various organizations that play an important role in this approach have come to the forefront. From these, thirteen respondents were selected for an interview: two SIP resident advisors, two managers of the Slotervaart submunicipal authority, a staff member from the Order Maintenance Department of the municipality; three staff members of municipal services; two staff members from housing associations; two staff members from welfare organizations, and a staff member from a job agency. House visits were carried out and resident consultation sessions attended over a period of two days. Finally, three meetings were also attended in which work agreements were made with partners of the submunicipality.

2. Institutional robustness also plays a role among tenants who receive a visit from an intervention team. For instance, the coordinator of the Slotervaart Centre for Support for Parents and Children refers to the preferences of certain residents: "People wish to hold on to the first discussion partner they meet at the Centre. 'That lady was pleasant and I don't mind sharing my worries with her.'" Another respondent emphasizes the risk of stigmatization: "As soon as parents hear that a submunicipal council is engaged and people from Youth Care are also part of the group, all the doors firmly

close. It's a question of stigma: 'Make sure you avoid Youth Care.' Because the next step is that your children will be taken away. That's not true, but the stigma is there."

CHAPTER 9. THE COLLECTIVE SHOP BAN

1. Eighty-seven discussions were held with respondents. Seventy-four shopkeepers who participate in the CSB were interviewed. These shopkeepers have businesses on the Gedempte Gracht, Gravenstraat, Grote Markt, Grote Marktstraat, Haagsche Bluf, Hoogstraat, Spui, Turfmarkt, Venestraat, Vlamingstraat, and Wagenstraat. The shops in this area vary from large department stores and electronics chains such as Mediamarkt to small specialist businesses such as a tobacconist's. Studying such a large area enabled the researchers to gain a representative picture of a part of the city center where the measure is in force. Besides interviews with shopkeepers, discussions were also held with six security officers of enterprises, and with the head of the private security service of a major commercial chain in the area; a district police officer of the (local) Haaglanden police; a staff member of the Public Prosecutor's Office who was involved in the formulation of the CSB; a legal member of staff for communications from the Dutch Data Protection Authority; the head of CSB Registration; and the head of The Hague City Centre Shopkeepers Association. In addition, a meeting of The Hague City Center Board was attended, which covered the issue currently under discussion.

2. Nowadays an entrepreneur who catches a shoplifter red-handed can force him or her to pay damages of 151 euros for the time the shop owner has lost in handling the matter. This time includes the time spent observing the shoplifter, arresting him or her, and reporting the matter to the police.

CHAPTER 10. CITY AND CITIZENSHIP

1. The literature presents different ideas on the social contacts in sealed and private living domains. Anglo-Saxon literature states that the extent of community forming in gated communities is rather disappointing. Edward Blakely and Mary Snyder speak of "living by contract rather than by contact" (1997: 20, 129–35). Dutch research into privately managed living domains points to the fact that social cohesion among the residents is not self-evident (Hamers & Tennekes 2008: 28–31). In contrast, Jasper Eshuis et al. (2011) emphasize that the residents know one another relatively well and that people interact with one another in a pleasant manner.

2. The project of the Dutch philosopher Henk Oosterling (2009b) in the Rotterdamse Bloemhof district is a good example of a successful translation of the French philosophy of difference to the problems of the big city. At the primary school of the same name in that district, the children have been receiving lessons in judo, gardening, cooking, and philosophy since 2008, with the aim of building up self-confidence and self-respect.

REFERENCES

Abrahamsen, R., and M. C. Williams (2009) "Security beyond the State: Global Security Assemblages in International Politics." *International Political Sociology*, 3, 1–17.

Agamben, G. (2004) "Non au tatouage biopolitique." *Le Monde*, 10 January.

Alliez, E. (2001) "Différence et répétition de Gabriel Tarde." *Multitudes* 4 (4), 171–76.

Anderson, B. (1983) *Imagined Communities. Reflections on the Origin and Spread of Nationalism*. London: Verso.

Appadurai, A. (1996) *Modernity at Large: Cultural Dimensions of Globalization*. Minneapolis: University of Minnesota Press.

Augé, M. (1992) *Non-Places: Introduction to an Anthropology of Supermodernity*. London: Verso.

Bachelard, G. (1958) *La poétique de l'espace*. Paris: Presses Universitaires de France.

Badiou, A. (1993) *L'éthique: Essai sur la conscience du mal*. Paris: Hatier.

—— (2009) *Second manifeste pour la philosophie*. Paris: Fayard.

Balzacq, T. (ed.) (2011) *Securitization Theory: How Security Problems Emerge and Dissolve*. London: Routledge.

Barham, E. (2003) "Translating *Terroir*: The Global Challenge of French AOC Labeling." *Journal of Rural Studies*, 19, 127–38.

Barry, A., and N. Thrift (2007) "Gabriel Tarde: Imitation, Invention, and Economy." *Economy and Society*, 36 (4), 509–25.

Bauman, Z. (1999) *In Search of Politics*. Stanford, CA: Stanford University Press.

—— (2000) *Liquid Modernity*. Cambridge, UK: Polity Press.

Bayley, D. H., and C. Shearing (1996) "The Future of Policing." *Law and Society Review*, 30 (3), 585–606.

—— (2001) *The New Structure of Policing: Description, Conceptualization, and Research Agenda*. Washington, DC: National Institute of Justice.

Beavon, R., and A. Jarvis (2003) *Nelson Advanced Science: Structure, Bonding, and Main Group Chemistry*. Cheltenham, UK: Nelson Thornes.

Beccaria, C. (1963) *On Crimes and Punishments*. New York: Prentice-Hall (first published: 1764).

Beck, U. (1992) *Risk Society: Towards a New Modernity*. London: Sage.

—— (1999) *World Risk Society*. Cambridge, UK: Polity Press.

Beck, U., and J. Willms (2004) *Conversations with Ulrich Beck*. Cambridge, UK: Polity Press.

Beckett, K., and S. Herbert (2008) "Dealing with Disorder: Social Control in the Post-Industrial City." *Theoretical Criminology*, 12 (1), 5–30.

——— (2009) *Banished: The New Social Control in Urban America*. New York: Oxford University Press.

Beirne, P. (1987) "Between Classicism and Positivism: Crime and Penalty in the Writings of Gabriel Tarde." *Criminology*, 25 (4), 785–819.

——— (1993) *Inventing Criminology: Essays on the Rise of "Homo Criminalis."* Albany: State University of New York Press.

——— (2001) "Introduction to the Transaction Edition." In: G. Tarde, *Penal Philosophy* (1912). New Jersey: Transaction, xi–xix.

Bennet, T., D. Farrington, and K. Holloway (2003) *The Effectiveness of Neighbourhood Watch*. Pontypridd, UK: University of Glamorgan.

Berg, M. van den (2008) "Boeventuig of vernieuwers? Rotterdamse interventieteams zetten rechtvaardigheid op het spel." *Tijdschrift voor sociale vraagstukken*, 1–2, 8–12.

Bergmans, S. (2007) *De juridische gevolgen van hennepteelt in (huur)woningen: Verdere regulering- een verbetering van het softdrugsbeleid*. Tilburg, Netherlands: Celsus Juridische Uitgevers.

Bey, H. (1991) *T.A.Z.: The Temporary Autonomous Zone; Ontological Anarchy, Poetic Terrorism*. New York: Autonomedia.

Bijlsma, L., M. Galle, and J. Tennekes (2010) "De herbergzame ruimte van de stadswijk." *Justitiële verkenningen*, 5, 90–111.

Blakely, E. J., and M. G. Snyder (1997) *Fortress America: Gated Communities in the United States*. Washington, DC: Brookings Institution.

Blandy, S., D. Lister, R. Atkinson, and J. Flint (2003) *Gated Communities: A Systematic Review of Research Evidence*. CNR Summary 12: Sheffield Hallam University and University of Glasgow.

Boccaccio (1835) *The Decameron; or, Ten Days' Entertainment*. London: William Sharp and Son (first published: 1470).

Boomkens, R. (2006) *De nieuwe wanorde: Globalisering en het einde van de maakbare samenleving*. Amsterdam: Van Gennep.

Boone, M., and R. van Swaaningen (2013) "Regression to the Mean: Punishment in the Netherlands." In: V. Ruggiero and M. Ryan (eds.), *Punishment in Europe: A Critical Anatomy of Penal Systems*. Basingstoke, UK: Palgrave Macmillan, 9–32.

Borgers, M. J. (2007) *De vlucht naar voren*. The Hague: Boom.

Bourdieu, P. (1979) *La distinction: Critique sociale du jugement*. Paris: Minuit.

Boutellier, H. (2004) *The Safety Utopia: Contemporary Discontent and Desire as to Crime and Punishment*. Dordrecht, Netherlands: Kluwer.

——— (2011) *De improvisatiemaatschappij: Over de sociale ordening van een onbegrensde wereld*. The Hague: Boom.

Bovenkerk, F. (2008) "De commerciële teelt van hennep in Nederland en het probleem van de georganiseerde misdaad." In: T. Decorte (ed.), *Cannabisteelt in de lage landen. Perspectieven op de Cannabismarkt in België en Nederland*. Leuven, Belgium: Uitgeverij Acco, 175–84.

Bovenkerk, F., and W. I. M. Hogewind (2002) *Hennepteelt in Nederland: Het probleem van de criminaliteit en haar bestrijding*. Utrecht, Netherlands: Willem Pompe Instituut voor Strafrechtswetenschappen.

Braithwaite, J. (1989) *Crime, Shame, and Reintegration*. New York: Cambridge University Press.

Brooks, L. (2008) "Volunteering to Be Taxed: Business Improvement Districts and the Extra-Governmental Provision of Public Safety." *Journal of Public Economics*, 92, 388–405.

Brouwers, J. (1981) *Bezonken rood*. Amsterdam: De Arbeiderspers.

———(2007) *Datumloze dagen*. Amsterdam: Atlas.

Brown, P. (2008) "Business Improvement Districts: An Overview." *Local Economy*, 23 (1), 71–75.

Bruinsma, G. J. N., and F. Bovenkerk (1996) "Deelonderzoek II: Branches." In: *Parlementaire enquêtecommissie Opsporingsmethoden, Inzake Opsporing: Enquête opsporingsmethoden, Eindrapport*. The Hague: Sdu Uitgevers.

Bryson, B. (2003) *A Short History of Nearly Everything*. London: Doubleday.

Bullock, K., and B. Jones (2004) *Acceptable Behaviour Contracts Addressing Antisocial Behaviour in the London Borough of Islington*. London: Home Office.

Bunt, H. van de, and R. van Swaaningen (2004) "Van criminaliteitsbestrijding naar angstmanagement." In: E. R. Muller (eds.), *Veiligheid: Studies over inhoud, organisatie, en maatregelen*. Alphen aan den Rijn, Netherlands: Kluwer, 663–77.

Burchell, G., C. Gordon, and P. Miller (eds.) (1991) *The Foucault Effect: Studies in Governmentality*. Chicago: University of Chicago Press.

Burney, E. (2002) "Talking Tough, Acting Coy: What Happened to the Anti-Social Behaviour Order?" *Howard Journal*, 41 (5), 469–84.

Burris, S. (2004) "Governance, Microgovernance, and Health." *Temple Law Review*, 77, 335–62.

Burris, S., P. Drahos, and C. D. Shearing (2005) "Nodal Governance." *Australian Journal of Legal Philosophy*, 30, 30–57.

Burris, S., M. Kempa, and C. Shearing (2008) "Changes in Governance: A Cross-Disciplinary Review of Current Scholarship." *Akron Law Review*, 41 (1), 1–66.

Burroughs, W. S. (1959) *Naked Lunch*. New York: Grove (12th printing).

———(1990) *Interzone*. New York: Penguin.

———(1999) *Conversations with William S. Burroughs* (ed. A. Hibbard). Jackson: University Press of Mississippi.

Buzan, B., O. Wæver, and J. de Wilde (1998) *Security: A New Framework for Analysis*. Boulder, CO: Rienner.

Castells, M. (1996) *The Information Age: Economy, Society, and Culture*. Volume 1, *The Rise of the Network Society*. Oxford: Blackwell.

———(1997) *The Information Age: Economy, Society, and Culture*. Volume 2, *The Power of Identity*. Oxford: Blackwell.

———(1998) *The Information Age: Economy, Society, and Culture*. Volume 3, *End of Millennium*. Oxford: Blackwell.

Chavis, D. M., J. H. Hogge, D. W. McMillan, and A. Wandersman (1986) "Sense of Community through Brunswick's Lens: A First Look." *Journal of Community Psychology*, 14 (1), 24–40.

Christie, N. (1993) *Crime Control as Industry: Towards Gulags, Western Style*. New York: Routledge.

Chun, Y. H., and H. G. Rainey (2005) "Goal Ambiguity in U.S. Federal Agencies." *Journal of Public Administration Research and Theory*, 15 (1), 1–30.

Clarke, V., and J. Eck (2003) *Become a Problem-Solving Crime Analyst in 55 Small Steps*. London: Jill Dando Institute of Crime Science.

Cohen, S. (1979) "The Punitive City: Notes on the Dispersal of Social Control." *Contemporary Crises*, 3, 339–63.

——— (1985) *Visions of Social Control: Crime, Punishment, and Classification*. Cambridge, UK: Polity.

Coleman, J. S. (1990) *Foundations of Social Theory*. Cambridge, MA: Harvard University Press.

Colquhoun, P. (1806) *A Treatise on the Police of the Metropolis*. London: Printed for J. Mawman.

Cornelissen, E., and T. Brandsen (2007) *Handreiking "Achter de voordeur": Een verkennend onderzoek naar zeven grootstedelijke Achter de voordeur-projecten*. Rotterdam, Netherlands: SEV.

——— (2008) "Kritiek op huisbezoeken is vrijblijvend." *Tijdschrift voor Sociale Vraagstukken*, 5, 6–9.

Crawford, A. (1999) *The Local Governance of Crime: Appeals to Community and Partnerships*. Oxford: Oxford University Press.

——— (2003) "'Contractual Governance' of Deviant Behavior." *Journal of Law and Society*, 30 (4), 479–505.

——— (2006a) "Networked Governance and the Post-Regulatory State? Steering, Rowing, and Anchoring the Provision of Policing and Security." *Theoretical Criminology*, 10 (4), 449–79.

———. (2006b) "Policing and Security as 'Club Goods': The New Enclosures?" In: J. Wood and B. Dupont (eds.), *Democracy, Society, and the Governance of Security*. Cambridge: Cambridge University Press, 111–38.

——— (2009) "Situating Crime Prevention Policies in Comparative Perspective: Policy Travels, Transfer, and Translation." In: A. Crawford (ed.), *Crime Prevention Policies in Comparative Perspective*. Cullompton, UK: Willan, 1–37.

Davis, M. (1992) *City of Quartz: Excavating the Future in Los Angeles*. New York: Vintage.

——— (1998) *Ecology of Fear: Los Angeles and the Imagination of Disaster*. New York: Vintage.

De Cauter, L. (2004) *The Capsular Civilization: On the City in the Age of Fear*. Rotterdam, Netherlands: NAi.

DeLanda, M. (1991) *War in the Age of Intelligent Machines*. New York: Swerve Editions.

—— (2006) *A New Philosophy of Society: Assemblage Theory and Social Complexity.* London: Continuum.

Deleuze, G. (1953) *Empirisme et subjectivité: Essai sur la nature humaine selon Hume.* Paris: Press Universitaires de France.

—— (1962) *Nietzsche et la philosophie.* Paris: Presses Universitaires de France.

—— (1963) *La philosophie critique de Kant: Doctrine des facultés.* Paris: Presses Universitaires de France.

—— (1966) *Le Bergsonisme.* Paris: Presses Universitaires de France.

—— (1968) *Différence et répétition.* Paris: Presses Universitaires de France.

—— (1969) *Logique du sens.* Paris: Minuit.

—— (1981) *Francis Bacon: Logique de la sensation.* Paris: Éditions de la Différence.

—— (1983) *Cinema-1: L'Image-mouvement.* Paris: Minuit.

—— (1986) *Foucault.* Paris: Minuit.

—— (1988) *Le pli: Leibniz et le Baroque.* Paris: Minuit.

—— (1990) *Pourparlers 1972–1990.* Paris: Minuit.

—— (1993) *Critique et clinique.* Paris: Minuit.

—— (2001) *Pure Immanence: Essays on a Life.* New York: Zone.

—— (2002) *L'île déserte et autres texts: Textes et entretiens, 1953–1974.* Paris: Minuit.

—— (2003) *Deux régimes de fous: Textes et entretiens, 1975–1995.* Paris: Minuit.

Deleuze, G., and F. Guattari (1972) *Capitalisme et schizophrénie.* Volume 1, *L'Anti-Œdipe.* Paris: Minuit.

—— (1975) *Kafka: Pour une litterature mineure.* Paris: Minuit.

—— (1980) *Capitalisme et schizophrenie.* Volume 2, *Mille plateaux.* Paris: Minuit.

—— (1991) *Qu'est-ce que la philosophie?* Paris: Minuit.

Deleuze, G., and C. Parnet (1991) *Dialogen.* Kampen, Netherlands: Kok Agora.

Derrida, J. (1970) "Structure, Sign, and Play in the Discourse of the Human Sciences." In: R. Macksey and E. Donato (eds.), *The Structuralist Controversy: The Languages of Criticism and the Sciences of Man.* Baltimore, MD: Johns Hopkins University Press.

—— (1972) *Marges de la philosophie.* Paris: Minuit.

—— (1994) *Force de loi: Le "fondement mystique de l'autorité."* Paris: Galilée.

Donzelot, J. (1977) *La police des familles.* Paris: Minuit.

Downs, A. (1967) *Inside Bureaucracy.* Long Grove, IL: Waveland.

Dupont, B. (2004) "Security in the Age of Networks." *Policing and Society*, 14 (1), 76–91.

Durkheim, E. (1900) "Deux lois de l'évolution pénale." *Annee sociologique*, 4, 65–95.

—— (1960) *De la division du travail social.* Paris: Presses Universitaires de France (first published: 1893).

—— (1968) *Les règles de la méthode sociologique.* Paris: Presses Universitaires de France (first published: 1895).

—— (1979) *Le suicide: Etude de sociologie.* Paris: Presses Presses Universitaires de France (first published: 1897).

Edelenbos, J., and E. H. Klijn (2007) "Trust in Complex Decision-Making Networks: A Theoretical and Empirical Exploration." *Administration & Society*, 39 (1), 25–50.

Edwards, A., and G. Hughes (2005) "Comparing the Governance of Safety in Europe: A Geo-Historical Approach." *Theoretical Criminology*, 9 (3), 345–63.

Eggen, A. Th. J., and W. Van der Heide (2005) *Criminaliteit en rechtshandhaving 2004: Ontwikkelingen en samenhangen*. The Hague: Ministerie van Justitie/WODC en CBS.

Ekblom, P. (1995) "Urban Crime Prevention: Development of Policy and Practice in England." In: K. Miyazawa and S. Miyazawa (eds.), *Crime Prevention in the Urban Community*. Deventer, Netherlands: Kluwer Law and Taxations Publishers, 99–114.

Elder-Vass, D. (2008) "Searching for Realism, Structure, and Agency in Actor Network Theory." *British Journal of Sociology*, 59 (3), 455–73.

Elias, N. (1978) *What Is Sociology?* London: Hutchinson.

Elias, N., and J. L. Scotson (1994) *The Established and the Outsiders: A Sociological Enquiry into Community Problems*. London: Sage.

Engbersen, G. B. M. (2006) "Sociale uitsluiting en sociale herovering in Rotterdam." In: K. van Beek and Y. Zonderop (eds.), *30 Plannen voor een beter Nederland: De sociale agenda*. Amsterdam: Meulenhof, 130–47.

——— (2009) *Fatale remedies: Over de onbedoelde gevolgen van beleid en kennis*. Amsterdam: Amsterdam University Press.

Ericson, R. V. (2007) *Crime in an Insecure World*. Cambridge, UK: Polity.

Ericson, R. V., and K. Haggerty (1997) *Policing the Risk Society*. Toronto: University of Toronto Press.

Eshuis, J., E-H. Klijn, and M. van Twist (2011) "Privaat beheerde woondomeinen: Beloftevol of beangstigend fenomeen?" *Beleid en Maatschappij*, 38 (1), 30–46.

European Parliament (2007) *Organised Theft of Commercial Vehicles and Their Loads in the European Union*, May. Available at www.stavc.nl/pdfdb/publicaties/EU%20 report.pdf. Last accessed September 2014.

Ewald, F. (1986) *L'Etat providence*. Paris: Grasset.

——— (2002) "The Return of Descartes' Malicious Demon: An Outline of a Philosophy of Precaution." In: T. Baker and J. Simon (eds.), *Embracing Risk: The Changing Culture of Insurance and Responsibility*. Chicago: University of Chicago Press, 273–301.

Farrías, I., and T. Bedner (eds.) (2010) *Urban Assemblages. How Actor-Network Theory Changes Urban Studies*. London: Routledge.

Feeley, M. M., and J. Simon (1992) "The New Penology: Notes on the Emerging Strategy of Corrections and Its Implications." *Criminology*, 30 (4), 449–74.

——— (1994) "Actuarial Justice: The Emerging New Criminal Law." In: D. Nelken (ed.), *The Futures of Criminology*. London: Sage, 173–201.

Ferrell, J. (2013) "Cultural Criminology and the Politics of Meaning." *Critical Criminology*, 21 (3), 25–271.

Ferrell, J., K. Hayward, and J. Young (2008) *Cultural Criminology: An Invitation*. London: Sage.

Fijnaut, C., and B. de Ruyver (2008) *Voor een gezamenlijke beheersing van de drugsgerelateerde criminaliteit in de Euregio Maas-Rijn*. Tilburg, Netherlands: Euregio Maas-Rijn.

Fineman, S. (2000) *Emotion in Organizations*. London: Sage.

Flint, J. (2006) "Surveillance and Exclusion Practices in the Governance of Access to Shopping Centres on Periphery Estates in the UK." *Surveillance & Society*, 4 (1/2), 52–68.

Flusser, V. (2002) *Writings*. Minneapolis: University of Minnesota Press.

Foucault, M. (1966) *Les mots et les choses: Une archéologie des sciences humaines*. Paris: Gallimard.

—— (1972) *Histoire de la folie à l'âge classique*. Paris: Gallimard.

—— (1975) *Surveiller et punir: Naissance de la prison*. Paris: Gallimard.

—— (1976) *Histoire de la sexualité*. Volume 1, *La volonté de savoir*. Paris: Gallimard.

—— (1980) *Power/Knowledge: Selected Interviews and Other Writings, 1972–1977* (C. Gordon, ed.). New York: Pantheon.

—— (1983) "The Subject and Power." In: L. H. Dreyfus and P. Rabinow, *Michel Foucault: Beyond Structuralism and Hermeneutics; With an Afterword by Michel Foucault*. Chicago: University of Chicago Press, 208–26.

—— (1984a) *Histoire de la sexualité*. Volume 2, *L'usage des plaisirs*. Paris: Gallimard.

—— (1984b) *Histoire de la sexualité*. Volume 3, *Le souci de soi*. Paris: Gallimard.

—— (1997a) *Ethics, Subjectivity, and Truth* (P. Rabinow, ed.). New York: New Press.

—— (1997b) *The Politics of Truth* (S. Lotringer and L. Hochroth, eds.). New York: Semiotext(e).

—— (2000) *Power* (J. D. Faubion, ed.). New York: New Press.

—— (2003) *Abnormal: Lectures at the Collège de France, 1974–1975*. New York: Picador.

—— (2004a) *"Society Must Be Defended": Lectures at the Collège de France, 1975–1976*. London: Penguin.

—— (2004b) *Breekbare vrijheid: Teksten & interviews*. Amsterdam: Boom/Parrèsia.

—— (2008) *The Birth of Biopolitics: Lectures at the Collège de France, 1978–1979*. New York: Palgrave Macmillan.

—— (2009) *Security, Territory, Population: Lectures at the Collège de France, 1977–1978*. New York: Picador.

Froestad, J., and C. Shearing (2013) "Meditative Reflections on Nils Christie's 'Words on Words,' through an African Lens." *Restorative Justice: An International Journal*, 1 (1), 31–46.

Furedi, F. (1997) *Culture of Fear: Risk-Taking and the Morality of Low Expectation*. London: Cassell.

Gallie, W. B. (1962) "Essentially Contested Concepts." In: M. Black (ed.), *The Importance of Language*. Englewood Cliffs, NJ: Prentice-Hall, 121–46.

Garland, D. (1985) *Punishment and Welfare: A History of Penal Strategies*. Aldershot, UK: Gower.

—— (1990) *Punishment and Modern Society: A Study in Social Theory*. Chicago: University of Chicago Press.

—— (1996) "The Limits of the Sovereign State: Strategies of Crime Control in Contemporary Society." *British Journal of Criminology*, 36 (4), 445–71.

———(1997) "'Governmentality' and the Problem of Crime: Foucault, Criminology, Sociology." *Theoretical Criminology*, 1 (2), 173–214.

———(2001) *The Culture of Control: Crime and Social Order in Contemporary Society.* Chicago: University of Chicago Press.

———(2003) "Penal Modernism and Postmodernism." In: T. G. Blomberg and S. Cohen (eds.), *Punishment and Social Control.* New Brunswick, NJ: Transaction, 45–74.

Giddens, A. (1979) *Central Problems in Social Theory: Action, Structure, and Contradiction in Social Analysis.* London: Macmillan.

———(1984) *The Constitution of Society: Outline of the Theory of Structuration.* Berkeley: University of California Press.

———(1991) *Modernity and Self-Identity: Self and Society in the Late Modern Age.* Cambridge, UK: Polity.

Gilling, D. (1994a) "Multi-Agency Crime Prevention: Some Barriers to Collaboration." *Howard Journal*, 33 (3), 246–57.

———(1994b) "Multi-Agency Crime Prevention in Britain: The Problem of Combining Situational and Social Strategies." *Crime Prevention Studies*, 3, 231–48.

Ginneken, J. van (1992) *Crowds, Psychology, and Politics, 1871–1899.* Cambridge: Cambridge University Press.

Gluckman, M. (1963) "Gossip and Scandal." *Current Anthropology*, 4, 307–16.

Goffman, E. (1961) *Asylums: Essays on the Social Situation of Mental Patients and Other Inmates.* Chicago: Aldine.

———(1968) *Stigma: Notes on the Management of Spoiled Identity.* London: Penguin.

Goldschmidt, W. (2006) *The Bridge to Humanity: How Affect Hunger Trumps the Selfish Gene.* Oxford: Oxford University Press.

Graham, S. (2010) *Cities under Siege: The New Military Urbanism.* London: Verso.

Graham, S., and S. Marvin (2001) *Splintering Urbanism: Networked Infrastructures, Technological Mobilities, and the Urban Condition.* London: Routledge.

Grail, J., and G. Dawkins (2008) "Business Improvement Districts in London." *Local Economy*, 23 (1), 76–80.

Grant, J., and L. Mittelsteadt (2004) "Types of Gated Communities." *Environment and Planning B: Planning and Design*, 31 (6), 913–30.

Guattari, F. (1984) *Molecular Revolution: Psychiatry and Politics.* New York: Puffin.

———(1992) *Chaosmose.* Paris: Galilée.

———(2009) *Chaosophy: Texts and Interviews, 1972–1977.* Los Angeles: Semiotext(e).

Haan, W. J. M. de (1995) "Integrale veiligheid: Beleidsvernieuwing of beleidsvervaging?" *Justitiële verkenningen*, 5, 25–48.

Haggerty, K. D., and R. V. Ericson (2000) "The Surveillant Assemblage." *British Journal of Sociology*, 51 (4), 605–22.

———(eds.) (2006) *The New Politics of Surveillance and Visibility.* Toronto: University of Toronto Press.

Haggerty, K. D., D. Wilson, and G. J. D. Smith (2011) "Theorizing Surveillance in Crime Control." *Theoretical Criminology*, 15 (3), 231–37.

Hajer, M., and A. Reijndorp (2001) *In Search of New Public Domain: Analysis and Strategy*. Rotterdam, Netherlands: NAi.

Hallsworth, S., and J. Lea (2011) "Reconstructing Leviathan: Emerging Contours of the Security State." *Theoretical Criminology*, 15 (2), 141–57.

Hamers, D., K. Nabielek, S. Schluchter, and M. van Middelkoop (2007) *Afgeschermde woondomeinen in Nederland*. Rotterdam, Netherlands: NAi.

Hamers, D., and J. Tennekes (2008) "Voor een beperkt publiek: De effecten van besloten wooncomplexen op het publieke domein in Nederland." *Krisis: Tijdschrift voor actuele filosofie*, 2, 18–36.

Hamilton, J. T. (2013) *Security, Politics, Humanity, and the Philology of Care*. Princeton, NJ: Princeton University Press.

Hammar, T. (1990) *Democracy and the Nation State: Aliens, Denizens, and Citizenship in a World of International Migration*. Aldershot, UK: Avebury.

Hannigan, J. (1998) *Fantasy City: Pleasure and Profit in the Postmodern Metropolis*. London: Routledge.

Harvey, D. (2008) "The Right to the City." *New Left Review*, 53, 23–40.

Hayward, K. (2004) *City Limits: Crime, Consumer Culture, and the Urban Experience*. London: Glass House.

——— (2012) "Five Spaces of Cultural Criminology." *British Journal of Criminology*, 52 (3), 441–62.

Hayward, K., and M. Schuilenburg (2014) "To Resist = to Create? Some Thoughts on the Concept of Resistance in Cultural Criminology." *Tijdschrift over Cultuur & Criminaliteit*, 4 (1), 22–36.

Heliview Research (2011) *Ontwikkelingen in de beveiligingsbranche: Branchescan particuliere beveiliging 2010*. Breda, Netherlands: Heliview.

Henry, S., and D. Milovanovic (1996) *Constitutive Criminology: Beyond Postmodernism*. London: Sage.

——— (1999) *Constitutive Criminology at Work: Applications to Crime and Justice*. Albany: State University of New York Press.

Hobbes, T. (1963) *Leviathan*. Cleveland, OH: World (first published: 1651).

Hoogenboom, A. B. (1991) "Grey Policing: A Theoretical Framework." *Policing and Society*, 2, 17–30.

——— (2009) "Dingen veranderen en blijven gelijk." *Justitiële verkenningen*, 1, 63–77.

Hughes, E. C. (1961) "Tarde's *Psychologie économique*: An Unknown Classic by a Forgotten Sociologist." *American Journal of Sociology*, 66 (6), 553–59.

Huisman, W., and M. L. Koemans (2008). "Administrative Measures in Crime Control." *Erasmus Law Review*, 1 (5), 121–145.

Johnston, L. (2006) "Transnational Security Governance." In: J. Wood and B. Dupont (eds.), *Democracy, Society, and the Governance of Security*. Cambridge: Cambridge University Press, 33–51.

Johnston, L., and C. Shearing (2003) *Governing Security: Explorations in Policing and Justice*. London: Routledge.

Jones, T., and T. Newburn (2002) "The Transformation of Policing? Understanding Current Trends in Policing Systems." *British Journal of Criminology*, 42 (1), 129–46.

—— (2006) *Plural Policing: A Comparative Perspective*. London: Routledge.

—— (2007) *Policy Transfer and Criminal Justice: Exploring U.S. Influence over British Crime Control Policy*. New York: Open University Press.

Jong, A. de, and M. Schuilenburg (2006) *Mediapolis: Popular Culture and the City*. Rotterdam, Netherlands: 010-Publishers.

Jong, J. D. de (2007) *Kapot moeilijk: Een etnografisch onderzoek naar opvallend delinquent groepsgedrag van "Marokkaanse" jongens*. Amsterdam: Aksant.

Kane, A. A., L. Argote, and J. M. Levine (2005) "Knowledge Transfer between Groups via Personnel Rotation: Effects of Social Identity and Knowledge Quality." *Organizational Behavior and Human Decision Processes*, 96, 56–71.

Kant, I. (2008) *The Critique of Judgement*. Radford, VA: Wilder (first published: 1790).

—— (2010) *The Critique of Pure Reason*. University Park: Pennsylvania State University Press (first published: 1781). Electronic Classics Series.

Kelling, G. L., and C. Coles (1996) *Fixing Broken Windows. Restoring Order and Reducing Crime in Our Communities*. New York: Random House.

Kempa, M., R. Carrier, J. Wood, and C. Shearing (1999) "Reflections on the Evolving Concept of 'Private Policing.'" *European Journal of Criminal Policy and Research*, 7 (2), 197–223.

Kempa, M., P. Stenning, and J. Wood (2004) "Policing Communal Spaces: A Reconfiguration of the 'Mass Private Property' Hypothesis." *British Journal of Criminology*, 44 (4), 562–81.

Kemshall, H. (2003) *Understanding Risk in Criminal Justice*. Berkshire, UK: Open University Press.

Kimmerle, H. (2000) *Philosophien der Differenz: Eine Einführung*. Würzburg, Germany: Königshausen and Neumann.

Korf, D. (2010) *Coke bij de vis: Misdaad en moraal*. Amsterdam: Vossiuspers UvA.

Korf, D. J., and M. Wouters (2008) "Ontmantelen van hennepkwekerijen in Nederland." In: T. Decorte (ed.), *Cannabisteelt in de lage landen: Perspectieven op de Cannabismarkt in België en Nederland*. Leuven, Belgium: Uitgeverij Acco, 87–103.

Krausse, J. (1998) "Informatie in één oogopslag: Over de geschiedenis van diagrammen." *Oase*, 48, 3–30.

Kubbinga, H. (2003) *De molecularisering van het wereldbeeld*. Part 1. Hilversum, Netherlands: Verloren.

Kupchik, A. (2010) *Homeroom Security: School Discipline in an Age of Fear*. New York: New York University Press.

Kuppens, J., E. de Vries Robbé, I. van Leiden, and H. Ferwerda (2006) *Zware jongens op de weg: Een onderzoek naar georganiseerde diefstal in de wegtransportsector*. Arnhem, Netherlands: Advies- en onderzoeksgroep Beke.

Laermans, R. (1995) "Sociologie vandaag: Enkele stellingen en notities." *Tijdschrift voor Sociologie*, 16 (2), 133–41.

——— (2009) "Soevereiniteit, biopolitiek, en moderniteit: Een kritische lezing van Giorgio Agambens *Homo sacer.*" *Krisis: Tijdschrift voor actuele filosofie*, 3, 52–67.

Latour, B. (1991) *Nous n'avons jamais été modernes: Essai d'anthropologie symétrique.* Paris: Découverte.

——— (2002) "Gabriel Tarde and the End of the Social." In: P. Joyce (ed.), *The Social in Question: New Bearings in History and the Social Sciences.* London: Routledge, 117–32.

——— (2005) *Reassembling the Social: An Introduction to Actor-Network Theory.* Oxford: Oxford University Press.

Lefebvre, H. (1972) *Le droit à la ville: Suivi de espace et politique.* Paris: Anthropos.

——— (1996) *Writings on Cities.* Oxford: Blackwell.

Lefort, C. (1992) "La question de la démocratie." In: *Essais sur le politique (XIXE–XXE Siècles).* Paris: Seuil, 17–31.

Levi, M., and M. Maguire (2004) "Reducing and Preventing Organised Crime: An Evidence-Based Critique." *Crime, Law, and Social Change*, 41 (5), 397–469.

Levi, R., and M. Valverde (2008) "Studying Law by Association: Bruno Latour Goes to the Conseil d'Etat." *Law and Social Inquiry*, 33 (3), 805–25.

Levi, M., and D. Wall (2004) "Technologies, Security, and Privacy in the Post-9/11 European Information Society." *Journal of Law and Society*, 31 (2), 194–220.

Lévi-Strauss, C. (1949) *Les structures élémentaires de la parenté.* Paris: PUF.

Liddle, A. M., and L. Gelsthorpe (1994) "Crime Prevention and Inter-Agency Co-Operation." *Crime Prevention Unit Series Paper 53.* London: Home Office Police Department, Police Research Group.

Lint, W. de, and S. Virta (2004) "Security in Ambiguity: Towards a Radical Security Politics." *Theoretical Criminology*, 8 (4), 495–519.

Lipsky, M. (1980) *Street-Level Bureaucracy: Dilemmas of the Individual in Public Services.* New York: Russell Sage.

Loader, I. (2000) "Plural Policing and Democratic Governance." *Social and Legal Studies*, 9 (3), 323–45.

Loader, I., and N. Walker (2001) "Policing as a Public Good: Reconstituting the Connections between Policing and the State." *Theoretical Criminology*, 5 (1), 9–35.

——— (2007) *Civilizing Security.* Cambridge: Cambridge University Press.

Lohof, S., and A. Reijndorp (eds.) (2006) *Privéterrein: Privaat beheerde woondomeinen in Nederland.* Rotterdam, Netherlands: NAi.

Low, S. (2003) *Behind the Gates: Life, Security, and the Pursuit of Happiness in Fortress America.* New York: Routledge.

Lupi, T., and D. Schelling (2010) *Eerste hulp bij sociale stijging: Een literatuuronderzoek naar "achter de voordeur"-aanpakken.* The Hague: Ministerie van VROM/Nicis Institute.

Machiavelli, N. (2008) *The Prince: Bold-Faced Principles on Tactics, Power, and Politics.* New York: Sterling (first published: 1513).

Manunta, G. (1999) "What Is Security?" *Security Journal*, 12 (3), 57–66.

Marks, M., and A. Goldsmith (2006) "The State, the People, and Democratic Policing: The Case of South Africa." In: J. Wood and B. Dupont (eds.), *Democracy, Society, and the Governance of Security*. Cambridge: Cambridge University Press, 139–64.

Marx, G. T. (2001) "Murky Conceptual Waters: The Public and the Private." *Ethics and Information Technology*, 3 (3), 157–69.

Maturana, H. R., and F. J. Varela (1980) *Autopoiesis and Cognition: The Realization of the Living*. Dordrecht, Netherlands: Reidel.

Maurutto, P., and K. Hannah-Moffat (2006) "Assembling Risk and the Restructuring of Penal Control." *British Journal of Criminology*, 46 (3), 438–54.

Mauss, M. (2004) "Essai sur le don: Forme et raison de l'échange dans les sociétés archaïques." In: *Sociologie et anthropologie*. Paris: PUF, 145–79.

Mazerolle, L., and J. Ransley (2005) *Third-Party Policing*. Cambridge: Cambridge University Press.

McLaughlin, E., and K. Murji (1995) "The End of Public Policing? Police Reform and the New Managerialism." In: L. Noaks et al. (eds.), *Contemporary Issues in Criminology*. Cardiff, UK: University of Cardiff Press, 110–27.

McLuhan, M. (1964) *Understanding Media: The Extensions of Man*. New York: McGraw-Hill.

Megginson, W., and J. Netter (2001) "From State to Market: A Survey of Empirical Studies on Privatization." *Journal of Economic Literature*, 39, 321–89.

Metaal, S., M. Delnoij, and J. W. Duyvendak (2006) *Een Amsterdamse benadering: Vooruitkomen, samenleven, en thuis voelen in Nieuw West*. Amsterdam: Bureau Parkstad.

Mill, J. S. (1989) *On Liberty and Other Writings*. Cambridge: Cambridge University Press (first published: 1859).

Mitchell, D. (2003) *The Right to the City: Social Justice and the Fight for Public Space*. New York: Guilford.

Mitchell, J. (2001) "Business Improvement Districts and the 'New' Revitalization of Downtown." *Economic Development Quarterly*, 15 (2), 115–23.

Mouffe, C. (2005) *On the Political*. London: Routledge.

Muller, B. (2008) "The Biometric State: Securing the Political Imagination; Popular Culture, the Security Dispositif, and the Biometric State." *Security Dialogue*, 39 (2–3), 199–220.

Nelen, H. (2008) "Demystificeren en Verstehen: De toegevoegde waarde van culturele criminologie voor het evaluatieonderzoek." In: D. Siegel, F. van Gemert, and F. Bovenkerk (eds.), *Culturele criminologie*. The Hague: Boom, 69–79.

Neocleous, M., and G. S. Rigakos (eds.) (2011) *Anti-Security*. Ottawa, Canada: Red Quill.

Newman, J. (2001) *Modernising Governance: New Labour, Policy, and Society*. London: Sage.

Nietzsche, F. (1994) *Götzen-Dämmerung; oder, Wie man mit dem Hammer philosophiert*. In: F. Nietzsche, *Werke in drei Bänden*, Volume 3. Cologne, Germany: Könemann, 279–384 (first published: 1889).

———(2007) *On the Genealogy of Morality*. New York: Cambridge University Press (first published: 1887).

Notitie Integrale Aanpak Hennepteelt (Memo for the Integral Approach to Hemp Cultivation, 2006). Drugbeleid. Brief van de minister van BZK aan de voorzitter van de TK inzake Notitie Integrale aanpak hennepteelt. Tweede Kamer, vergaderjaar 2005–2006, 24 077, nr. 184.

Oenen, G. van (2008) "Babylonian Social Engineering: How Contemporary Public Space Can Learn from New Babylon." *Open: Cahier on Art and the Public Domain*, 15, 36–59.

O'Malley, P. (1996) "Risk and Responsibility." In: A. Barry, T. Osborne, and N. Rose (eds.), *Foucault and Political Reason: Liberalism, Neo-Liberalism, and Rationalities of Government*. London: University College London Press, 189–208.

———(2004) *Risk, Uncertainty, and Government*. London: Glasshouse Press.

O'Malley, P., and S. Hutchinson (2007) "Reinventing Prevention: Why Did 'Crime Prevention' Develop So Late?" *British Journal of Criminology*, 47, 373–89.

Ombudsman Rotterdam (2007) *Baas in eigen huis: "Tja, wij komen eigenlijk voor alles"; Rapport van een ambtshalve onderzoek naar de praktijk van huisbezoeken*. Rotterdam, Netherlands.

———(2011) *Kijken en bekeken worden: Een onderzoek naar de dagelijkse praktijk van de Rotterdamse interventieteams*. Rotterdam, Netherlands.

Oosterling, H. (1996) *Door schijn bewogen: Naar een hyperkritiek van de xenofobe rede*. Kampen, Netherlands: Kok Agora.

———(2009a) "Rizoom." In: E. Romein, M. Schuilenburg, and S. van Tuinen (eds.), *Deleuze compendium*. Amsterdam: Boom, 188–204.

———(2009b) *Woorden als daden: Rotterdam vakmanstad/skillcity, 2007–2009*. Rotterdam, Netherlands: Jap Sam.

Osborne, D., and T. Gaebler (1992) *Reinventing Government*. New York: Plume.

Paine, R. (1967) "What Is Gossip About? An Alternative Hypothesis." *Man*, 2, 278–85.

Park, R. E., and E. W. Burgess (1921) *Introduction to the Science of Sociology*. Chicago: University of Chicago Press.

Peters, A. A. G. (1972) "Het rechtskarakter van het strafrecht." In: Y. Buruma (ed.), *100 jaar strafrecht. Klassieke teksten van de twintigste eeuw*. Amsterdam: Amsterdam University Press, 271–87.

Pierre, J. (ed.) (2000) *Debating Governance: Authority, Steering, and Democracy*. Oxford: Oxford University Press.

Piret, J. M. (2002) "Het recht op veiligheid: Fundamenteler dan een sociaal grondrecht." In: K. Rimanque (ed.), *Het recht op vrijheid*. Antwerp, Belgium: Maklu, 11–37.

Politie (1977) *Politie in verandering: Een voorlopig theoretisch model*. The Hague: Staatsuitgeverij.

———(2003) *Tegenhouden troef: Een nadere verkenning van tegenhouden als alternatieve strategie van misdaadbestrijding*. Tilburg, Netherlands: Projectgroep opsporing.

——— (2004) *Tegenhouden als nieuw paradigma voor de politie?* Amsterdam: DSP.

——— (2005) *The Police in Evolution: Vision on Policing.* The Hague: NPI.

Pols, R. (1997) "Pokken." *Trouw,* 22 October.

Presdee, M. (2000) *Cultural Criminology and the Carnival of Crime.* London: Routledge.

Prigogine, I., and I. Stengers (1984) *Order out of Chaos.* New York: Bantam.

——— (1988) *Entre le temps et l'éternité.* Paris: Fayard.

Prins, R., and L. Cachet (2011) "Integrale veiligheidszorg en de burgemeester." *Tijdschrift voor Veiligheid,* (10) 1, 43–58.

Purcell, M. (2002) "Excavating Lefebvre: The Right to the City and Its Urban Politics of the Inhabitant." *GeoJournal,* 58, 99–108.

Raad voor Maatschappelijke Ontwikkeling (RMO) (2008) *De ontkokering voorbij: Slim organiseren voor meer speelruimte.* Amsterdam: Uitgeverij SWP.

Räkers, M. (2008). "Hulpverleners moeten niet meegaan in stoere taal." *Tijdschrift voor sociale vraagstukken,* 10, 26–29.

Rancière, J. (1995) *La mésentente: Politique et philosophie.* Paris: Galilée.

Reagans, R., and B. McEvily (2003) "Network Structure and Knowledge Transfer: The Effects of Cohesion and Range." *Administrative Science Quarterly,* 48 (2), 240–67.

Reichman, N. (1986) "Managing Crime Risks: Towards an Insurance-Based Model of Social Control." *Research in Law, Deviance, and Social Control,* 8, 151–72.

Reiner, R. (2010) *The Politics of the Police.* New York: Oxford University Press.

Ricoeur, P. (1965) *De l'interprétation: Essai sur Freud.* Paris: Seuil.

Rigakos, G. S., and D. R. Greener (2000) "Bubbles of Governance: Private Policing and the Law in Canada." *Canadian Journal of Law and Society,* 15 (1), 145–85.

Romein, E., and M. Schuilenburg (2008) "Are You on the Fast Track? The Rise of Surveillant Assemblages in a Post-Industrial Age." *Architectural Theory Review,* 13 (3), 337–48.

Romein, E., M. Schuilenburg, and S. van Tuinen (2009) *Deleuze compendium.* Amsterdam: Boom.

Rose, N. (1999) *Powers of Freedom: Reframing Political Thought.* Cambridge: Cambridge University Press.

——— (2000) "Government and Control." *British Journal of Criminology,* 40 (2), 321–39.

Rose, N., and P. Miller (1992) "Political Power beyond the State: Problematics of Government." *British Journal of Sociology,* 43 (2), 173–205.

Rosenbaum, D. P. (2002) "Evaluating Multi-Agency Anti-Crime Partnerships: Theory, Design, and Measurement Issues." *Crime Prevention Studies,* 14, 171–225.

Rozemond, N. (2010) "Beccaria's Dream on Criminal Law and Nodal Governance." In: J. Blad, M. Hildebrandt, N. Rozemond, M. Schuilenburg, and P. Van Calster (eds.), *Governing Security under the Rule of Law.* The Hague: Eleven International Publishing, 37–51.

Salter, M. (ed.) (2008) *Politics at the Airport.* Minneapolis: University of Minnesota Press.

Sampson, A., P. Stubbs, D. Smith, G. Pearson, and H. Blagg (1988) "Crime, Locali-
ties, and the Multi-Agency Approach." *British Journal of Criminology*, 28 (4),
478–93.

Sassen, S. (1991) *The Global City: New York, London, Tokyo*. Princeton, NJ: Princeton
University Press.

——— (1999) *Globalisering: Over mobiliteit van geld, mensen, en informatie*. Amsterdam: Van Gennep.

——— (2006) *Territory, Authority, Rights: From Medieval to Global Assemblages*. Princeton, NJ: Princeton University Press.

Saussure, F. de (1986) *Course in General Linguistics*. Peru, IL: Open Court.

Schinkel, W. (2007) *Denken in een tijd van sociale hypochondrie*. Kampen, Netherlands:
Klement.

——— (2011) "Prepression: The Actuarial Archive and New Technologies of Security."
Theoretical Criminology, 15 (4), 365–80.

Schinkel, W., and M. van den Berg (2011) "City of Exception: The Dutch Revanchist
City and the Urban *Homo Sacer*." *Antipode*, 0 (0), 1–28.

Scholte, R. (2008) "Burgerparticipatie in veiligheidsprojecten." In: H. Boutellier and R.
Van Steden (eds.), *Veiligheid en burgerschap in een netwerksamenleving*. The Hague:
Boom, 223–41.

Schuilenburg, M. (2008a) "Citizenship Revisited: Denizens and Margizens." *Peace
Review: A Journal of Social Justice*, 20, 358–65.

——— (2008b) "The Dislocating Perspective of Assemblages: Another Look at the Issue
of Security." *Open: Cahier on Art and the Public Domain*, 15, 18–35.

Schuilenburg, M., and P. Van Calster (2009) "De Collectieve Winkelontzegging: Een
antwoord van willekeur op overlast." In: H. Boutellier, N. Boonstra, and M. Ham
(eds.), *Omstreden ruimte: Over de organisatie van spontaniteit en veiligheid*. Amsterdam: Van Gennep, 137–55.

Schuilenburg, M., and R. van Steden (2014) "Positive Security: A Theoretical Framework." In: M. Schuilenburg, R. van Steden, and B. Oude Breuil (eds.), *Positive
Criminology: Reflections on Care, Belonging and Security*. The Hague: Eleven International Publishing, 19–30.

Sennett, R. (2008) *The Craftsman*. New Haven, CT: Yale University Press.

SEV (2010) *Internationale vergelijking achter de voordeur: Professionals in de frontlijn
tussen burgers en instanties*. Rotterdam.

Shearing, C. D. (2001) "Punishment and the Changing Face of Governance." *Punishment & Society*, 3 (2), 203–20.

——— (2005) "Nodal Security." *Police Quarterly*, 8 (1), 57–63.

——— (2006) "Reflections on the Refusal to Acknowledge Private Governments." In:
J. Wood and B. Dupont (eds.), *Democracy, Society, and the Governance of Security*.
Cambridge: Cambridge University Press, 11–32.

Shearing, C. D., and P. C. Stenning (1981) "Modern Private Security: Its Growth and
Implications." In: M. Tonry and N. Morris (eds.), *Crime and Justice: An Annual
Review of Research*. Chicago: University of Chicago Press, 3: 193–245.

—— (1983) "Private Security: Implications for Social Control." *Social Problems*, 30 (5), 493–506.

Shearing, C., and J. Wood (2003a) "Governing Security for Common Goods." *International Journal of the Sociology of Law*, 31, 205–25.

—— (2003b) "Nodal Governance, Democracy, and the New 'Denizens.'" *Journal of Law and Society*, 30, 400–419.

Sijbesma, R. (2007) *Pakkende verbindingen: Zelf-organiserende moleculen voor functionele materialen*. Inaugural lecture, delivered on 23 February 2007 at the Technical University Eindhoven, Netherlands.

Simmel, G. (1968) *Soziologie: Untersuchungen über die Formen der Vergesellschaftung*. Frankfurt, Germany: Suhrkamp.

—— (1968) "Das Geheimnis und die geheime Gesellschaft." In: *Soziologie: Untersuchungen über die Formen der Vergesellschaftung*. Frankfurt, Germany: Suhrkamp, 383–455.

Simon, J. (1987) "The Emergence of a Risk Society: Insurance, Law, and the State." *Socialist Review*, 97, 61–89.

—— (1988) "The Ideological Effects of Actuarial Practices." *Law and Society Review*, 22 (4), 771–800.

—— (2007) *Governing through Crime: How the War on Crime Transformed American Democracy and Created a Culture of Fear*. Oxford: Oxford University Press.

Simon, J., and M. M. Feeley (2003) "The Form and Limits of the New Penology." In: T. G. Blomberg and S. Cohen (eds.), *Punishment and Social Control*. New Brunswick, NJ: Transaction, 75–116.

Simons, M., and J. Masschelein (2009) "In de ban van het leren: Over biopolitiek en beleid van levenslang leren." *Krisis: Tijdschrift voor actuele filosofie*, 3, 23–38.

Sloterdijk, P. (1998) *Sphären I: Blasen, Mikrosphärologie*. Frankfurt, Germany: Suhrkamp.

—— (1999) *Sphären II: Globen, Makrosphärologie*. Frankfurt, Germany: Suhrkamp.

—— (2004) *Sphären III: Schäume, Plurale Sphärologie*. Frankfurt, Germany: Suhrkamp.

Smith, A. (1976) *An Inquiry into the Nature and Causes of the Wealth of Nations* (R. H. Campbell and A. S. Skinner, eds.). Oxford: Clarendon (first published: 1776).

Smith, K. G., S. J. Carroll, and S. J. Ashford (1995) "Intra- and Interorganizational Cooperation: Toward a Research Agenda." *Academy of Management Journal*, 38 (1), 7–23.

Solà-Morales, I. de (1996) "Terrain Vague." Quaderns, 212, 34–44.

Spapens, A. C. M., H. G. van de Bunt, and L. Rastovac (2007) *De wereld achter de wietteelt*. The Hague: WODC.

Steden, R. van (2007) *Privatizing Policing: Describing and Explaining the Growth of Private Security*. The Hague: Boom.

Steenhuis, D. W. (1984) "Strafrechtelijk optreden: Stapje terug en een sprong voorwaarts." *Delikt en Delinkwent*, 14, 395–414 and 497–512.

Stokkom, B. van, M. Becker, and T. Eikenaar (2012) *Participatie en vertegenwoordiging: Burgers als trustees*. Amsterdam: Pallas.

Swaaningen, R. van (2005) "Public Safety and the Management of Fear." *Theoretical Criminology*, 9 (3), 289–305.

—— (2008) "Sweeping the Street: Civil Society and Community Safety in Rotterdam." In: J. Shapland (ed.), *Justice, Community, and Civil Society: A Contested Terrain*. Cullompton, UK: Willan, 87–106.

Szymborska, W. (1998) *Poems: New and Collected, 1957–1997*. New York: Harvest.

Taleb, N. N. (2007) *The Black Swan: The Impact of the Highly Improbable*. New York: Random House.

—— (2012) *Antifragile: Things That Gain from Disorder*. New York: Random House.

Tarde, G. (1895) "Criminalité et santé sociale." *Revue philosophique*, 39, 148–62.

—— (1912) *Penal Philosophy*. Boston: Little, Brown (first published: 1890).

—— (1924) *La criminalité comparée*. Paris: Alcan (first published: 1886).

—— (1962) *The Laws of Imitation*. Gloucester, MA: Peter Smith (first published: 1890).

—— (1969a) "The Public and the Crowd." In: G. Tarde, *On Communication and Social Influence* (ed. and intro. T. N. Clark). Chicago: University of Chicago Press, 277–94 (first published: 1901).

—— (1969b) *On Communication and Social Influence* (ed. and intro. T. N. Clark). Chicago: University of Chicago Press.

—— (1999) *Monadologie et sociologie*. Paris: Les empêcheurs de penser en rond (first published: 1893).

—— (2000) *Social Laws: An Outline of Sociology*. Kitchener, Ontario: Batoche Books (first published: 1898).

Teisman, G. R. (2005) *Publiek management op de grens van chaos en orde: Over leidinggeven en organiseren in complexiteit*. The Hague: Sdu Uitgevers.

Terpstra, J. (2008) "Police, Local Government, and Citizens in Local Security Networks." *Police Practice and Research*, 9 (3), 213–25.

—— (2010) *Het veiligheidscomplex: Ontwikkelingen, strategieën, en verantwoordelijkheden in de veiligheidszorg*. The Hague: Boom.

Terpstra, J., and R. Kouwenhoven (2004) *Samenwerken en netwerken in de lokale veiligheidszorg*. Zeist, Netherlands: Uitgeverij Kerckebosch.

Terpstra, M. (2002) *Omstreden besluiten: Filosofische aspecten van het besturen*. Amsterdam: SUN.

Tonkens, E. (2003) "'Achter de Voordeur' als opdracht en taboe." In: *Mondige burgers, getemde professionals: Marktwerking en professionaliteit in de publieke sector*. Amsterdam: Van Gennep, 201–15.

Tonkens, E., J. Uitermark, and M. Ham (eds.) (2006) *Handboek moraliseren: Burgerschap en ongedeelde moraal*. Amsterdam: Van Gennep.

Tops, P. (2007) *Regimeverandering in Rotterdam: Hoe een stadsbestuur zichzelf opnieuw uitvond*. Amsterdam: Uitgeverij Atlas.

Trommel, W. A. (2009) *Gulzig bestuur*. The Hague: Boom/Lemma.

Tweede Kamer der Staten-Generaal (1985) *Samenleving en criminaliteit: Een beleidsplan voor de komende jaren*. Vergaderjaar 1984–1985, 18 995, nrs. 1–2.

Valverde, M. (2011) "Questions of Security: A Framework for Research." *Theoretical Criminology*, 15 (1), 3–21.

Van Calster, P. (2006) "Re-visiting Mr. Nice: On Organized Crime as Conversational Interaction." *Crime, Law, and Social Change*, 45 (4–5), 337–59.

——— (2010) "Studying Society, Safety, and Security: Notes on Observer Involvement." In: R. Lippens and P. Van Calster (eds.), *New Directions for Criminology: Notes from Outside the Field*. Antwerp, Belgium: Maklu, 17–39.

Van Calster, P., and M. Schuilenburg (2009) "Burgernet vanuit een nodal governance perspectief." *Justitiële verkenningen*, 1, 93–113.

——— (2010) "On Gabriel Tarde, Complexity Theory, and Complex Interactions." In: R. Lippens and P. Van Calster (eds.), *New Directions for Criminology: Notes from Outside the Field*. Antwerp, Belgium: Maklu, 171–89.

Verhage A. (2009) "Corporations as a Blind Spot in Research: Explanations for a Criminological Tunnel Vision." In: M. Cools et al. (eds.), *Governance of Security Research Papers Series I: Contemporary Issues in the Empirical Study of Crime*. Antwerp, Belgium: Maklu, 80–108.

Vindevogel, F. (2005) "Private Security and Urban Mitigation: A Bid for BIDs." *Criminal Justice*, 5 (3), 233–55.

Vollaard, B., P. Versteegh, and J. van den Brakel (2009) *Veelbelovende verklaringen voor de daling van de criminaliteit na 2002*. Apeldoorn, Netherlands: Politie & Wetenschap.

Von Hirsch, A., and C. Shearing (2000) "Exclusion from Public Space." In: A. Von Hirsch, D. Garland, and A. Wakefield (eds.), *Ethical and Social Perspectives on Situational Crime Prevention*. Oxford: Hart, 77–96.

Voorbeeldconvenant integrale aanpak hennepteelt (2007) Available at www.hetccv.nl/dossiers/Hennepteelt/zeeland-en-west-brabant---convenant-hennepteelt-2013. Last accessed September 2014.

Wacquant, L. (2009) *Punishing the Poor: The Neoliberal Government of Social Insecurity*. Durham, NC: Duke University Press.

——— (2010) "Crafting the Neoliberal State: Workfare, Prisonfare, and Social Insecurity." *Sociological Forum*, 25 (2), 197–220.

Wakefield, A. (2003) *Selling Security: The Private Policing of Public Space*. Cullompton, UK: Willan.

Walters, R. (1996) "The 'Dream' of Multi-Agency Crime Prevention: Pitfalls in Policy and Practice." In: R. Homel (ed.), *The Politics and Practice of Situational Crime Prevention*. Crime Prevention Studies. Monsey, NY: Criminal Justice Press, 75–96.

Wastell, D., P. Kawalek, P. Langmead-Jones, and R. Ormerod (2004) "Information Systems and Partnership in Multi-Agency Networks: An Action Research Project in Crime Reduction." *Information and Organization*, 14, 189–210.

Welch, M. (2010) "Pastoral Power as Penal Resistance: Foucault and the Groupe d'Information sur les Prisons." *Punishment & Society*, 12 (1), 47–63.

Wesselink, L., M. Schuilenburg, and P. Van Calster (2009) "De Collectieve Winkelontzegging." *Tijdschrift voor Veiligheid*, 8 (1), 6–19.

Wetenschappelijke Raad voor het Regeringsbeleid (WRR) (2005) *Sociale herovering in Amsterdam en Rotterdam: Eén verhaal over twee wijken*. Amsterdam: Amsterdam University Press.

White, A., and M. Gill (2013) "The Transformation of Policing: From Ratios to Rationalities." *British Journal of Criminology*, 53 (1), 74–93

Whitehead, A. N. (1964) *The Concept of Nature*. Cambridge: Cambridge University Press (first published: 1920).

Williams, R. G. (1996) "Strike It Niche! Business Improvement Districts." *Journal of Property Management*, 61 (3), 21–22.

Williams, R., and D. Edge (1996) "The Social Shaping of Technology." *Research Policy*, 25, 865–99.

Willrich, M. (2011) *Pox. An American History*. New York: Penguin.

Wilson, J. E. (1998) *Terroir: The Role of Geology, Climate, and Culture in the Making of French Wines*. London: Reed Consumer Books.

Wilson, J. Q., and G. L. Kelling (1982) "Broken Windows: The Police and Neighborhood Safety." *Atlantic Monthly*, 127, 29–38.

Wittebrood, K., and P. Nieuwbeerta (2006) "Een kwart eeuw stijging in geregistreerde criminaliteit: Vooral meer registratie, nauwelijks meer criminaliteit." *Tijdschrift voor Criminologie*, 48 (3), 227–42.

Wood, J. (2006) "Research Innovations in the Field of Security: A Nodal Governance View." In: J. Wood and B. Dupont (eds.), *Democracy, Society, and the Governance of Security*. Cambridge: Cambridge University Press, 217–40.

Wood, J., and M. Kempa (2005) "Understanding Global Trends in Policing: Explanatory and Normative Dimensions." In: J. Sheptycki and A. Wardak (eds.), *Transnational and Comparative Criminology*. London: Glasshouse, 288–316.

Wood, J., and C. D. Shearing (2007) *Imagining Security*. Cullompton, UK: Willan.

——— (2009) "De nodale politiefunctie." *Justitiële verkenningen*, 1, 11–28.

World Health Organization (1980) *The Global Eradication of Smallpox: Final Report of the Global Commission for the Certification of Smallpox Eradication*. Geneva: World Health Organization.

Wouters, W., D. J. Korf, and B. Kroeske (2007) *Harde aanpak, hete zomer: Een onderzoek naar de ontmanteling van hennepkwekerijen in Nederland*. The Hague: WODC.

Young, J. (1999) *The Exclusive Society: Social Exclusion, Crime, and Difference in Late Modernity*. London: Sage.

——— (2007) *The Vertigo of Late Modernity*. London: Sage.

Zedner, L. (2003) "The Concept of Security: An Agenda for Comparative Analysis." *Legal Studies*, 23 (1), 153–75.

——— (2006a) "Liquid Security: Managing the Market for Crime Control." *Criminology and Criminal Justice*, 6 (3), 267–88.

——— (2006b) "Policing before and after the Police: The Historical Antecedents of Contemporary Crime Control." *British Journal of Criminology*, 46, 78–96.

——— (2007) "Pre-Crime and Post-Criminology?" *Theoretical Criminology*, 11 (2), 261–81.

——(2009) *On Security*. London: Routledge.

Žižek, S. (2000) *The Ticklish Subject: The Absent Centre of Political Ontology*. London: Verso.

Zuijlen, R.W. van (2008) *Veiligheid als opdracht. Een onderzoek naar veiligheid als fundamenteel recht en als positieve verplichting van de staat in het licht van de politietaak tot strafrechtelijke rechtshandhaving*. Nijmegen, Netherlands: Wolf Legal Publishers.

INDEX

actor-network theory (ANT), 305n2

actuarial justice, 68

affect, 51, 147, 268–269, 309n1; affect hunger, 268

airport, 9, 11, 251, 255, 265; John F. Kennedy airport, 38; Schiphol airport, 36, 38, 187

American Institute of Criminal Law and Criminology, 133

ancien régime, 262

Antisocial Behavior Order (ASBO), 230–231

Appadurai, Arjun, 35

Aristotle, 57, 98, 117

Asia, 106, 254

assemblage, 4–7, 24, 56–58, 97–131, 250, 287, 291–292, 308n3, 309n4; interassemblage, 194; intra-assemblage, 235–236; security assemblage, 125–131, 148, 155–161, 163–164, 166, 171, 173, 181–186, 189, 191, 193–194, 197, 205, 234–236, 245, 247, 250–251, 261, 264, 285, 293–294, 296–300, 311–312n9; self-assemblage, 152; surveillant assemblage, 5, 125–126

astronomy, 144

auspices, 30

autopoiesis, 176–177

Avogadro, Amedeo, 148–149

Bachelard, Gaston, 246

Badiou, Alain, 159, 282

banishment, 6, 9, 23–24, 40, 62, 83, 89, 111, 165, 226–244, 257, 260, 264, 266–267, 287, 295, 297–300

Banksy, 113

barrack, 55

Bateson, Gregory, 105

Baudrillard, Jean, 306n3

Bauman, Zygmunt, 67, 153–154

Bayley, David, 82

Beccaria, Cesare, 29, 43, 91, 132, 154, 157, 229, 238, 287, 289, 310n4

Beck, Ulrich, 82, 92, 124

Beckett, Katherine, 298

"behind-the-front-door," 6, 9, 206, 209, 212, 218, 293

Beirne, Piers, 132, 136, 309n2

Belgium, 307n6

belonging, 268; sense of belonging, 269

Bentham, Jeremy, 114

Bergson, Henri, 18, 57, 118, 131

Bey, Hakim, 270

Bible, 60

biology, 110, 113, 176

biopolitics, 73–74, 76, 78, 124, 213–215, 224; biocontrol, 123; biopower, 73–74; life politics, 214

Black Muslims, 30

Blakely, Edward, 269, 314n1

Blood and Land, 276

Boccaccio, Giovanni, 61

boot camp, 93

Borgers, Matthias, 94

bottom-up, 48, 128–129, 227; top-down, 1, 41, 128–129, 189

Bourdieu, Pierre, 68, 246, 311

Braithwaite, John, 238

Brandsen, Taco, 209, 211

ABOUT THE AUTHOR

MARC SCHUILENBURG is Assistant Professor in the Department of Criminal Law and Criminology at the VU University Amsterdam.

Lightning Source UK Ltd.
Milton Keynes UK
UKOW04n0621140715

255132UK00011B/160/P